I0816737

The History of Hentai Manga

An Expressionist Examination of Eromanga

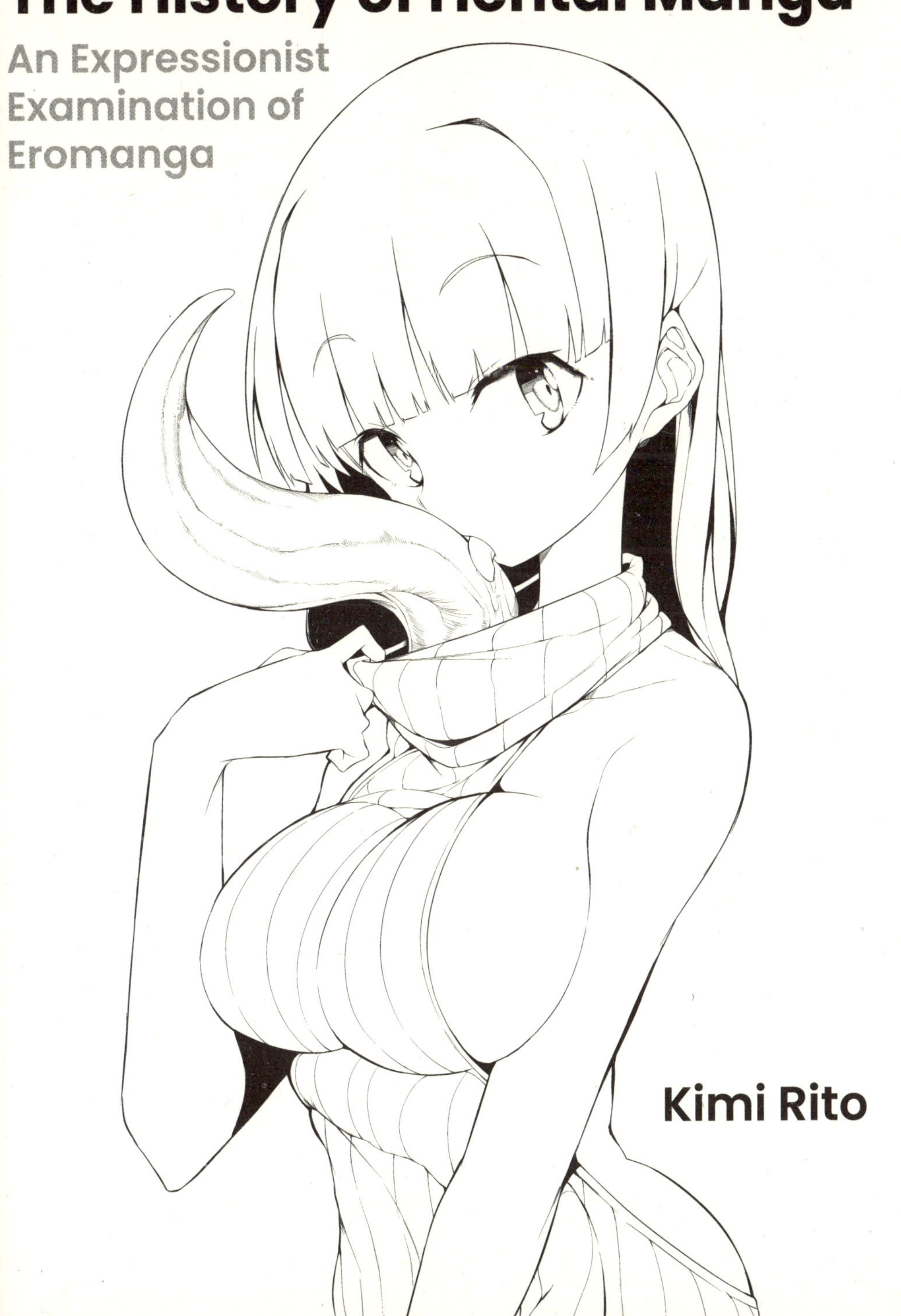

Kimi Rito

Preface

The contents of this book are not exactly the usual manga-oriented representation theory material one would see in a book about eromanga. One could call it an unusual look into the genre, using material that looks into expressions influenced by the medium as well as its expansion, evolution, and its variations from the times of their invention and discovery forward through the vehicle of manga. As a result, this book has turned into more of an attempt to look at its semiotics, into the symbols (something that someone can look at and naturally understand in an instant, that also has shared common meaning or generalizations applied to it) that have stuck within the genre of eromanga.

At the same time, it's also a document that contains a multilateral investigation into the creators and situations that helped shape those expressions, while directly looking at other elements that have given those expressions their meaning, and questioning the circumstances that birthed them.

Nevertheless, let me declare my refusal to the statement that in the end this book is merely consideration and research of the visual aspects and perception of the expressions that lie at the heart of eromanga. Nor is it one that also looks at the plots and characters of what has been allowed to develop within the genre.

If we are to think that eromanga as a genre is but a series of stories serving as the crossbeams to construct our masturbation media, then I believe it would be correct to say that we are looking at but only one of its many facets. To the reader, the most important thing when it comes to the genre may lie in its usefulness and practicality. It is also the place where creators within the genre are able to execute their implementation of these varied expressions, as well.

It is a genre where the exploration of both genders' sexualities, as well as the act itself, serves as the lynchpin to these stories. Complementing that, this genre is a place where the sky's the limit when it comes to content. Historically, eromanga has been the vanguard of progressive values, overflowing with innovative expressions, as it has been a testing ground for both of these things in the past.

Hiroya Oku, the author of ***GANTZ*** (Shueisha/Dark Horse) and ***Inuyashiki*** (Kodansha/Kodansha Comics USA), once put forth the idea that when a breast shakes, the nipple is like a headlight in the dark as the locus of a picture with the idea of the "nipple afterimage."

There is also the concept of the "cross-section view"—a view at the moment of insertion during intercourse where, because anatomical drawings or MRI-like realistic imaging on behalf of the artist can't be fully achieved, the artist instead tries to make those inner workings visible to the audience. Few people know that the cross-section view as a visual expression is a holdover from the *shunga* (lit. "spring pictures") art of the Edo period.

The seed of the expression that once shocked the world from that same time period of the *ukiyo-e* master Hokusai has fully blossomed into modern gekiga master Toshio Maeda's ***Legend of the Overfiend*** (*Urot-*

sukidouji, Wanimagazine/FAKKU); that is to say, the expression of a girl being assaulted, having her every hole, both inside and out, mentally and physically filled by tentacles.

The illustrated sound effects of sweat, semen, and other bodily fluids become continuously entangled within the story in a visually fresh and vibrant manner. The sound of the vagina opening, "kupaa," from the art of Akazawa RED has shown itself to be a classic example of this particular form of expression. The loss of words the moment she reaches orgasm known as "*misakura-go*" (Misakura-speak) comes from the works of Nankotsu Misakura. Misakura managed to distill that sound into a single "movement" on the page.

All of the above examples are but just a small offering within the genre, but they are excellent examples of expressions that had they not been within the purview of eromanga, they would've most likely never become what they are today. They were invented, copied, improved, and finally, codified within manga history. After that they were polished and condensed, becoming the symbols they are today.

If we are to say that the "encoding" process of manga expressions is a rough one, then we are, broadly speaking, talking about the process of distortion, deformation, economization, abridgment, and compression. Examples of this process that readily come to mind are that moment when a character is so surprised that their eyes seem to just fly open wide, or when they're so angry that the anger seems to ripple throughout every muscle in their body, or when they're befuddled, the drop of sweat that slides down their forehead, or when they're surprised, the mark that appears near the top of their head, and so forth. All of those are examples of the encoding process.

Another example is the moment in a romantic-comedy genre work when a male character sees a female character naked and subsequently gets aroused, and as a result, has a nosebleed. This is an example of what we call abridgment within the scene as a whole, because the reader, by seeing those signs, can put two and two together as to what is going on inside of the male character's head. Without explicitly explaining what is happening inside of that character's mind in that moment step by step, the story is becoming compressed and abridged into something easy to understand.

When we speak of deformation and distortion, it would be not entirely inappropriate to look at it as exaggeration, a department well within eromanga's purview. No, perhaps it would be better to say that it is a bluff that goes past exaggeration.

A female character's breasts that are so large they seemingly extend beyond the panels—no, the pages themselves. Semen that seems to gush and fill every square inch of the insides of the human body. The moment when a female character orgasms and it seems to go beyond that to a state of pleasurable madness and anguish.

Apparently, when deformation approaches that degree, there are some readers out there that seem to think that process becomes a killjoy of sorts. But when the deformation goes beyond mere exaggeration and into foolishness, it is precisely at that point where a new expression for the genre is born; one that will allow the reader to experience a level of passion to that degree depending on how clever and creative the author can be with it. How much can they increase the female character's cuteness, but also show that she's "enjoying herself so much that she [seems to be] tormented by it"? How much more realistic can they have those sensations play out, and have that get across to the reader as such?

Within the domain of being so eccentric that the possibility of the author's message not getting across to the audience, there is also within the realm of expression evolution the power of those expressions that increase the audience's literacy (as it relates to eromanga). More specifically, it is the power to make the impossible possible, and make it charming. It is also because the audience can directly confront the author, and the lower halves of those bodies they draw, that one can add that exaggeration into the mix during the encoding process. It is precisely within this realm of things that can only be drawn within eromanga that this reality exists. It is the realm where the audience can easily take all of these expressions in, and it is also the realm where the artists who draw these expressions can mix and influence each other.

All of these things make up the encoding process.

Depending on the encoding process and how it differs with each new expression, the inventors and discoverers of those new symbols that may have similar processes are no different (or perhaps greater) than each other when it comes to the importance of the mechanism of the transmission of said expressions.

But within that transmission process, it is also important to note that just as an earthquake radiates from an epicenter, that still does not mean that the process itself as it radiates from the origin of the expression will be a linear one. There are complex waves, which at times will jump over areas vacant of these ideas, seemingly easily leaping over time itself to create their own periods, which at that point, will continue to spread out.

Nor does it mean that there is only one epicenter during the encoding process. Waves from other hypocenters will interfere with each other, bump into each other and against each other, and will simultaneously, cause even more complex waves to transmit themselves. Those more complex waves will swallow everything in their path and change, then evolve, and at times will even alter those expressions' meanings (but also sometimes unintentionally, as the audience misinterprets these expressions and is mistaken about them). That particular process can cause a mutation of that expression as well.

To borrow from one of the few research books on the topic of eromanga, ***Erotic Comics in Japan*** (*Eromanga Studies;* Kauro Nagayama, 2006 East Press/ Amesterdam Univ. Press), if there are indeed cultural genes that are the same as memes, then perhaps we can safely say that even as one of these genes has small changes and mutations, and there are many hands involved during that process, that if the many hands that share this content rapidly begin to support it for as long as it lasts, then it is also safe to say that the content that is culled and forgotten completely also can quickly disappear for good.

And yet within that process, it would be incorrect to compare the fight for a meme's life with the biological fight for existence. Mostly due to the fact there are other factors in play when it comes to how to compare a meme's lifecycle, including reasons relating to societal issues, technological issues, and sometimes, just plain old happenstance has its place in these factors and reasons.

As someone who is writing a treatise on these expressions, I can't very well ignore some of these reasons and factors altogether. I feel that it is my duty to painstakingly collect data on all of these factors involved for the themes of this book.

When it comes to the encoding process within the manga medium, there has been a great deal of prior research already done. However, when it comes to eromanga as a genre, there has been almost no research done whatsoever.

If compared to a long time ago, the non-fiction genre of manga research has become ridiculously popular. Manga research scooped up large fiction genres like *shonen* (boys' comics) and *shojo* (girls' comics) manga and examined them from all sides. Manga panels, speech bubbles, hand-drawn lettering, sound effects, onomatopoeias, as well as the approach an author takes when drawing their characters have been topics for research in the past. The way the plot of manga has changed throughout various eras, as well as the system of values we read, take in, and assign things, has been thoroughly examined in sociological circles.

Manga is connected to many other forms of media, and as a medium one can approach it from nearly any school of thought or subject for research, as it is a medium that we become quite familiar with from an early age onward (the author sure has). Perhaps it would be better to say that because it is a medium with which we are all, as Japanese citizens, familiar from an early age on, and we are in a time where that relationship does have such value, that it has become quite the attractive candidate for research in general.

However, it should be said that even within the bulk of academic manga research and study, eromanga as a genre is not unlike black matter residing in space.

That is to say, it is nearly entirely invisible to the human eye.

I realized this when I began my research on *bishojo* manga (manga that focuses on young women, often as sex symbols) in 2008. No, to be honest, it's something I had always known, deep down. So perhaps it would be better to say that I had always known but it wasn't until I started to actually do the research that I really noticed. Any prior work I found was small in number, and the number of specialized experts on the topic weren't even worth counting at all there had been so few.

But the biggest issue had been about gathering data, as many academic archives had no material regarding eromanga in their libraries at all. And of course, there weren't really any academics or researchers within the field, either. While I understood that all of these things meant that information about the field would be hard to come by, I also understood that "erotic" part of manga, in a way, was being protected, and should not be overly disturbed.

Eromanga authors and artists weren't exactly being called to appear on those "behind-the-scenes" TV documentaries about how they ply their trade. When someone put out a call for a generic manga artist in their hometown, the only artist excluded from the search was one who had drawn erotic content. When the Cool Japan soft power initiative was announced by the Japanese government in 2010 (to be implemented in 2013), the only manga artists that were actively excluded were those who had drawn erotic content, it seemed, by intentional design.

It seemed it was a genre beyond redemption with regard to research, and even experts seemed to feel and understand that this was the norm.

Is eromanga as a genre, itself, the exception? No, that doesn't seem to be the case.

The amount of eromanga that started out as bishojo comics aren't very few in number. So I chased that feeling knowing that the eromanga artists that can discuss the topic say that the concept of "eromanga" itself isn't something that is seen in other genres and that birthed the freedom for them to draw "whatever they wanted, as long as they made it erotic." That breeding ground was very fertile, becoming the reason why the eromanga genre is as varied as it is in terms of the content of the works within it.

Therefore, while the genre is one that shows both content about sex and sexuality, it also speaks of human desire, fate, and despair, usually using the character's physical bodies as the vehicle to do so. The artist is able to tell us these stories, putting their hearts down on paper (or increasingly, on tablets). Occasionally that erotic content can be funny, but even that element has a righteous and valid power to it, and in the end, it can emerge as a persuasive element in storytelling.

Just as we cannot unravel the mystery of the construction of the universe without also analyzing dark matter, one cannot understand manga without taking a tour through the expressions of eromanga. New expressions are continuously being born and are disappearing, leaving behind only the expressions that have been validated by their readers in each era. These expressions of eromanga flow hot and passionately like magma under the dark and enigmatic earth's crust and mantle.

In recent years, we have figured out the potential of Japan's eromanga as a genre as countries overseas have appraised works in its canon (to the point of affecting this document in question). This has been done by looking at the unique expressions of eromanga as the amount of material that has been published worldwide has been enough to attest to as examples. I firmly believe that looking at the visual expressions of the genre via research is the main way to understand manga expressions as a whole.

While I progressed through my research of bishojo comics, I discovered that a lot of adult manga authors were quite enamored with editors and other fans of the eromanga genre. This was later collected into a self-published book called ***Eromanga no Genba,*** which I researched and contains content from 2011 to 2015. In 2016 it was republished in Japan in trade paperback form as a compilation of eromanga author interviews by Sansai Books. As someone who is a big fan of the eromanga genre, I thought that I knew enough on the subject and with that in mind I started to compile data and write this book.

But as I started to speak with people involved with the genre, on the other side of those conversations I found the passionate thoughts of those people, which I used as nails to drive things home within this book. In the spirit of providing my readers entertainment, along with wishing to enchant with the cute and the erotic, this book was forged into existence.

In the past, there was an age when it was thought that there was little point in comparing eromanga to regular manga, and that the artists working in eromanga had no choice but to do so. Perhaps it would be better to say that there are probably still those cool-headed rookies that think that unconsciously when they enter the industry.

However, I think it would be safe to say that from a creator's point of view, there isn't really anyone who thinks that out there creating eromanga right now. Rather, I would say that because they have the freedom to create eromanga, that's why we're constantly seeing a rejuvenation of the industry and new products are continuously being pushed out as well. Because those products are being pushed out, we're seeing a continuous birthing of new expressions. These new works are becoming broadcasting platforms, in a way, when it comes to constantly creating new expressions. People who work those hints into their creations, and as a result, we are seeing a gathering of artists putting out these works with what might be called greed, are standing on the cutting edge of eromanga expressions.

I firmly believe, and this is not an exaggeration, that out of all of the genres of manga out there, eromanga is the genre that has perhaps the most power when it comes to being able to birth these new expressions the most.

I'm not sure when it was when I started feverishly researching eromanga. It was as if I'd been sucked into the world of these creators, feeling their pride as well. When I began to write this book but before I'd started unraveling the mysteries of these expressions and researching them, I now find myself standing on the front lines alongside these creators who taught me about their passion and their work, and perhaps that in itself was its own motive.

I believe this book may be the first to compile many of the expressions of eromanga thus far. I'm sorry to say that as far as a history of manga expressions, this is pretty limited in scope. However even in this limited scope, I did want to write about these expressions' deep history, as well as reveal the origins of its main structures and the incidents tied to them, which are both very deeply intertwined. I hope that throughout this book I have managed to capture the charm of eromanga as a genre.

Though at the same time, I find myself at the foot of the mountain of as-yet untouched eromanga research, earnestly hoping that its vistas will finally stretch out before me. ❁

Table of Contents

The History of Hentai Manga

CHAPTER ONE

How Breast Expressions Have Changed over Time

Breast Expressions Are the Barometers of the Times

Even though this is a chapter on the history of breasts in eromanga, I would say it isn't an exaggeration to say that "how they are expressed" has a history of its own apart from eromanga.

According to many mangaka, the creation, development, problem-solving, and expansion of these symbols continue to take place across the industry. Anyone can weaponize their own dreams and delusions when they draw breasts. And depending on how those breasts get drawn, it becomes akin to hoisting one's flag, inviting an investigation of your work by others.

To draw breasts, it isn't enough to simply be an artist in pursuit of the shape of the body. It instead calls for a look at what men are looking for when it comes to women; both their ideals and dreams about them, against the backdrop of the current societal norms of their eras. It also calls for a look into how women perplex men in regard to their sex appeal as well as the secrets about women they have buried deep down within them and women's awareness of both of those things. Therefore, it would not be an exaggeration to say that in those ways, the expressions of breasts in manga are the barometers of the times.

The creators that help birth and advance these expressions put their desires and complex internalized relationships with women into their work. At times, they also confront their betrayals, failures, and frustrations as well during the artistic process, and in doing so, they try to draw the greatest breasts of their time.

Breasts, chest, bust, titties...are mounds of attraction that nearly become swollen with hidden meaning, and thus, are parables unto themselves. These are the ways that women's breasts are referred to by these artists. For the sake of this book, I'd like to simply call them "breasts."

Though perhaps the word "breasts" isn't the most ideal word given the kindness of the secrets wrapped deep within them, how they burst with elasticity on the outside, and pose, facing front, with apparent dignity. When the word "breasts" first came about, one could feel the hopes and dreams it held within it…at least, that's what I would like to assert.

Within the realm of the history of breast expressions, there's one simply indispensable topic to handle regarding breasts that is so important that I need to address it first. Which is to say, I'd like to look at how they're drawn, and from there on, how they have evolved as symbols in Japanese comics.

If we are to look at and trace the origins behind the way breasts are drawn, we also must consider when they were drawn, for that is connected to the eromanga genre itself. Even now, *kyounyu* (big breasts), *bakunyu* (enormous breasts), *chonyu* (hyper breasts), *kinyuu* (freakish breasts), *binyuu* (flat-chested), *hinnyu* (small breasts), and *binyu* (well-shaped breasts) are all connected to some sort of feeling or emotion individually that happened when they were named.

Perhaps it's better to say that since the dawn of manga itself, those emotions that became expressions of breasts have always existed, just in a far murkier form.

When researching breasts in manga, there's also something quite unexpected that we can learn. In old shonen magazines, we can see that works depicting magnificent breasts that wouldn't hide their nipples started to appear more frequently around thirty years ago. They became something of a fad for people who found it hard to otherwise proclaim they loved huge breasts. These people pushed back when others claimed that big breasts were a sign of being a *mothercon* (having an Oedipal complex). When we circle back around to current times, we can see that the current image of (big) breasts is completely different.

Indeed, it is safe to say that the system of values and common sense when it comes to breasts has undergone a rather drastic change over the years. The oppression of the system of values centered around big breasts, as well as conjecture around those values have helped unleash what some have called a "big boobification" within the genre. It has also helped mold a new concept of those huge breasts into something more solid by its own volition.

It can be said that breasts and their expressions are sex-sensitive symbols. They can also be targets, and along with the time they were drawn in, can be reactions to those symbols/targets. And those reactions can be just as sensitive as the material in question they're reacting to in themselves.

From the position of looking at the history of these expressions within this book, we can look at expressions that emerged in the 1980s. Such expressions emerged representations depicted within *lolicon* (Lolita complex) magazines, *bishojo* comics, and the like. We can also see how these representations and the axis on which they were drawn have changed and compare them to other genres (in this case, I specifically mean shonen magazines). As it influenced other genres, people began to investigate the origins of these influences. And in that way, I think, that's how these expressions began to extend their reach into manga as a whole.

But as a practical matter, breasts and their expressions existed in all of the manga genres at the time, including content in children's magazines, shonen magazines, *seinen* (young adult comics) magazines, and shojo magazines. The only things amongst all the manga genres that differed were representation, usage, messages, and philosophy regarding how the breasts were expressed.

Now, as we consider that expressions of breasts exist in all of these genres, the theme of breasts seemed to widen as the sea stretches out over the earth. As it widened, the deeper the subject became. And as such, I must admit that it has become such a topic that I cannot possibly completely cover in this one book.

So, I would like to admit that this one chapter on these specific expressions within eromanga will be limited to one of my wheelhouses, which is bishojo comics.

That being said, I'd like to move on to "the theory of breasts." It's possibly one of the most exciting areas within manga as a whole. I believe that everyone has their own separate theory of breasts, including you, dear reader. I do believe you'll compare your theory to mine, but as long as you would continue to read it, I'd be happy regardless.

In terms of visual expressions of breasts, there has been prior research done on the subject and in no small numbers. Some of this research includes works like the ***Tits Art Museum*** (*Chibusa Bijitsukan*, Gin Shiro, 1999, Kyoto Shoin), ***The Cultural Theory of Breasts*** (*Chibusa Bunkaron*, Chibusa Kenkyuukai, 2014, Tankousha), ***A History of the Breast*** (Marilyn Yalom, 1997, Knopf), *Erotic Comics in Japan*. All of these are a great place to start on the subject.

From Ero-Gekiga to Bishojo Comics

I know I said that for this section we'd be looking at material from the 1980s forward, but since the birth of eromanga occured before then, that possibly needs some further explanation.

The first magazine in Japan dedicated to eromanga debuted in 1973 and was called *Manga Bestseller (*KK Bestsellers). It changed its name to *Manga Erotopia* (KK Bestsellers, Wanimagazine) soon after.

Erotopia's strategy was simple: take the *gekiga* (a noir and realism art movement within manga) that had been in the magazine and was quite popular up until that point, and strengthen the presence of the sex and/or violent elements within the story. What resulted was a new genre, a fusion of the two, named *ero-gekiga*.

However, the initial ero-gekiga magazines took little from the methods used within the eromanga genre, and instead, focused on switching to packing their magazines full of manga as well as gekiga, 4-koma (four-panel comic strips), and other similar types of manga that were common back then. Gradually that petered out into its own style. By 1975, there were many *ero-gekiga* magazines, enough to cement this style into its own genre.

The circulation for these ero-gekiga magazines officially peaked in

1978, and when you include the special issues of those magazines into the numbers, it is believed that somewhere between eighty to one hundred different ero-gekiga magazines were actively being published annually.

The 1980s would see the rise of lolicon and bishojo magazines, which grew from otaku fan culture, and their growth would happen in inverse proportions to ero-gekiga, which started to decline in circulation.

The reason for ero-gekiga's decline was that the baby boomer readership was beginning to start families of their own, and naturally started to separate from that genre when it came to reading material. Various theories suggest that instead they migrated to seinen publications like *Young Magazine*, and when it came to masturbation aids or material, that readership was stolen by *gravure* (models who pose suggestively) and/or skin magazines.

At the dawn of the 1980s, the forces that extended in the place of ero-gekiga were so-called *lolicon* comics, and after that, *bishojo* comics, which became a genre unto itself. As ero-gekiga declined, new genres took its place; it wasn't that the ero-gekiga readership moved towards them. Instead, a brand-new readership emerged for these brand-new genres. They were different from realistic gekiga. Instead these new genres primarily employed the use of deformed characters, and anime-like motifs in the form of cute girls (for bishojo comics), and in that way, the bishojo comic genre readership (and its subsequent fans) expanded rapidly.

At the center of these new genres stood a layer of *otaku* (nerds/fans), who bought and sold *doujinshi* (self-published zines) at events like Comic Market (the world's largest zine and indie art festival). Though it would be better to say that with the arrival of the founding father of the bishojo comic genre, Hideo Azuma, the expansion of the genre began at an explosive pace.

From his early days in the '70s, Azuma utilized deformed characters in slightly naughty scenes in order to present his sci-fi and comedy stories. As those around him centered him in their movement, in 1979 he wrote a zine named *Cybele* (picture 1-1), which got mixed up with the otaku who went to events like Comic Market; as a result, he ended up kicking off the *lolicon* boom in manga altogether.

The movement of these excited otaku did not escape the notice of publishers. The first issue of *lolicon* comic magazines in Japan was a new venture called *Lemon People* (1982, AMATORIA; 1-2AB). The first issue's cover stated that it "had the monopoly on lolicon comic content in 1982," expressing the excitement over the very word *lolicon* itself.

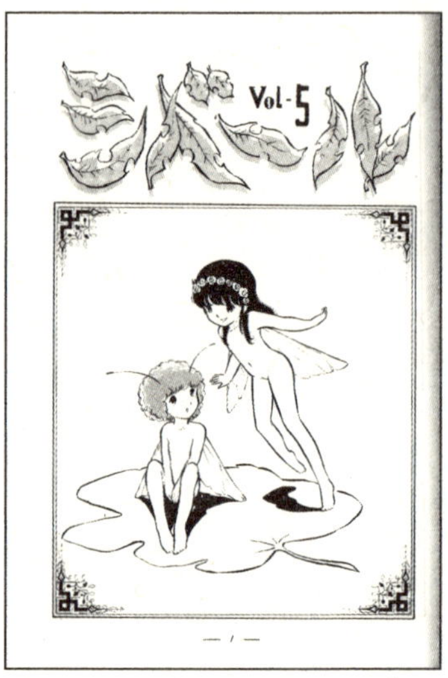

1-1: *Cybele* Vol. 5 (1980, Cybele editorial)

What I would like to caution here is about the nuance of the term "lolicon"... The current term denotes, in a broad sense, "perverts who get off on little girls," with a wholly negative image stuck to this nuance from a societal level. And these days it is more or less defined as "eromanga with schoolgirls younger than middle school as the object of lust."

However, 1980s-era *lolicon* as a term wasn't as limited in scope to the one we have now, but rather something more like "the cuteness of beautiful girls, precious comrades taking co-ownership of and having experiences that can be called ephemeral and are touchingly lovely."

It should be noted, though, this definition did not divorce this "cuteness" from the sexual charm of girls of this age, but instead, if we were to put it in modern terms, it would not be incorrect to say that it was most likely something closer to the *moé* (blossoming beauty) aesthetic boom that happened in the early 2000s rather than possessing the same definition as today.

Some were literary in style, filled with intoxication over the stage of self-consciousness we experience when we go through puberty, yet at the same time, quite masochistically the otaku who consumed these comics often called themselves "sick."

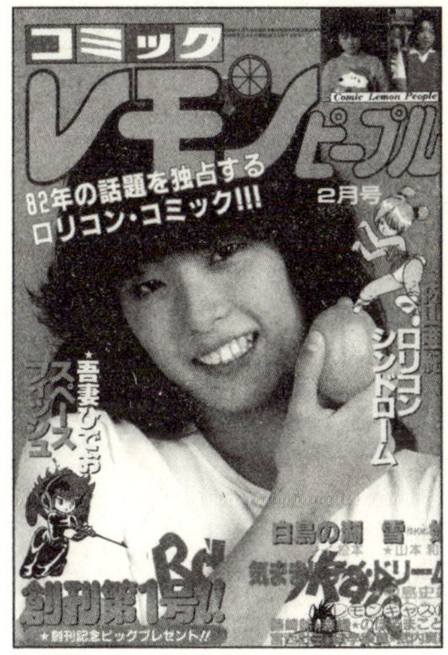

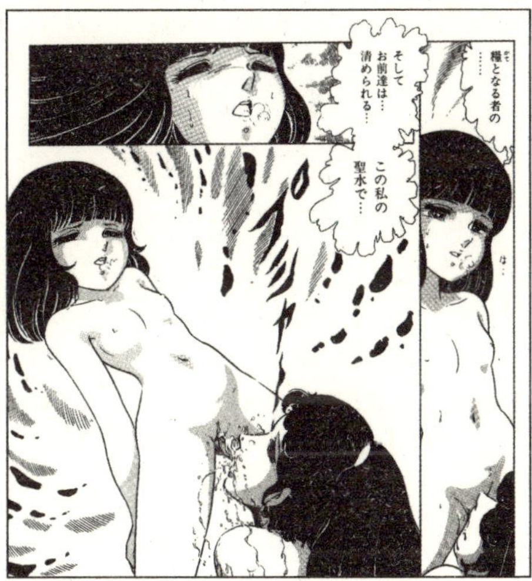

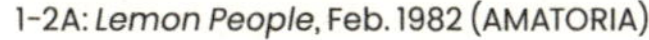

1-2A: *Lemon People*, Feb. 1982 (AMATORIA)

1-2B: ***Rasen Kairou*** (Waho Konoma 1983, AMATORITA)

Bishojo comics, on the other hand, the other genre that debuted at the beginning of the '80s alongside lolicon comics, would find itself maturing as its own genre in the eromanga mainstream thereafter.

The Lolicon Outlook on Breasts

As we talk about how eromanga has changed over the ages, I'd like to turn to the expressions of breasts within the dawn of bishojo comics and how they were drawn.

But even within the lolicon genre, the age limit of these characters was very ambiguous. Just as high school girls call old men lolicon for their interest in them, in the '80s the field was cast widely with regard to age (ranging anywhere from elementary schoolers to high school-age girls, or possibly even young adults). Lolicon was not a term necessarily used to denote the age of these girls, but rather, these girls that were drawn in (cute) anime styles became the icons of the genre. Therefore, the way these girls were engaged with was accordingly divided into lolicon and bishojo comics.

The pretty girls that appeared in lolicon comics at the time had, in most cases, what was undoubtedly the secondary sex characteristics that appeared only within the realm of 2D, with tender buds swelling from chests. The "big-breasted loli" trope was rarely seen in work at that point in time. As for lolicon as a semiotic symbol, one could not even say that their breasts were depicted as swellings from their chests, but instead we are focused more on the characters' innocent, pure existence according to the feeling readers got at the time from the ideals of the artists that worked within this genre.

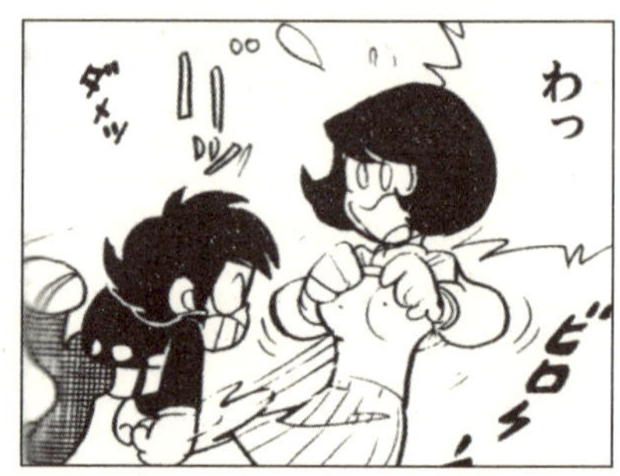

1-3: ***Futari to 5-nin***, Vol. 1 (Hideo Azuma 1974, Akita Shoten)

Within Hideo Azuma's works, in a narrow sense we see him refusing to define the stereotypical age range for lolicon, and instead we have him projecting his ideals in his work, drawing comparatively plump breasts on many of his characters (1-3). In the so-called *diaper manga* produced by the famous Aki Uchiyama, the female characters of his work were drawn to look as if they had no breasts at all so that they could be kept to a visually specific age (1-4). In Senno Knife's work, the dainty characters are drawn with a coldness that is bewitchingly reminiscent of dolls with unassertive breasts and without panties (1-5). Rei Aran was a pioneer of blending beautiful girls and *mecha* (robotics; 1-6); as was Moriwo Chimi (1-7). The breasts they drew tended to be, once again, just one part of a girl's body, and stopped at that when it came to drawing the expressions of them.

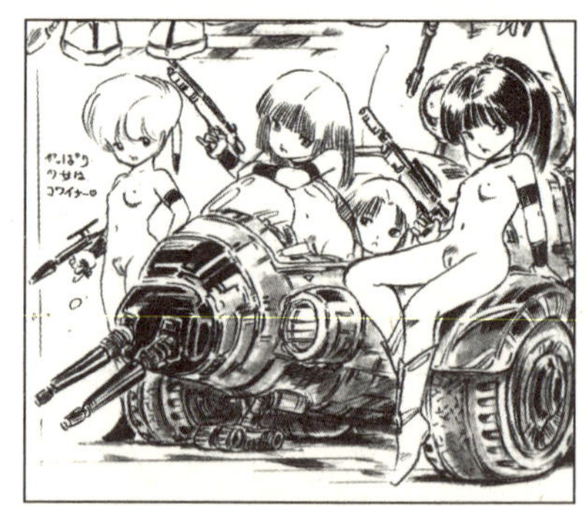
1-4: ***Kawaii GIRL no Kaki-kata Kyoshitsu*** (Aki Uchiyama 1983, AMATORIA)

All of these different artists had different ways of drawing breasts, to the point where I would like to say that there's as much individuality in their work as what you would find in eromanga today.

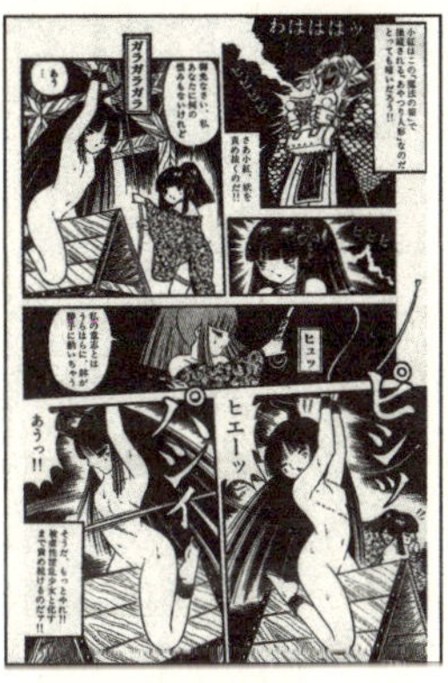

1-5: ***Kuchu Rokaku no Majitsushi*** (Senno Knife 1982, AMATORIA)

However, actual depictions of sex were few and far between. In shonen magazines, they couldn't show the lower half of a girl's body, so it might be correct to say that to certain readers who wished to read works featuring sex acts, loli con comic magazines had the advantage there. In that sense, by suggesting the girls' innocent pubic hair, crevices, and veins (within lolicon material) might have stolen readers' hearts with that strategy.

An artist who would later make it big in the bishojo comic world, Giyugun (1-8), explained his work and how he draws by saying, "Within the revolution that is bishojo comics, there wasn't the ability to make sexual depictions a reality, even in eromanga, up until now. After this, you won't be able to miss the tendency towards private part-oriented material!"

This does not mean "genitals that have been drawn without modification," but is more like, "when using the super-deformed style, instead of drawing realistic genitals, the modification to the drawings were more dilute in nature."

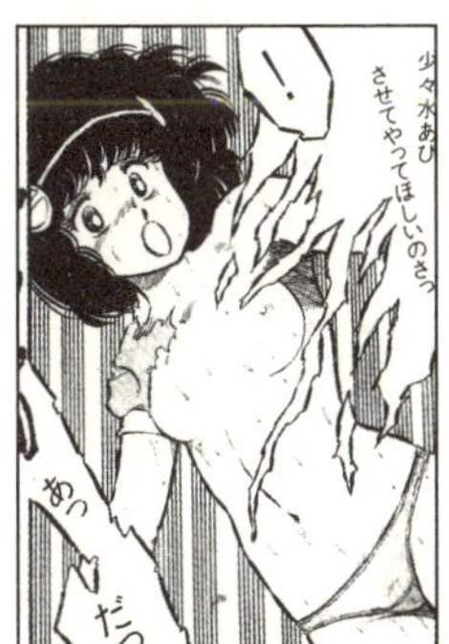

1-6: ***Iczer One*** (*Tatakae!! Ikusa 1*; Rei Aran 1983, AMATORIA)

When it came to drawing the expressions of breasts within manga, back then it meant that bishojo comics fully waded into a pool of ideas reflecting female genitalia for the first time. In this way, Giyugun watched bishojo comics pioneering these expressions within the genre, making his words testimony to that event.

Of course, breasts, and without peer, the expressions of breasts, were not making light of the actual body parts. Within the early days of bishojo comics, each expression itself had differences in size to the next. However, it was thought that shonen magazines generally did not have too many differences within their expressions. Nonetheless, to conclude that shonen magazines had little difference within their expressions, does not resolve or explain the circumstances behind that lack of difference of expressions. In reality, the representations of breasts within shonen magazines from the '70s on had exploded compared to the previous era, and those expressions entered the age of "breast inflation."

So, let's get into why expressions of breasts in both shonen and children's magazines suddenly exploded, shall we?

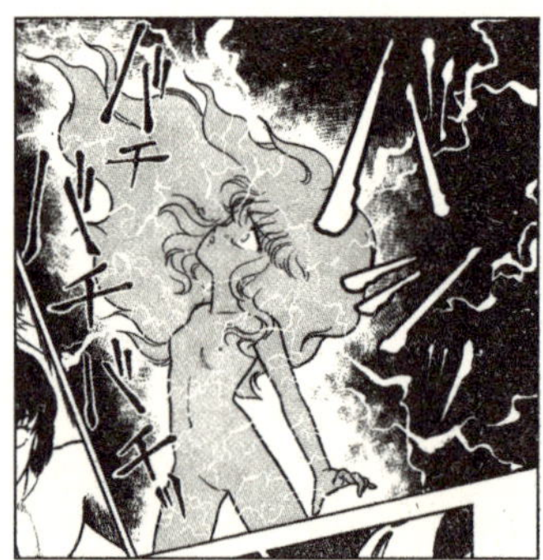

1-7: ***Hades Project Zeorymer*** (*Purojekuto Zeoraima*, Moriwo Chimi 1984, AMATORIA)

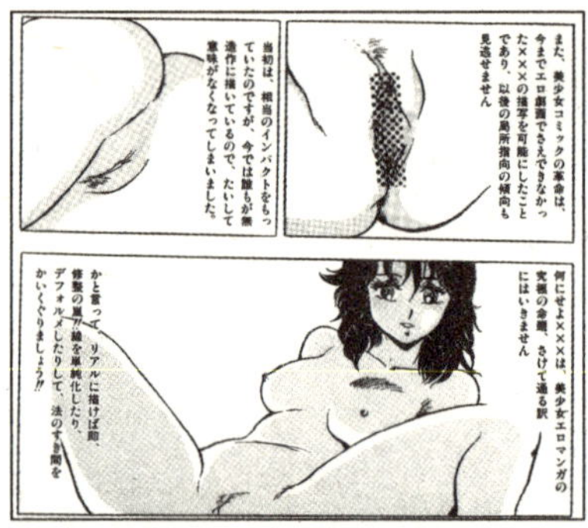

1-8: ***Joyful Koshinaka & "Eiken" Gang*** (*Eiken no Koshinaka-kun*; Giyugun 1987, Shoubunkan)

Shonen Magazines Were Treasure Troves of Breasts!

Though this cannot be said for all manga, most of the content in shonen, ero, and seinen magazines throughout the second half of 1970s were for diehards of the gekiga comics. One could say the tide turned in a major way where most magazines went from carrying gekiga to manga mostly featuring carefree playboys and ladies' men, cute erotic comedies, and just generally erotic content.

A number also featured content that had the protagonist going up against a giant evil force or an extraordinarily strong rival before eventually knocking them down. There were also stories about sports teams giving it their all.

Others focused on characters that didn't want stoic lives but rather wished for a fun school experience with their female companions; those that wanted to live a carefree life; and some who had delusions they shared with the audience, too, and so on.

Did the young men that read these magazines suddenly have a change of heart in terms of what they wanted from them? I ask because shonen magazines were now actively bringing heroines to the forefront of these stories. These new comics would feature love stories, slapstick comedies, and slightly erotic content about youth and one's school days, all of which became quite popular.

And then there were the anime adaptations of stories like Rumiko Takahashi's ***Urusei Yatsura*** (1978, Shogakukan/Viz Media), Fujihiko Hosono's ***Sasuga no Sarutobi*** (1980, Shogakukan), Hisashi Eguchi's ***Stop!! Hibari-kun!*** (1981, Shueisha), and many others. I suppose one could make the argument that these works accelerated how the genre started to spread.

Up until that point, even shonen magazines would have their share of panty shots, breasts, and nudity drawn as *fan service* (sexually alluring scenes). But within the school life genre, all of these scenes could be collected in a single comic for the first time, as they tended to cluster together naturally within the flow of a story. And, of course, the stories with fan service were very popular with younger male readers.

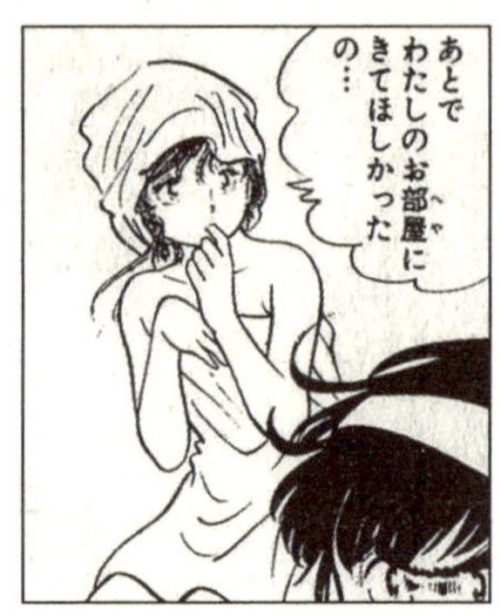

1-9: ***Izumi-chan Graffiti,*** Vol. 1 (Tatsuo Kanai 1981, Shueisha)

Imagine you go diving only to miraculously see a pair of beautiful breasts exposed to you by some lucky turn of fate. This is an example of the beauty of form for this genre, the "lucky pervert" trope that flourished within it starting in the 1980s.

The heroine of Tatsuo Kanai's ***Izumi-chan Graffiti*** (1980, Shueisha; 1-9) Izumi Tamura; Yoshie, the heroine of Yasuhiro Nakanishi's ***Oh! Tohmei Ningen*** (1982, Kodansha; 1-10); and Izumi Harada from Hikaru Tooyama's ***Heart ♥ Catch Izumi-chan*** (1982, Kodansha; 1-11)...are girls in the same grade as the male protagonist for each of their series. They are a little perverted but still quite pure, and compared to the late-bloomer male protagonist, they are often forward and positive about things. And all of whom expose their nude forms to these protagonists at their convenience.

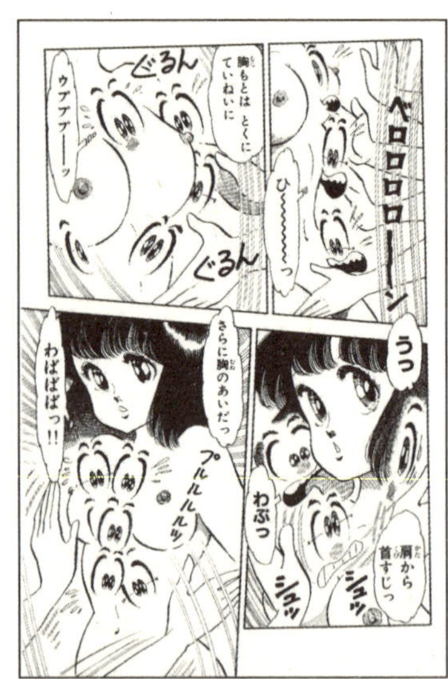

1-10: ***Oh! Tohmei Ningen***, Vol. 3 (Yasuhiro Nakanishi 1983, Kodansha)

Whether it would be better to say that in this genre at this time, it was all about the plot twists happening between the protagonist and heroine. Or was it the goal of the readers to see the heroine's breasts and/or underwear? Or for them to be able to touch/fondle them or see them strip nude? Either way, it is safe to say that it would be difficult for shonen magazines to show any more than that back then.

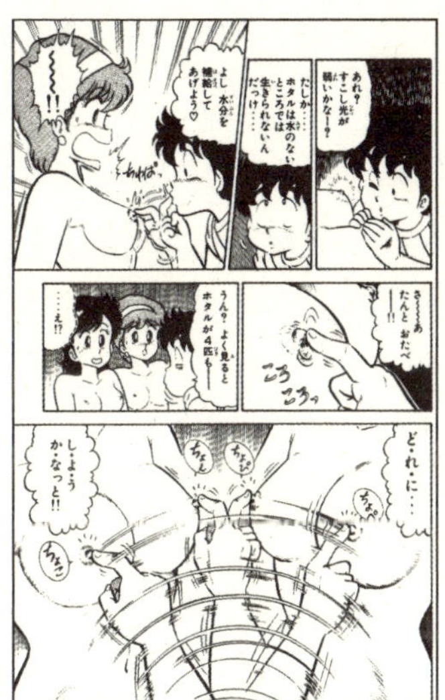

1-11: ***Heart ♥ Catch Izumi-chan***, Vol. 6 (Hikaru Tooyama 1986, Kodansha)

And going along with that, whatever plot twist was needed to get to that payoff was important, to say the least. The size, shape, and softness of the breasts was not something people got overly into, as is evidenced by the fact that most artists drew breasts of the average size in these series. Though I can say that among the three previously mentioned artists, Nakanishi almost always drew nipples on his breasts.

In the shonen magazines of this era, most stories within them were allowed to draw nipples on their breasts. Outside of the other option of spilling shadows over the breast to tease the reader, there was no other intentional, unnatural censorship done before publication. While it varied from magazine to magazine, most shonen publications only started to enforce what was later called the "Nipple Code" (banning the direct portrayal of nipples) as a tacit, self-inflicted agreement after 1980.

But it wasn't only in shonen publications where that was happening. The early waves of breasts within publishing also began crashing upon the shores of children's magazines as well. However, it's important to say that the meaning of "breasts" and their representation here is different from what was appearing in shonen properties.

Compared to the "accidental" phenomenon happening in shonen, expressions in children's manga were drawn more in the spirit of skirt flipping, practical jokes, and children's games in general. The heroine in Takeshi Ebihara's ***Miss Machiko*** (*Maicchingu Machiko-sensei* 1980, Gakken; 1-12), Miss Machiko, has a trick played on her by a student and her punishment is to allow him to touch her breasts. While this is sexual harassment, *Miss Machiko* is largely about a mischievous, playful, shy teacher who plays tricks on others.

While the frequency Miss Machiko has to let a student touch her breasts seems rather high, the instances she shows her nude breasts are actually quite small. Throughout the eight-volume series, the audience can only see her nipples in the first volume.

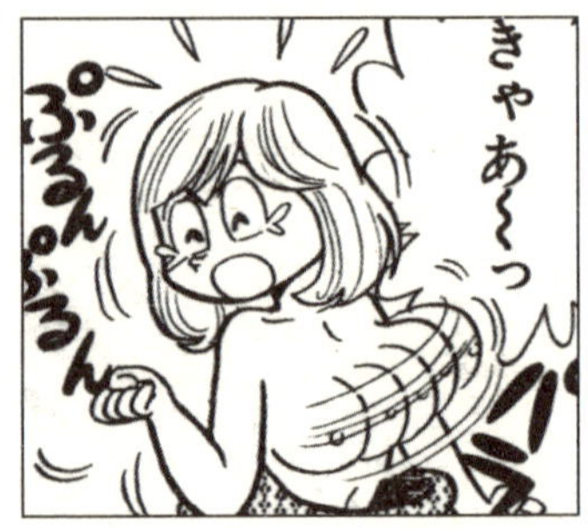

1-12: ***Miss Machiko,*** Vol. 1 (Takeshi Ebihara 1981, Gakken) This is the debut of Ebihara's unique breast expression.

However, Miss Machiko is an adult woman. And the size of her breasts is rather large. They're drawn quite simply in the manga, and that style isn't just limited to children's magazines at that time. Instead, in manga in general, it might be more appropriate to say they're inserted as representative of something more.

Shonen publications had quite a few expressions of breasts within them, but the lewd breast revolution didn't really kick off until Go Nagai's assistant, Susumu Yoshikawa (1-13) and his comic that was serialized in *Monthly CoroCoro Comics*, ***Ojama Yurei-kun*** (1979, Shogakukan) appeared on the scene. While it was serialized in a children's comic publication, it did have a high number of sexy scenes in it.

Within its debut in the magazine, the protagonist, who had been hit by a car and was now a ghost, went to haunt and eventually possess his female classmate, Kodama Yamano (who, it turns out, is the only one who can see him). In that way, they become stuck with each other in the vein of a sexy slapstick comedy as different sexy plot twists build.

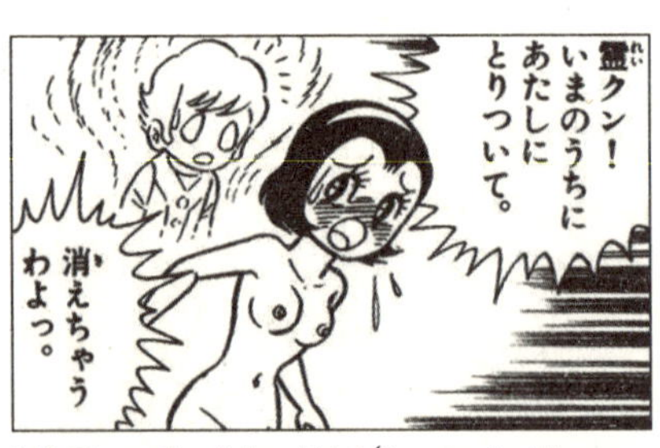

1-13: ***Ojama Yurei-kun***, Vol. 2 (Susumu Yoshikawa 1980, Shogakukan)

Various sexy scenes happen, but is the protagonist, a shy, weak boy? Or is he a pervert? Why would there be so many sexy scenes for a children's series? And how does it differ from shonen comics from that point in time (aside from the protagonist being dead)?

Well, the heroine, Kodama Yamano, is an elementary schooler and she has large breasts. It is almost as if the expressions were the artist's inheritance from his time with Go Nagai (a legendary artist known for his own scandalous shonen series). On top of that, those breasts have nipples very clearly and visibly drawn on them.

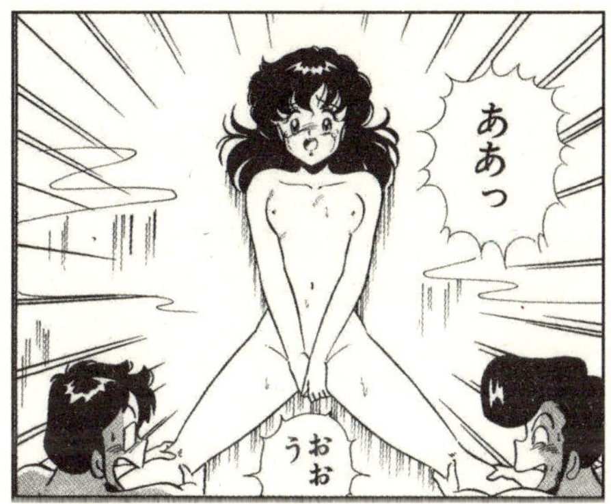

1-14: ***Paradise Gakuen***, Vol.1 (Masatoshi Kawahara 1985, Kodansha)

By the end of the decade, the karate manga ***Shura no Mon*** (1989, Kodansha) by Masatoshi Kawahara had become famous. But before that, in 1985, Kawahara launched the bishojo title ***Paradise Gakuen*** (1985, Kodansha; 1-14). Shinobu Hiromori, also known as Lolicon Maker, debuted in a shonen magazine under the pen name Nonki Miyasu with ***Yarukkya Nnight*** (1987, Shueisha; 1-15), a bishojo comic. Sumiko Kamimura launched ***Ikenai! Luna-sensei*** (1986, Kodansha; 1-16), the first real comic of the genre to come under fire for its eros was also launched at this time. All of these titles, serialized in shonen publications, were popular, cheerful and sexy school life comedies, proving that particular story formula was gold for drawing in readers.

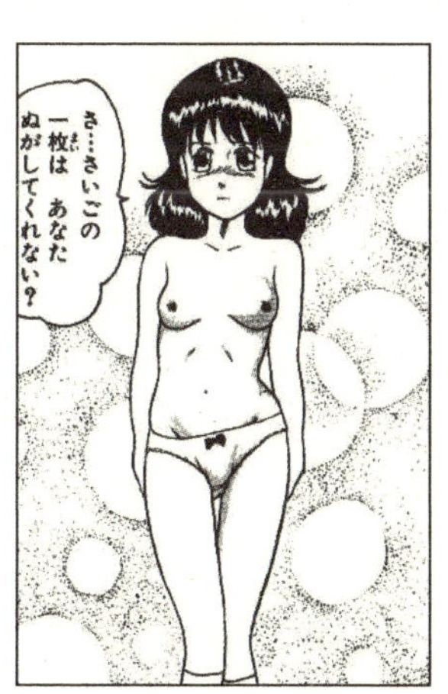

1-15: ***Yarukkya Nnight***, Vol. 1 (Nonki Miyasu 1985, Shueisha)

Manga breasts from the beginning of the 1980s to its midpoint were, and this is a rather abrupt summary, on the whole, rather large and soft in shape and texture, though readers weren't yet seized with thoughts of jiggle physics as of quite yet. The dynamics of how the unseen would become seen was of great importance to readers. So, when the unseen was finally visible, the character (and the readers) would be thanking their lucky stars and varying representations of such would be also just as important to readers as they spread like wildfire throughout the genre by 1985.

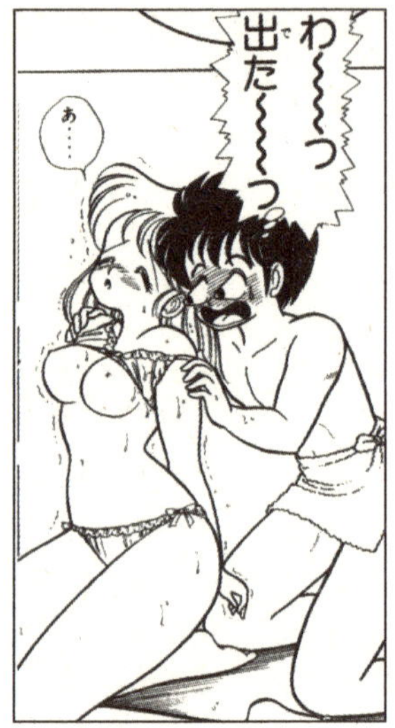

1-16: ***Ikenai! Luna-sensei***, Vol 1 (Sumiko Kamimura 1987, Kodansha)

I don't think that the readers' obsession with how artists drew their breasts was quite there yet like it would be in later years, but then again, the conscious effort on behalf of artists to differentiate how they draw breasts wasn't quite there yet either.

After this, the breasts in shonen comics would carve out a different (evolutionary) path than the ones followed by seinen and bishojo comics, but out of the remaining two, the one to undergo drastic changes in style first would be bishojo comics.

Meanwhile, the '80s began with the founding of the lolicon genre and continued with the cultivation of that new genre. But midway through the lolicon boom, the "lolicon theory proclamation" was made.

Bishojo Comics with Newfound Freedoms

When the lolicon boom began in the 1980s, the word otaku was not yet in the general lexicon as a term for fans. Fans, who went to events like Comic Market, created a marketplace for doujinshi, and soon, started to crank out bishojo comics like no one's business.

However, while there were many monthly serialized bishojo comic magazines out there by this time, it was still a category that was centered in fans' passion for the material, and not very popular yet. For these were folks who did not read your usual shonen and seinen magazines.

While still calculating the spread of this new genre, people working within it found themselves soon standing at a fork in the road in terms of which path the genre should take in order to advance and ultimately, evolve it.

The two forks were: One, about reflecting their pure love for girls, which focused on beauty rather than eros. This fork aimed to become the image of the genre for bishojo comics, or the "lolicon fundamentalism sect." And the second, which wanted to find their desire and sense of eros in their ideal girls put to the page, or the "ero supremacy sect."

These two sects within bishojo comics warred quite visibly in the pages of the monthly magazines, and the places where these two did not fight were reflected in magazine sales.

Bit by bit, by looking at this data, it became apparent that over time, work being published had a bias that listed in the direction towards the ero supremacy sect. It seemed that the male readers that were so passionate about these subjects were honest to their desires for eros after all. And in this way, the lolicon fundamentalism sect was destroyed in a blink of an eye. Which is why by the midpoint of the decade, there would be a proclamation made—*lolicon theory*.

But that being said, it wasn't like the proclamation went ahead and automatically hard coded everything into eromanga. Perhaps it would be better to call it the "unloliconification" of eromanga. It wasn't about taking beautiful girls and shutting them solely within the framework of lolicon concepts, either. It was more about giving the otaku their own space, so they could fully project their ideals onto these works, as well as the process of that shift.

In terms of how this movement started to gain traction and how it started to accelerate, in 1984 the debut of Tou Moriyama had a huge effect on making all of that happen. In regular, non-eromanga magazines, he worked under the name Naoki Yamamoto, a pen name (which many other artists who did/or do ero content can relate to as many have different names used for different content). Moriyama's manga was the heralding of a new style that hadn't been seen before, up until this point in time (1-17).

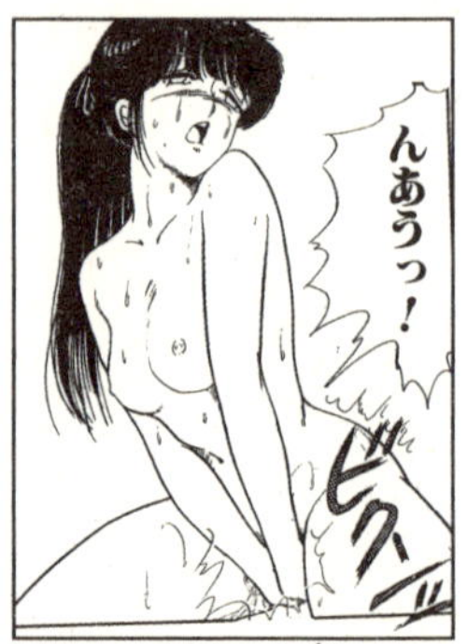

1-17: ***Rough & Ready*** (Tou Moriyama 1986, Tsukasa Shobo)

It was different from the ero-gekiga and lolicon manga styles, as it was cutting-edge with a different context entirely. There were large parts of it that used bishojo designs as a base to build upon. While it was close to bishojo content, there was a mercilessness to it. There was a hard, unforgiving edge that had not been seen in any of the aforementioned genres before, ever.

It had an eros ethic along with mysterious plot twists, and it felt as if someone had set it to be *lolicon-free*, bringing about a new vision for bishojo comics to that audience.

Tou Moriyama's books flew off the shelves when they were published, creating the chance to create ever more fervent fans for the genre for the first time ever.

The magazines that took the chance to collect these brand-new bishojo comic artists who remade the genre were *Monthly Penguin Club Magazine* (1986, Tatsumi Publishing later Fujimi Publishing), and *Manga Hot Milk Magazine* (1986, Byakuya-Shobo). These two magazines would help the bishojo comic world to gain traction in publishing from this point forward, and became quite popular with their readership, drawing in new fans.

A new vision for what constituted bishojo also meant a new vision for expressions of breasts to be born. Until this point in time, when it came to the image of lolicon most fans thought of, it was bound to a framework of ideals with girls with small breasts. Soon, that image would be freed from that one particular framework.

And it was at this point in time, that big breast expressions were born.

The Dawn of Big Breasts

According to *lolicon fundamentalism*, it was at this time that breast expressions, which had been tightly bound since their inception along with the genre, had been set free. And there was a new freedom of possibilities as to what one could desire and project within the genre. So along with the growing popularity of Moriyama's works, it started to spread outside of its previous limits with a new vigor. In order to do that, breasts began to be drawn bigger as a way to appeal to new readers, causing yet another transfiguration within the genre.

Bishojo comics had more of an affinity to eromanga than most thought, and as they began to become *eromanga-fied*, bigger breasts were tied to sex appeal, and expressions that were thought to exercise one's sexual drive were backed in greater numbers.

It was the first step in the "big boobification" of the eromanga genre. Except this time, the driving force of this new movement within the genre definitely wasn't just resistance to lolicon fundamentalism. It didn't stay within the bounds of the manga world. It spread across Japan, bringing prosperity with it, and brought the omen of the *big breast bubble* along with it.

I should probably explain the term "big breasts" here. By the mid-1980s, the term "kyounyu," or big breasts, was another term not really in the Japanese lexicon. I will not say that it was not in the lexicon at all, as copywriters for Japanese pornography (Japanese adult-videos or JAV) used the term in summaries on packaging to get the potential watcher's attention. But it was mostly isolated to that world back then. So, in the real world, most people weren't pointing at large pairs of breasts and calling them *kyounyu*.

I think I may have said this already but to repeat myself: the year that the term *kyounyu* entered the mainstream Japanese lexicon was 1989.

Japanese porn star Kimiko Matsuzaka (1-18) debuted in 1989, and the weekly tabloid magazines that introduced her used the term kyounyu to describe her intense bust. After that, across most of the (male) world, use of the term spread quite rapidly. Before then, the other term that originated from adult media used the most was "D-cup," so that by that point terms like "boin" (the onomatopoeia for the sound of a big bust bouncing) and "dekapai" (huge titties) had already made their way into the mainstream. It is thought that the term kyounyu started to spread from the year 1985 onward, eventually ending up in the Japanese lexicon.

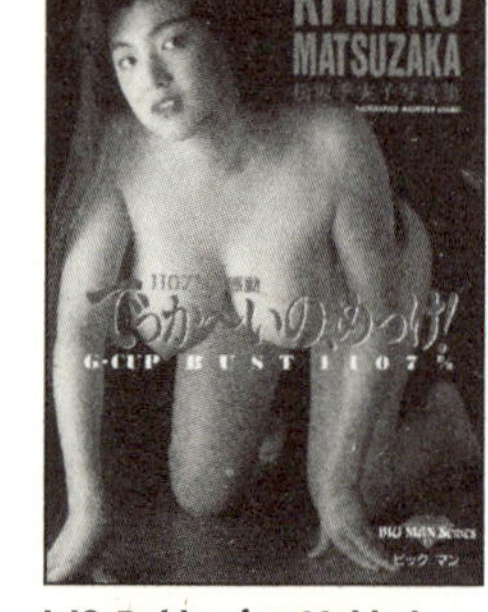

1-18: ***Dekka~i no Mekke!*** (Kimiko Matsuzaka 1989, Big Man)

Amongst kyounyu researchers, it is thought that the influence export of foreign gravure magazines such as *Bachelor* (Dia Press; 1-19) and *Dick* (Taiyou Shobo) was no small thing. Like Perry's black ships that opened Japan, blonde-haired foreigners would from the land of breasts to throw open the doors like her ancestors did.

Of course, going backwards a little, the idol models that are considered the pioneer *kyounyu idols* are Ikue Sakakibara, foreign entertainment personality Agnes Lum and the new era kyounyu idol models are Naoko Kawai and Yoshie Kashiwabara (who did it all underground, of course).

After that, the amount of porn videos that used the term D-cup as a selling point would increase. Which makes me wonder, was there something like the "long-awaited kyounyu theory" that existed to explain the amount of fervor generated by these fans, and how they embraced it?

But let us return to the issue of eromanga.

To the concepts and expressions of breasts that had been set free and newly allowed in scope and shape, the stream and path of the culture-wide big boobification became something of a tailwind to the movement as a whole, spurring it along.

1-19: *Bachelor*, Feb. 1992 (Dia Press)

And that's where the debut of "baby-faced kyounyu characters" comes in.

But it wasn't just within bishojo manga that this happened. This was a brand-new idea in general to eromanga.

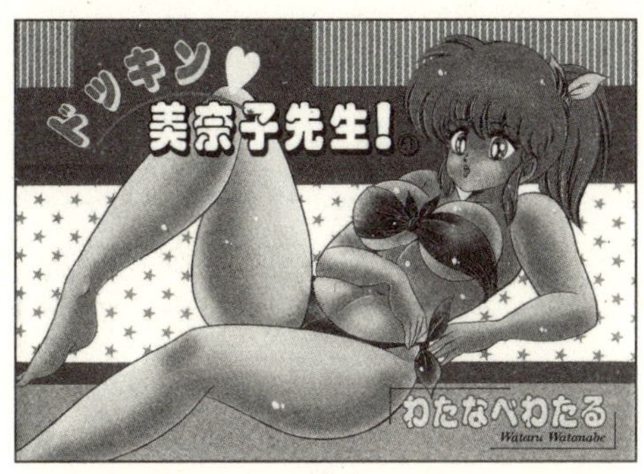

1-20: ***Dokkin ♥ Minako-sensei*** (Wataru Watanabe 1987, Byakuya-Shobo)

When we talk about early kyounyu artists, there's one we absolutely can't remove from the rest of the list: Wataru Watanabe (1-20, 21). The breasts he drew were so overwhelming in their existence that it was hard to tear one's eyes away from them. Watanabe's breasts have a round, very plainly distinctive contour to them; as if you'd touch them and they'd ripple with an effect much like an overfilled water balloon. As semiotic symbols go, they have a very manga-like shape to them, much like those that belonged to those beautiful blonde-haired actresses that Japan became so enamored with. Many eromanga readers suddenly became obsessed with this new character type, an existence that charmed as many as it drew in. The new design was the combination of a blonde actress's body with the face of a bishojo comic character.

Wataru Watanabe had, in a magazine interview ("Chotto Ecchi na Fukubukuro, Vol. 2"; *Comptiq* 1989, Kadokawa), declared that the one character that had influenced him was Machiko from Takeshi Ebihara's *Miss Machiko.* In Watanabe's first collected work, ***Dokkin ♥ Minako-sensei*** (1989, Byakuya-Shobo), the main character Miss Minako had been influenced by

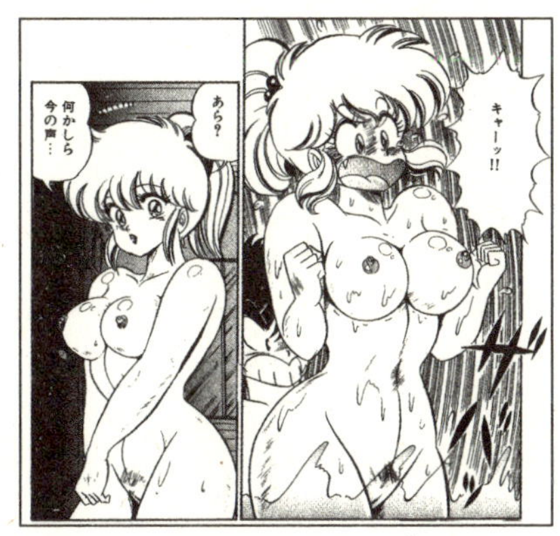

1-21: ***Dokkin ♥ Minako-sensei***, Vol. 2 (Wataru Watanabe 1987, Byakuya-Shobo)

a very popular idol at the time, Minako Honda. It was as if someone had fused Miss Machiko with Minako Honda's body. Yet at the same time this new teacher type of character was quite different from that blonde-haired kyounyu actress from *Bachelor*. Was Watanabe trying to create a new type of teacher when he created Miss Minako?

Minako was Watanabe's ideal bishojo. She was one with a gloriously free bust and one with a childlike face, and precisely because of that, she became a symbol of the genre. The conclusion of this expression was as if this new bishojo character was disrupting a loli expression's body with the size of her breasts.

With that, a new type of expression, the *kyounyu loli*, was born.

The Post-80s Big Breast Emancipation Movement

After Wataru Watanabe's debut, two more new artists would leave their mark on the genre and their influence would ripple throughout it for years to come.

Kei Kitamimaki would open the way for the development of the overwhelming shapes of bodies of big-breasted *shemales* and *futanari* (hermaphrodite) characters, as well as attractive mature women (1-22).

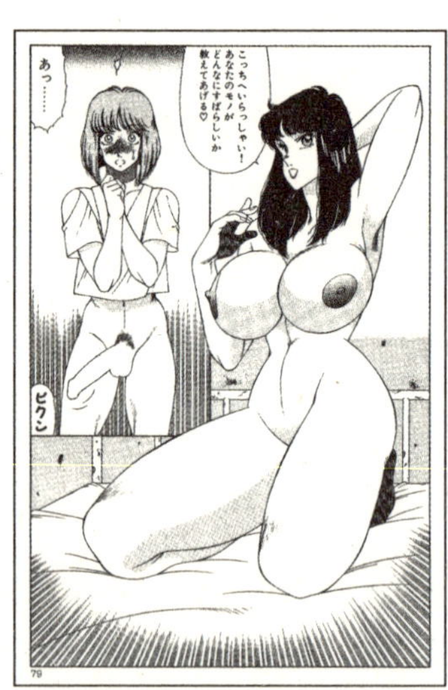

1-22: ***Aphrodite no Yu-utsu*** (Kei Kitamimaki 1988, Byakuya-Shobo)

Then there were the school life love comedy series with a kyounyu heroine. It has been said that this work introduced yet another brand-new concept, *bakunyu* (explosively large breasts). Seemingly exceeding human intellect at that time, these overwhelming big breasts outclassed the rest. The man behind this glorious new expression was Tohru Nishimaki (who uses the name Takeshi Kajiwara for regular manga; 1-23).

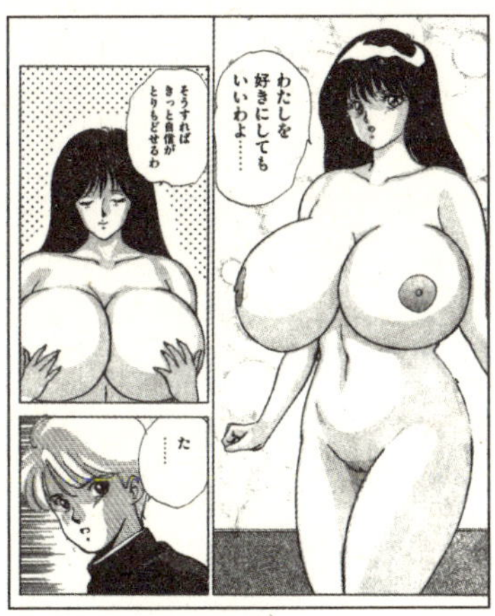

1-23: ***D-Cup LOVERS*** (Tohru Nishimaki 1993, Hit Publishing)

The kyounyu anthologies they both participated in, considered a pioneering force in the genre, were published in 1988: Byakuya-Shobo's *D-Cup Collection* (1-24) and Outou Shobo's *D-Cup Club* (1-25). These were published before kyounyu as a word became part of the lexicon, so instead they used the term D-cup for their style of drawing (though kyounyu did exist at the time).

Looking at the covers for *D-Cup Collection*, it's easy to see that Kitamimaki's busts are more than a D-cup. If I were to be distasteful in describing them, they are more than a G-cup in size. In Kei Yoshida's covers for *D-Cup Club*, the breasts he drew were of a completely impossible to measure size, as if ignoring the limits of how large they could be.

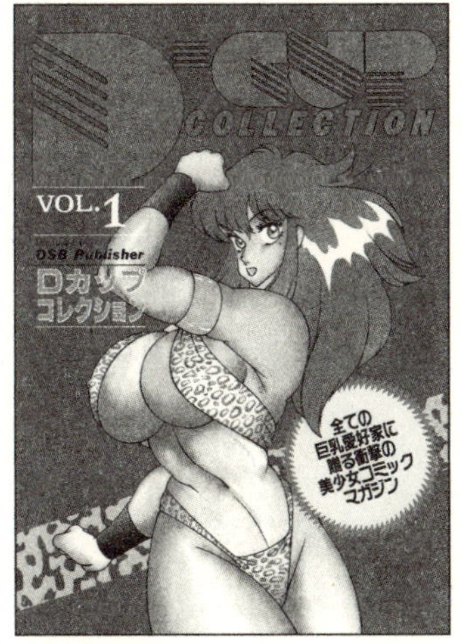

1-24: *D-Cup Collection*, Vol. 1 (1988, Byakuya-Shobo)

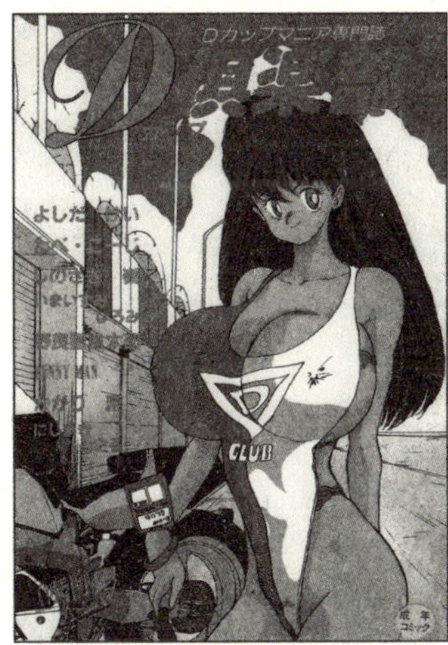

1-25: *D-Cup Club*, Iss. 1 (1988, Outou Shobo)

In terms of how men saw this at the time, when they thought of the word "D-cup," a bra size did not come to mind. It was more in the vein of "obviously, huge breasts." Most likely, when they saw the single letter "D," then the term "dekkai" (massive) most likely came to mind. So you understand that an image of largeness took priority when it came to the term.

There is also the theory that the reason why these breasts were drawn larger than needed was possibly because men misunderstood how bra sizes worked.

As I said previously, from the '80s on, there was a second invasion of Japan; this time filled with skin magazines featuring buxom foreign women, and this had a great amount of influence and impact when the big-breasted boom really kicked off. Many gravure magazines leapt upon the term D-cup, and there was even a magazine called *D-Cup* in publication at one point, but at the time, a foreign D-Cup bra was roughly two sizes larger than a Japanese one (mostly due to the fact that there are apparently many ways to measure for a bra). It's been said that maybe Japanese readers really saw an F-size, not a D-cup and paid it no mind as they possibly did not know the difference.

I am of the mind that male readers didn't really think much of bra sizes, though I can guess that images of the F-size and above gravure models they'd seen previously had been burned into the backs of their minds. Delusions can change one's understanding of things. I'm not quite sure if there had been an artist at that time that would've been able to draw a correct D-cup.

These anthologies that had been planned became the backdrop to the fact that kyounyu as a concept was beginning to be accepted by the masses, and the comics the artists drew became their own personal endorsement as such.

In an interview I had with *D-Cup Collection* artist, Kei Kitamimaki, he spoke about the details of what made him wake up to the allure of big breasts. He had been aware of the existence of the *lolicon boom* that had started at the beginning of the 1980s and the bishojo comic genre that had sprung up shortly thereafter. But when it came to influences on his own work, he told me that *ero-gekiga* had more of an influence on his work than the other two genres. However, what had truly shocked him the most had been the imported skin magazines similar to Bachelor. He had been buying them in bookstores since he was in middle school, and thus kyounyu became his favorite fetish.

I can guess that that shock he received upon seeing kyounyu for the first time was quite considerable. The bodies he drew with their large breasts and glamorous bodies were so removed from the smaller Japanese body type. Their shoulders especially seemed far closer to the American and European body types instead. When all of this is considered, one can see the big impact those magazines had on Kitamimaki's style.

Similarly, we can see the same with Tohru Nishimaki's style. An avid reader of magazines like *Playboy* and *Bachelor* that he had started buying in his teens, he too awoke to the allure of the big breast trope. However, his art was different than Kitamimaki's in that while he drew *bakunyu* American/European pornstar-grade breasts, he still tried to cultivate the rest of his character to resemble the sweet cuteness of a Japanese idol.

Perhaps it would be better to call them the heaven-sent saints of the kyounyu genre, the heads of a newly rising movement with regard to fetishes. And perhaps their rise to fame was natural that way. However, both have testified to the fact that they battled with their inner demons, wondering if it was okay for them to draw big breast content like this. Yet at the same time, their testimony to how much they loved kyounyu as their own personal favorite fetish was something embarrassing and perhaps it went to the point of mania, but there was that sense that they should claim that mania regardless.

Perhaps as proof of that, one person wrote that the covers of *D-Cup Club* should instead be called "D-Cup Mania Magazine" as an instigating phrase, scratching a bit of the surface (at least of the hardcore fans' part) of the fetish that people desperately loved and showing that.

At this time, kyounyu as a word, was instead referred to by the onomatopoeic "boin" (boing, the sound a bouncing bust makes) and *dekapai* (a portmanteau of *dekai* [huge] and *oppai* [tits]) a great deal of the time. When used with women in conversation, these words were also used in banter with women with large breasts who had a complex about it. With men, a great deal of the time it had come to be used to make fun of the men who were big fans of the trope. At the end of Kitamimaki's *D-Cup Club* run, his thoughts about this were recorded as thus in an interview.

> **Editor:** Do people give you the cold shoulder when you tell them you're a fan of *dekapai*?
>
> **Kitamimaki:** Yes. I suppose it's because this feeling is hidden inside of normal folks, so they tend to think I have an Oedipal complex.

From how this article was written, it is easy to see in such phrases as "[getting] the cold shoulder," "Oedipal complex," and "maniac" and other such negative terms have been connected to having an interest in this trope. Anyone can see that.

But out of the artists who said to themselves, "I want to draw kyounyu, but I'm hesitant to do so," the first of those artists that tore down that wall in his heart was none other than baby-faced big breast artist Tohru Nishimaki.

His debut came about due to asking Kitamimaki if it was not only okay to draw a bishojo character with big breasts, but if he'd approve putting one in their anthology. One truly gets the feeling that Nishimaki was seeking permission, which was in turn granted by Kitamimaki.

As if the anthology were an exercise to gain citizenship to the land of drawing big-breasted characters and to continue to spread the movement, he was inheriting the will to do that from Kitamimaki himself. As if he were pushing back against the curse laid upon artists all who had wished for more freedom within the bishojo genre movement but could not run from the framework set forth by strict *lolicon* fans. As if he were pushing back against the real-life kyounyu boom in Japanese porn and imported pornography. Or as if he were gathering the troops and doing so in order to take back the vision of his own bishojo characters from that lolicon curse.

After the 1980s, these new eromanga breast expressions spread, like a signal across the spectrum. It was as if the "Big Breast Emancipation Movement" was a real thing happening in real time (1-26). The media began to run columns about the first kyounyu anthology in Japan, *D-Cup Collection*. Here is an excerpt from one of them:

> *Forgive me for dispensing with the preliminaries, but right now, we seem to be in the process of reclaiming the image of girls with plump chests. And please note, this is happening within the lolicon fan-founded world of bishojo eromanga. It is not a revolution nor is it a fad, but rather it is a true and legitimate return to these values.*
>
> *Thank you, lolicon fans. Because of you we have been able to witness the birth and development of this world.*

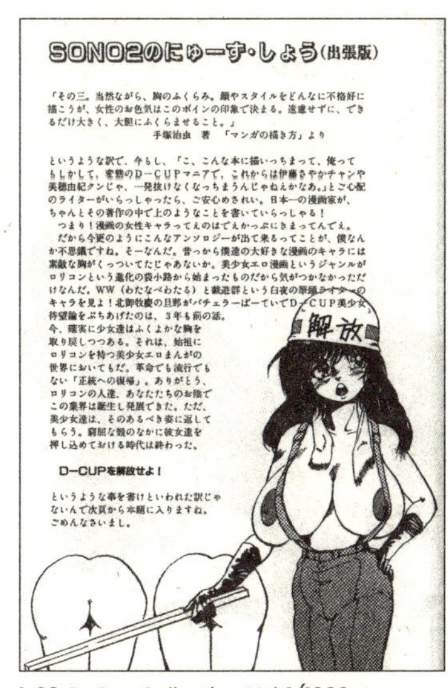

SONO2のにゅーず・しょう(出張版)

「その三。当然ながら、胸のふくらみ。顔やスタイルをどんなに不格好に描こうが、女性のお色気はこのボインの印象で決まる。遠慮せずに、できるだけ大きく、大胆にふくらませること。」

手塚治虫　著　「マンガの描き方」より

というような訳で、今もし、「こ、こんな本に描いっちまって、俺ってもしかして、変態のD－CUPマニアで、これからは伊藤さやかチャンや美穂由紀クンじゃ、一発抜けなくなっちまうんじゃねえかなあ。」とご心配のライターがいらっしゃったら、ご安心めされい。日本一の漫画家が、ちゃんとその著作の中で上のようなことを書いていらっしゃる！

つまり！漫画の女性キャラってえのはでえかっぷにきまってんでえ。

だから今更のようにこんなアンソロジーが出て来るってことが、僕なんか不思議ですね。そーなんだ。昔っから僕達の大好きな漫画のキャラには素敵な胸がくっついてたじゃあないか。美少女エロ漫画というジャンルがロリコンという進化の袋小路から始まったものだから気がつかなかっただけなんだ。WW（わたなべわたる）と戯遊群という白夜の筆頭ライターのキャラを見よ！北御牧慶の旦那がバチェラーばーていでD－CUP美少女待望論をぶちあげたのは、3年も前の話。

今、確実に少女達はふくよかな胸を取り戻しつつある。それは、始祖にロリコンを持つ美少女エロまんがの世界においてもだ。革命でも流行でもない「正統への復帰」。ありがとう、ロリコンの人達、あなたたちのお陰でこの業界は誕生し発展できた。ただ、美少女達は、そのあるべき姿に返してもらう。窮屈な殻のなかに彼女達を押し込めておける時代は終わった。

D－CUPを解放せよ！

というような事を書けといわれた訳じゃないんで次頁から本題に入りますね。ごめんなさいまし。

1-26: *D-Cup Collection*, Vol. 1 (1988, Byakuya-Shobo) This is the column from which I pulled that excerpt.

> *We thank you, but now we must return to how those bishojo images should be, rather than what you have made of them. The time of you shoving them into such slender, skinny shells is over.*
>
> ***Release the D-Cup!***

While this article was part joke and part news, I believe that there is some truth to it; honesty not found on the surface with some fans. Kyounyu, a new expression for breasts, helped birth new possibilities within bishojo comics. And many artists would end up doing battle on those fields in the future.

The Leaping Flames of the Big Breast Boom in Seinen Magazines

Meanwhile, regular manga (especially *seinen* magazines) too was heeding the call and a new wave of big boobification within it.

It was still publishing its stories of lucky perverts with accidental breast exposure, worshiping that particular story trope within its sacred *shonen* magazine. But with seinen magazines, there was a slow but steady influx of new works heavily influenced by the real life kyounyu boom in gravure and pornography.

In seinen magazines, it wasn't simply about exposing breasts; it was about drawing them bigger, and correspondingly, value added. This became a point that charmed fans greatly, creating a direct link between breast size and the popularity of the work in question. If the breasts were bigger, that work tended to be more popular.

Haruka Inui's ***Ogenki Clinic*** (1989, Akita Shoten; 1-27), and its voluptuous female nurse character was immensely popular for that reason. Even though it was written before the generalization of the term kyounyu, the word appears many times within this series as a term.

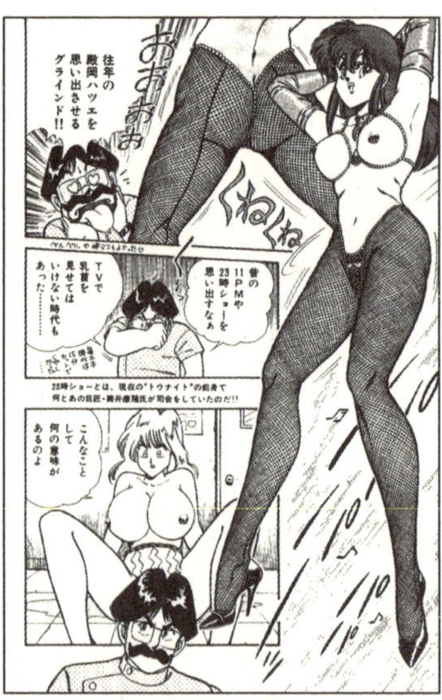

1-27: ***Ogenki Clinic***, Vol. 1 (Haruka Inui 1987, Akita Shoten)

Within shonen magazines, Tohru Nishimaki debuted as Takeshi Kajiwara in *Weekly Shonen Magazine* with his serialized title, ***Kanojo wa Delicate!*** (1989, Kodansha; 1-28). By this point, someone had already overcome kyounyu heroines with a *bakunyu* heroine, and readers couldn't take their eyes off of her. Apparently, with breasts so large that they had smashed their editor's expectations completely. Even he had not expected that her breasts would be this large.

After those titles and Kimiko Matsuzaka's (the original JAV kyounyu actress) debut in the late '80s, kyounyu became a generalized term in the '90s.

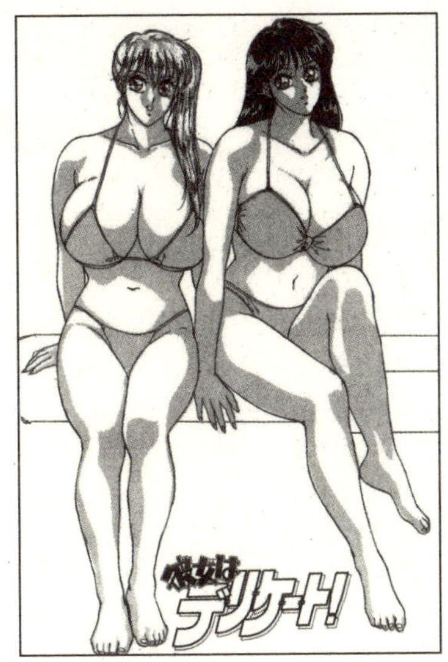

1-28: ***Kanojo wa Delicate!***, Vol. 8 (Takeshi Kajiwara 1990, Kodansha)

Within the manga world, the first kyounyu title debuted. It was Koichiro Yasunaga's ***Kyounyu Hunter*** (1989, Shogakukan, 1-29). In this slapstick comedy, a flat-chested girl who has a complex about her breasts becomes a super-heroine who takes revenge on well-endowed ladies. While we know that its selling point in terms of interests was its big-bosomed characters, I cannot help but wonder if it was also because the shirt that the Kyounyu Hunter wore herself had a "D-Cup" logo on it. This was proof that the term kyounyu was now firmly linked to the term *D-Cup.*

I must note, however, that the size of the kyounyu characters' breasts in that series was above a D cup. And as per usual, men's understanding of how bra sizes work is quite dismal at best.

With the birth of the term kyounyu, most likely came one more word along with it: *hinnyu*, or flat-chested. Though when this term was born, and when it was fixed into the general lexicon, is still under investigation. At this point in time, not many people used

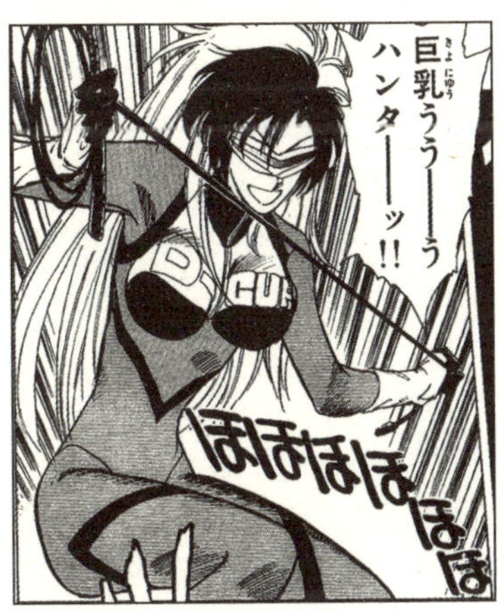

1-29: ***Kyounyu Hunter***, *Right Breast* (Kouichirou Yasunaga 1990, Shogakukan)

the term. Instead they are thought to have used terms like *pechapai* (petite tits), *naichichi* (no-breasts), *pettanko* (flat-chested), or *sentakuita* (flat as a washboard) as expressions for the opposite of large breasts.

Shortly after the kyounyu concept emerged in manga, so did the opposite concept: women with small chests, complexes, and jealousy with regard to big chests. *Kyounyu Hunter* is a story that starts with that concept. While it is a story about being jealous towards large breasts, it is also a story that, as a contrast, shows women with large breasts who also struggle with them (as in, they are too large).

Kyounyu became a big factor within seinen manga. At times, the size of the protagonist's breasts would determine their position within the story, and perhaps this was when expressions of breasts as a representation of a character's personality became an element in manga.

In the same seinen magazines, the big boobification of things began to accelerate, but the way those breasts were drawn, and the evolution of style took a bit longer to develop in comparison. Wataru Watanabe and general manga-style breast expressions were obvious to the eye, and the size of those breast expressions were usually the heart of their appeal.

One who sang the praises of having an objection to the big breast trope was Hiroya Oku. Oku himself has declared his love of the trope, but at the same time, he was the one person unsatisfied with the way they were drawn. He was of the mind that they should have a softness and feel to them. But at this point in time, he was drawing large breasts on otherwise washboard-flat girls. Oku's breasts would inflate when the character was asleep, their growth progressing as if it were an oscillation. In other words, Oku's breasts came alive when his characters slept! Using the trope as an icon, and as far as kyounyu expressions go, it was brilliantly done.

After this assertion of kyounyu ideals was made on his part, one can see the huge impact it had on seinen comics.

By the way, in Oku's debut series (which is considered a masterpiece), aside from a girl with kyounyu, ***HEN*** (1992, Shueisha; 1-30) had men bonding with each other and women falling in love with each other. In the early '90s, his work was one of the first to cover transgender issues in a major seinen magazine. Visual expressions aside, he was possibly one of the most ambitious artists of the era, as he would touch upon issues and themes like transgender people, and challenge others to do so as well.

All of this would, like the way one would prepare one's opening moves in the game *go*, prepare him for greatness when arguably his biggest work, *GANTZ,* was serialized later on.

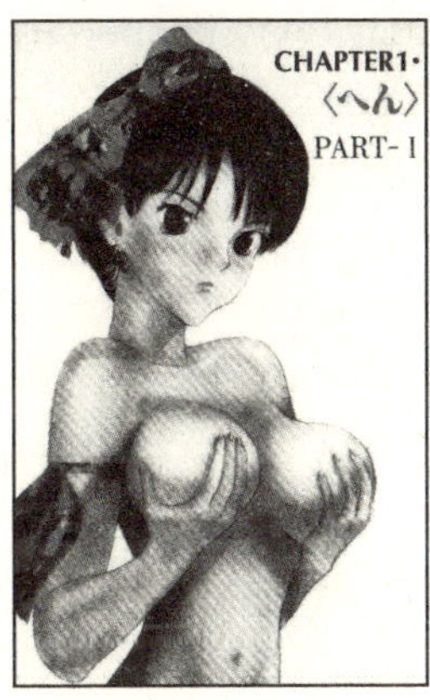

1-30: ***HEN*** (Hiroya Oku 1992, Shueisha)

But let us leave any further analysis of how Oku's visual expressions, and the influence they had on works to come for the next chapter.

Seinen magazines became the link between the 2D and 3D world with regard to the kyounyu boom, and also became the facilitator for the pace it spread at. They implemented a variation of kyounyu characters (breasts as personalities), which continued after this time. Of course, within that there was the shape of the kyounyu trope, and while the expressions of those breasts became abundant, the male-oriented seinen genre itself within manga helped speed up the spread and development of this trope more than the expressions themselves did.

To the Age Where Big Breasts Are Common

After the end of the 1980s, the world of seinen comics were released from the lolicon curse, and a new trope, kyounyu, thrown into the mix was quickly absorbed by its readers. This made the field in which expressions of breasts were flourishing widen greatly.

The age of daring to release big breast anthologies and the hardcore fans' inclination for them had already passed, and a within bishojo comic magazines had now been secured. The propensity for kyounyu had earned its citizenship within the realm of bishojo comics at last. As it did so, kyounyu-centered artists were continuously releasing their own material.

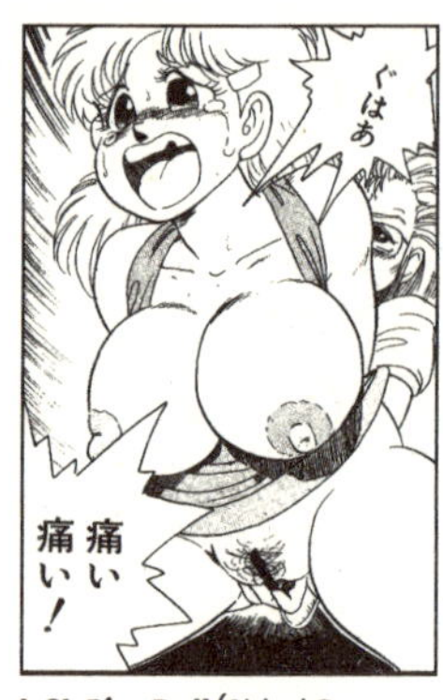

1-31: ***Piss Doll*** (Shiroi Gunpan 1988, Byakuya-Shobo)

The first half of the '90s saw Kei Kitamimaki and Wataru Watanabe continue to put out big-breasted content simply because they could. With other artists starting to mass produce their own large-breasted characters, the genre would rush headlong into its first warring states period.

The beginning of kyounyu as a genre also was the beginning of a period where differentiation was introduced into the genre. Various new types of breast expressions began to appear, and furthermore within seinen magazines, the idea of breasts as personalities naturally sprang up within the genre as well.

The first harvest of the plump kyounyu genre came from artist Shiroi Gunpan (1-31). Then there was Minor Boy, who went from drawing lolicon material to becoming a master of S&M kyounyu content (1-32). Hiroshi Kawamoto (1-33) and Yu Asai (1-34) drew their girls plump, cheerful, and very much in a shonen style. There was Yoshimasa Watanabe, who fused anime with big breasts (1-35). Mugi Tokisaka is the magician behind *throbbing breast* content (1-36). Kazuki Kotobuki fused gekiga with the bishojo genre and big bosoms extremely well in his stories (1-37). Kazu Tomonaga, whose style was much like *young seinen* (comics aimed at older teens) magazines, drew large drooping breasts (1-38). Kozou Youhei was the progenitor of fantasy mixed with kyounyu. HindenBURG fused erotic parody with kyounyu (1-39). Kiyoshi Shimizu drew his girls slender with big breasts (1-40). Yumisuke Kotoy-

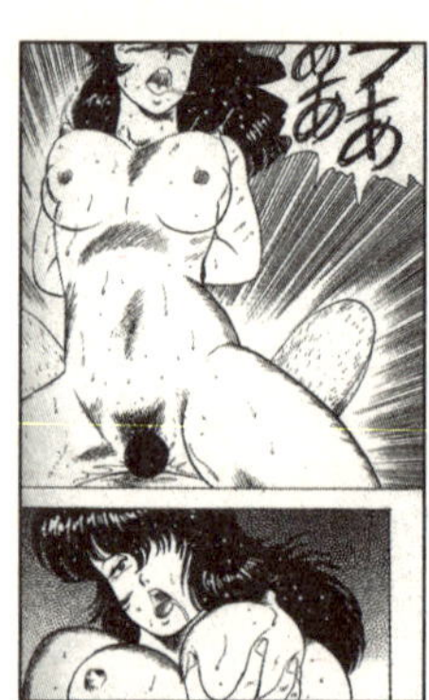

1-32: ***Keiko-sensei no Kagai Jugyo*** (Minor Boy 1988, France Shoin)

oshi developed characters with hanging breasts and a fragile state of mind (1-41). DISTANCE created their massively busty characters with an overwhelming feeling of existence to them, who also had pounding sex (1-42). Ryohta Magaki loves kyounyu and *Gundam,* and won the ultimate prize by marrying a big-breasted editor (1-43). miyabitsuzuru made the charms of busty older women known to the world (1-44). ...All of these artists I've captured here, and more, are only but one piece of the whole when it comes to the world of the kyounyu genre.

While today's kyounyu genre readers might see this and wonder, "Is this the only level of kyounyu artists we have?" I would like for them to go ahead and remember that when the genre emerged, this was the same generation that decided that D-cups equaled kyounyu in size. Back then, readers saw large breasts and thought they were weapons.

In the first half of the '90s, they were pillars that helped support bishojo comics, which along with the readers' needs and demands, helped develop a line of products expected to sell well over time. Together in turn, they helped develop and cement the kyounyu genre and trope as a brand. Halfway through the decade, somehow kyounyu became the expected default for eromanga.

But by the midpoint of the decade, *hinnyu* (small breasts) became a minority trope, as it had anthologies created about it. It became a niche genre, and its disposition as a genre changed the slightest bit.

At this point, things started to slow down a bit with the *big boobification* movement, however. More than kyounyu, more than bakunyu, no, even more than *chonyu* (hyper breasts) had the genre gone through an evolution in size of breasts in content. Kyounyu as a trope had seemingly evolved beyond human wisdom in terms of (breast) size. The vertical axis was still going strong.

Then, things took a turn towards a horizontal axis vector (of growth).

In other words, a new era was on the horizon and it would continue the progression of "breasts as personality types" birthing out new content and tropes.

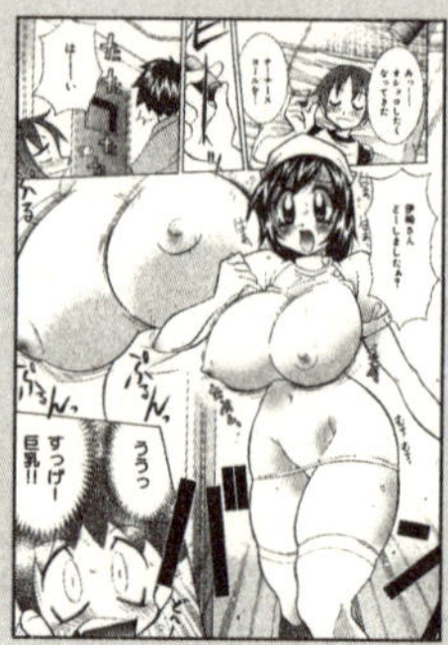

1-33: ***Oshioki Bakunyu Nurse*** (Hiroshi Kawamoto 2002, Toen Shobou)

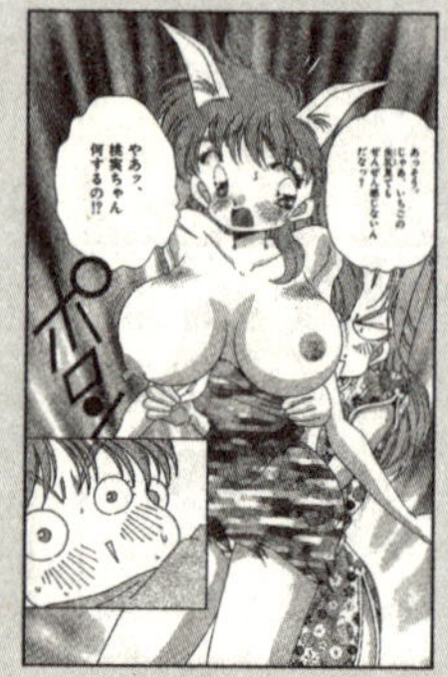

1-34: ***Ichigo ♥ Channel*** (Yu Asai 1996, Cybele Publishing)

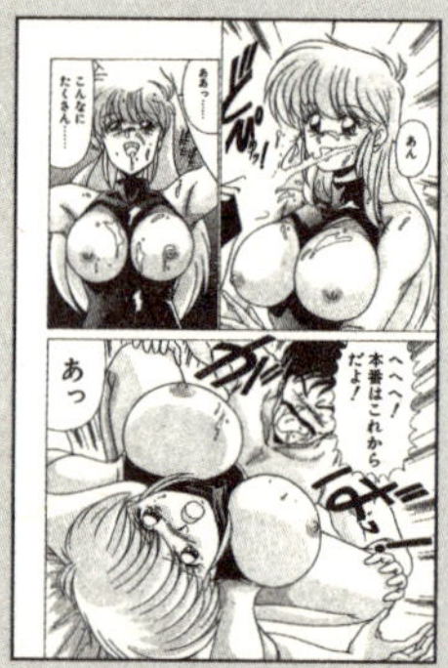

1-35: ***Midnight Program*** (Yoshimasa Watanabe 1992, Akaneshinsha)

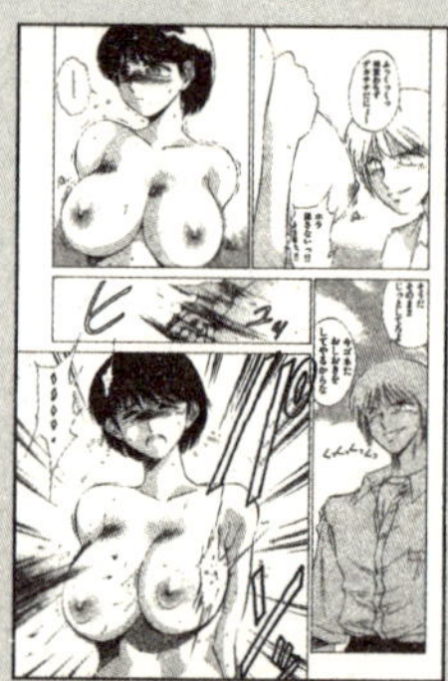

1-36: "NyuMan" (Mugi Tokisaka 1997, Wanimagazine)

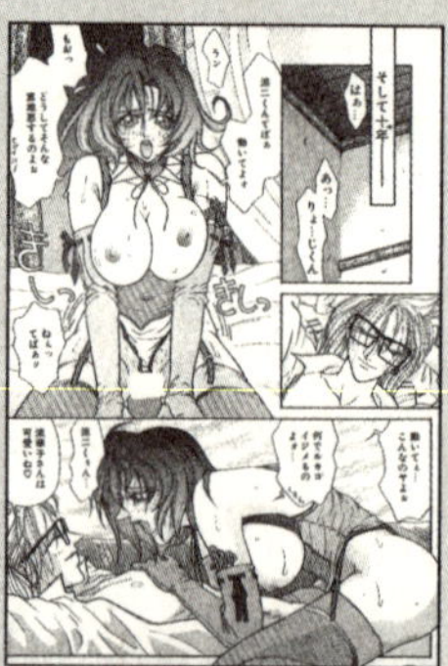

1-37: ***NIGHT VISITOR*** (Kazuki Kotobuki 1994, Tsukasa Shobo)

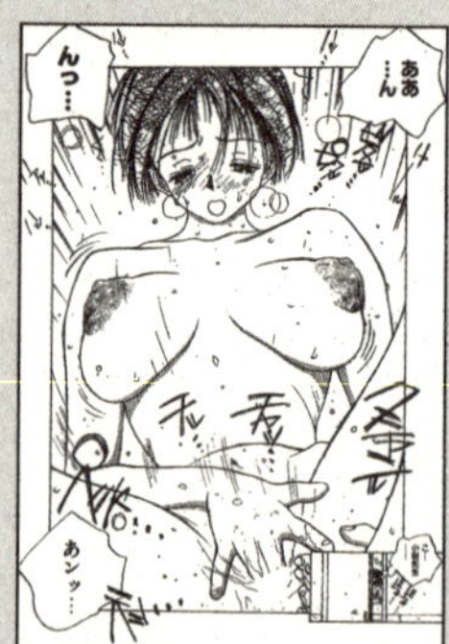

1-38: "Futarikkiri no" (Kazu Tomonaga 1993, Tsukasa Shobo)

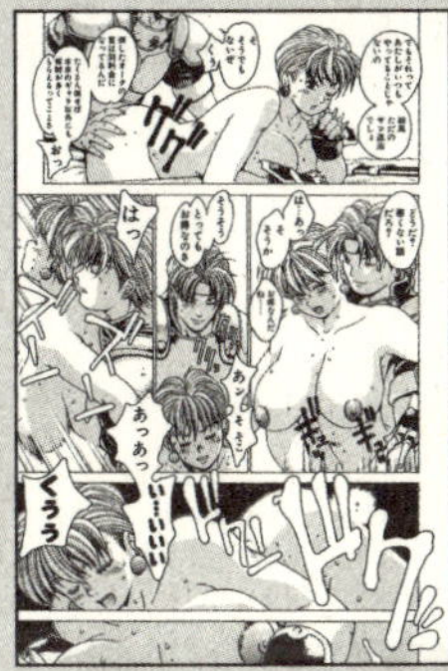

1-39: ***PUNKY KNIGHT*** (Kozou Youhei 2001, Akaneshinsha)

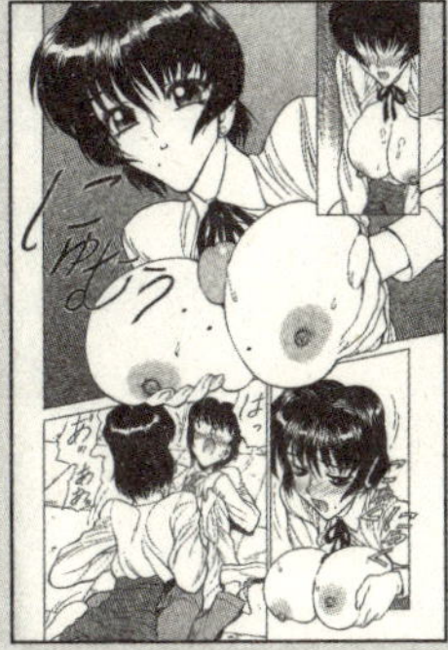

1-40: ***Sensei no Tsuyabukuro*** (Kiyoshi Shimizu 2005, JC Publishing)

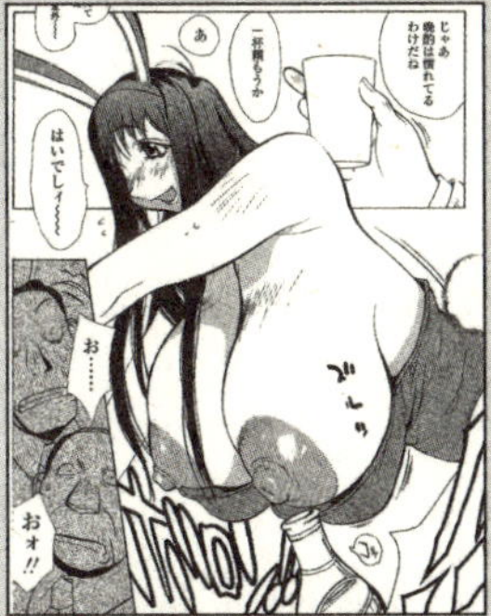

1-41: ***INSULT!!*** *(In INSULT!!,* Yumisuke Kotoyoshi 2001, Fujimi Publishing)

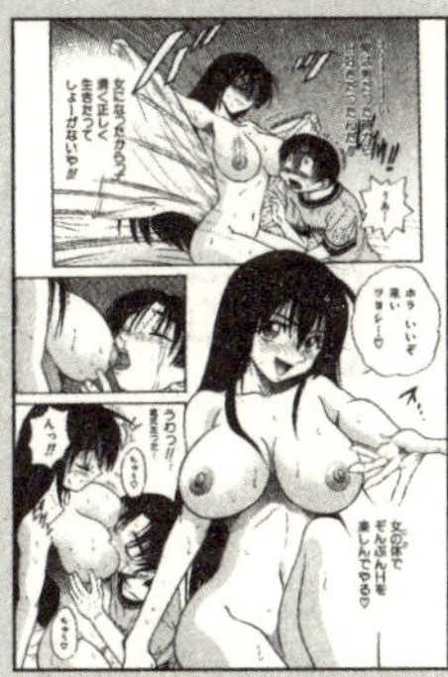

1-42: ***Mikaeru Keikaku*** (DISTANCE 2002, JC Publishing)

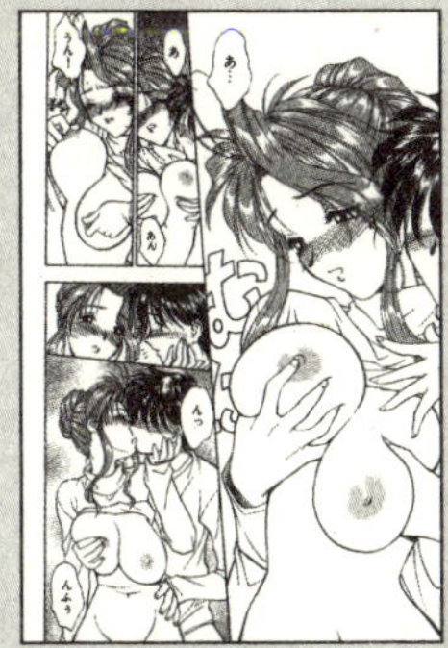

1-43: ***WITCH!***, Vol. 1 to ½ (Ryohta Magaki 1998, Tsukasa Shobo)

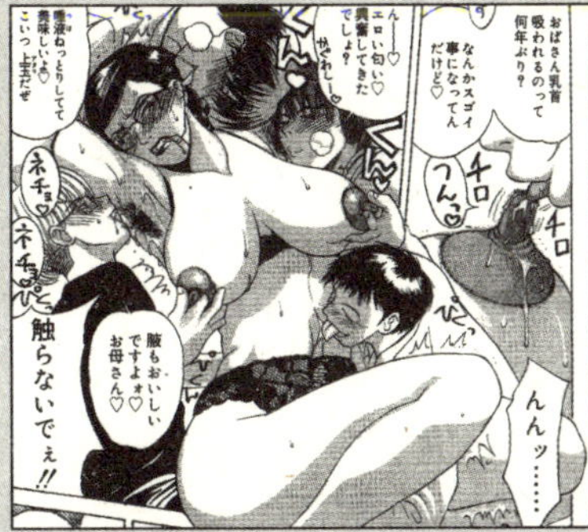

1-44: ***Innocent Children*** (miyabitsuzuru 2001, Tsukasa Shobo)

Which Are the "Correct" Breasts?

Within the *big boobification* of breasts, the idea was to basically draw characters with an increased bust size, and things started to evolve from that point forward. It was a feeling as if the parameters for largeness were to be manipulated.

Of course, taking breasts like Hiroya Oku's into consideration, rendering softness along with size, there were quite a lot of creators who had a great deal of originality in their work.

But let us start with those who enlarged their breasts as a base. One could say that this was the age that explored the parameters that determined how artists enlarged their breasts and searched for answers as to how those breasts were fixed on the body. However, to their credit, these artists did understand that there were other elements in play with regard to this issue.

Namely, these artists would, one by one, search for these answers for their bishojo comic characters by asking which breasts were "lawful" or "correct," and then would go on to find their individual truths in a fusion of "breasts as personality."

Up until then, artists had moved toward using an anime style, pulling away from a realistic interpretation of these bodies and parts in their art. Instead they had embraced drawing deformed-styled characters as an underlying theme, using that as a base for their manga, they therefore looked at art by Wataru Watanabe and his "overfilled water balloon-like" style (which was very manga-like, very semiotic sign-like) and started from there. We will go into changes that happened by way of exploring for these solutions.

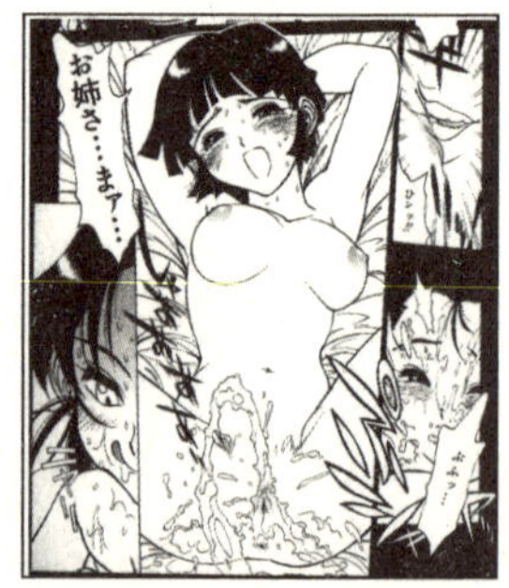

1-45: ***G-gai Kitan*** (Yuichirou Tanuma 2000, Core Magazine)

From the beginning of the 1990s until its midpoint, we saw a flurry of artists like Hiroyuki Utatane, Yuichirou Tanuma (1-45),

Tetsuyaro Shinkaida (1-46), Range Murata (1-47), and OH! Great (1-48) debuted. Their style was overwhelming and not photorealistic, and more than all of the artists before them who drew with delicate lines, these artists took things in a completely new direction. Theirs were not photo-realistic nor "correct" breasts, but instead were the ones the most appropriate for their bishojo characters. Yet they did not lose a sense of realness to them.

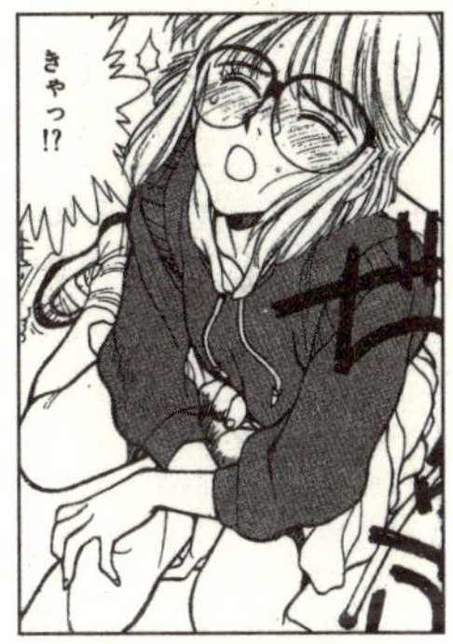

1-46: ***Encyclopedia of Tetsuyaro Shinkaida*** (*Daihyakka;* Tetsuyaro Shinkaida 1989, Byakuya-Shobo)

This was the age when the radicalization of these breast expressions began.

Up until that point, much like oil and water in a cup that did not mix, there had been a mismatch of *big breasts* and *bishojo characters* co-existing in a similar space. This was the age when they were finally fused together. The lines of these breasts, along with their softness, curvature, and size, finally found the appropriate style to be applied to them.

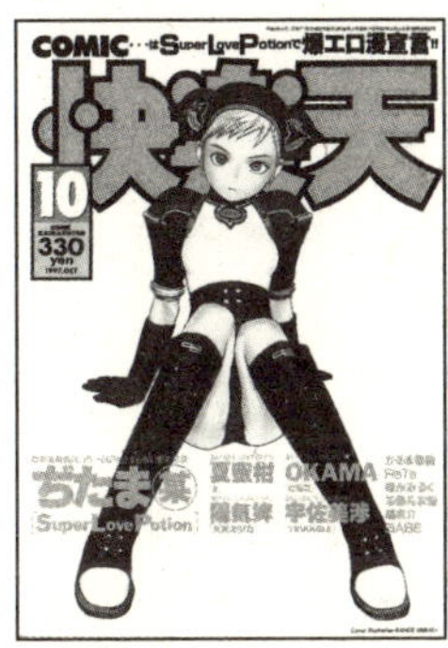

1-47: *Comic Kairakuten*, Oct. 1997 (Range Murata, Wanimagazine)

I can't help but wonder if many artists realized that this was the route they were taking when creating these works. And it wasn't just with kyounyu that this happened, nearly all breast expressions that have happened have taken routes similar to these before.

According to critic Gou Sakakibara, this evolution of the fusion occurred to spread these expressions of breasts over time. He calls these characters ones that "possess lewd bodies on internalized characters." Meaning their faces were

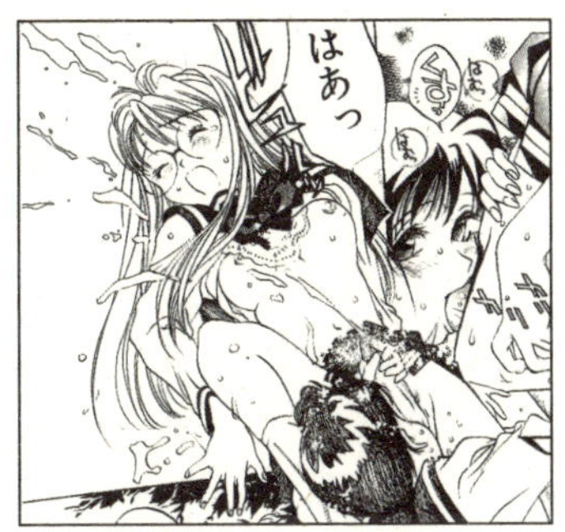

1-48: ***Engine Room*** (OH! Great 1999, Core Magazine)

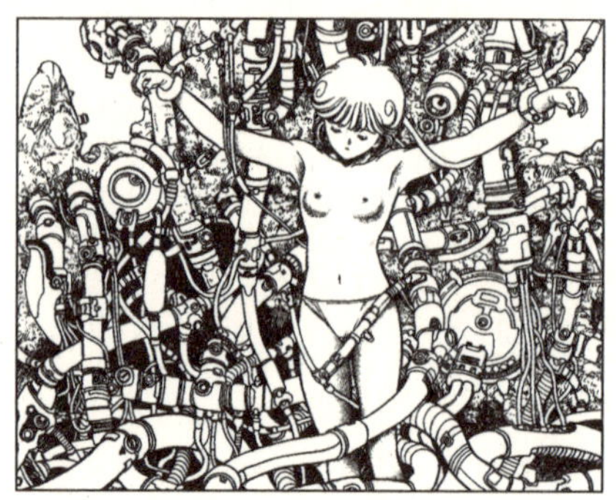

1-49: ***Video Girl Ai,*** Vol. 3 (*Denai Shojo*; Masakazu Katsura 1990, Shueisha/Viz Media)

ones that displayed the inner characteristics of the bishojo genre as symbols, whereas their bodies were manga-like, at odds with their faces.

We see this with heroines like Masakazu Katsura's ***Video Girl Ai*** (Denei Shojo 1989, Shueisha/Viz Media, 1-49) and Masamune Shirow's ***Ghost in the Shell*** (Kokaku Kidotai 1989, Kodansha/Kodansha USA). But according to Sakakibara in **Bishojo *no Gendaishi*** (2004, Kodansha), these can be seen as unbalanced "chimera-like" characters.

Each attempt to give characters the most "correct" body and breasts was not just limited to eromanga in as so far as it was a struggle for both regular manga artists and eromanga artists alike. With works like *Video Girl Ai,* there were obviously stages of trial and error with the artists. However, for the readers the fusion between breasts and body type was quite unbalanced.

The mid-'90s on the whole saw not just a rising trend in the quality of drawing, but also the debut of a bunch of artists that focused on dainty lines, stylish designs, and very visually-focused characters. It also saw the debut of high-end artists like OKAMA (1-50), and Douman Seiman (1-51).

A lot of new artists like the aforementioned helped bring an anime-style revival to eromanga with non-photorealistic characters featuring extremely slender bodies, with big hands and feet.

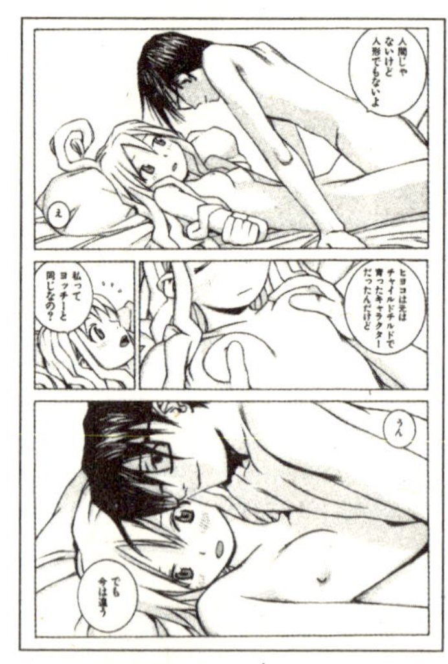

1-50: ***Meguri Kuru Haru*** (OKAMA 1998, Wanimagazine)

This was not a return to the previous style when I say it was a revival, but rather the feeling that all of this was new was very strong.

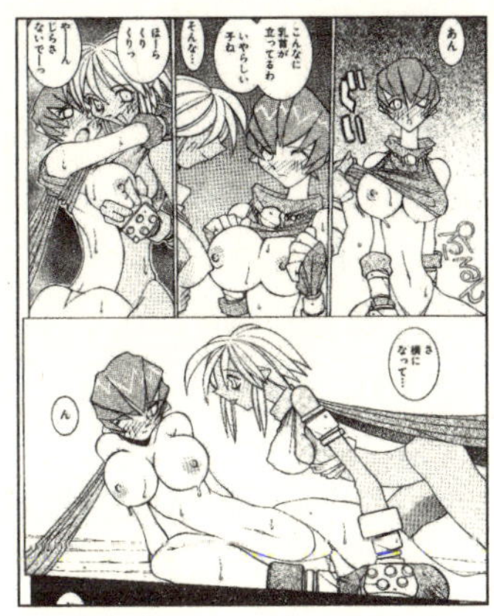

1-51: ***VAVA*** (Douman Seiman 1996, Hit Publishing)

Now, these stylish characters with breasts that were finally matched *correctly* with each other also had a physical sense of softness to them as well. Within this pedigree, we had artists like Tachibana Seven (1-52), Heppoko-kun (1-53), UonaTelepin (1-54), Kanikani (1-55), and Koichi Kusano (1-56) suddenly stepping up to take their inheritance. Under their watchful eyes, bodies became slender again, returned to a loli-type shape, which became the protagonist for the moé-style boom in the early to mid-'00s. Soon, the *moé form* would come to be fused with breasts, too.

One more thing happened within the latter half of the '90s. Within the *breast expression revolution* that was starting to happen was a change of the "textural feel" for a lot of this art. The idea of the "feel" of depictions and expressions of breasts up until this point really hadn't been present in eromanga. It was not unlike what we saw in food critique reporting where there was a new value of a sense of "richness" to food.

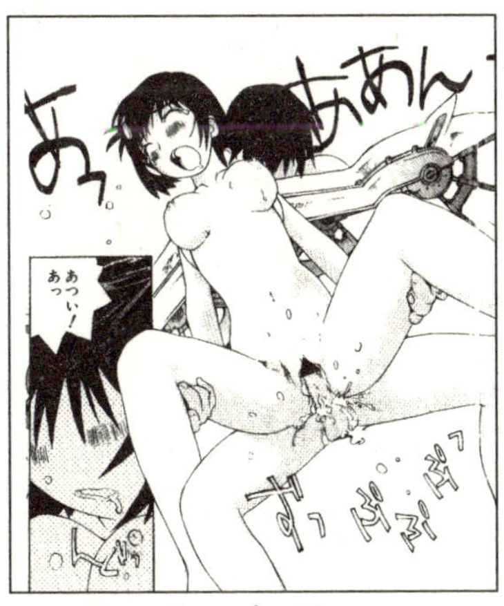

1-52: ***Otome Kaihatsu*** (Tachibana Seven 2002, Oakla Publishing)

However, even though we call it "texture," it's hard not to explain it as such as a parameter. In terms of actual elements such as highlights and shadows, the effects of light and such on images, it might be easier to explain that feel is really just all of these things rolled into one in terms of how they affect how the reader "perceives" them.

In terms of another development in the '90s when it comes to making manga is a huge leap in the development of CG technology. Rather than the advance of CG canvas and subject material, instead a revolution in coloring occurred. This affected eromanga in illustrations, but also within the world of bishojo genre games, as CG illustrations are often inserted into those games. With CG, this enabled artists to bring forth the sense of a texture and evolved to being able to apply highlights to these images.

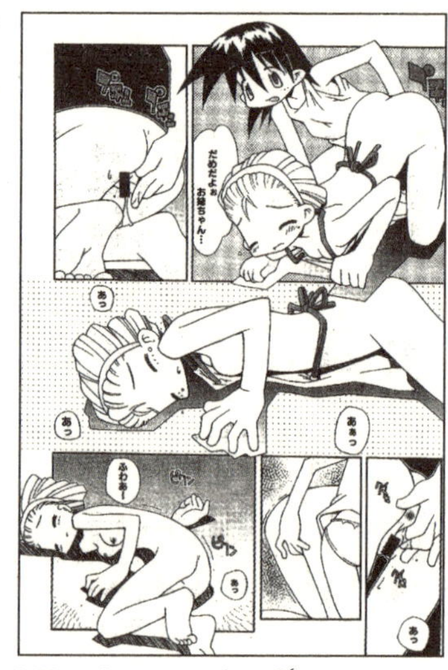

1-53: ***Muku na Tenshitachi*** (Heppoko-kun 2001, Shobunkan)

Even within the monochrome world of manga, the beginning of the '90s onward saw a shift in the amount of variation within gradation and screen tones used. This happened within the world of manga as a whole and not just eromanga, and this advanced the standard level of manga as a result.

One artist that cultivated the use of this new available spectrum of texture was Masamune Shirow, who used these tones to bring a realistic textural feeling to the science fiction stories he drew. Bishojo comic artists used these tones to give a sense of texture, of realness to their breasts with nipples, finally having found that they were able to (I know this is redundant, but this is the first era where we see artists using gradation shading and screen tones so aggressively. At first it was only one artist doing so, as the *Bach-*

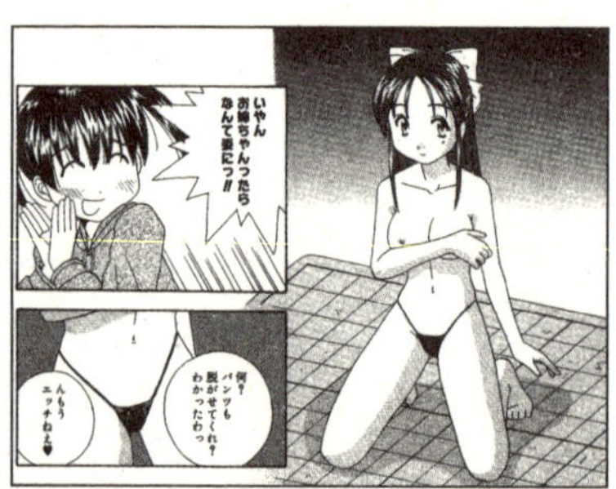

1-54: "Un, Yappari Nurse shika!!" (UonaTelepin 2001, Core Magazine)

elor-reading founder of kyounyu Kei Kitamimaki says…himself).

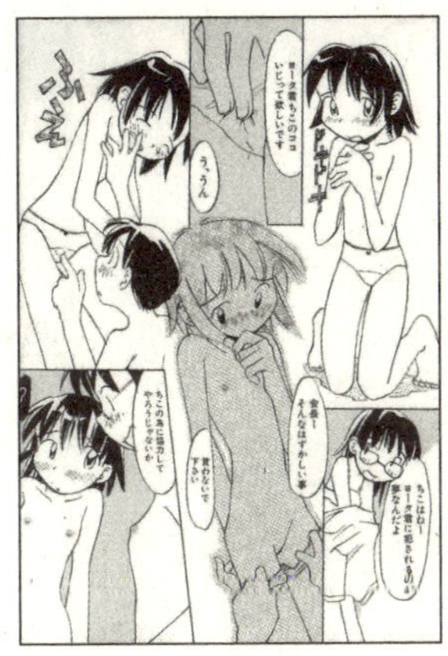

1-55: ***CHI CHI POCKET*** (Kanikani 2001, Kubo Shoten)

This became the era of CG, and I can't help but wonder if the obsession with texture became a bit obvious. This obsession being, of course, with the natural fusion of big breasts and the characters that resulted from it, as well as the technological advances that helped make texture a value that readers judged their manga reading material with.

This is how breast expressions that had a real feel and actual physics to them (jiggle physics, that is) were born, using bishojo characters as a base to build on.

It might be better to say that before the 21st Century, it took roughly ten years to find answers to *breast questions* like these, and now we had all of these answers amassing as one single solution.

The '90s birthed these new breast expressions, and one artist from this era that continues to have a huge impact on artists today is Ishikei. When asked to describe the breasts that he drew, the best I can do is say that he interwove shadows and highlights in his illustrations. He appeared obsessed with achieving a thoroughness to the texture in his work.

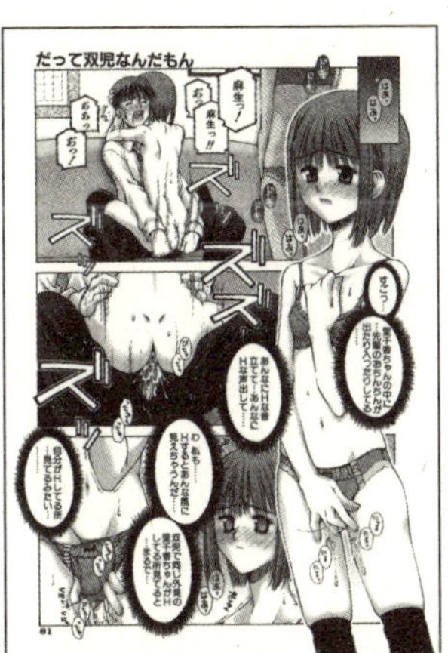

1-56: ***Delusion Love Device*** (*Muso Renai Sochi*; Kouichi Kusano. 2006, Hit Publishing)

For manga, while he combined bishojo characters with kyounyu, way before the VR era, it was almost as if one could reach out and touch his characters, which earned him many fans.

How were Ishikei's characters born? I went straight to the source to find out.

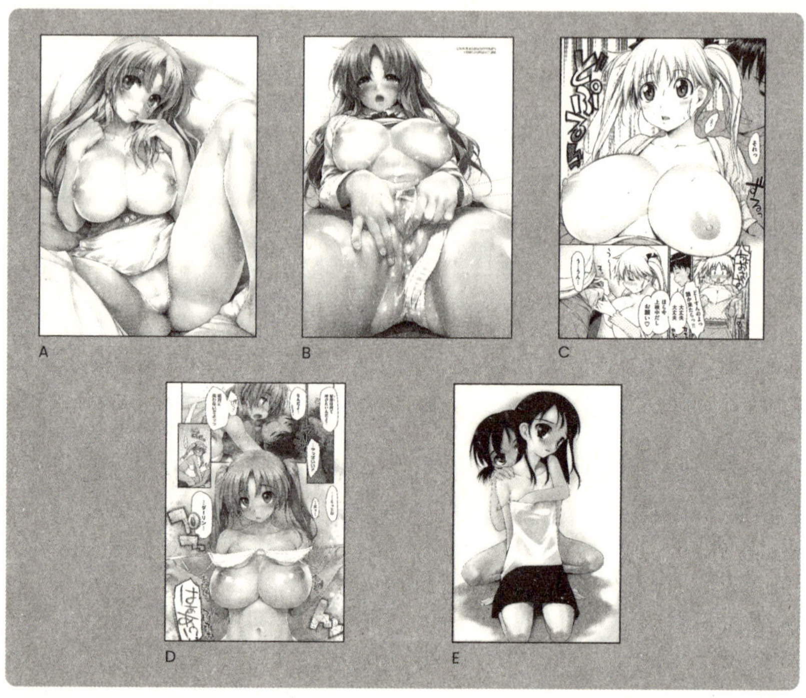

INTERVIEW WITH **ISHIKEI**

"When There were Highlights, Breasts Seemed to Come Alive"

PROFILE

Video game graphic designer and independent illustrator, made his illustration debut with *COMIC Moe* (Shobunkan) in 2000. His foray into manga was in 2004 with Sanwa Publishing's *Comic Mashou.* Known for his color and texture work, specifically with the breasts and nipples he draws, his works feature highlights and details that are unique to him. His best-known work is ***TiTiKei*** from Wanimagazine.

A: ***TiTiKei*** (2013, Wanimagazine/FAKKU)
We can't see the color here, but I'm still grateful.

B: ***TiTiKei*** (2013, Wanimagazine/FAKKU)
Ishikei's beloved puffy nipples.

C: ***TiTiKei*** (2013, Wanimagazine/FAKKU)
Overwhelming and brilliant breasts.

D: ***TiTiKei*** (2013, Wanimagazine/FAKKU)
Faint but still impressive in monochrome.

E: *Comic Mo-e* (Oct. 2000, Shobunkan)
Ishikei's illustration debut.

—Many artists revere you for your superior expressions of breasts in manga. Do you have any influences when it comes to manga?

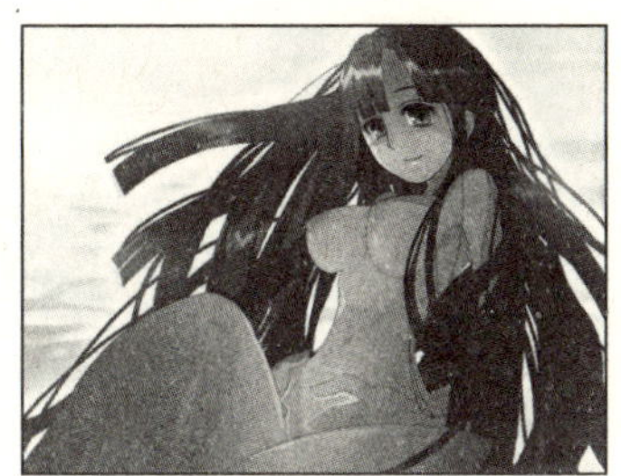

1-57: ***KO・KO・RO...***, 0 (Rio Jinguji 2004, Aaru; video game)
The highlighting on the breasts that influenced Ishikei.

ISHIKEI: Because I've done a lot of h-games and the like, I'd have to say Rio Jinguji (1-57). I really love his art. What really left an impression on me was that he used highlights on his breasts.

When I saw his art, I realized something. I remember thinking, "Wow, breasts that have highlights and those that don't look totally different." Like they'd come alive all of a sudden.

So I decided to copy that and see what happened. However, depending on where you put those highlights, breasts can change. There are never two same breasts with highlights. So, when I draw, I constantly think of where those highlights should go.

—So it wasn't a theoretical approach that you used, but an intuitive one instead?

ISHIKEI: I would say so, yes. I would consider how light would hit the object I drew and try to picture it in my head. Because there were people who always put their highlights in the same place regardless of the shape of the object, and you have to take the pose of the body and the light source into account when you draw. And if you don't, then it looks pretty weird. So I'd think about that and get really pissed off (laughs).

I think people need to put a bit more thought into things like this.

—That sounds like you're using a textbook approach to things when you draw.

ISHIKEI: I mean, if you think about it, it's probably the worst thing, right? If you're finally able to draw a beautiful girl, you should think about it. And there are people out there who don't. I'm not saying you should be strictly thinking about realistic sources of light, but there are a lot of people who throw things in because they think it'll look more charming that way.

In order to portray things beautifully, I think that you just need to consider everything as you draw, is all.

—We've gotten used to seeing it in our time but in the 1980s, we didn't really see artists putting highlights on nipples when they drew breasts. We've come to see this become standard practice since then, but it wasn't until fairly recently that artists have consciously drawn and started to highlight the whole of their breasts in their art. Of course, they were able to shade three-dimensional objects, but when they first started doing that, there was definitely a dullness in that shading. Now that we have a better sense of gradients, we've been able to start fine-tuning that process. But in terms of highlights, well, we didn't really see the efficacy of using highlights until fairly recently.

ISHIKEI: Shou Kitagawa's style of tonework comes to mind here (1-58). The parts he didn't apply it to were pretty rough, weren't they?

—The way that he drew breasts was that he didn't just draw them. Instead, he made sure the rest of his women's bodies firmly existed on their own, and in that way, he was able to

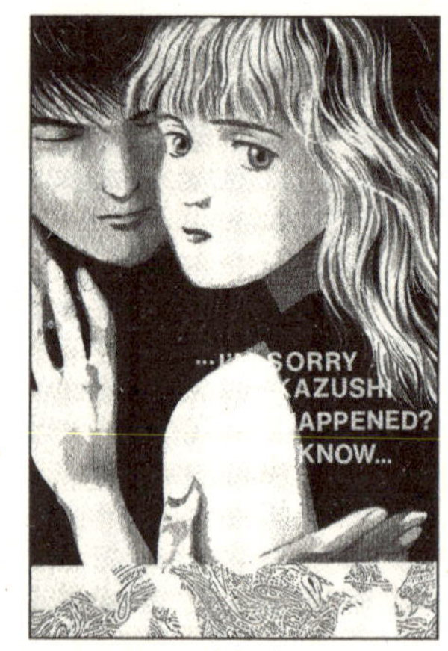

1-58: ***NINETEEN*** (Shou Kitagawa 2005, Shueisha)
A manga pioneer of tonework.

achieve symmetry. The highlights and the way light hits Kitagawa's bodies really gave breasts a sense of actual existence. You can actually feel it.

ISHIKEI: When you're drawing, you have to consider where the point of view, where one's line of sight is being drawn to is going. I'd really like for it to go towards the breast. That's why I tend to draw things a bit bigger. When you see something like that on a magazine cover, it's really something remarkable to behold. So that's why I'd like the line of sight to be focused on the breasts.

I really want my work to stand out if it's in a magazine that's carried by a convenience store. Because if it stands out, someone buys it, and that money goes to the publisher. I want to be able to contribute to publishers in that way. So, I always try to stress the points where I want the readers' eyes to go and put my whole heart into it.

However, it seems that there are some artists out there that use my drawings for reference. I always try to pluck things from the 3D world and drop it into the 2D world. So, I'm not sure about artists who use my 2D work as a reference for more 2D work. I wonder what they're thinking.

—If it's for mere mimicry, there's no point in doing that, but if it's to imagine what their drawing would look like with a textural feel to it, then perhaps they're doing it to work on their techniques? I think there's an element to how your breasts meet your bodies, and perhaps that's why. And maybe that's how they find their own, perhaps.

ISHIKEI: That's definitely been made as an argument before. When I was drawing parody comics of ***Strawberry 100%***, the breasts I drew were like rubber balloons, with no sense of softness. But I gave them a shot and that in itself was pretty effective.

I always want to try things, because I really didn't like my art all that much, you see. And it remains that way to this day, mostly because I'm always aware that my art may be appraised at any time.

—But the fact that you're aware of that at your level of things is amazing! People say that one shouldn't get complacent about one's work, so I think this is fantastic.

ISHIKEI: If you do things that way, you can watch yourself continue to change and grow. When I see young artists with amazing, polished art, and I look at my art from where they're standing, I think, "They must really think my art is garbage." So, I always kind of have a complex about it (laughs).

On shedding light on areas that aren't breasts

ISHIKEI: Even though I was highly influenced towards drawing breasts, I tried putting highlights on penises, too. There was a lot of trial and error involved, but I got to the point where I could draw things more realistically, and it slowly became a whole lot more fun to do so (laughs). And that's when I understood that when you only draw breasts, it gets kinda grotesque and you reach a truly filthy place. But anything goes when it comes to penises!

—In a certain sense, this is lawless territory.

ISHIKEI: It's okay for penises to be grotesque. You shouldn't need to regulate that, and it becomes more fun to draw that way. That's why I can draw dicks so fast. I kind of do it while humming, too (laughs).

—I don't get that sense at all. I get the sense that you draw it firmly and deliberately. But I do think that having a buoyant, lighthearted attitude

about drawing them does raise the quality of your work.

ISHIKEI: I mean, it's the same for drawing breasts, as well, but when you highlight the head of a penis, you bring it to life!

—And in that way you kind of breathe life into it!

ISHIKEI: You can, yes, but that does tend to disappear when you start revising your designs of it (laughs).

—Now I can see what you mean. The way you draw the female form, as well as breasts and penises, despite having technology that aids you.

I think that the one specific characteristic of your art is your highlights, and where you include how light hits objects. I do not think it would be an exaggeration to call you the Vermeer of bishojo art.

On the ideal breasts

—When you start drawing breasts, is there a certain type or shape of them that you get hung up on?

ISHIKEI: Deep down, I'm obsessed with Russian breasts. They're pale, white, with slightly thick nipples, and hang downward slightly.

—You tend to give the areola a great deal of gradation.

ISHIKEI: I also tend to draw the nipples slightly swollen because I like puffy nipples. I think it's good to draw nipples with a solid sense of real existence to them. Anyway, I like to draw soft breasts. Not just because those are the types of breasts I get the most requests for. But if I'm to accept reality and draw them smaller, it feels like I've lost a battle with myself (laughs). I'm aiming to draw breasts with integrity to them and a larger-than-life sense of them actually existing.

—You draw breasts with a real sense of feeling to them, especially this sense of softness. That comes across quite well in your work. I do think that using highlights helps communicate this feeling of texture well, too.

The only other artist I can think of at the moment that manages to also achieve that is Shirow Masamune (1-59). Mr. Shirow doesn't express softness the same, but rather the muscular body of a woman instead. And he achieves that because of the way he uses highlights. It's a stark contrast to your work.

ISHIKEI: Of course, I love large, soft breasts, but in reality, this size of breast would droop far more, I think. When I say that, if you look at how a lot of 2D stuff is drawn in terms of how the human skeleton works, things like eye size and the like are pretty inconsistent versus real life. I often wonder how to show that in my work.

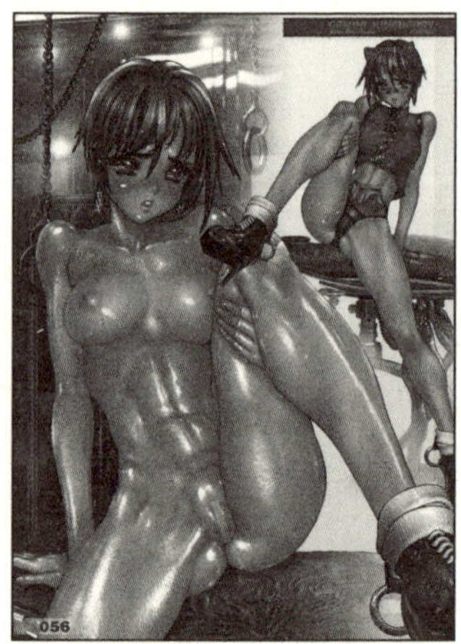

1-59: ***GREASEBERRIES***, Vol. 1 (Masamune Shirow 2014, GOT)
A muscular beauty with highlights.

—It seems that evolution in style is something you've awakened to in recent years. You have manga-style characters that have manga-style breasts attached to them. When it comes to research of the most erotic female bodies, I firmly believe you are one of the foremost artists that were so dedicated to bringing a new era to bishojo characters. In the cup that was eromanga, manga-like, moe characters were water, and erotic breasts were oil. You managed to fuse the two together, and I often wonder how difficult it was to do that.

But I believe that you quested towards the erotic with a spirit of inquiry, and earnestly developed these new expressions. Because you had that attitude, I believe you were able to make that fusion possible. To me, it was on the same level as that fellow that developed plastic that's able to biodegrade. That's how important this advancement in eromanga was to me.

"Eromanga was the newest form of media"

ISHIKEI: In terms of the many expressions up until this point, I won't deny that so much of that was aided by young people developing technology to help push it all forward. Even when you skip over that, said technology has still made it easier for people in general. And because now people have that extra time that technology gave them, I hope they devote time and work together so that they can help develop more technology and expressions.

—But wouldn't you say that the amount of young people has been decreasing?

ISHIKEI: I too have gotten that impression. When you slack on cooperating with others, the whole industry will wither away. You know, the industry is counting on those young people!

—When it comes to the meticulous task of creating new work and developing it, they can't forget their spirit of inquiry when making it.

ISHIKEI: Long ago, I thought the newest form of media we had were eromanga magazines. I used to happily read those because the cutest pictures were always printed inside of them. But now I wonder, what's it like now? I get the sense that the latest forms of media are non-erotic in nature. And because of that, I get the feeling that they're not as cheerful.

—Especially when it comes to otaku culture. Before, so many of them loved

the erotic, and I know you and I turned towards things of that nature. Everything erotic was new, and there definitely were a lot of fans out there made as a result of that

(Compiled April 2016)

All Breasts Are Connected

And of course, the evolution of breast expressions as seen in bishojo comics didn't stop there. Even now, it continues to evolve, and is affecting and influencing many genres as a result.

In the '90s, seinen comics were the first to take in this stream of new kyounyu content from the eromanga world as an influence. Shonen magazines, however, continued with *the lucky pervert trope*, which only increased after big breast influences started to spread to that genre, but there were otherwise no large changes seen in the genre. Rather, due to the influence of comic regulation and policing, nipples on breasts were sealed away along with the textural feel of breasts. Which led to a time when a large swath of those expressions was lost.

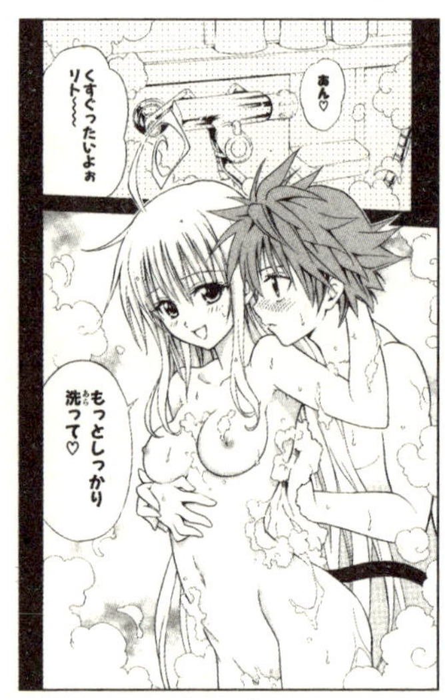

1-60: ***To LOVE Ru***, Vol. 1 (Kentaro Yabuki & Saki Hasemi 2006, Shueisha/Seven Seas Ent.)

Entering the 21st Century, the wall between regular manga magazines and bishojo magazines crumbled, and artists actively started to overcome those walls. This led to a sudden dramatic advancement in the speed in which the propagation and transmission of expressions happened. Before, when symbolic breasts were published in shonen magazines, comics like *Strawberry 100%* (*Ichigo 100%*; Mizuki Kawashita

2002, Shueisha/Viz Media), ***To LOVE Ru*** (Kentaro Yabuki,& Saki Hasemi 2006, Shueisha/Seven Seas Ent., 1-60), thought to have obvious bishojo comic influences, started to debut one after the other.

And then the largest breasts in shonen history debuted...

The heroine of Seiji Matsuyama's ***Eiken*** (2001, Akita Shoten/Media Blasters, 1-61), Chiharu Shinonome was, in the early days, drawn with an 88cm bust (an F-cup), but due to the editor's request and the artist's interests, all of the characters's breasts were abruptly inflated, and *bakunyu* in shonen were born.

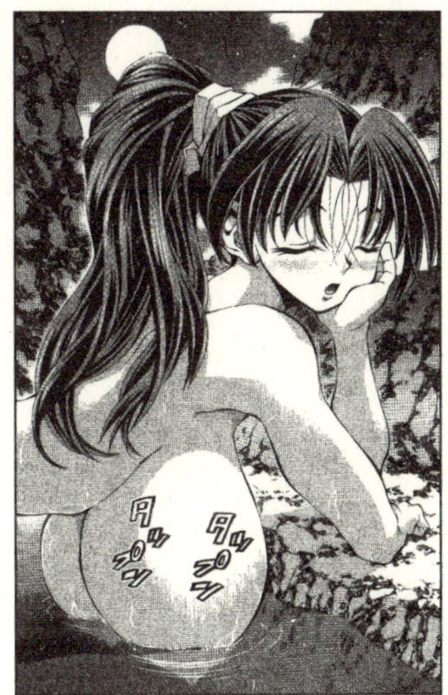

1-61: ***Eiken***, Vol. 10 (Seiji Matsuyama 2003, Akita Shoten/Media Blasters)

And it wasn't just breasts undergoing these changes. Renderings of pseudo-semen were put in place due to the *nipple code*. Eventually, unimaginable erotic expressions became the talk of shonen magazines, to the point where original video animations (OVAs) had been approved for production based on content in these magazines.

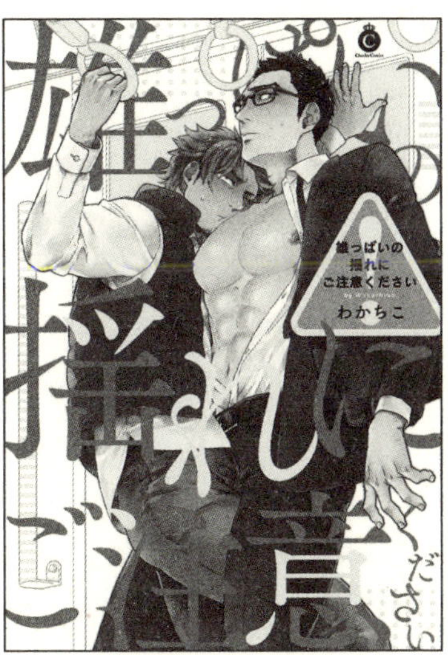

1-62: ***Oppai no Yure ni Go-Chui kudasai*** (Wakachiko 2017, Sankosha)

Even in the *boy's love* (comics featuring gay couples, often written for a female audience) genre, men's chests were also called *oppai* (a pun using the kanji for male; 1-62) comparatively making light of men's pectoral muscles. Sometimes that word wasn't used, putting a more serious emphasis on expressions of male nipples, developing those and other concepts based on sexual play.

In recent years, in public libraries, increasing numbers of more morbid boy's love books like ***Oppai Danshi*** (Kento Asaba 2017, Shusuisha) and others talking about male breasts have officially been designated as obscene.

Even in the world where the most breasts were making their appearances, bishojo comics, new breasts were always being invented.

There was a wide variation of both nipples and areolas. Huge areolas, puffy areolas, puffy nipples, inverted nipples, and all other representations of such are so numerous that in order to properly consider them, I had to write a whole chapter about them. *Bakunyu, kinyuu,* and *chounyu*—which were breasts so large you couldn't even fit them in a room, all increased in number. If these expressions of largeness were the vertical axis of the equation, then their feel was the horizontal axis, growing in parallel. A third axis would be *fukunyu* (multiple animal-like breasts), which only show up as *hinnyu* in size and mostly exist only in the realm of the fictional; or *kyonyu* (breasts that exist in an imaginary space; 1-63), which usually exist in empty space and are drawn in the form of big breasts.

...Breasts are everywhere, are all connected, and are free.

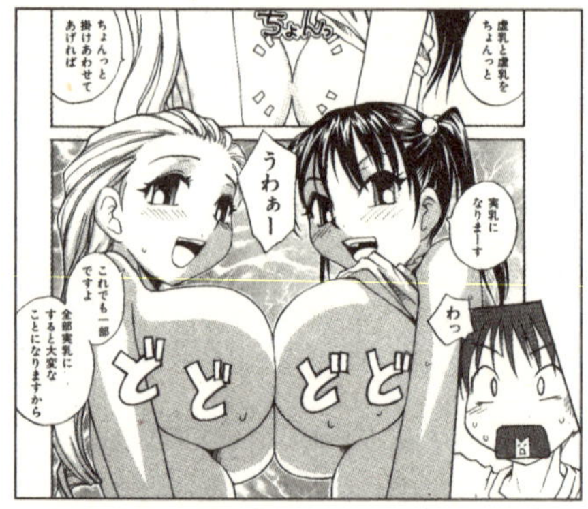

1-63: ***Nihon Kyounuto*** (RaTe 2007, Wanimagazine)

The Most Vital Place of the Body Conceived 2D Breasts

And so we've come to see a huge amount of development, spread, expansion, and evolution of breasts within the eromanga genre. However, their fatal point in eromanga is that they are manga themselves. Breasts' static feel, largeness, softness, elasticity…have all undergone a large amount of evolution, but the dynamics that go hand-in-hand with elements weren't any match for actual pictures or anime. In manga, no matter how dynamic a scene might have been, it was still drawn on a piece of paper. Even if it's a sexy scene with dynamically moving kyounyu elements, you would still need manga-like three-dimensional technology to make that look real.

Of course, within manga's history, from the early days onward, lines of flow and efficacy, sound effects and other elements were developed to that end. But when it comes to breasts and manga symbols, I can't help but wonder.

Within the kyounyu trope that was around in the '80s, flowing lines got across how those big breasts moved. Meanwhile wave-like lines also related how that movement appeared to the point where the curvature of those breasts could help make them look alive. I cannot help but wonder if someone talked about that when these works were in the concept stages.

Along with the dynamics of big breasts, there was the development of movement that wouldn't mar the feel of those breasts when transmitting that information to the reader, which as a result, birthed and evolved brilliantly into expressions that could evoke visualization of those breasts after the end of the decade.

What was more surprising was that some of those expressions from the '90s weren't a product of eromanga necessarily, but rather ones of regular manga instead.

And those expressions that became the default for breasts were none other than the "nipple afterimage." ❁

The History of Hentai Manga

CHAPTER TWO

The Spread of the Nipple Afterimage

How to Overcome the Breasts' Greatest Weak Spot

Within manga's representation of breasts, there were those expressions within *ero-gekiga* that saw huge growth in the 1970s, which were exaggerations chasing after real breasts. There were also the expressions seen in *shonen* magazines at the time, blooming within school set romance comedies, which, as a major theme, tended to take the sexier route of things with a deformed style.

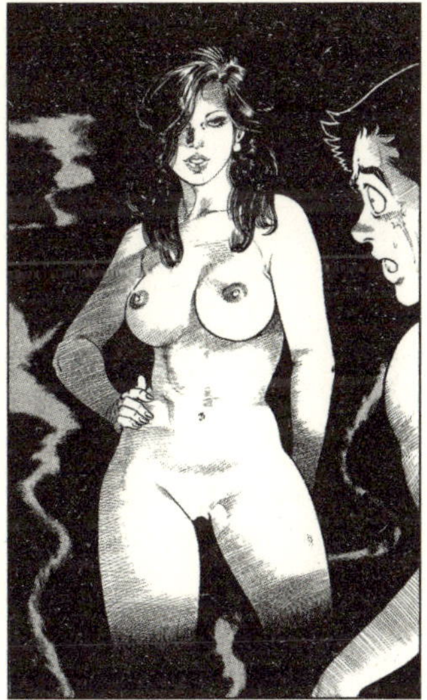

2-1: ***Ma-monogatari Aishi no Betty***, Vol. 1 (Seisaku Kano & Kazuo Koike 1980, Shogakukan)

In the previous chapter we looked at the rise of *lolicon* manga within shonen in the 1980s, as well as the genealogy of *bishojo* manga breasts. And of course, the exaggeration of breasts didn't stop at that point.

In two of Kazuo Koike's popular '80s *gekiga* works, ***Ma-monogatari Aishi no Betty*** (Shogakukan, 2-1), and ***Shikken Ningyo Dummy Oscar*** (Shogakukan, 2-2), his artist Seisaku Kano chased after reality to the point where it was if a golden-haired beauty had leapt straight from the pages of a foreign skin magazine like *Playboy* onto his pages.

Meanwhile in the shonen world, we h ad the rise of Buichi Terasawa's ***Cobra*** (2-3) from the pages of *Weekly Shonen Jump* magazine. The popular boys' comic featured beautiful women, along with burly men and a heavy dose of eros, leaving a powerful impression on its readers.

With regard to the breasts of the gekiga genre, there was the question of how real they could make those breasts, as well as the question as to whether or not they could recreate said breasts. One can see a clear sign within gekiga when it comes to these questions in terms of the pursuit for realistic breasts.

On the other hand, when it came to manga's deformed breasts, one can see a clear transition between styles as well as an evolution. I spoke about this in the previous chapter but whether realistic, deformed, or exaggerated, the weak link when encoding these breasts as expressions was: how do we get them to move intensely? This was an issue that had to be overcome to progress further.

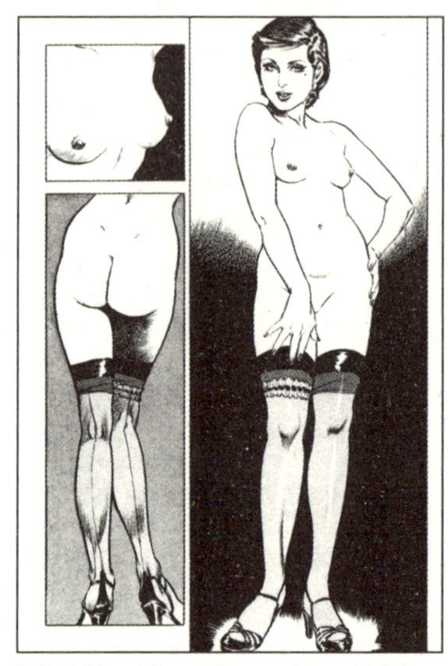

2-2: ***Shikken Ningyo Dummy Oscar***, Vol. 3 (Seisaku Kano & Kazuo Koike 1979, Studio Ship)

Motion pictures allow for the appearance of natural movement, so when it came time for breasts to move within a scene, this depended on the acting skills of the performer.

Which brings us to our next questions: what was the first anime work that animated the movement of breasts? And what manga was the first to do the same? These are age-old questions that continue to rage on between fans of both mediums, argued with white-hot flames of passion.

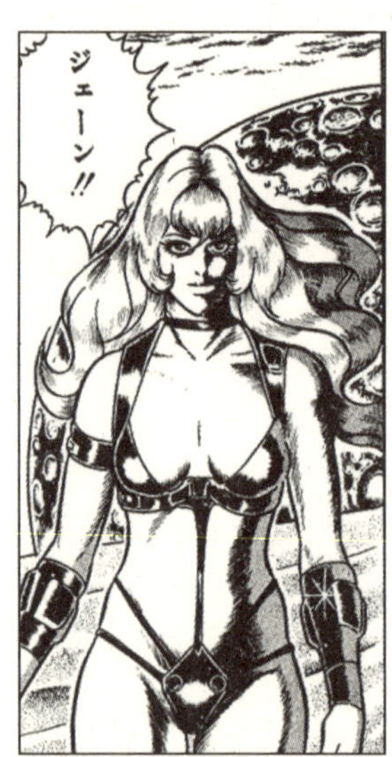

2-3: ***Cobra***, Vol. 1 (Buichi Terasawa 1979, Shueisha)

For a long time in the world of anime research, Hideaki Anno's creation for the Nihon SF Taikai (Japan's premiere science fiction convention), ***Daicon IV: Opening Animation*** (2-4) has been the long-accepted answer for the question of which anime work depicted the movement of breasts. However, in recent years, if the question turns to simply being about breasts moving in anime, period, there have been multiple reports of works before *Daicon IV* that depict just that.

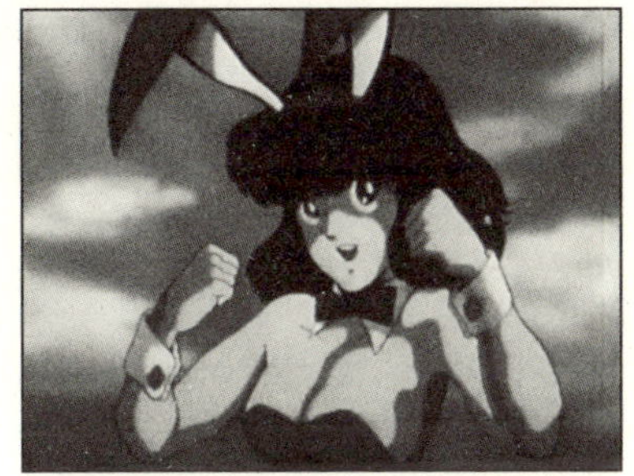

2-4: ***DAICON IV: OP FILM*** (DAICON4 EXECUTIVE COMMITTEE 1983, animation)

And do we have a standard about how breasts physically move? If so, is it an organized, clear depiction of them moving at their core? Did the creator who animated them have a fetish for breasts? Those sorts of questions start to emerge when we shift the focus of the question ever so slightly.

Just like with manga research, the question after that is of just as great interest: if this representation is the same as the other, and that expression's connotation and meaning is clear, has it succeeded the other?

There is that point of view which turns this debate into a set of facets (with regard to structure and discovery) to examine further. This avenue of thought has revitalized part of manga research as a whole and has helped further anime archival as a practice. It has given researchers context and easier access to data on the subject.

Which has made eromanga researchers quite jealous.

This will be a bit of a digression, but when one compares manga expressions to actual filmed content and anime, the expressiveness of the symbols that get these movements across to the audience are splintered. To compensate for that, many manga expressions have been developed. However, in the case of breasts, to say that creators have been thick-headed about doing so wouldn't entirely cover it.

And as if it were a comet appearing for the first time, brand-new expressions of breast movement, with the breast's main protagonists, nipples, appeared. It was a bold changeover to a new way of thinking, a paradigm shift that was called the "chikubi zanzou" (*nipple afterimage*).

On the Nipple Afterimage

In a literal sense, this visual expression is when a nipple is used to create an afterimage visible to the reader. More precisely, it is a technique used to draw manga to point out that when a breast shakes, the areola and the nipple are the locus in those lines of flow, much like a car's taillights leave an afterimage in the dark, thus nipples would do the same thing in this situation.

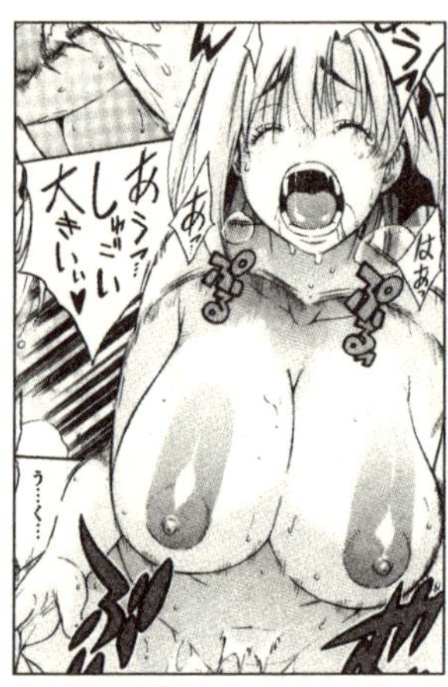

2-5: ***DAISY!*** (Amatarou 2009, Core Magazine)

When reviewing the four examples I've included (2-5~8), it should become apparent to you. It's mainly when the primary use of screentone in a panel (often nipples and areola) is rendered into becoming the locus of the panel creating an afterimage to the reader. Though there are also times when the technique blurs or dilutes lines to have a similar effect.

This technique has been used by artists since 1994, and as if chasing artists over the years, the frequency of its use has increased quite a bit. It would be odd to look in one of the current eromanga magazines being published and not see the technique in active use. It's the one expression used by anyone who's anyone in the world of eromanga; a fixture within the genre.

If there were to be a how-to-draw-eromanga book published, I don't think it would be an exaggeration to say that amongst breast expressions, this one would be a headliner and have its own section. That's just how well known a technique it is.

As of 2017, there are multiple how-to-draw-breasts books in print, but none of them have noted the afterimage, nor given it its own category. I am expecting a quick response to this observation on my part.

Speaking of the term "nipple afterimage," it was coined by manga creators. It originates from a conclusion based on all of the nipple expressions of eromanga categorized together and was formally named as such in 2009.

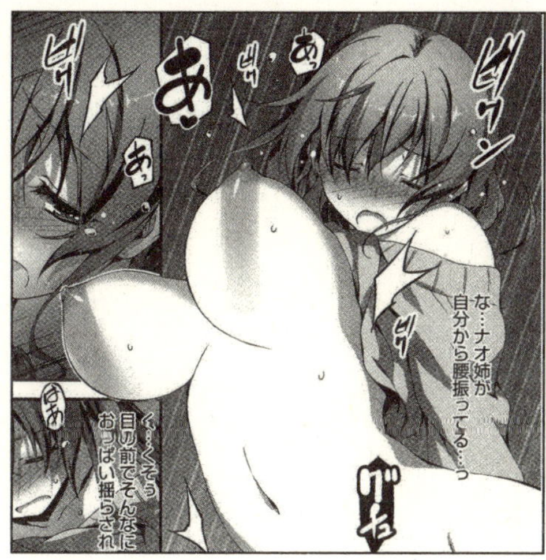

2-6: "Nao to Ecchi" (Kikurage 2014, GOT)

However, I would like to note that this term has existed since before I started to look into everything *nipple afterimage*.

There is no specific manga work to attribute or link to the coining of this term, but there is an adult video title released in 2008, ***Chikubi Zanzou Bomb! 4 Hours*** (h.m.p; roughly translated as *4 Hours of the Nipple Afterimage!*) that is connected. On the packaging for this title there is a savagely moving breast, where the camera blur is to the point where not only does the nipple have an afterimage, but rather the entire breast itself has one. If I were to compare it to the manga expression, I would say that the usage of the term in this case is a bit harder to nail down in use.

I have heard reports that even in 2008, on eromanga-related internet bulletin boards, the term *nipple afterimage* was used in relation to the manga expressions of the same name. However, a choice of words does not necessarily equal a proper use of the term.

The next question is, were there other similar terms that existed that artists and editors of the original *nipple afterimage* used?

While there is not much discourse on the subject, Kaoru Nagayama, the author of *Erotic Comics in Japan*, left the following words in a special feature on breasts in 2000:

There have been countless kyounyu *drawn. Within that amount, there are so many different minute variations of those expressions that I could write a whole book on those alone. Globe-shaped breasts, bell-shaped breasts, slightly hanging breasts, breasts with silicone in them, breasts with button-like nipples, bolt-like breasts, sombrero-like breasts, breasts that shake in sync with each other, breasts that have a discrepancy in size...all of these on top of the expressions using the nipple afterimage technique in the toning of the nipples...*

—"Comic JUNKYS"; Manga Hot Milk, *Jan '00 (Kaoru Nagayama, Core Magazine)*

Here we have Nagayama using the phrasing "the nipple afterimage technique in the toning of the nipples," but it is thought that there wasn't a degree of familiarity with the formalized term yet. Though this expression has been around roughly since 1994 and people have knowledge of it, it seems that perhaps in 2000 the formalized name itself was still very ambiguous in its existence. However, if one were to say that same idea of "the nipple afterimage technique in the toning of the nipples," there is no doubt that ordinary people in the eromanga industry, as well as readers, would have a concrete image of what that expression was.

While it is thought that these creators had subtle differences in their methods and styles of work, if one of them were to tell their assistant, "Give this nipple an afterimage!", most likely the idea would have translated just fine to that assistant in terms of what kind of expression they were being asked to create.

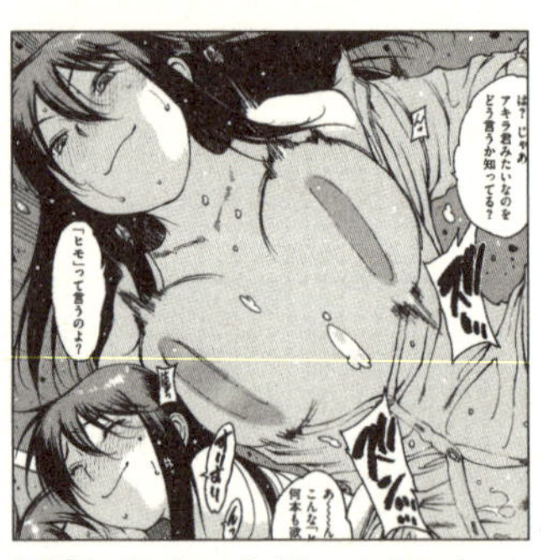

2-7: "The Feeling of a Woman Begging for Bareback" ("'Nama' wo Shucho-suru Onna no Nama no Kanshoku"; Nishi Iori 2017, Wanimagazine)

I did mention before that this had become a specialized term, and although this background did in fact exist at the time, I would like the audience to understand that it was 100% set in stone as a specialized term.

If you search for the term online, it may turn into "nipple afterimage technique" when you try to find results. The term itself debuted online approximately in 2010 and was added to *pixiv*'s ***pixiv Encyclopedia*** as a searchable term shortly thereafter. The definition of the concrete term as published by *pixiv* is as follows:

> *Nipple afterimage technique: A phenomenon where when a breast shakes, the nipple leaves an afterimage. There is no particular "killer technique" meaning to the use of "technique" here. A similar term is "breast tail lights."*
>
> *—http://dic.pixiv.net/a/乳首残像拳 (Jan 2017)*

The *pixiv Encyclopedia* also has information about the details relating to when the term was born:

> *Moreover, the puzzling term "nipple afterimage technique" came about in the vicinity of the term "nipple afterimage," and also perhaps is a play on words with the* Dragon Ball *term of "the afterimage technique* (zanzouken)," *a killer martial arts technique from the series.*

That explanation is the same as the one for the *nipple afterimage*, more or less. And when the word "technique" is added to the term, there is a greater deal more impact than without it. That is why the wordplay element was recorded.

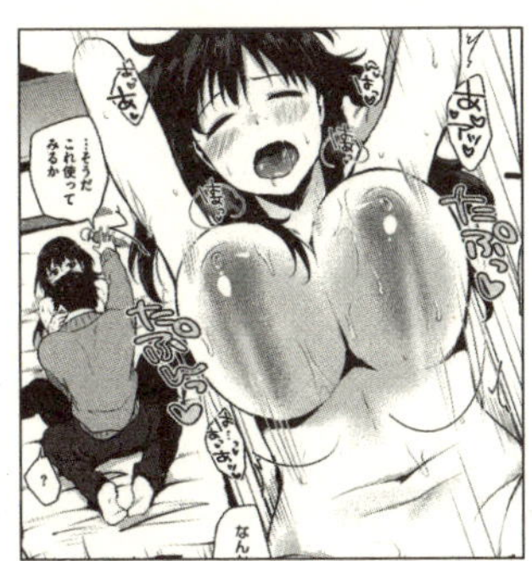

2-8: ***Love Sign?*** (*Suki na Sign wa*; Uekan 2017, Core Magazine)

To the *Dragon Ball* generation, this altered term is unforgettable now that it has merged with this other term. Personally, I think that it's quite the interesting concept, and it's a great way to explain it within the framing of this book.

Breast Mechanics and Jiggle Physics

And now, I would like to go a little deeper into detail on an important point regarding the formalized term *nipple afterimage*.

At first, I spoke about it in the framing of a savagely moving breast, to the point of it looking like a camera blur. However I would like to assert that I believe that framing it only as an afterimage is insufficient.

When a breast moves from point A to point B, the nipple moves with it. The degree of that movement's vibration, to put it simply, is the locus, between its starting point and ending point. It is the place where the nipple's afterimage appears and is expressed, and one can think of it as the first nipple afterimage. But what's important here is that making sure the reader can figure out the locus of the afterimage on the breast and understand it. Regardless of how much it moves, making sure that the audience understands this with the least amount of information but the maximum amount of effectiveness.

I believe that every new afterimage of the nipple and its route, as well as its speed and acceleration, and everything else that is needed to create and reflect this vector value, is more perfect than the first nipple afterimage ever drawn.

Of course, looking backwards over our shoulders at the history of the development of the nipple afterimage as an expression, there have been a number of these expressions where the starting point and terminus of the afterimage is poorly defined by the artist, but with regard to the modern day usage, one could say most of the expressions put forth these days meet

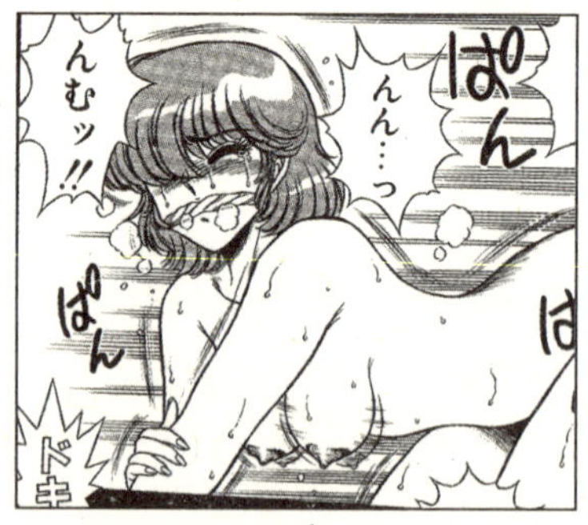

2-9: ***To Meet Someday*** (*Itsu ka Aetara*; Jacky Kameyama 1994, Kubo Shoten)

the requirements as established with the specialized term itself. While I cannot say that "the expressions that do not meet these requirements are not those that are nipple afterimages," I do believe there are more perfect versions of the defined expression out there currently compared to the amount of versions that do not make the cut.

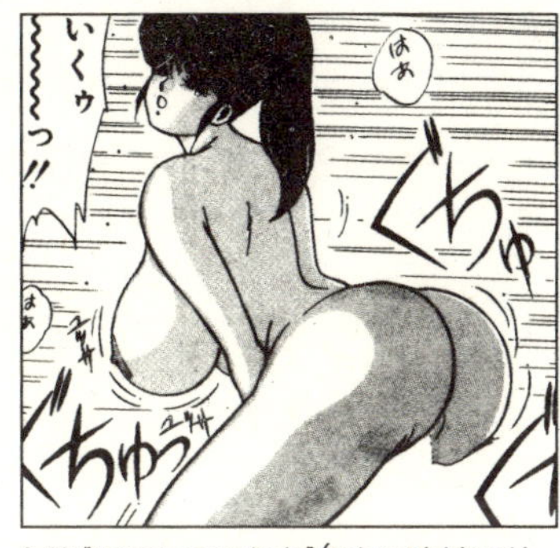

2-10: "Natsu no Prelude" (Tohru Nishimaki 1988, Byakuya-Shobo)

While there are some versions of this expression out there that one cannot feel awareness on behalf of the artist regarding the mechanics of how fiercely that breast is moving, depending on the expression, there is a visualization above what is considered to be only within 2D art.

If you were to ask me, "Well, until the birth of this expression, was it just that breasts within manga didn't move?" Of course I would say that isn't the case.

Breasts in manga have always moved. Comparing manga to mediums that move in real time (like movies and anime), by all rights, even a non-moving picture must show dynamics of some sort, so someone needed to come up with an expression that could express that. It goes without saying that that is where someone needed to help manufacture expressions that could highlight movement with oblique lines, lines of flow, and the wavy lines of oscillation... All of which became a fixed technique of manga.

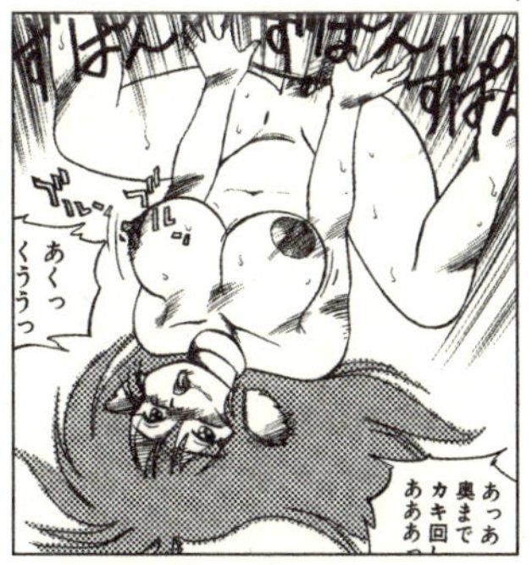

2-11: "Jukenshi Tina no Yutsu" (Hitoshi Funato 1988, Byakuya-Shobo)

In the early days of manga, there was heavy use of expressions with moving breasts. Most likely in terms of oscillation, the contour of the breast itself would be shaking when used. That is where sound effects like "poyon poyon," "tayun tayun," “pururun,” “boin boin,” and other such sounds were used in concert to help highlight the expression. We saw this a lot in the early days where expressions with the natural shaking of the breast were used (2-9~11). Sometimes, during sex when bodies moved intensely, both the maximum and minimum line sizes for contouring were used at the same time. Readers understood the frequency of that movement this way but now it has become a classical manga technique.

However, as a technique, it never went extinct. In shonen and seinen magazines, that technique is still on active duty within artists’ arsenals and has a different pedigree in terms of evolution compared with that of the nipple afterimage.

The Discovery of Vertical Movement

Another bit of unravelling we need to do about the history behind the sudden paradigm shift in eromanga, the new expression of the way breasts moved – the nipple afterimage. This gets quite interesting in my opinion.

Let’s talk about seismology.

Originally when it came to breasts and movement, if we were to make the oscillation of the contouring of the breasts into waves, we would have horizontal movement (the surface wave, or “S-wave”). The dynamics that would help give nipples afterimages, vertical movement (the primary wave, or “P-wave”) were discovered later. It has been said that this discovery was revolutionary.

However, if you really, really think about it, if a breast were to move quite intensely, it is possible that a nipple alone would leave an afterimage. This was the question born in the aftermath of the *afterimage* itself.

Currently, with taillight afterimages, we have the phenomenon of the taillights as a source of light in the darkness that leaves an image in the dark. Just as we can see the effect of these lights leaving a trail behind them, in this case, the nipples may also be the luminous paint that lights up the night when a breast is shaken. However, in reality, the entire breast would shake along with the nipple, and if it is dark out (and we're going with this analogy), it could be that it's not visible at all to the audience.

Most likely, the first example of the two just compared would only be a situation that could happen in porn. Within manga, even if an expression were used to replace a realistic situation, the probability of that expression being a boring one is quite high.

Then why is the nipple afterimage as an expression used so much by eromanga creators and authors? How did it become commonly used?

It is because manga is a place where your wildest delusions can become real, possibly due to the fact that the libido in manga easily overcomes what it would be in reality. I want to see breasts move intensely, I want to feel that movement directly, I want to feel that movement more completely, I want to know the softness of those breasts. This visual expression (and others) was born from wishes like these on behalf of the readers, fused with artists' ability to churn out delusional material. And as far as protocols go, that method of doing things seems to bring results. The eromanga of old that prioritized bringing eros into manga possibly utilized this method and that is what is owed to its success.

The ability that manga has to render and convince, along with collective libido that brings eros to these works most likely helped birth the miracle of this locus.

The Dawn of the Nipple Afterimage

I know that by this point I've explained the nipple afterimage expression at length, but I haven't yet covered who invented this expression in 1994. As a matter of fact, that answer is still being confirmed. Let me explain...

Every new expression has an origin point; a first page to their story. I'm not sure about how people in regular manga feel, but when it comes to eromanga expressions, it definitely is not always easy to discover origin points for some expressions. When one defines that first page, it involves researching all past materials with brute force, and of course, there are no guarantees that the subject of reference is even still there at all. Looking at prior research and archives can take so much time that one would easily get overwhelmed while doing an investigation into things. And when it's an early expression? Even then, when it comes to the origins of those expressions it can be nearly impossible to define them sometimes.

Even with very eromanga-specific expressions, there are not many cases where one can definitively state the works that serve as their places of origin. The reason for that is that compared to regular manga, a lot of eromanga content hasn't been archived, so there is little to no data to look up.

However, in the case of the nipple afterimage, we do know the inventor, when it was invented, and the work it first appeared in. Which is exceedingly rare. What's even more surprising is that I discovered which original works it is attributed to, and that the two inventors of the nipple afterimage both arrived at their unique versions of this expression at more or less the same time.

Because these both came out at roughly the same time, it's hard to think that one saw the other's expression and was influenced by that. And if it was a case of unconscious inspiration, that's hard to determine at this time.

Those two creators are the creator of *GANTZ* and other manga, Hiroya Oku, and the creator of ***Seraphic Feather*** (Kodansha/Dark Horse), Hiroyuki Utatane. From both of these artists' testimonies, I can conclude that the first emergence of this expression happened in the summer of 1988. Due to the fact that it is does not happen and they are similar by utter chance, we run into the next issue of how hard it is to determine the historical links these have to each other both going forward and going back. With regard to the nipple afterimage, the design of the expression and its goals are strongly inherited, with no interruption in its genealogy.

This expression's *starting and ending points* before its invention act as its P-wave, and because I haven't found any other manga before with afterimages drawn in them, I believe that it is correct to say that they are definitely the inventors of the nipple afterimage.

Why did God bestow the nipple afterimage when the violent shock of the Showa Era ending happened? I would like to inspect the testimony of both creators to find out what kind of expression the early nipple afterimage was.

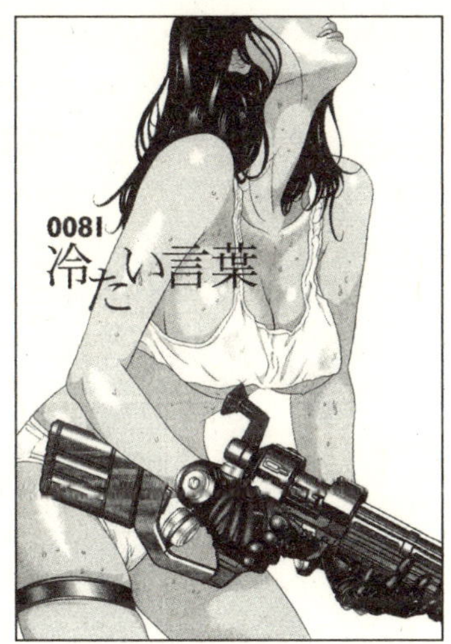

2-12: ***GANTZ***, Vol. 7 (Hiroya Oku 2002, Shueisha/Dark Horse)

Now, speaking of Hiroya Oku's most important work, I think it is safe to say that *GANTZ* is an utterly charming sci-fi story with novel battle scenes, and circles of mysteries that unfolded along with the chapters to the reader. Truly, it was a story no one had ever seen before. While the fact that it used 3DCG in its process was talked about quite a bit, personally, I enjoyed the *bishojo* characters with *kyounyu* that decorated the beginning of each new chapter (but was not always particularly related to them), and to me, it was quite impressive and I always looked forward to it (2-12).

I can't help but wonder when Oku stumbled upon the nipple afterimage. The first time he used it was, quite surprisingly, in 1988 with his debut, an award-winning *Young Jump* seinen manga title called *HEN.* It was a work that was so popular it even had a live-action TV drama adaptation and is the origin point for all his works.

As this was his debut title, the fact that he invented a new expression when he was basically still an amateur is quite shocking.

When one sees the use of the nipple afterimage in practice (2-13, 14), it is a magnificent expression where the *starting and ending point* as well as the locus are clearly defined to the reader's eye. The lines of flow of the fallen protagonist reflect the highlights of the afterimage for the right nipple, and consequently the state of the dislocated *kyounyu* breast with left nipple is clearly transmitted as an expression to the reader. I would also like to point out that it is not just the breasts moving here, but the whole body of the character as well to compensate for the expression.

As a very early era expression, with it being as effective as it is, all I can say is…that's Oku's work for you.

In the next panel, the most basic nipple afterimage appears from the depiction of intense sex.

But what was the impetus that helped birth this expression, I wonder? I wanted to know the answer to that question, so I dared to carry out an interview with the legend, Mr. Oku himself. Even though he was quite busy now that his new title, *Inuyashiki* had just gotten a serialization, I received two replies to my puzzling request.

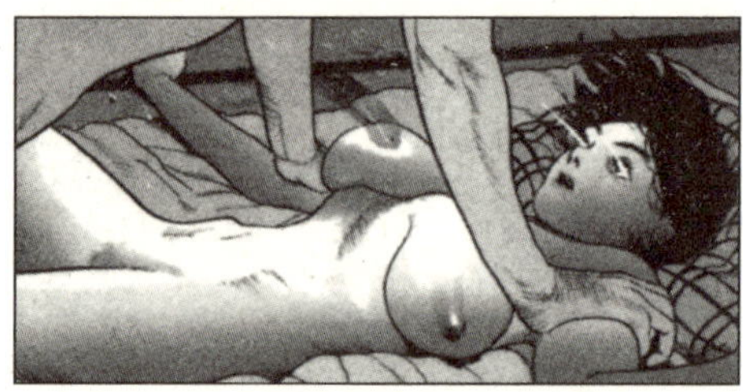

2-13: ***HEN*** (Hiroya Oku 1989, Shueisha)

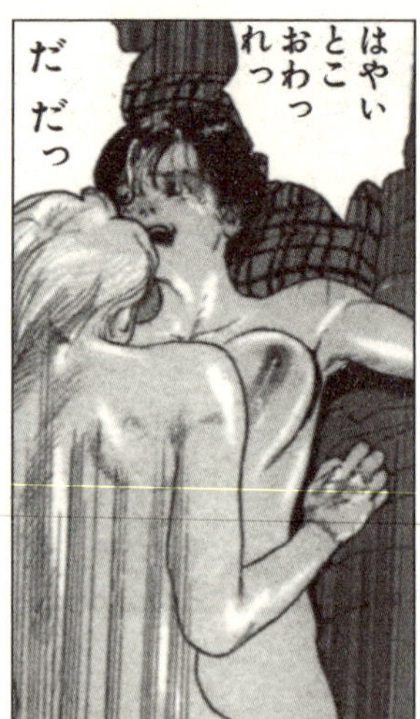

2-14: ***HEN*** (Hiroya Oku 1989, Shueisha)

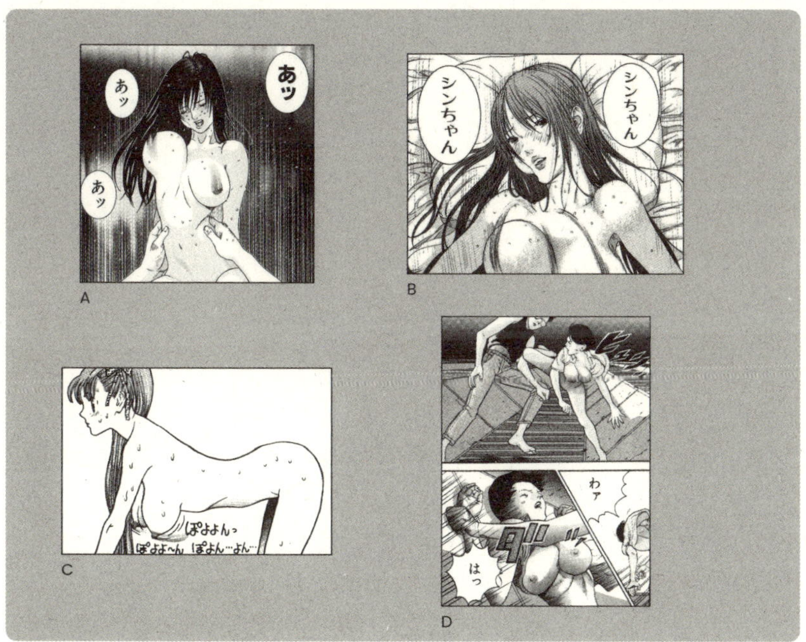

***A: GANTZ**, Vol. 17* (2005, Shueisha/Dark Horse) The asymmetrical left to right nipple afterimage.

B: Maetel no Kimochi, Vol. 3 (2007, Shueisha) A nipple afterimage using oblique lines.

C: *HEN*, Vol. 2 (1989, Shueisha)

D: *HEN*, Vol. 3 (1989, Shueisha)

INTERVIEW WITH **HIROYA OKU**

"I wanted to invent my own expression."

PROFILE

Debuted in 1989 and won Shueisha and *Young Jump Magazine's* 19th Annual Seinen Manga Award with *HEN. HEN* remade and reconstituted BL, trans, and lesbian components within seinen manga and became a huge hit. His next series, which he promptly used 3DCG for character modeling, was the very popular *GANTZ.* It got both an anime and a live-action movie adaptation. Even in his debut work, there was a fastidiousness about his breast expressions. He is a self-admitted fan of the *kyounyu* trope.

—The nipple afterimage *has made its way into adult comics, and one could argue that it's become the default in terms of widely used expressions.*

Hiroya Oku: Oh, is that how it's being used these days? I really am not up on all of that.

—And while it's been used in many works, I've been able to determine the first use of it was within your work, Mr. Oku. To be more precise, I haven't been able to find any record of any other artist using it before you did, so currently, that makes you the first artist to use this.

Oku: I see! And is that a good thing? (laughs)

—In adult-targeted manga, there aren't many particularly apparent expressions that one can catch a glimpse of, but it's rare to have a case like this where it's quite clear-cut where to attribute things in terms of origin works and artists.

Oku: Is that so... Well, when it comes to the *nipple afterimage* as an expression, I drew it because I hadn't seen anyone else drawing anything like it at that point in time. So I'm honestly happy to see that no one before me had drawn something like it. I suppose because had someone beat me to the punch on that one and used it before I did, I wouldn't have had any reason to use it at all in my work.

—Let's get into the first nipple afterimages you drew. It would be these (2-13, 2-14). According to your afterword in this book these are from summer 1988.

Oku: Yes, that's correct.

—In your debut work, HEN, *aside from the nipple afterimage, it seems you were trying out various new expressions. If I may ask, what was the impetus behind developing these new expressions within your work?*

Oku: With regard to the nipple afterimage, I hadn't really seen any expressions that involved breasts moving in manga up until that point. The only ones I had seen that had anything to do with breasts, or the chest area at all, were ones that involved a chest being crushed by something, or the chest moving in the direction of its movement. Because of that I wondered, "How can I make a chest move and portray its (heavy) weight?"

As lines used for moving chests and breasts that I'd seen in manga had been well drawn, I had decided that it wasn't about the lines. Instead, I figured out that I needed to focus on the tone of the nipples and making them the locus point for movement. I think the reason why I used an afterimage is that, in my head, afterimages leave trails of what looks like light behind them

"The nipple afterimage was born from a place of carnage before a deadline."

—Which means that you created a clearer expression than just moving breasts from point A to point B.

Oku: That's right. Things happened in that way, I suppose.

—So then the previous expressions you'd been tempering were more accidental in terms of their creation?

Oku: My debut work was drawn carefully from the first page onward. However, while the first half of the book was drawn at a reasonable pace, the second half I was being rushed by my deadline, and I found myself in the situation where I had to put the finishing touches on the book within three days or less. So, the nipple afterimage expressions I drew in that part of the book were more or less at the end of it. I was really trying to just churn out my pages in time. I didn't even use proper ink for the main lines; I think I used a fineliner pen.

At first, I used a G-Pen to draw everything, but then my deadline came and I hadn't really used any tones or gradation. So it was like doing construction at top speed, but I still wanted to be really precise with the nipple afterimage. So, after some trial and error, the nipple afterimage was born. That's just kind of how it happened.

And of course, at that time, it wasn't an expression I used very heavily or anything. After the manga award I won, it was around that time I was getting requests from the eromanga world, and that's how I got involved, as someone helping behind the scenes.

I remember talking to someone within that world and he said, "Oh, Oku-sensei, you know everyone in the eromanga world is using your expressions, right?" Apparently they thought favorably of me. When I heard that, I was so surprised, mostly because I hadn't thought my expressions had spread that far out into various other spheres of manga.

—It really, really has become a standard. I believe that when you first started using that expression, no one could've known how popular it was going to become.

Oku: I wonder if it was the case of them just imitating each other. In terms of not caring who used this expression first, I mean. It's kind of a mysterious phenomenon to me. After all of the expressions I used in that book, this one expression that was slightly different from the rest in the manga world ends up spreading to all corners of it.

—You mean, it's more like a feeling where instead of saying that you tempered that expression and then put it in your work, it's more like you chased it down, and went with what happened afterward but also the fact

that you ended up going down in history as the creator of this expression with your name tied to it as it spread? Something like that?

Oku: I mean, I'm not sure I've gone down in history as the creator of this expression or anything… (laughs) But regardless, it still feels quite strange.

"Going where no man has gone before" was something that happened only in stories

—You've stated that Katsuhiro Otomo's work has influenced you quite a bit.

Oku: That's right. But at that time, Mr. Otomo's work had so many expressions drawn in them that no one had really seen before. I really admired his approach to things. So in my debut work, I wanted to include lots of expressions no one had seen before as much as I possibly could, as well. So I ended up throwing a lot of them in there, and only one turned out big (laughs).

—But because you had that zeal in you to do something historic and leave your name behind in the annals of history, you ended up creating the nipple afterimage as an expression.

Oku: That theme of going where no man has gone before wasn't just limited to expressions. I also applied it to content as well. In *HEN*, we have a man changing his gender. Stories about gender swaps have been in manga a lot over the years, so I wanted to look at a story about a sudden gender swap but more in the vein of it's a symptom of a progressing illness. Like that movie, ***The Fly***, except in my story a boy realizes he's changing more and more into a girl. It was something no one had ever drawn before, and I wanted to draw it. And I did. But the fact that only the afterimage expression remained out of all of that…

—Still I think that "going where no one has gone before" is the theme of your manga on the whole. In HEN, *you were able to draw homosexual love in a seinen magazine. In* ZERO ONE *(1999, Shueisha) and* GANTZ, *you aggressively used CG. So in that sense, you definitely did many things no one else had done before. I think that by challenging the norm, you were able to give birth to those expressions.*

"I might be uncomfortable with the idea of continually drawing the same expressions over and over again"

—Back to the nipple afterimage for a moment.

I looked into how much you've used that expression, and it was not very often. Perhaps source materials have gotten lost over time, but out of what I was able to find, you haven't used it even ten times.

Oku: It's true that I haven't really used it all that much. It's easy to tire those kinds of expressions out, so I might be uncomfortable with the idea of continually drawing the same expressions over and over again. I don't know.

—In GANTZ, *you used the nipple afterimage left to right, in a symmetrical fashion with your breasts you drew. Currently within eromanga, it's still considered a novel technique, and within regular manga, it tends not to show up very often.*

The afterimages in Maetel no Kimochi *aren't the current gradation-heavy afterimages, but rather ones done with an oblique line instead. So, they're like different expressions when drawn that way.*

Oku: Ah, okay, I get you now! Yeah, I didn't really do that consciously. It was just me going with the flow again. (laughs)

—This is just my own selfish little inquiry, but because of the way that breasts move within the nipple afterimage in terms of distance, the way the breasts up until now have been drawn with it certainly look very dynamic. As someone who loves kyounyu, I would say that this is a rather magnificent invention.

Oku: Is that so? Thank you very much. (laughs)

"When I saw Fujiko Mine, I thought, 'Oh, it's okay to draw breasts that big after all!'"

—When I think of you, Oku-sensei, I think of the nipple afterimage, but also someone whose breast expressions are generally quite fastidious.

Oku: Really? I've loved big breasts for quite a long time, since I was a kid!

—I keep thinking of your debut, and how in 1988, there weren't a whole lot of folks out there who used the kyounyu trope in regular manga magazines back then. Gravure magazines and the Yellow Cab talent agency didn't really become a thing until the '90s, and even in the late '80s, there wasn't a whole lot of kyounyu manga within eromanga as a whole. In terms of content, I did manage to find a magazine from 1988, the August edition of Penguin Club *and brought it with me today.*

Oku: Ah, (Ran) Hiryuu! Me and Mr. Hiryuu were both assistants for Naoki Yamamoto back in the day. That name brings back memories... (pages through magazine) Yeah, a lot of this couldn't be called *kyounyu* material.

—After re-reading HEN, *I had a thought. Your breast expressions were at least ten years ahead of anything in eromanga at the time. And when you add to*

that the fact that this was drawn in a seinen manga, it's really quite shocking.

Oku: I've been drawing characters with pretty big breasts from that point onwards.

Speaking of breasts, I was really influenced by the ***Lupin III*** character, Fujiko Mine. When I saw Fujiko, I thought, "Oh, it's okay to draw breasts that big after all!" At that point, I hadn't really drawn any characters with big breasts yet, so I tried my hand at it. When I did, it felt really good to do so.

When I looked at other breasts and compared them, smaller ones just didn't stack up the way I wanted them to. Something just didn't feel right, like something was missing. I started thinking that they looked really stiff.

—Like they were big breasts, but they looked as if they felt stiff, you mean?

Oku: I started growing more and more unsatisfied with things, so I thought that I would start drawing breasts with weight but express how soft they were. I became obsessed with that thought. After that, there was some trial and error, but I managed to draw things the way I wanted to in my debut.

—The textural feel of the breasts you draw seem quite supple yet flexible. The kyounyu and gravure booms would both come with the beginning of the 1990s, but their breasts still somehow looked very hard texture-wise.

Oku: The image of breasts that I have in my head is that they're like water balloons. In order to get a feeling for how those would move, I tried drawing various versions of those breasts in a simulation. They're soft, but you can feel their weight. That was the ideal I became obsessed with when it came to drawing.

—That's really realistic, too. Especially when rendering breasts on a person who's asleep on their backs. Their breasts are kind of horizontally offset.

Oku: Yeah!! There weren't any images out there at the time that showed that. I thought, why didn't anyone think of that sooner? It felt like there weren't too many breasts out there that seemed like they were the result of someone's obsession. So I stepped in to make that a reality.

(Compiled May 2014)

The Continued Evolution of Oku's Nipple Afterimage

As you heard in the interview, the amount of times that Hiroya Oku has used the nipple afterimage expression is less than ten times, so it wasn't like he used the expression he invented as a trademark within his own work. His serializations often appear in regular manga magazines, and it's not like his work is specifically marketed towards adults within the sphere of eromanga, and that's likely the reason why this is the case. But aside from that, to the point where he mentioned his fellow assistant, it seems that Mr. Oku was completely unaware that he is in fact the inventor of the nipple afterimage.

So, when he did use the expression, it wasn't with the mindset of "this is a thing that I created."

It seems that when Oku is interested in something, he ends up creating an expression or an idea in the process, and he isn't just hung up on one single type of expression.

So, when I think of things that way, about how the nipple afterimage as an expression isn't too heavily used by its creator and why, I'm satisfied.

Of course, I haven't forgotten about how this artist evolved this expression.

In *GANTZ*, the asymmetric nipple afterimage – where the breasts move left to right and swing at half height repeatedly – was an expression technique not seen very often even in eromanga and took a high degree of skill in drawing. The same with *Maetel no Kimochi*, where the afterimage is not colored with tones, but rather overwritten with thin drawn lines. This became known as the "slash afterimage" expression. This expression isn't "patented" but more of a self-presented new model for practical use, and as if it were a policy, it was not used a second time. One can feel the pride emanating from that expression.

I touched upon this briefly in the previous chapter about kyounyu, but when it comes to self-proclaimed big breast fan Oku, many expressions that we did not have until now, particularly ones of breasts, are because of his obsession with them. As far as simple signs go, he was dissatisfied with the deformed style breasts that had been drawn so far, and instead was in pursuit of the soft material feeling of breasts, their curvature, and so forth. I can't help but wonder if Oku's love for breasts, coupled with two wheels of unparalleled expressionability, helped pull these grand inventions towards him.

There is one more inventor when it comes to the nipple afterimage: Hiroyuki Utatane. His most known works are *Seraphic Feather* and ***Heaven's Prison*** (*Tengoku;* 2002, Shueisha). He's established his reputation as an artist that draws bishojo characters with very delicate lines, and a great deal of his fans have been charmed by those curious beauties.

While recently he's been doing work in general manga magazines and zines, his debut was in bishojo comics and seinen manga. Up until then his female characters had deviated from the norm, with tall proportions, and dainty, beautiful lines.

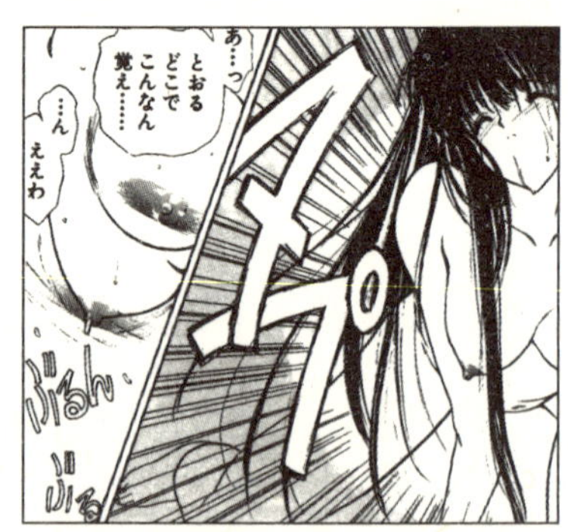

2-15: ***COUNT DOWN*** (Hiroyuki Utatane 1992, Fujimi Publishing)

With an aggressive manga style, his first collected work, ***COUNT DOWN*** (Fujimi Publishing), became popular at the drop of a hat. *COUNT DOWN* was reprinted no less than forty times, in a very short amount of time; to the point where each additional run started to expand, and according to anecdotes, the printing machines at the supplier broke. To say it became a huge hit would be an understatement.

The most popular chapter was a short named "Yuwaku ni Tsuite," where the nipple afterimage is clearly on display (2-15). The special characteristic of Utatane's version of that expression is that it doesn't quite have a clear locus but instead blurs nipples with breasts in motion. And thus, began the trend of shaving down varying gradation tones on the nipples themselves.

The intensity of the shaking breast, along with retaining the beauty of the nipple itself while creating the taillight effect was a novel new approach to the nipple afterimage. Just as taillights, Utatane's nipple afterimage had the nipple gradually fading out and gives a sense of *wabi-sabi*.

The first trade book with the nipple afterimage that Utatane released was *TEA TIME 6* (1989, Byakuya-Shobo), and within this anthology collection was his first short story with the expression, "MIRROR" (2-16). The details about this are noted down in the next interview, but "MIRROR" wasn't his only short to be reprinted, and the script for this work dates back to 1988.

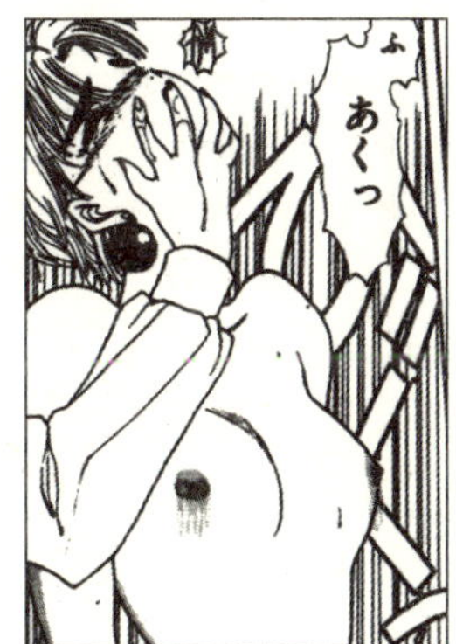

2-16: "MIRROR" (Hiroyuki Utatane 1989, Byakuya-Shobo)

Surely, this coincided with Hiroya Oku's release, and just like with Oku, Utatane's variation on the expression dates back to his debut. That's one thing they share in common.

In Oku's case, the nipple afterimage was born out of his deadline rushes, and he used lines to show the new kyounyu trope with his shaking breasts.

I wonder what it was in Utatane's case?

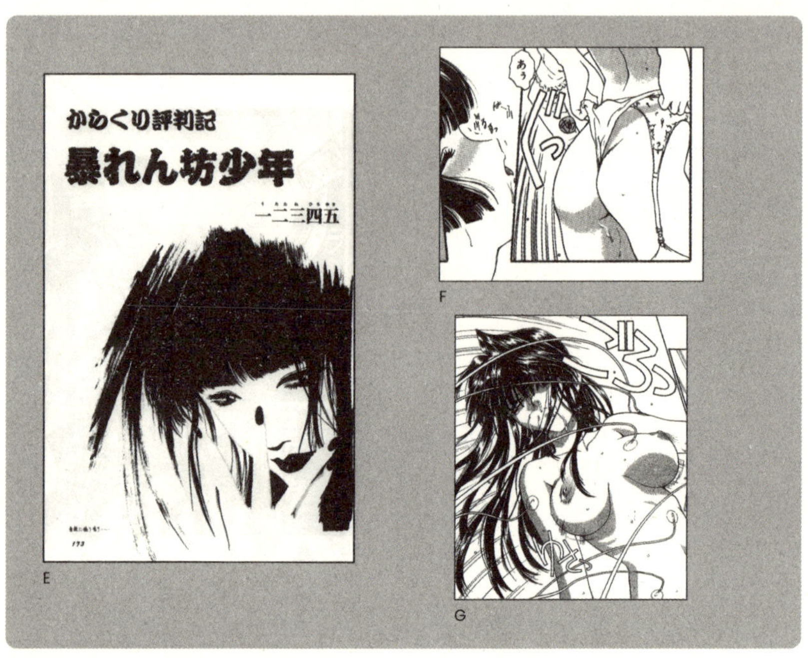

E. *TEA TIME 6* (1989, Byakuya-Shobo)
The short-story "Abarenbo Shonen."

F. ***Countdown: Sex Bombs*** (*COUNT DOWN*; 1992, Fujimi Publishing/Fantagraphics)
Utatane's obsession with buttocks.

G. ***Seraphic Feather***, Vol. 9 (2005, Kodansha/Dark Horse) The nipple afterimage with gradation.

INTERVIEW WITH **HIROYUKI UTATANE**

"The feel of breasts was personally quite important to me."

PROFILE

His other pen name is Hozumi Watanuki. He has also gone by the names IchiNi-SanShiGo and Shigatsu-tsuitachi Hachigatsu-tsuitachi. He made his debut in the 1988 Byakuya-Shobo anthology, *TEA TIME 5*. After that, he tried looking for a new job and found one that didn't suit him well, so he retired early. After moving to Tokyo, he then became a full-time mangaka. His first book, *Countdown: Sex Bombs*, was a huge hit. While continuing activities in the zine world, he also appeared often in regular manga magazines. He doesn't just restrict himself to manga, but has also branched out into anime, illustrations, and games.

—What was the process behind you figuring out your version of the nipple afterimage?

Hiroyuki Utatane: Well, chronologically, it was before *TEA TIME 5* (1988, Byakuya-Shobo), which was my trade debut. But before that, in the eromanga sphere, I took part in ***Banana Kids*** (Byakuya-Shobo), an anthology that had been slated to go on sale that September. So that means I worked on that anthology somewhere between June and July that year. But then, it went on hiatus, and now I had an amorous manuscript on my hands. So, it became this strange thing where I did it first for an indie anthology, but that fell through, so it ended up going into a manga anthology. Yu Toyama, this editor who is famous in the zine world, looked out for me and put together two collections.

—It certainly sounds like there were a few plot twists for those. I had a bit of trouble figuring out the chronological order of things, but now you've helped clear that up a bit.

Utatane: My debut was printed, but I don't know if you could call it a *debut*. But my ero debut, "Abarenbo Shonen" was probably the earliest of the bunch that came out.

Two years before that, though, I won an award for a contribution I made to Shogakukan, and it made news. I started doing doujin stuff later, around my sophomore year in college, I think. A senior member of my group made a whole work dedicated to researching the USSR's military affairs in our zines. I participated in the issue before that, and Hitoshi Okuta and I experimentally drew a bishojo-themed spread. The next issue, to tease that prudish colleague that was so into USSR stuff, I drew an even more lewd spread than the one before, and somehow the conversation turned to me. That's how I started drawing serialized illustrations.

Actually, the illustrations from that time made it into *COUNT DOWN*, on the table of contents page and at the end of the book (2-17). But the version that was illustrated in our circle's publication was slightly different. The girl was still on all fours with her butt in the air, and behind her butt we had the USSR flag.

—That's certainly something adulthood cannot erase.

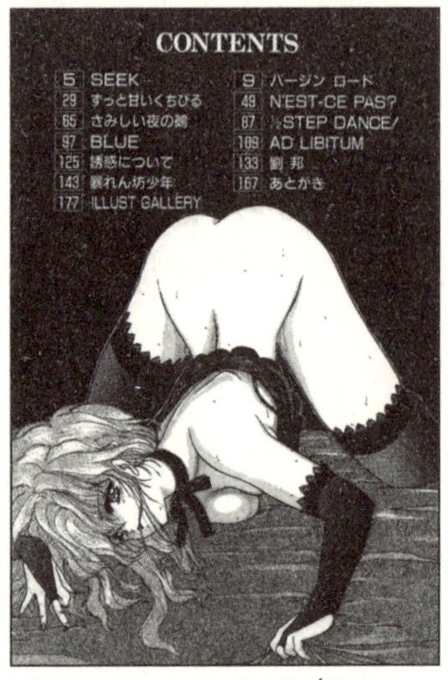

2-17: ***Countdown: Sex Bombs*** (*COUNT DOWN*; Hiroyuki Utatane 1992, Fujimi Publishing/Fantagraphics). Redrawn material from the USSR zine.

Utatane: The editor of that zine anthology (Yu Toyama) had seen those illustrations and apparently tried to get in touch with me. I say "apparently" because his invitation never reached me, and I found out halfway through that it got shelved. I wasn't really aware at the time of how adult this was in terms of content, and it pissed me off that it got shelved, so I thought that I'd get back at him by drawing it anyway (laughs). If he'd asked me more directly to draw something in the eros sphere, I might've given up entirely.

—To have such high-quality work in your debut... I'm aware of the quality of the doujin zines from this time period, and yours, quite frankly, is outstanding.

Utatane: But you also have to take into account that I'd won that award a few years before, and I'd been steadily chugging along in terms of drawing. Two years onward, I'd already been featured as a guest in three of a friend's doujin works, and before long with one of them, everyone had dropped out so it became a solo doujin work instead. Aside from \

the spreads, I did everything else myself, and it turned into something a bit strange. I was selling it at zine shows like Manga Gallery & Market (MGM). And selling right next to me was none other than Gosho Aoyama, the creator of ***Case Closed*** (*Meitantei Conan*; Shogakukan/Viz Media).

"Playing leapfrog with Masamune Shirow's textural tones and applying them to nipples"

Utatane: Now going back to manga for a moment, but before I started college was when Masamune Shirow weaponized tones, using them in techniques that would create texture in manga. The tones before then were limited to ones mainly for patterns and shadows, but even so, I think that Shirow managed to use those to help create a weight and feel to his manga expressions quite well.

—At around the time he released **Appleseed,** *he managed to render the texture of things. Which as an expression wasn't very common in manga at the time.*

Utatane: The first volume of *Appleseed* (1985, Seinshinsha) was shocking, quite frankly. I was taking my college entrance exams at the time and had to go to Tokyo to do so. So, I went to the Shinjuku branch of *Manga no Mori* (a now-defunct manga specialty bookstore chain), and that's where I got to see an exhibition of Shirow's work. I saw the tones and went, "Wow, these are amazing," and they left a deep impression on me.

About two years later, ***Bastard!!*** (1988, Shueisha) by the great Kazushi Hagiwara debuted. Hagiwara's tonework also made a deep impression on me because it was just so great. It struck me as especially polished tonework. At around that time or maybe a bit after it seemed like many people were using gradations in their work. The only work up until that point that I felt used gradation well to achieve a textural feel to their expressions was the intergalactic ship in ***Locke the Superman*** (*Chojin Locke*, Yuki Hijiri 1987~, Sakuga Group). While there sure were a lot of shading expressions that were used in that work, to me, it unlocked a world of possibilities regarding the use of tones I thought that if used correctly, I might be able to achieve an expression that looked like a camera blur.

—So you thought that you could use shading to create a camera blur?

Utatane: Early on, I thought that if tones were applied to nipples it might have an interesting effect. Because on curved surfaces, the coloring on the upper and lower parts are different, right?

The tone I used the most back then was IC #430. It was a series of thin gradated bars, and at that time, my precision wasn't too good, so conversion to fainter lines was difficult. *MAXON* had a far smoother feel to it. So, I thought I'd use the rougher gradation for the nipples. The conversion point on curved surfaces is where shadows are the palest, so it's where gradation would be palest, too.

In terms of whether I would cut off the excess parts, or scrape them off… I wondered if I were to leave those excess parts on, would it create an afterimage? And that was the impetus behind me using this visual expression in my work.

—I see. Hiroya Oku said he was struck by the urge to create an expression when he saw the way that large breasts moved. For you, it was because you could see how gradations could be used with nipples to make a great nipple afterimage that would convey texture.

As you said, there are also other nipple expressions aside from the afterimage that use tone really well, too. And at this point in time, I think that there weren't many techniques that used highlights on nipples, either.

Utatane: That's true. There was mostly only just planing (shaving off excess areas of tones) and regular net tones in use at this time. When you use gradation, that's when you can really sense the texture of things. To me, the feel of things was quite important.

—So what you're saying is that within the diversification of gradation, there were changes within techniques for texture. Shirow used gradation expressions on the mechanical parts of his work as a way to contrast, whereas you applied gradation to highlight the human form.

Utatane: I didn't have a shaving technique down at that point and Hagiwara's gradation he used on his crosses didn't turn out very good. There were lots of gradation techniques that made skin very pale, but they weren't very good, and tended to make things look dirty. I wasn't a fan of initial missteps like that, but at the same time, I knew one sheet of tone wouldn't be enough on my own work, so I used more than that.

—I see! And out of that skillful use of gradation tones, the nipple afterimage was born.

Utatane: Just like I did with the nipple afterimage, I had to carefully draw the buttocks as well. And at that time, there weren't a whole lot of expressions for drawing something from the front to the buttocks at all. So the crevice in the delta area is visible. I liked that a fair bit, so I drew it. I think it's pretty erotic, so why did other people not like it? (laughs)

(Compiled July 2014)

Were Both Nipple Afterimages the Same?

After finishing those interviews with Oku and Utatane, I got a taste of feelings so profound it felt as if they were going to cut me down where I stood.

My main takeaway from the interviews with those two was that both their approach and how they each arrived at their own versions of the nipple afterimage expression were in completely different ways.

In Oku's case, it was based on the observation of real shaking breasts, which he converted to flowing lines in his drawings. And in Utatane's case, it was him seeing the possibilities of how gradation tones could be used and believed he could create a sense of textural feel to make breasts more beautiful.

These differences are very interesting.

My original theory was that one had seen the other's work, and that it was an unconscious thing they did during the creation process. But that theory had been betrayed, in a good sense of the word. Both had come up with this expression during their debuts, and even if you think about it, one cannot deny their work.

This really was pure coincidence in terms of timing. In their debut works, it was as if a divine revelation had happened to both of them, encouraging them to create the nipple afterimage expression. Both versions of the expression were completely original, as I have confirmed myself.

Since I started researching on the internet in 2008, many occurrences of Oku's version of the nipple afterimage have appeared, even in articles. Possibly due to that, Oku has been acknowledged for his great feat as the inventor of the nipple afterimage.

However, this piece has confirmed and acknowledged both Oku and Utatane as inventors of the nipple afterimage. Here I would like to once again recognize that due to the effort of these two artists, the nipple afterimage expression was born.

The Two Sides that the Inventors of Manga Expressions Possess

I said before that both inventors of the nipple afterimage rarely used it in their own work after inventing the expression. I think that in their present state, they are still inventing expressions not being satisfied with things as they are in this moment. It might have something to do with their pride as artists. Additionally, neither shows signs of slowing down their chase after other body expressions, drawing on the very power of manga to charm and draw in readers.

Just as Japan felt during the '90s bubble; just as it still feels after the most recent bubble that they do not live within one; these artists did not feel as though they had finally discovered the nipple afterimage.

Ultimately, due to them being focused on "making interesting manga," this expression was part coincidence, and because of that, were finally acknowledged for having created such an important expression.

In the afterword of the fifth volume of *GANTZ*, Mr. Oku said that when he recognized that he had invented the nipple afterimage, he hadn't felt very good about it: He relates:

> Afterwards, all of the other artists around me couldn't stop talking about this expression. While I did draw it to render the movement of breasts, and to that end, drew the trajectory of the afterimage created by the nipples, hentai and other manga genre artists also made use of it. I think they all used it not knowing where it came from, probably. Anyway, after I drew this, I was a bit concerned that people would start saying, "but the breasts, the breasts!".
>
> *Hiroya Oku*
> (*GANTZ*, Volume 5; 2002)

As an artist, I'm sure that having attention paid to nothing but the parts of one's work that one didn't necessarily wish for couldn't have been a good feeling at all.

In Hiroyuki Utatane's case, he seems to be a bit puzzled as to why the first expression he really put all of his might into (the cheeks of the buttocks) was never really valued. In reality, Utatane instead turned his focus to resolutely creating almost stupidly beautiful buttocks expressions. Since his release of *COUNT DOWN*, I think he worked more within mainstream manga, instead of drawing directly erotic material. However, it is important to note that there are instances of the nipple afterimage inside of his next work, *Seraphic Feather.*

While these two cases are different, it seems that when the impact of a certain invention becomes great, the more it seems to absorb the inventors in stress and trouble, as if they have had a curse laid upon them. But I'm sure there are also cases where when those expressions have brought them attention, that may not be the case of their works as a whole, or even to the heart of them. Instead it becomes a situation where the specific images are the only things to be remembered.

There are also cases where something misconstrued therein takes on a life of its own. There has also been the theory that when creators invent an expression, they may also try to simultaneously figure out how to rid themselves of it. I'm sure in the case of new creators that don't have many other weapons at their disposal, this goes double for them.

When a manga expression is born, and especially, the bigger it is, the more artists are influenced by it. It begins to spread, and at some point, it becomes shared property between the creator and the readers seeing it. Once one becomes generalized, it undergoes encoding. That process begins with changes within the expression, then evolves, is essentially given meaning and also undergoes a transfiguration of sorts.

With these expressions, there also may be the issue of how its original inventors and the artists that gained fame by making use of the expression may be concerned about having a divergence between the original intent and meaning meant by those parties, and then the intent and meaning as interpreted by the readers. Whichever expression it may be, the encoding process of it will always have its points and demerits.

That is the alternate theme of this book.

The Afterimage Window Period

It would be incorrect to say that the nipple afterimage, upon its debut in 1988, had such a big impact as an expression that upon its transmission to the eromanga world became mainstream in popularity as an erotic expression in one fell swoop.

The origin of the nipple afterimage that year was more or less decided. I used to believe that consequently, if you were to thoroughly look into eromanga presented from that year on, you'll naturally figure out how this expression spread. However, I have since moved away from that line of thought. After thorough research, I found that the wider spread of the nipple afterimage as an expression didn't start happening until roughly sometime around 1993.

The movement of breasts were, as usual, accompanied by sound effects like " poyon poyon" and "purun purun," but there was absolutely no indication there was an afterimage at all. I wonder what was happening there.

One might say that the "four year-long window period" is the greatest mystery of the nipple afterimage as an expression.

As to why this window period happened, I have two theories. The first theory: at the beginning of the 1990s, with the unforeseen kyounyu boom happening, smaller windows began to accumulate. It began to swell mainly with the gravure and adult video booms that were happening adjacent to the kyounyu boom, and that wave crashed into seinen and shonen comic magazines, just as I explained in the previous chapter. When someone brings up kyounyu today, the next image that comes to mind is that of plump chests in motion. But in the realm of manga at the time, that desire had not yet been realized.

In other words, the artists that drew kyounyu were only concentrating on their sensitivity. To the readers, seeing that alone satisfied them. Perhaps for both parties, as much as they wanted to see kyounyu moving, I can't help but wonder if it was because the desire to pursue this particular fetish was more pressing.

Of course, just like Mr. Oku, we know that it wasn't necessarily the issue of not having an artist, whose enthusiasm for the material feeling of breasts and their movement, creating content. Instead it might've been an issue of artists like Oku being too ahead of their time. Another possibility is that to begin with, the world needed to get used to the kyounyu trend.

My second theory (and this may be the more credible of the two): as it happened with that era on the whole, there was an ice-age of sorts for eromanga at the same time. Due to the effect of the Miyazaki Murders of 1989, within the shonen and seinen genres there was a severe chilling effect on extreme realistic depictions, to the point that there was removal of certain content at the time. This was also the time of content being sold under the label of erotica but it wasn't very erotic at all due to this chilling effect. Even in eromanga magazines, editors gave orders to creators to "lessen the sexual content as much as possible."

But of course, people still wanted to challenge the eromanga world with new expressions. However, due to everything that happened as a result of the Miyazaki Murders, there were people concerned that someone might come in and alter eromanga so that it no longer had the erotic part of it. It may be what made many quite sensitive about the topic, and perhaps it helped steal the initial thunder, the velocity of those ideas, effectively decelerating them.

At this point, the eromanga world aside, there were some concerned that was the only thing that it was spending its time on. It is thought that the strategy that was used in order to stick it out until the chilling effect thawed was as long as no one released anything that would stand out, they laid low, and kept their mouth shut, things would be okay. That sort of tense situation wouldn't exactly be fertile breeding ground for new expressions.

It has been said that the ice age began to thaw around 1993, and suddenly the nipple afterimage spread like wildfire. If one thinks about it, that would be expected for that to happen.

In non-adult manga, especially within the seinen and shonen genres, as to how the nipple afterimage would evolve as an expression, well, not even the reflection of the expression was able to be seen at the time. While there was Hiroya Oku's groundbreaking expression work and the methods with which he produced them in regular seinen manga, after that, the only other work that used his expression in that genre in the '90s was the seventh volume of Kentaro Miura's ***Berserk*** (1989~, Hakusensha/Dark Horse), where there was a nipple afterimage used with the character Charlotte (2-18).

While the first appearance of the nipple afterimage was in mainstream manga, it hadn't spread much within that category. Instead it ended up becoming a specialized technique in eromanga. If one follows that line of thought, then perhaps it's natural to think that the evolved form of the nipple afterimage would have been just as unique.

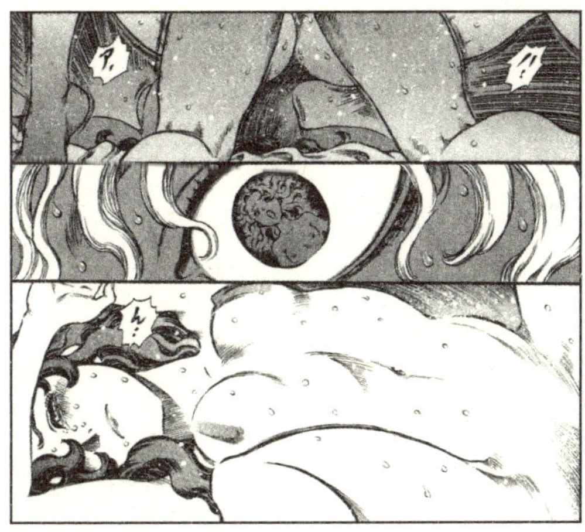

2-18: ***Berserk***, Vol. 7 (Kentaro Miura 1995, Hakusensha/Dark Horse)

Nipple Afterimage Inflation

Finally, the nipple afterimage had been revived, and a time where the eromanga world would be honored came into being.

The thawing effect began around 1993, and in 1995 explosive growth occurred. At that time, it was clear that there were repeated occurrences of the nipple afterimage in use. Had one opened an eromanga magazine, it seemed nearly every single magazine had it drawn within it.

In the early days of the nipple afterimage, the afterimage part of the expression seemed to have little confidence as to whether it would be able to convey its message to the reader; more times than not it would have classic sound effects like "purun" (jiggle) and "burun" (tremble) accompanying it to make sure the reader knew what they were seeing.

But even within those versions of the expression, that approach wasn't uniform. This early period of trial and error on behalf of creators, especially for those who wanted to take the expression in their own direction, can be seen as an open "cementing period" in its own right.

There was a type of nipple afterimage where the nipple was not blurred, but rather the entire contour of the breast was (2-19). There's another type where the nipple was left alone and complemented (2-20, 21). Another novel approach was by way of fusing small breasts with the nipple afterimage (2-22). Even if they were small breasts, warping movement lines around the upper body gave the nipples a sense of weight and existence, and the dynamics of movement improved.

Around this time, yet another type of nipple afterimage made itself known, the "asymmetrical nipple afterimage" (2-23, 24). It turns out that breasts move a lot more freely than we think they do.

In this era there might have been creators who decried that the nipple afterimage had become boring, and that a new, more free type of breast movement expression was needed. Though whether there really were creators who felt this way is anyone's guess. Regardless, the creators who

Renewal of the Nipple Afterimage

2-19: "VIVID FANTASY" (Rei Arou 1993, Mediax)

2-20: "Jigoku Kyoshi O'en Senjuraku" (Heaven-11 1993, Byakuya-Shobo)

2-21: "SOAP" (Ran Hiryuu 1994, Tatsumi Publishing)

2-22: "BATH COMMUNICATION" (Hiromi Egawa 1995, Mediax)

2-23: "HAPPY BIRTHDAY TO MY GIRL" (DISTANCE 1994, France Shoin)

2-24: "Ai no Tame ni" (Douman Seiman 1995, Hit Publishing)

were the most active were the ones who loved and took pride in kyounyu. Like fish taking to water, they began to draw breast expressions that were more intense and dynamic.

It was as if Mugi Tokisaka (2-25), Minor Boy (2-26), Kazuki Kotobuki (2-27), Kazu Tomonaga, Seiji Aura (2-28), Kengo Yonekura (2-29), and many other kyounyu creators had gained a new weapon to fight with, vividly wielding their pens across the page. This is also the age where we see Wataru Watanabe's version of the nipple afterimage, where his busty youngsters helped create an era of water balloon breasts. All of these artists rushed to cozy up to this new culture and ended up helping to renew the expression (2-30).

After a roughly four year-long window period, the afterimage appeared to be reverting to its ancestral form as it descended into the world of eromanga. I did relate before that the short window was possibly a side-effect due to the Miyazaki Murders, but it also might be that because this expression was so heavily policed that it exploded into activity once the restrictions were lifted. The post-window era was like the Big Bang for eromanga.

However, the next issue that pops up in wake of that theory is: was there a sense of inheritance (in terms of the creators that were deeply influenced by this expression) with the nipple afterimage that Oku and Utatane invented, which also underwent inflation during the *eromanga bubble era?*

Even though there was a four-year window, that doesn't necessarily mean that there was no activity around it; nor did it cease to exist. Through the medium of works not yet discovered, I still yet might find evidence to support the theory that inheritance and succession occurred. But at this point in time, I have no evidence to support the proliferation within the scope of mainstream manga. The only thing I can say is that my investigation into such is ongoing, even now.

Even if I were to gain hints from previous works to formally state that there was a proliferation of this expression, it may be that I'm being influenced on an unconscious level. Just as how the nipple afterimage resistance held its breath during the bubble era, I want to believe that perhaps

The Beginning of the Spread of the Nipple Afterimage

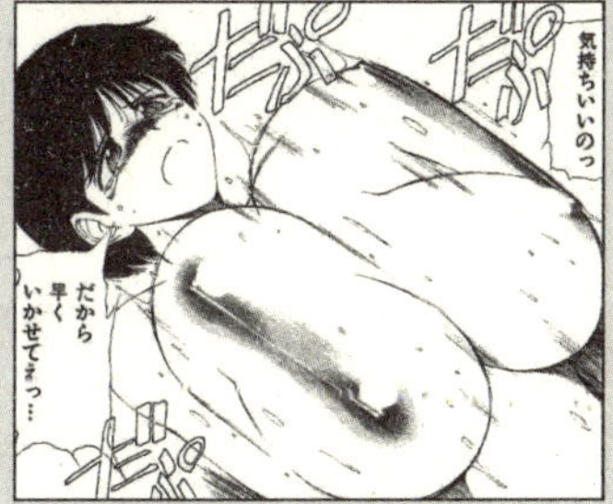

2-25: "NyuMan" (Mugi Tokisaka 1997, Wanimagazine)

2-26: ***Keiko-sensei no KagaiJugyo*** (Minor Boy 1988, France Shoin)

2-27: "NIGHT VISITOR" (Kazuki Kotobuki 1993, Tsukasa Shobo)

2-28: ***Imoto Play*** (Seiji Aura 2002, France Shoin)

2-29: "Shiritsu Seishitan Gakuen Renai!? Senka" (Kengo Yonekura 1998, Mediax)

2-30: ***Mama ni Dokkin*** (Wataru Watanabe 2001, Toen Shobou)

it will make itself known in time to me. But mixing personal emotions and research is absolutely something one must not do. So, I would like to go on investigating it for now.

The New Evolution of the Nipple Afterimage

Going into the year 2000, the nipple afterimage continues to evolve. At this point in time, the expression itself manages to barely follow the laws of physics. However, in 2000, it grows by not leaps but light years, and goes from following the laws of physics to seemingly move into the realm of sci-fi.

The afterimage wasn't that of taillights any longer as it now takes on the airiness of cellophane (2-31). This time, it isn't the only parts of the nipples influenced, but instead the nipple as a whole as part of the afterimage, which strengthened its sense of existence (2-32~34). Clothing was no longer a hindrance to creating the afterimage, but instead was drawn as the "clothed nipple afterimage," a brilliant plan that helped enhance the sense of material feeling to those breasts, and we start to see this a lot around this time.

There was also the moment that the breasts escaped their clothed confinement, which became the "flying nipple afterimage (2-35~37)." Other such modifications to the expression developed variations of it to use in differing situations. The same time that the *paizuri* (titty fuck) expression was developed, the nipple afterimage expression accommodated it, becoming the "titty fuck nipple afterimage (2-38)." The conventional wisdom-defying, vertical-only breast movement with the expression became the "horizontal movement nipple afterimage." There was also the version of the expression that eclipsed the locus of the afterimage, the "rolling nipple afterimage (2-39)."

The artists that helped create these modifications had seemingly

2-31: "Boku no Haigorei?" (Katsura Yoshihiro 2013, Core Magazine)

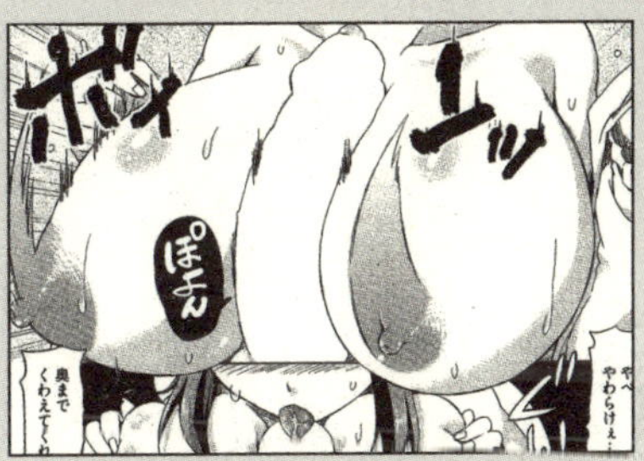

2-32: "Go-Keiyaku wa Kochira desu!" (Chiyoko Ayakase 2012, Core Magazine)

2-33: "Karate Ne-chan Monzetsu Suimin Kumite" (Drachef 2016, Angel Publishing)

2-34: "Real mo Game mo Kinshin Soukan" (Dai Uemukai 2017, GOT)

2-35: "Milky Queen" (Meguru Tsubakiya 2014, Issuisha)

2-36: "Kanojo wa Joji Happyochu" (URAN 2011, Core Magazine)

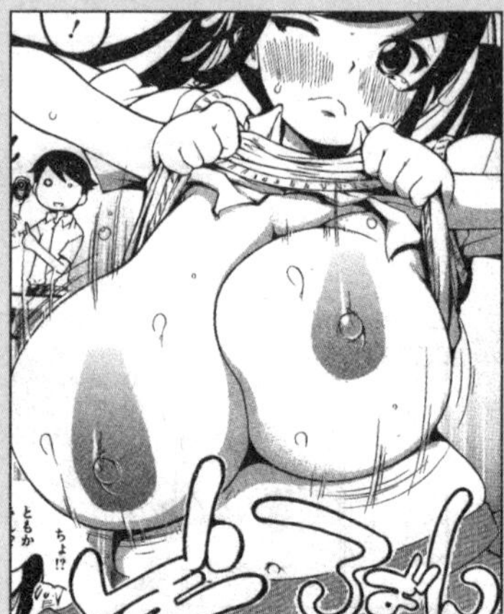

2-37: "Ani < Imoto" (Dorei Jackie 2010, Core Magazine)

2-38: "Zankou" (Kuroarama Soukai 1999, France Shoin)

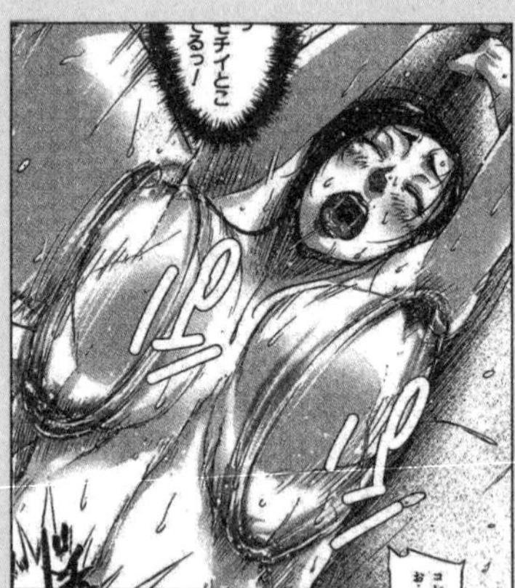

2-39: "Gyaku Rape Salon" (Saiyazumi 2017, TI NET)

believed in nearly every variation possible to make them.

But what really evolved during this period was the acceleration of the expression. It went harder, faster, stronger, as if it were the slogan of the national polity. The nipple afterimage started to carry a trademark at this time.

The afterimages that went up and down had three, four, or more afterimages, going through a *Super Saiyanization* of sorts. This version of the expression went up, down, right, and left, and was thus dubbed the "four-point afterimage," which helped the acceleration of the expression (2-40~45). When breasts were heavy like sandbags in their movement, the "sandbag afterimage" (2-46) was born. There was also the case of when there were too many afterimages, as if they'd been split into alter egos of each other and made the reader forget they were originally one afterimage. This was known as the "ninja nipple afterimage (2-47, 48)."

I introduced the concept of the "nipple afterimage technique" earlier in this chapter. When it comes down to it, when one takes all of these new versions of the expression into account, it seems that it may be the most accurate term for it after all. But now that we've come this far, it may be more appropriate (in the sense of "yes, there was a breast here after all" in a very real, physics-like way) to call it "Schrödinger's nipple afterimage."

And in this way, all these changes took roughly a decade as we enter the '00s.

For eromanga, the '90s were the era when the image of creating kyounyu manga itself was sold. However, in recent years, the more that people strove to sell such works without differentiating other themes, the fetish and its expressions continued to spread. As the eromanga genre's comprehensive skill at art rose, competition within popular categories intensified, and helped encourage that trend. This was the period where big breasts were the norm, as was the nipple afterimage, which meant that there was a fixing of the expression in place for use. On one hand, this was a revelation concerning the diffusion and spread of the nipple afterimage as an achievement. But when it came to the facets of change and evolution, one cannot deny that there was a sense of purification that came with it.

The Four Point (Nipple) Afterimage

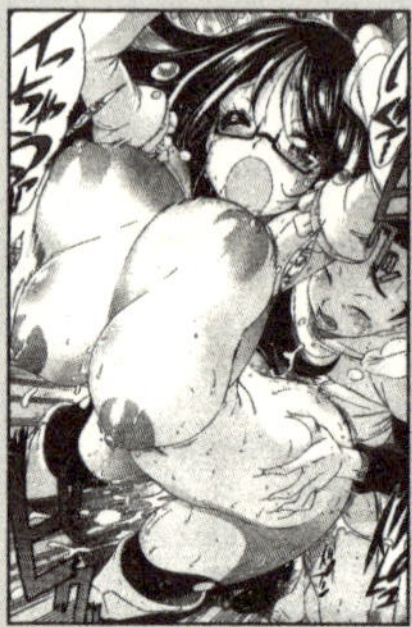

2-40: "METAMO SISTER" (Amatarou 2012, Core Magazine)

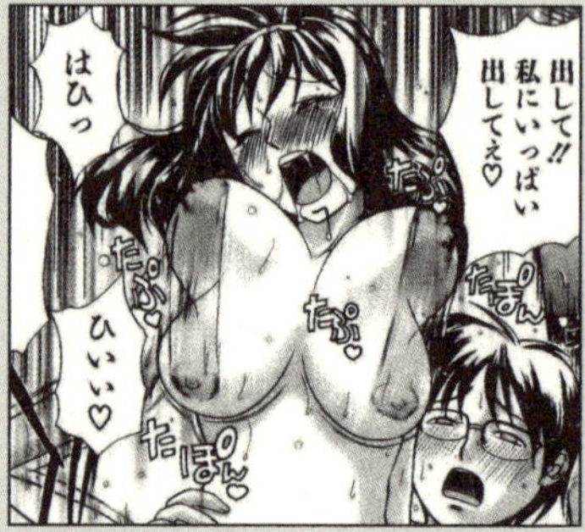

2-41: "NicoTama 2" (Yuki Takano 2006, Hit Publishing)

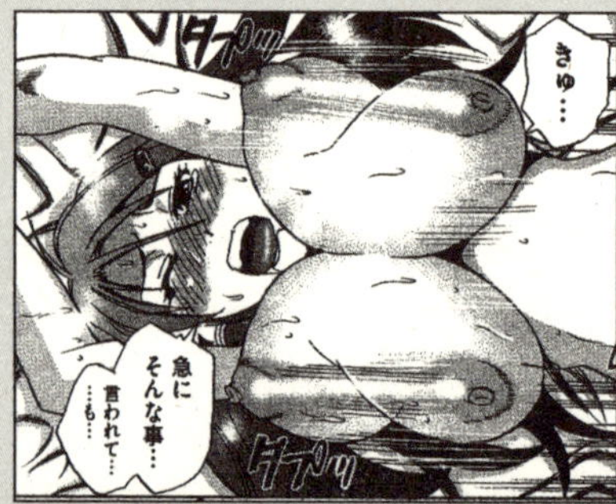

2-42: "HHH" (DISTANCE 2009, Core Magazine)

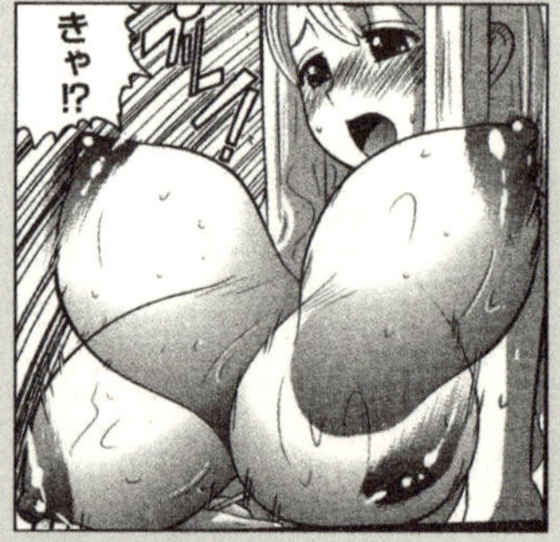

2-43: "Tooi Hi no Yakusoku" (Nero Norakuro 2007, Core Magazine)

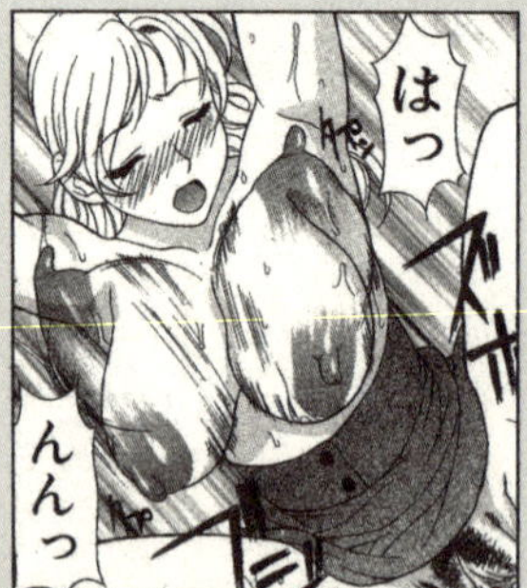

2-44: ***Saishu Kareshi Dangi*** (Yutakamaru Kagura 2003, Akaneshinsha)

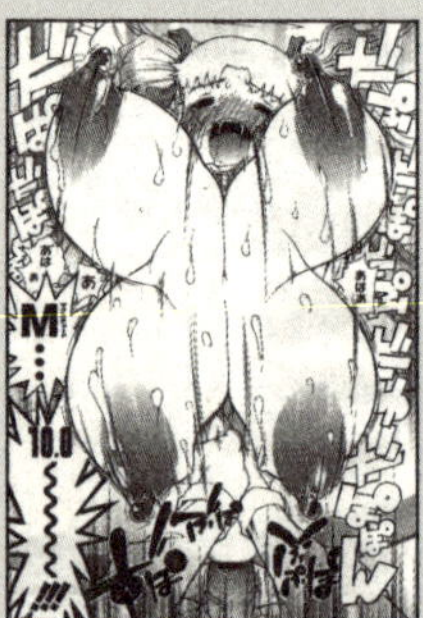

2-45: "Magnitude 10.0" (Dorei Jackie 2010, Core Magazine)

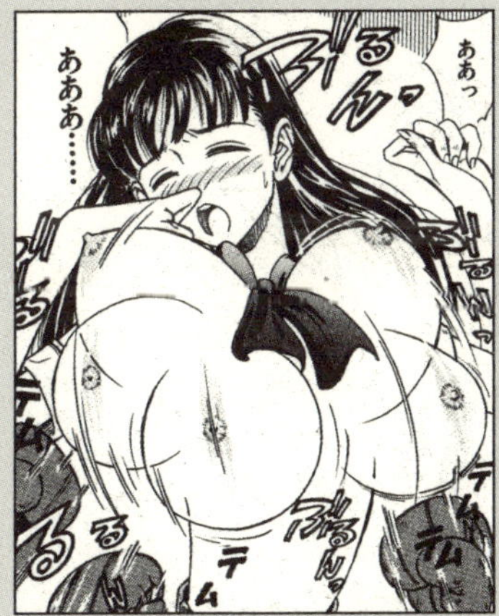

2-46: "RUSH!" (Chitose Sakuragi 1996, Wanimagazine)

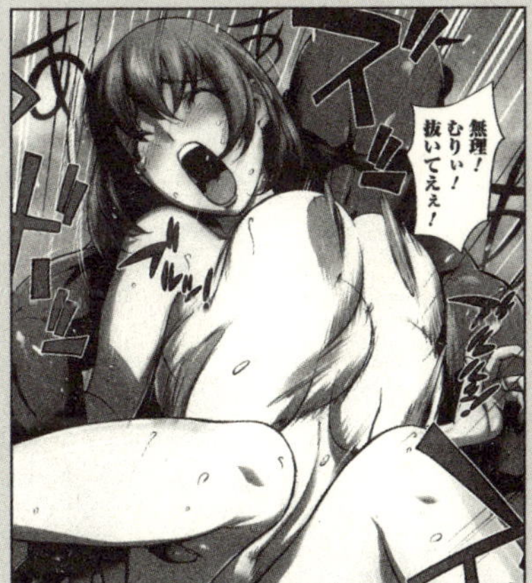

2-47: ***Netorare New Heroine*** (*Netorare Nyu Heroine*; KONKIT 2014, Issuisha/FAKKU)

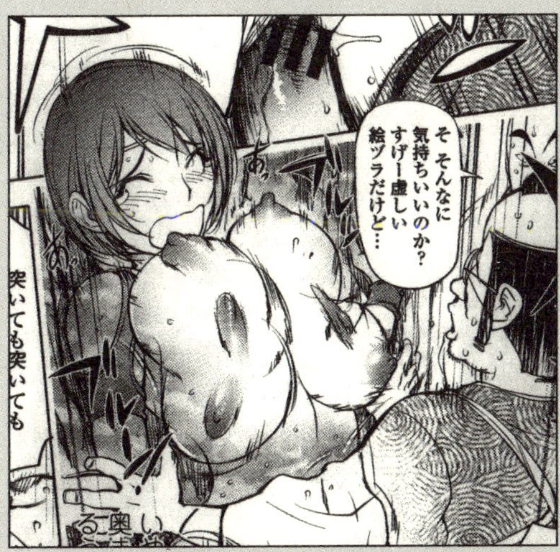

2-48: ***ToraChichi*** (KONKIT 2014, Fujimi Publishing)

If you think that this means the expression then comparatively calmed down within eromanga, that wasn't the case. Now that the nipple afterimage had conquered the genre, it sought out new frontiers. Born in mainstream publications, it became the most used expression in eromanga, only to once again cross back into regular manga territory.

Returning to Its Birthplace and Beyond

At this junction, I would like to look at the sudden mutation of the nipple afterimage by looking at a similar event that happened within *gekiga* scenes years before.

To begin with, I'm not sure the nipple afterimage can be seen in *ero-gekiga*. Truthfully, it cannot, but manga techniques of the time helped increase both whatever was in the creators' imaginations or delusions. It has been thought that even with those weapons available, that sort of expression just wouldn't mix with the reality-chasing styles of those genres. Therefore, it might be better to say that because of those factors, for the most part the nipple afterimage did not appear in *gekiga* and *ero-gekiga*.

However, within the process of evolution, different versions of the nipple afterimage appeared that people hadn't even dreamed of before. Perhaps it would be better to say that there were debates as to whether some of these groundbreaking new expressions could be considered part of the nipple afterimage canon.

If I were to attach a name to one of these new expressions, it would be best to call it the "mandala nipple afterimage," as if it were a religious painting; godly in its own right. If you were to look at it, I'm sure you would be shocked by this particular expression.

The person behind it is none other than veteran ero-gekiga artist, Taiyo Nemuri.

Taiyo Nemuri started drawing ero-gekiga in the beginning of the

1980s and is one of the few remaining creators on active duty for that genre. It's been said that they've been active since the '80s, but the nipple afterimage hasn't been around quite that long. Up until the beginning of the '90s, Nemuri has created conventional works for the ero-gekiga genre, but something happened between the early and mid-90s. Nemuri's art style experienced a huge shift, where they suddenly started drawing afterimages along with their nipples.

The unique characteristic of Taiyo Nemuri's nipple afterimages is that they share an unusual locus within their panels. Regular afterimages usually go from point A to point B, but Nemuri's go from C to D to E as well. They go right and left – wherever they please. It is as if Nemuri's afterimages occur in the sky, drawing mandalas. Hence, they are known as the "mandala nipple afterimage " (2-49). That being said, it's a bit more like a nimbus than a mandala, creating a scene that makes me wonder if it would open the way to Buddhist enlightenment if a reader were to see it.

Another afterimage-related expression is the "frame by frame afterimage," where it appears if the nipple is creeping onto the breast (2-50). There's also the "yin-yang afterimage," where it seems like the nipple's placement looks like something out of Yi Jing's ***Book of Changes.*** There's the "S-shaped afterimage," where the locus doesn't follow the nipple in a straight line, but rather in an S-shape (2-51). There's also the "cross afterimage," where the afterimage performs an utterly impossible feat by outlining the shape of a cross (2-52).

As you can see, a fair amount of very unique afterimage expressions came about in this period. Why Nemuri all of a sudden awoke to the possibilities of the nipple afterimage in the mid-90s is still unknown, but what we do know is that they were influenced by *bishojo* comics. The idea that "the afterimage is the starting point, everything but the ending point is a side-trip" is most likely uniquely something that Nemuri thought of. And within the genealogy of the afterimage, we can see all of this happening within the seinen genre, which is quite the interesting phenomenon indeed (2-53).

The Mandala Nipple Afterimage, From the World of Taiyo Nemuri

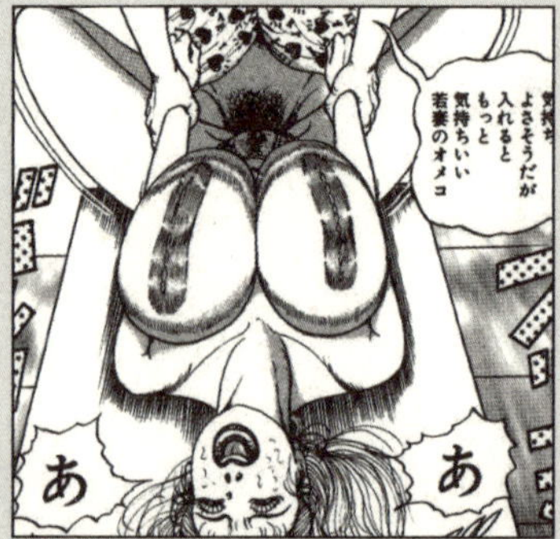

2-50: ***Bakunyu Jukujo Nikudan-Pai Panic*** (Taiyo Nemuri 2000, Toen Shobou)

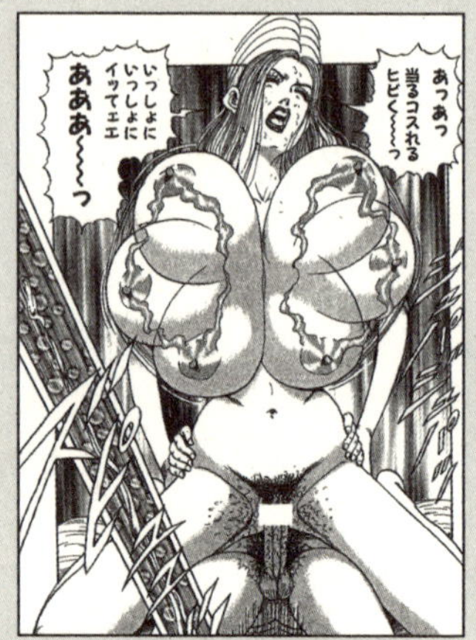

2-49: ***Mai no Kyounyu Ranbo*** (Taiyo Nemuri 2000, Cybele Publishing)

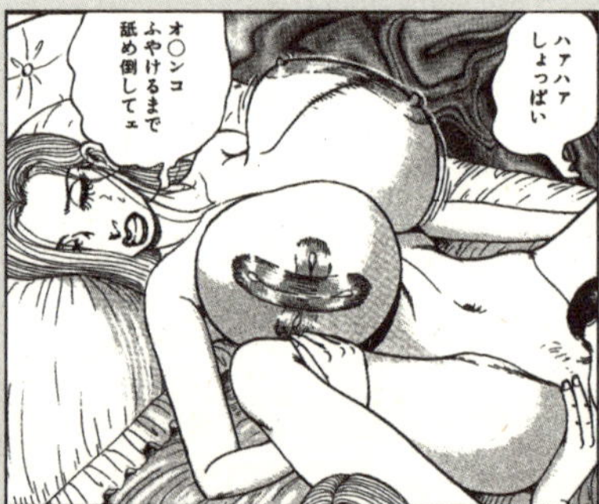

2-52: ***Mai no Kyounyu Ranbo*** (Taiyo Nemuri 2000, Cybele Publishing)

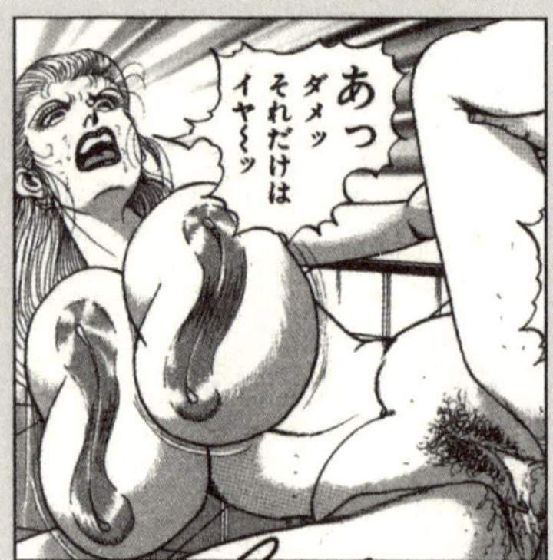

2-51: ***Bakunyu Jukujo Nikudan-Pai Panic*** (Taiyo Nemuri 2000, Toen Shobou)

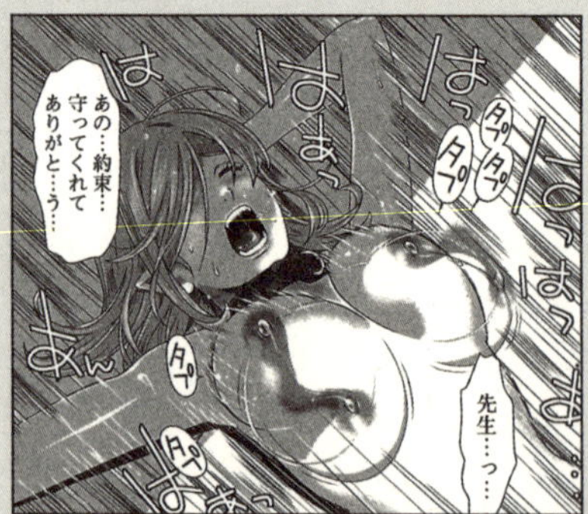

2-53: ***Love Junkies***, Vol. 2 (*Junai Junkie*; Kyo Hazuki 2015, Akita Shoten)

The Nipple Afterimages Created by Female Artists

When we think of the erotic manga genre, there is also the *TL* (teens' love) genre, and the adult female-targeted *lady-comi* as well.

Kanan Yamada was the one artist who brought the nipple afterimage, which up until then had only been in male-targeted genres, into the TL genre with the most enthusiasm (2-54). Yamada's work had been born in male-targeted regular adult manga magazines, and it's been thought that she knew the special characteristics of both the TL and mainstream manga genres well because of this fact. Artists that have experience in multiple genres tend to know the special characteristics of expressions used in those realms, as well as the cross-cultural communication that occurs.

While in recent years, the trend of manga creators not reading outside of their own genre isn't very large, I can't help but wonder if creators like Kanan Yamada that are active in multiple genres help assist the border migration and transgressions with these expressions as a result. Female artists in particular tend to take on more side projects in male-targeted genres and mediums, so it's been thought that due to that factor it's easier to yield a manga crop in that way.

These days, it's pretty easy to find an instance of the nipple afterimage in current TL comics (2-55~58). In recent years, there's been one more reason as to why the use of the nipple afterimage has risen in the TL genre, which is due to the fact that the *big boobification* that took place with the spread of the kyounyu trope throughout manga has finally landed in female-targeted genres like TL. If we are to go with this hypothesis, then we would know that as to female readers of shojo manga and TL, breast sizes had been drawn conservatively. At least, they had up until recent years where the amount of depictions of characters who didn't have complexes about having large breasts have definitely increased. This is thought of as a reaction to the kyounyu boom that had occurred throughout all genres of manga. This boom is also naturally connected to the movement of breasts.

Even within female-targeted genres, this change in awareness might've become an enticement towards these new expressions.

After the nipple afterimage migrated into TL, then the last (female-oriented) bastion as-yet untouched by this expression was *BL* (boys' love). I wrote before on how expressions of male breasts had rapidly spread and grew within the world of BL, I think that there is still a paradigm shift needed to make male nipples with afterimages in terms of matching in popular use.

Within independent works like fanzines, one can find uses of the male nipple afterimage, but I doubt that its use is as widespread as its progenitor in terms of being a standard expression. However, I do believe that there are many parts of BL with its challenging attitude with regard to expressions that the rest of the manga world could learn a thing or two from. From here on out, I am eagerly awaiting to see what happens next in that genre.

To LOVE Ru: The Shonen Nipple Afterimage

The increasing frequency in breast expressions that happened during the 1980s slowed at the beginning of the '90s. However, when it came to erotic content and shonen, they were like two peas in a pod.

There was a dangerous belief that had readers of that genre not opened their eyes, the future of the shonen and seinen genres would have been destroyed. Whether or not it would have actually happened is different. This idea was a flowing river, a peek into a largely unseen thought process that prioritized big breasts above all else. If neither were released, it meant that there would be a pursuit of erotic expressions.

It was in this atmosphere that the newly serialized *To LOVE Ru* debuted

The Nipple Afterimages That Set Teens' Love Ablaze

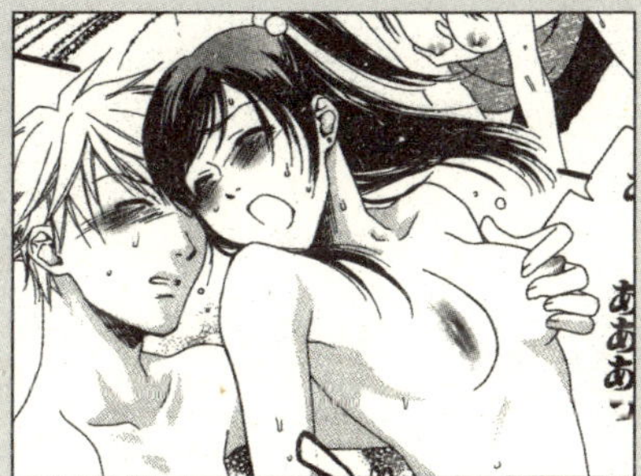

2-54: "Dare nimo Ienai" (Kanan Yamada 2002, Kousai Shobo)

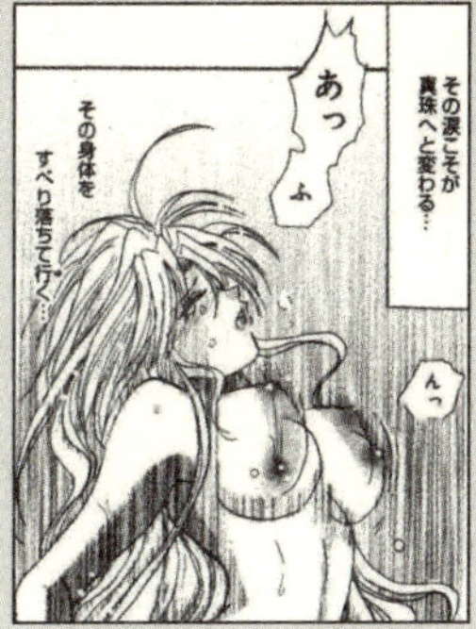

2-55: ***Beyond the Friend, Under the Lover*** (*Tomodachi Koibito Miman Ijo*; Natsuki Kuriyama 2004, Shobunkan)

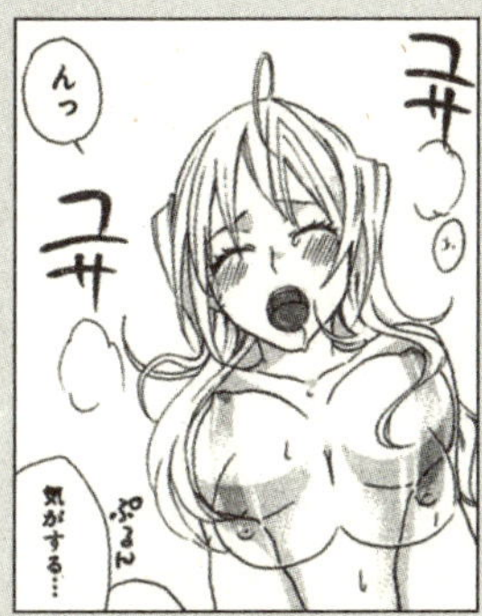

2-56: ***I Love You*** (*Kimi ga Suki*; Gyoe Suzumushi 2008, Shobunkan)

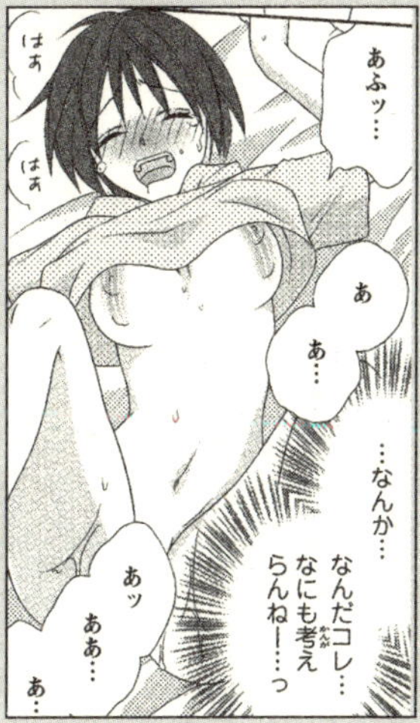

2-57: ***Bon-kyu-bon Danshi!*** (Kaya Aota 2014, Shusuisha)

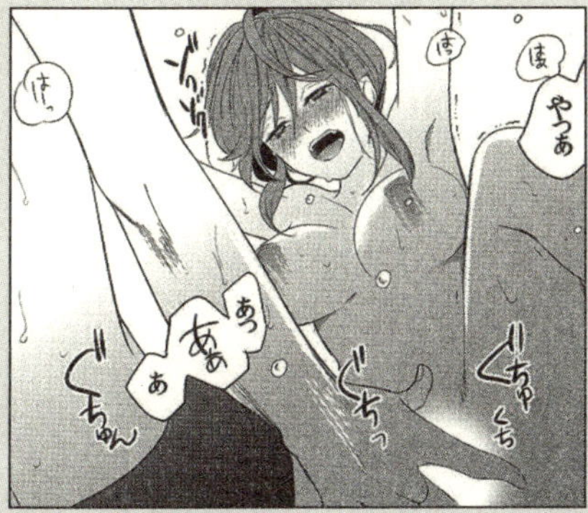

2-58: ***Futon to Kotatu 3*** (Tonari Toyama 2013, Screamo)

in *Weekly Shonen Jump*. The point of attention for *To LOVE Ru* was that it wasn't a design of shonen meets shojo like Matsukazu Katsura meets Mikan Momokuri in terms of genre fusion, but instead is part of the old guard of traditional shonen manga designs. Not in the sense that it used deformed, manga-like characters and breasts expressions, but more rather that it was reliable in its use of *bishojo* comic design tropes when it came to the female form. One can see the influence of those tropes in the depictions of breasts in this series.

Within its spinoff, ***To LOVE Ru: Darkness*** (2010, Shueisha/Seven Seas Ent.), a definite use of the nipple afterimage enters the scene (2-59). While *To LOVE Ru: Darkness* was serialized in a shonen magazine, it also completely lifted the ban on showing depictions of nipples. One could say then perhaps it was an issue of the meeting between uncensored nipple and afterimage being fated.

(I did touch briefly upon the breast expressions within this series in my previous chapter on breasts, but I would like to do it again once more in this chapter so that you may commit it to memory.)

Incidentally, it is important to note that the nipple afterimage within the shonen genre existed before this series was released, even before Kentaro Yabuki's work within it. From what I have been able to confirm, the oldest debut of the nipple afterimage in a shonen comic was in the pages of *Shonen Champion* magazine in 1999 from the 135th chapter of ***Oyama! Kikunosuke*** (Takahiro Seguchi 1996, Akita Shoten; 2-60). However, the nipples were censored in the graphic novel edition.

While there was a high chance of this magazine paying its respects to the expression from the jump, for a shonen comic I can't help but wonder if that was a deliberate decision on behalf of the editor to include within it. Just as with the 1997 *Pokémon Shock* incident on TV, this too was dangerous for children to look directly at. It might've been that even if adults felt the same way, the nipple afterimage might have had a simply herculean strength to it. Furthermore, Takahiro Seguchi made his initial debut in eromanga, and in the early period of *Kikunosuke*'s serialization was

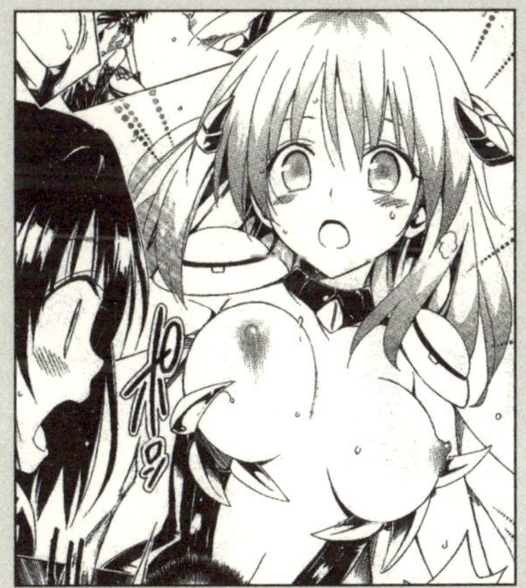

2-59: ***To LOVE Ru: Darkness***, Vol. 7 (Kentaro Yabuki & Saki Hasemi 2013, Shueisha/Seven Seas Ent.)

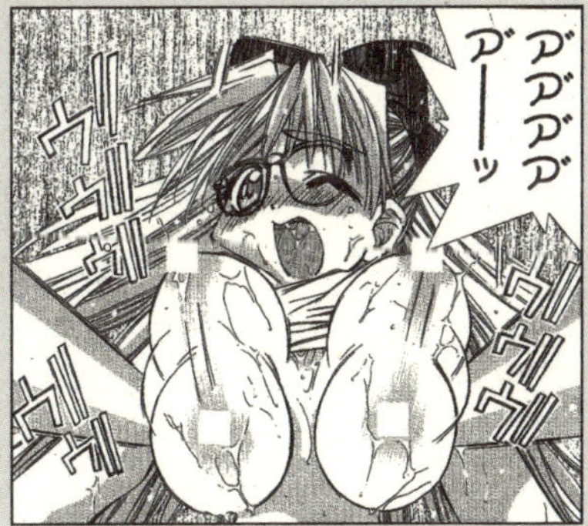

2-60: ***Oyama! Kikunosuke***, Vol. 14 (Takahiro Seguchi 1999, Akita Shoten)

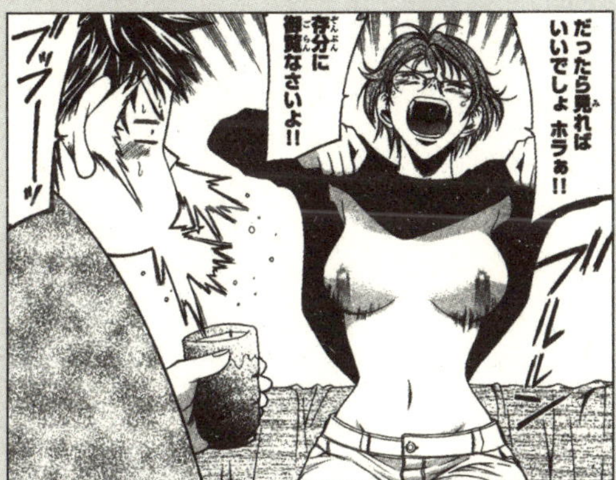

2-61: ***Suzuka***, Vol. 1 (Kouji Seo 2004, Kodansha/Del Rey)

also concurrently working for an eromanga magazine. Because of this concurrent serialization I can make peace with the fact that it appeared in a shonen publication.

After this, the nipple afterimage made an appearance in ***Suzuka*** (Kouji Seo 2004, Kodansha/Del Rey; 2-61). Much like with *To LOVE Ru*, it confirmed the spread of the nipple afterimage to shonen, and from there, it likely made many divergences then to spread to other categories as well. Because my investigation into categories other than shonen is insufficient, if you see a use of the afterimage elsewhere, please be kind enough to let me know.

Why Do Eromanga Expressions Tend to Spread?

The expression invented by both Hiroya Oku and Hiroyuki Utatane at the same time in 1988 had an incubation period, and after four years, exploded within eromanga, becoming one of the standards in the genre. It is an expression anyone can use, and as an understandable expression, it underwent an encoding process. After that, a new use of it was developed, and matured to the level where it became an inheritance of memory from the eromanga world within our larger manga industry as a whole.

Where manga genres distanced themselves from this expression, the eromanga world became the nipple afterimage's equivalent of Galapagos for Darwin. It became a specialized genre where many other expressions were also born. It is one of those expressions where though it originally was born in mainstream manga, it was hard to actually find an occurrence of that expression for a long time.

However, in recent years, the fences between manga genres have narrowed and there has been a lot of immigration (also known as border transgression) between genres. It's the same with artists, but also with readers and editors in terms of not having one fixed genre per person that they prefer to read. This has helped increase the desire for more free and interesting manga to be released into the world. And the main cause of this may be the fact that because it was an expression that dwelt for so long within eromanga, that helped along its diffusion process and provided a way to seep into other genres

I can't help but wonder what other deeply rooted eromanga expressions, like the nipple afterimage, will be released out into the world. I wonder how they will be born, evolve, and spread before our eyes.

Take for example… the "Mitsumine flat-chested nipple afterimage" (2-62). ❁

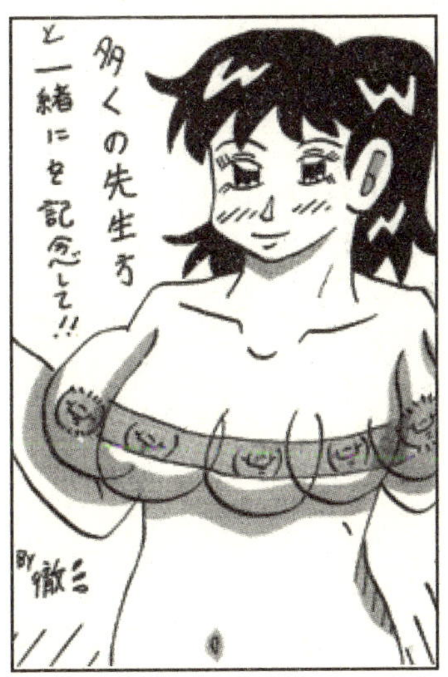

2-62: Original illustration (Tooru Mitsumine, 2015)

The History of Hentai Manga

CHAPTER THREE

Reinventing the Tentacle

What Is Tentacle Rape and Tentacle Play?

Mucus-soaked tentacles that elongate and tightly bind the female body, crawling like snakes to fill her secret places—her anus, her mouth—invading her every hole, raping her both inside and out…

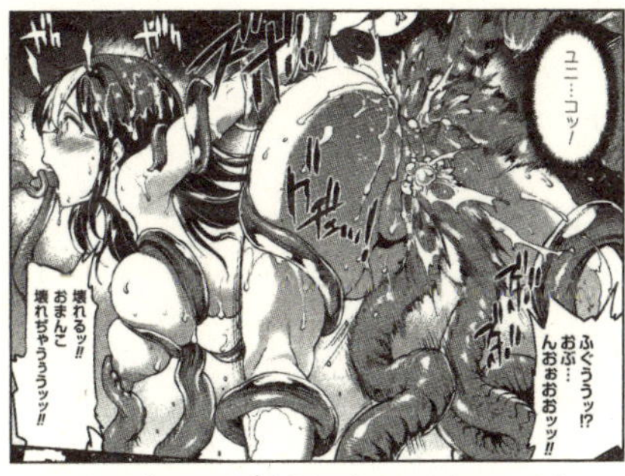

3-1A: ***The Grimore III*** (*Shinkyoku no Grimore III*; Erect Sawaru 2016, Kill Time Communications)

When eromanga fans hear the term "tentacle rape," a scene like this usually comes to mind. Modern-day tentacle rape and "tentacle play" usually involves a monster or mysterious lifeform with tentacles playing with a girl's body, usually developing into a scene where said woman gets violated by those tentacles.

Up until now many tentacle anthologies have been published within eromanga, enough to the point where it has formed another genre in its own right (3-1a~d). However, I wonder how the trope of the mysterious lifeform with tentacles violating the female body was born. Why did it need to take on the form of tentacles?

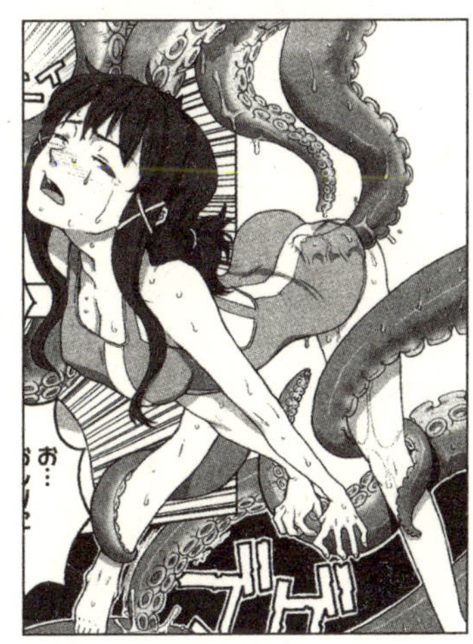

3-1B: ***LOAD OF TRASH*** (A-10 2010, Core Magazine)

First, let me go ahead and define "tentacles" as it is used for this book. A simple biological definition would be "belonging to a lifeform that does not possess hands, usually the protuberance in place of hands for an invertebrate," or in other words, a limb that is not a hand that is used to feel things is called a "tentacle." But the eromanga definition is different, namely combined another word, "tentacle rape." It does not characterize the nature of the creature that has it, unlike the biological definition, and instead the issue of how it behaves becomes part of the conflict of whatever work that it's in. When someone hears the terms "tentacles," "tentacle genre," or "tentacle play," what they think of as a result differs greatly in detail from person to person, but the first thing that I will address in this chapter is to unify all of these definitions for tentacle rape. Usually this definition hinges upon three conditions when it comes to depicting this term within eromanga.

These three conditions are:

1. **Regardless if it is a living organism or not, it will have long, narrow, sinuous limbs that can move freely.**
2. **These limbs will work independently, as if having a will of their own, and the owner of these limbs can operate them from long distances.**
3. **One can clearly tell that the woman (or sometimes, man) being attacked feels pleasure. The purpose of the attack is sexual assault, with the victim's will being violated, and the reader can understand this clearly.**

The first condition, simply, is that the host has long, narrow limbs that it can wind freely around its targets, but whether the host is defined or not is not a concern, and it doesn't necessarily need to be living for it to still be considered eligible to go under this condition. Rope or vines, even string or cord is fine, too. But because this would otherwise turn into an exercise in *kinbaku* (bondage rope play), we need that second condition.

Whether it be independently manipulated or from the outside, limbs that possess some sort of will must have a driving force behind them. Or to put it conversely, even if it is an inorganic cord and an alchemist or magician imbues it with power so that it moves freely, it can become

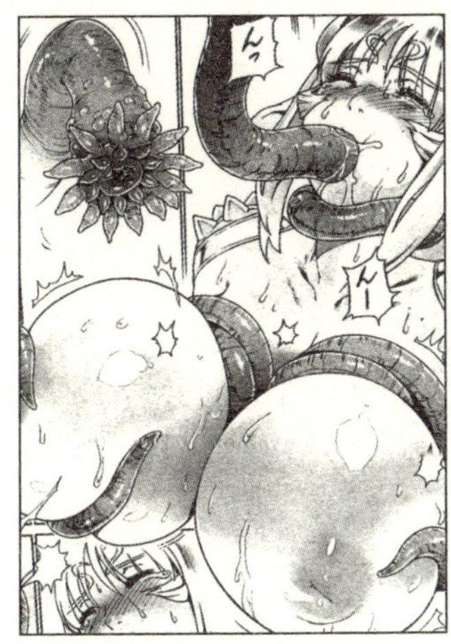

3-1C: "SECRET JOURNEY" (Po-Ju & Zappa Go 2009, Core Magazine)

tentacle-like in its existence. I purposely wrote "from long distances" in this case because while it denotes the chastity of the person being manipulated by touch, if the reader can't feel the creature's will, there isn't really a sense of them becoming "tentacles" established.

This makes the third condition even more important. Beyond the definition of tentacle rape that appears in eromanga, the reader wants the target to have sexual things done to them. If this is a standalone, the attacking creature needs a will to attack, and the victim needs their own motivations to defend themselves as well. The sexual service the artist knows fans want to see is present, and thus we have tentacle rape.

That said, if a Japanese Tentacle Rape Society academic conference existed (which as of writing this, doesn't seem to exist), I believe that there would be a white-hot debate about these conditions. However, here I would like to widen the scope of this definition of tentacle expressions that I've alluded to as quickly as I can, tracing back how people, especially women, came to be drawn in these expressions as well as inquire about the influences that this had on people.

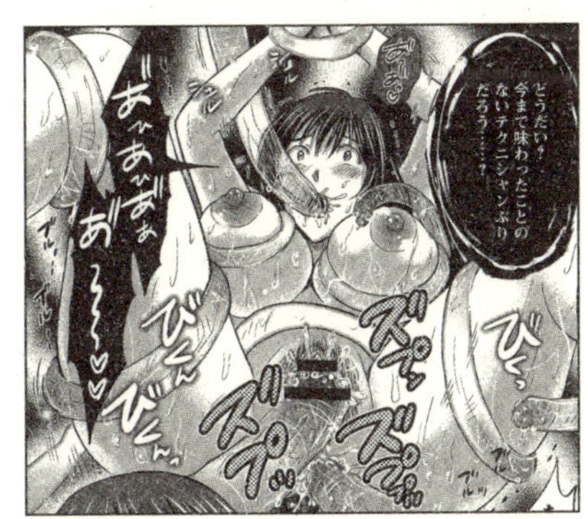

3-1D: ***Hitozuma Jigoku Rou*** (Hoshizuki Melon 2014, Sanwa Publishing)

Are Shunga the Roots of Tentacle Rape as a Trope?

Because there are currently living things on this planet that possess tentacles, I can't help but wonder if when people hear the word "tentacle" the first thing that comes to mind are octopi and squids.

In literary work, humanity has fought various giant tentacled creatures from the sea. An example of this is the Northern European legend of the kraken, a creature that is described as a mysterious marine organism (3-2). But many pictures of the kraken drawn by people look closest to a giant octopus or squid with giant tentacles that can easily overpower ships. The French author Jules Verne's ***Twenty Thousand Leagues Under the Sea*** (1870), and ***The Mysterious Island*** (1874) and other entries in his ***Voyages Extraordinaires*** series were inspired by those passed down tales of marine organisms, which debuted in his books. His works had them overpowering humans with their giant limbs.

Aside from this legend from Northern Europe, other cultures around the world have imagined giant octopi and squid in their folktales. Japan is no exception to this list. Edo period *ukiyo-e* woodblock prints and novels had octopus monsters in them. One such monster, the *umibouzu,* was thought of as a priest of the sea, and other such monsters were frequently the subject of folktales and anecdotes in fishing areas and shipping lanes.

But in these Japanese stories, it was never just about the octopus attacking people. Pictures of an octopus attacking a woman and doing sexual things to her were also drawn.

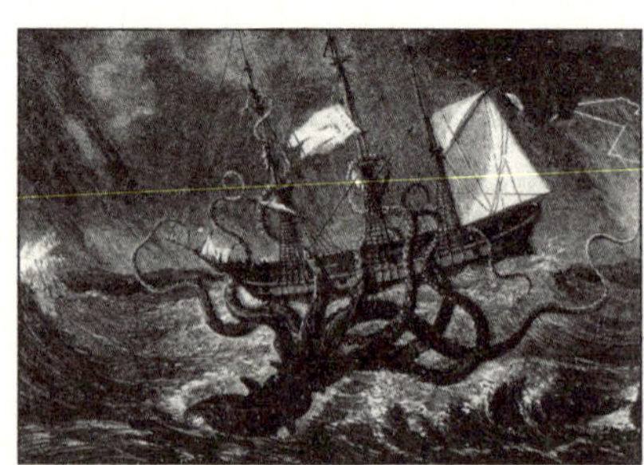
3-2: A kraken (Pierre Denys de Montfort 1810)

The Edo period ukiyo-e artist Katsushika Hokusai drew the famous *shunga* (erotic woodblock prints) ***The Dream of the Fisherman's Wife*** (*Tako to Ama*; 3-3) which features a diving girl being attacked by a giant octopus while entangled in its tentacles. *Fisherman's Wife* was published roughly circa 1820 in an *ehon* (erotic novel) series called ***Kinoe no Komatsu***. It was just a one-page illustration in a book, but it quickly made its way abroad, where it influenced many foreign artists at the time.

However, long before *Fisherman's Wife*, woodblock prints of women being attacked by octopi had been drawn, like Shigemasa Kitao's ***Programme of Erotic Noh Plays*** (*Yo-kyoku Iro Bangumi;* 1871, 3-4) and Shunsho Katsukawa's ***Lust of Many Women on One Thousand Nights*** (*Chiyo Dameshi,* 1786, 3-5) where diver girls are being violated by giant octopi.

Hokusai was influenced by Katsukawa and Shigemasa's work, making the recent theory that he drew *Fisherman's Wife* because of that influence stronger. In general, the people of the Edo era were heavily impacted by the idea of such creatures violating women, to the point where adaptations of that theme in art heavily increased.

As much as I would like to believe that there is a connection to current eromanga, the expressions of the tentacle rape trope, as well as the technology that helped further it are a continuation of a meme. I feel like that idea requires some very cautious thought. When it comes to explaining *shunga* as one of the big crazes of pop culture in the modern era, we also need to consider attitudes towards the sex industry, thought patterns, connections to animals and other things as they connect to sex as I believe that this is a multi-faceted issue.

I believe that it is dangerous to conclude that expressions of the current era and the designs that look like them are directly connected to current culture just because they have been used. Ultimately this book's goal is to make the reader aware of the tentacle rape trope, the designs that resemble it, as well as what was drawn in the past.

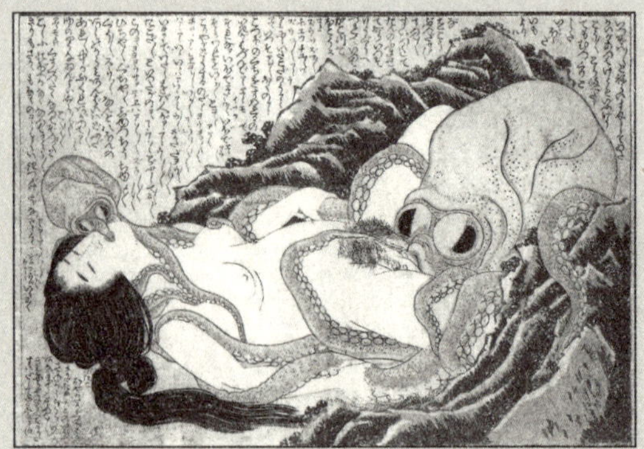

3-3: ***The Dream of the Fisherman's Wife*** (Tako to Ama; Katsushika Hokusai 1820)

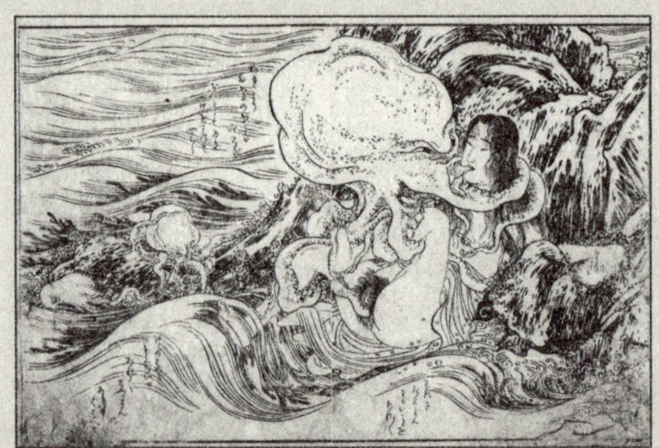

3-4: ***Programme of Erotic Noh Plays*** (*Yo-kyoku Iro Bangumi*; Kitao Shigemasa 1781)

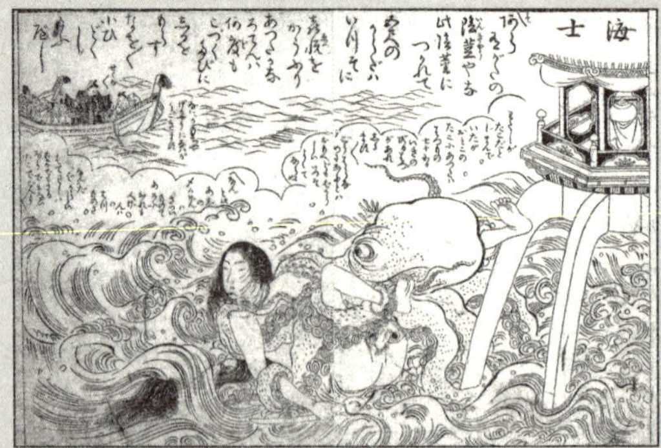

3-5: ***Lust of Many Women on One Thousand Nights*** (*Chiyo Dameshi*; Shunsho Katsukawa 1786)

The Octopus as a Symbol of Fear

Images of tentacle rape have been found within Edo period *shunga*, but I wonder what happened abroad?

As I related before, many tales of monster squid or octopi attacking humans exist throughout the world. The term "devilfish," while obsolete now, and also relegated to a regional term, meant octopus in the eras it was used, just as the term "demon" held a strong image of someone evil. Now, in many cases, the image of the octopus as the enemy in this trope is imagined as an alien or a monster.

In British sci-fi author H.G. Wells' 1898 novel, ***The War of the Worlds***, the Martian aliens' image is said to be similar to an octopus in appearance. They are described as having disembodied heads, while their arms and legs are said to be retrogressive; an image that seems like he's talking about octopi.

In Hollywood sci-fi and fantasy works, occasionally a film is released where hideous aliens who invade earth are shown to also have had tentacles. These sorts of stories became popular in the pulp magazines of the early 1900s, where one can find illustration spreads of monsters that made them look like octopi (3-6).

Pulp magazines covered a variety of genres of fiction, including sci-fi, fantasy, adventure, and mystery, becoming mass-market reading material. The pages were cheap (made of wood pulp), hence the name. The fiction written in those magazines came to be called "pulp fiction."

What was written in those magazines was basically fiction accompanied by delicately colored illustrations, which commanded quality over profits. In these illustrations, there is a focus on form, drawn with scenes of beautiful girls on the verge of being in danger. Fantasy

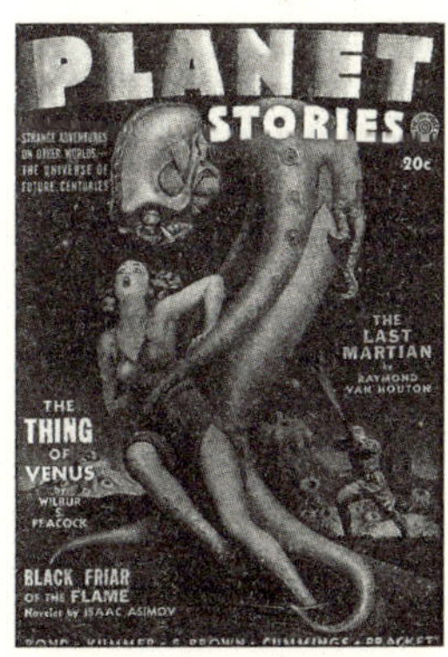

3-6: *Planet Stories*, Spring (1942 Fiction House)

and sci-fi illustrations would often feature unknown creatures with tentacles attacking mankind. There were no sex scenes illustrated in these magazines, but readers easily put two and two together in their heads upon seeing the images of beautiful girls being stalked or attacked by tentacles. And thus, procured these magazines in large numbers.

When one thinks about it, these illustrations, in the broad sense of it, perfectly captured the meaning of the term tentacle rape.

Meanwhile, in American horror, the conversation turned to tentacles and the myth of Cthulhu. This myth was written by H.P. Lovecraft as part of his novel ***The Call of Cthulhu***, about an evil god from space who descends upon earth. At the same time, Lovecraft, who desired to rise above hackneyed horror stories of that time, helped birth many atypical creatures like the chaotic evil god Yog-Sothoth, who impregnates a woman with his son in the story "*The Dunwich Horror.*" In ***The Shadow Over Innsmouth***, there is a disgusting manservant of one of the *Deep Ones* who helps breed hybrid fish people that can change into something truly terrifying. ***At the Mountains of Madness*** featured a protean monster. And in these settings, he created a shared space with his writer friends.

After Lovecraft's death, that shared space, where his writer friends also set some of their works, was systematically organized into the Cthulhu Mythos. One of the main characteristics in illustrations of Cthulhu are the many tentacles situated around his jaw and below his face (3-7). But there were also even more loathed creatures in western paintings, like octopi, anthropomorphized apes, dragons, and other evil things, that were mixed together when they were born.

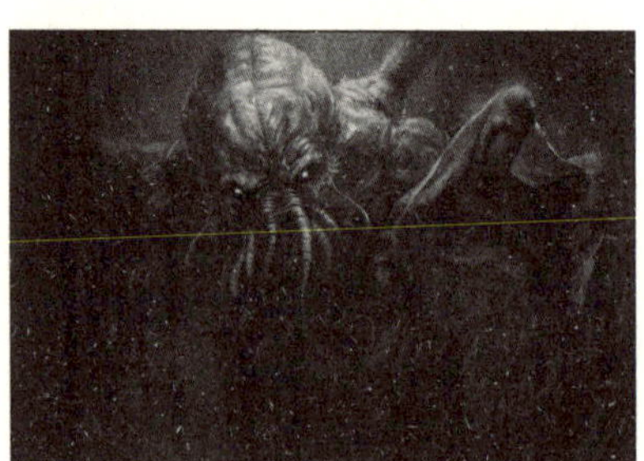

3-7: A monster from the Cthulhu myth (***The Call of Cthulhu and Other Weird Stories***; H.P. Lovecraft 1999, Penguin)

But Lovecraft's drawings of the Cthulhu Mythos did not depict sex, and the tentacles that were present were more about fear than sex in their purpose. They were emblems of horror. Unlike the Wellsian Martian, however, the Lovecraftian creatures were not purely octopus-types in body, but rather featured the head of an octopus, complete with tentacles, fused onto a human body and imbued with the evil intent one would find in a demon.

There were probably many people who saw the ***Pirates of the Caribbean*** franchise (2003) and were most likely reminded of both the kraken and Cthulhu.

In this way we can see how much tentacles have also shaped foreign media. It is important to note that throughout the pulp magazine period that tentacles were not seen as proxies for genitals, just as limbs that "wound around you" compared to Japanese tentacles, which were seen as "soaring erections." To that end, pulp sci-fi and horror that featured tentacles isn't directly connected to current Japanese tentacle media, only entering Japan by way of occupying forces immediately after postwar. American soldiers brought pulp sci-fi and horror magazines into Japan at the time, which became Japan's introduction to that form of media.

The Founder of Tentacle Rape, Toshio Maeda

In Japanese manga, heroes being attacked by monsters with tentacles has historically existed since the early period of manga. But when we turn the conversation to sexually imbued tentacle tropes, now I can confirm that the oldest portrayals of this trope in publication belong to "real-life" erotic comedy manga. This is the general term for magazines that ran adult-oriented manga content that predates *ero-gekiga* as well as sexually-related articles.

Weekly Manga Q was one of these magazines, and in the special edition for March 12, 1968, I found multiple scenes where various rare creatures with tentacle-like limbs were attacking young, beautiful girls (3-8). A lot of the content was also comedy related in nature, which still leaves behind the issue at hand: was this content using a tentacle rape trope?

Within this magazine there was the special edition ***Invasion of Sex Monsters from Outer Space!*** *(Kibatsu! Sexy Kaiju Oabare;* Ryuji Shima & Ken Kondo 1968, Shinju Shobo), which was later adapted into a book by Ohta Publishing, but at that time there was a *kaiju* boom, and it might be appropriate to think of as an erotic humor technique or parody interpretation of that trend.

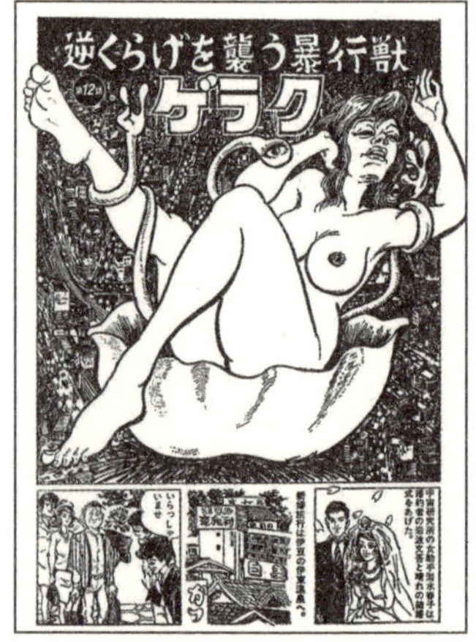

3-8: *Weekly Manga Q*, Mar. 12, 1968 ed. (Shinju Shobo)

Even in Osamu Tezuka's work, there is a scene that is thought to be part of the tentacle rape trope to be found within it. This scene can be found in "The Returnees" (*Kikansha*), which was serialized in 1973 in *Play Comics* (Akita Shoten). It is a sci-fi title, and a particular scene features a girl being assaulted by a mysterious space creature and subsequently becoming impregnated by it (3-9). However, this girl is not being violated for the purpose of rape. The tentacle rape is instead explained as the space creature needing to leave behind offspring, not for pleasure, though this stance is still rather weak as a proper explanation. However, I cannot deny that the fact that we can so quickly extrapolate that the girl becomes pregnant by the tentacle is no doubt a testament to the skill of the *God of Manga* (Tezuka).

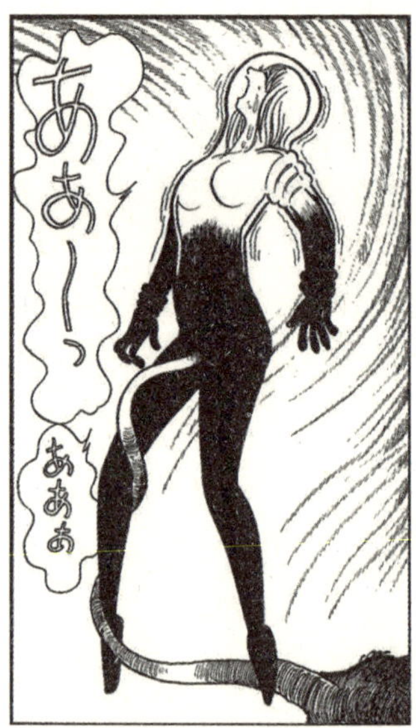

3-9: "The Returnees" ("Kikansha"; Osamu Tezuka 1973, Akita Shoten)

As we go into the early 1970s, Hideo Azuma, master of sci-fi gag manga, starts aggressively using tentacle expressions in his work in seinen and *mania* (fan) magazines. In his ***No Longer Human*** (*Ningen Shikaku;* 1978, Tokyo Sanseisha), there is a scene where a man that has turned to slime attacks a girl (3-10), In the short "Kaeri Michi" (1981, Kiso Tengaisha) too, a girl becomes wrapped up by seemingly mischievous tentacles (3-11). The shonen title ***Nanako SOS*** (1983, Koubunsha) is somewhat an homage to Hokusai's *Fisherman's Wife* (3-12). But in all of these examples, one strongly gets the sense that the role of the tentacle is one that is closer to that of gag material rather than anything sexual.

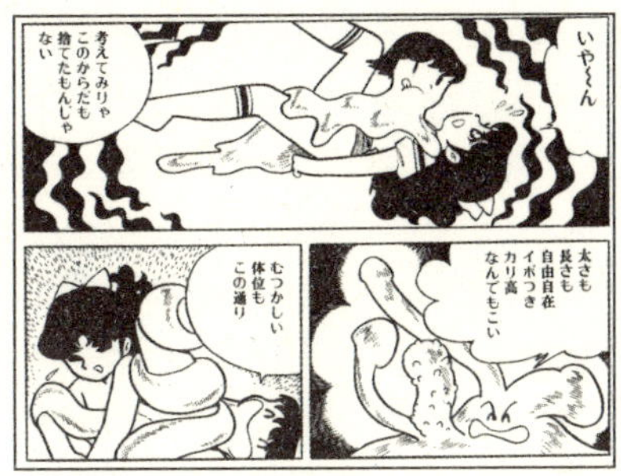

3-10: ***No Longer Human*** (*Ningen Shikaku;* Hideo Azuma 1978, Tokyo Sanseisha)

Continuing into the 1980s, we see the *bishojo* comic genre rise to power, leaving behind gekiga's realism and going more towards a simpler anime style, with lots of young heroines making their debut. We will later see a great many scenes accompanying those beautiful heroines with the tentacle rape trope, but before that happens a transitory period will be born. After that, the main representative early period of tentacle rape expressions may have traumatized many readers by now. I'm talking about the infamous gekiga manga *Urotsukidouji.*

Urotsukidouji, a title by *gekiga* artist Toshio Maeda, was serialized in the *ero-gekiga* magazine *Manga Erotopia* (1984~1986, Wanimagazine) and features a great fight between the therianthrope world, the demon world, and the human world. It is a romantic manga full of violence, action, and the erotic, however the scenes in which these creatures violated human women with their tentacles are what became the talk of the town. The release of the graphic novels was an unprecedented success. Because of this popularity, it

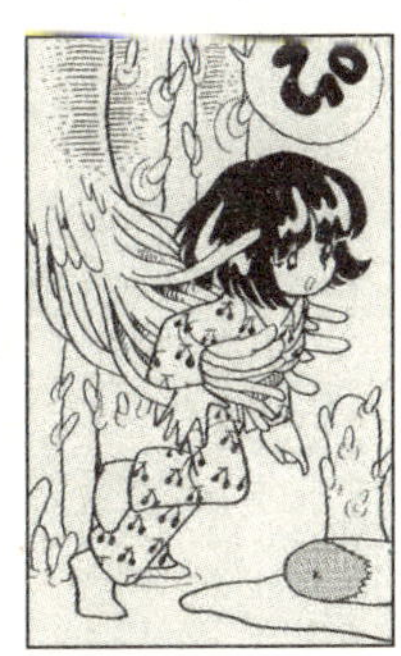

3-11: "Kaeri Michi" (Hideo Azuma 1981, Kiso Tengaisha)

even merited an original video animation release in 1987, ***Urotsukidouji: The Legend of the Overfiend*** (Phoenix Entertainment). This release hit the North American underground scene, and then became a worldwide phenomenon shortly thereafter. I believe this turned Maeda into the *Master of Tentacles*, an artist popular worldwide. And it seems as if in recent years he has started to attend international anime conventions, drawing for fans.

While Maeda is considered to be one of the artists active in the twilight of the gekiga genre, his development of the tentacle rape expression had a heavy impact on manga, and in turn *Urotsukidouji* heavily influenced Japanese eromanga.

The tentacles that Maeda drew in that series were not that of either an octopus nor a squid, but one of a being that possessed a will. His tentacles were creature-like, with a sticky viscosity to them much like a chameleon's tongue or birdlime. These tentacles creep around the girls, and instead of saying that they were fingering those girls, it's clear that the tentacles are copying male genitals, quickly becoming a situation where they can be inserted into them at any time. Because this expression was so progressive, many researchers, both Japanese and foreign, agree that because of its mix of sex, *bishojo,* and tenacles, it is the progenitor of the tentacle rape expression. However, in reality, six years earlier in 1978 was when Toshio Maeda drew his first work with tentacle expressions in it.

Published in *Special Young Comic* (Shonengahosha) was a short story called "SEX Tearing." In it there's a scene where a girl is sexually attacked by a monster with tentacles and is considered the origin point for *Urotsukidouji.*

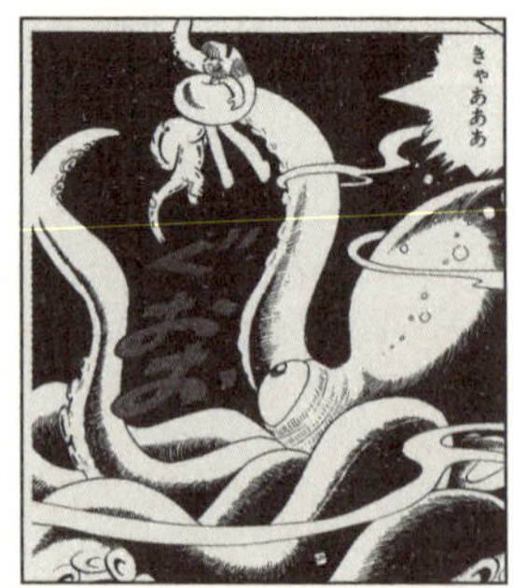

3-12: ***Nanako SOS***, Vol. 1 (Hideo Azuma 1983, Koubunsha)

Why did Maeda draw tentacles? Was there an image that became the seed for that idea?

I decided to ask Maeda himself about whether or not the reason why the tentacle genre came into being was in order to solve a larger problem within Japanese manga expressions. He spoke with me about it in the following interview...

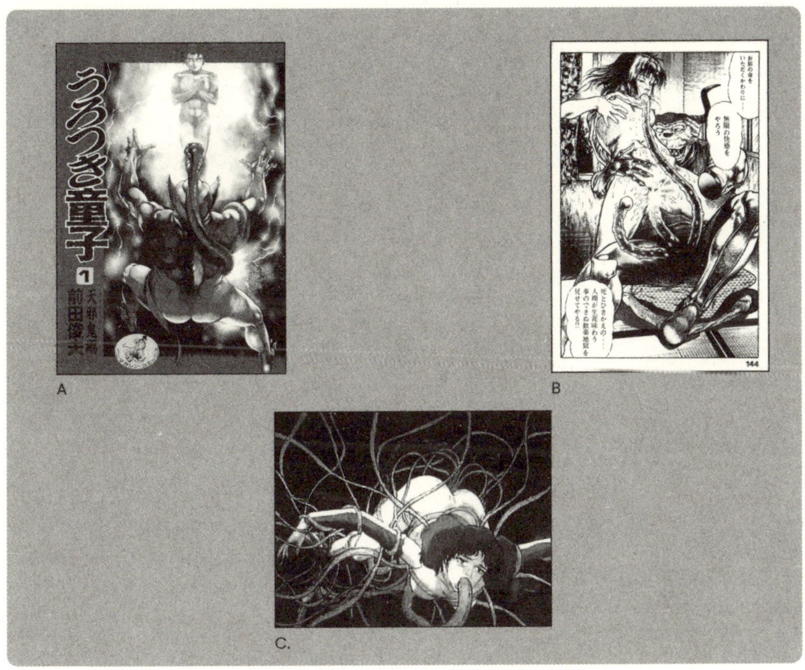

A

B

C.

INTERVIEW WITH **TOSHIO MAEDA**

"I thought tentacles would be able to lift women up"

PROFILE

Debuted in 1973. After that, he energetically worked for gekiga magazines. His manga *Urotsukidouji* launched in 1984 in Wanimagazine's *Erotopia* magazine and became a massive hit; even getting an anime adaptation of it in 1987. That same work became very talked about world-wide, and he is considered the pioneer of the erotic tentacle genre as a result. Currently, he likes to participate in international manga events, and has learned enough English to tell jokes at them. His other big works of note include ***Chi no Wana*** (1987, Sun Publishing), and ***Demon Beast Invasion*** (*Yoju Kyojitsu* 1989, Wanimagazine).

A: ***Urotsukidouji,*** Vol. 1 (1986, Wanimagazine)

B. ***Urotsukidouji,*** Vol. 5 (1987, Wanimagazine)

C. ***Urotsukidouji: Legend of the Overfiend*** (1987; animation)

"Tentacles are not genitals."

—*When you first started using tentacles in manga, was* Urotsukidouji *your first work that featured them?*

Maeda: Actually, it was an experimental short story, "SEX Tearing." That appeared in a magazine called *Special Young Comic* (3-13). I drew it because I couldn't really draw male genitals. So, I drew the girl's face, then the tentacle that would elongate and insert into her body with a sound effect like "gunyuu" (slurch). That experiment became the impetus behind creating that.

And in response, the head editor of the magazine called the police. But because it didn't feature actual genitals, apparently the policeman ran off. (laughs) My editor at the time was the man that's now in charge of Shonengahosha, Mr. Rikichiro Toda, but he told me, "Oh, since you're new, you can draw whatever you'd like…" So I warmed up by drawing a lot of jokes.

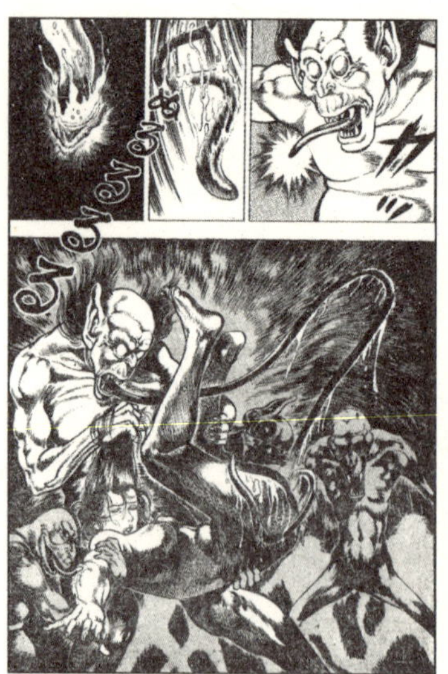

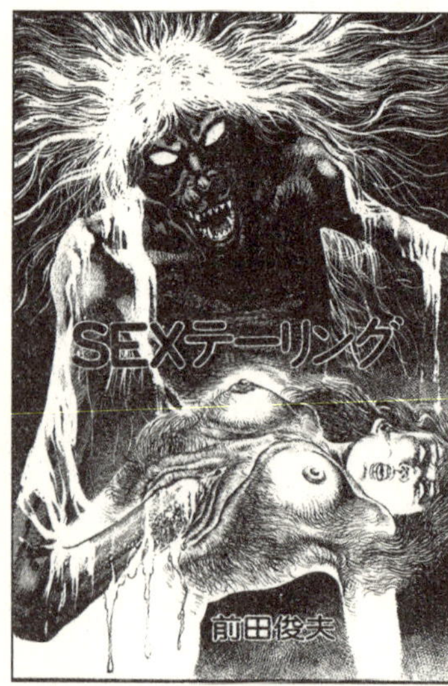

3-13, 14: "SEX Tearing" (Toshio Maeda 1976, Shonengahosha)

—*Which helped make* Urotsukidouji *bloom, right?*

Maeda: I think I've said this a lot in the past, but tentacles were born as a way to escape regulation in the first place. Tentacles are not penises. And as long as they aren't genitals, then there's no need to retouch them [for censorship]. Tentacles can wind around women and lift them up into the air, disregarding physics and gravity, and you can pose them whichever way you'd like. So as an artist, they're interesting because you get to draw lots of physiques with them. After all, there are only so many poses one can draw when there's a bed involved.

Readers don't want to see penises. Without decreasing sexual desire, male readers can easily imagine themselves in place of the tentacles, and you can show them. In that way, tentacles were fantastic (3-14).

—*They were definitely one of the longest lasting inventions within the history of eromanga. However, as of late, depending on the shape, tentacles have been undergoing retouching for censorship.*

Maeda: At first, my tentacles weren't octopus-inspired, but as time went on, I decided that octopus tentacles were easier to understand and went with those instead.

Lately though, I've been asked to "draw octopus tentacles." The ways to draw octopi have increased, but when I do draw one, someone ends up asking me if I'm Hokusai.

—*Would you say that your expressions haven't been influenced by Hokusai's* Fisherman's Wife?

Maeda: No, they aren't. As a child I often looked at Hokusai's art, but I never saw his octopus works. And if you ask why, it's because I was a child. There was no way to introduce me to *shunga* at that age. But lots of people seem to think that my work is influenced by Hokusai.

—*It's true that* shunga *has only really become mainstream as of recently.*

Maeda: When I told someone this was my first time hearing about this, they said, "Seriously?!" (laughs)

"The reason why I became so popular abroad."

—*Why do you think you became so popular abroad?*

Maeda: Because of the impact of my work, I'd say. My work tends to be the exact opposite in theme compared to famous Japanese animators like Hayao Miyazaki. "Love is great!" "People are great!" I went ahead and denied those themes. My themes said something like, "Love? What's that?" as a response. I think that *Urotsukidouji* went and smashed the hell out of the Japanese animator system of values.

—*Certainly, when you describe it that way, the only other Japanese anime movie previously exported that had a similar theme to your work was* **Akira.** *It might've been the first dark Japanese anime movie exported to the West.*

Maeda: My manga tends not to feature very good people, and you'll never find upstanding people in them. I'd rather draw people who live by their desires, which is a theme that comes up in *Urotsukidouji*. I asked the people working on the anime to incorporate that into their adaptation.

—*You'll have to forgive me if I remember incorrectly, but I think the regulation (in terms of banned content) for* Urotsukidouji *was a bit vague. I think it was the same in the States, too.*

Maeda: You're a bit off-base there, it's true. When I hear about the States, I usually hear about fans that had watched *Urotsukidouji* when they were ten or twelve years old. I do tell them that they shouldn't have watched it at that age (laughs), and that such behavior made my life crazy.

—And it definitely seems that the tentacle scenes leave a lasting impression on folks as well.

Maeda: It really did make an impact on people.

—I too went to the States to talk to anime fans, and it seems that the current younger generations there don't know about Urotsukidouji. *But many of them know about the tentacle genre, and the consciousness about it in those fans is rooted pretty deeply. Your adapted work is a starting point, and I had the thought that tentacles as a culture is being inherited.*

Maeda: In the States, even the average person knows about tentacles now. The fact that it started as a fad from my work has become pretty blurred, and instead tentacles have taken on a life of their own. But that's okay. I'm happy. And of course, while I don't think all tentacle content is derived from my work, I think many people are pretty aware that my work helped create an impact.

"America, where the censored becomes the uncensored."

—We spoke a bit before about how tentacles have evaded censorship, but in America, there really isn't a culture of censorship. In the American release for Urotsukidouji, *I have the feeling that they uncensored the material censored in Japan.*

Maeda: Oh, that was the original American licensee, Central Park Media, who decided to remedy that little problem on their own.

—On their own?!

Maeda: I believe I told them that I didn't really mind that it was censored, but it was the American licensee that made that call. But the crueler part of that was that it became an issue of how I had become infamous because of my work with tentacles. I had simply drawn tentacle manga, so it was like they were releasing a book under my name. Just stop it, already. (laughs)

—Aside from it becoming an issue within American publishing, I have the feeling it became an entirely different issue. I've heard that in the past that editors used to directly censor manuscripts themselves, but now in the States we have the problem of editors doing the reverse, redrawing censored material to look uncensored. It seems that it was a reverse phenomenon.

"You don't really need to demand that genitals be in manga, right?"

—Speaking of which, what are your thoughts on the historical Japanese practice of censoring material?

Maeda: I honestly don't really have a problem with it. If anything, I *want* certain material to be censored. When people remove regulation once, they stop seeing it altogether. In America, where there is no regulation, what's the point if you get to see genitals? When you're not able to see them, you want to see them. And I think that's perfectly fine.

—So what you're saying is that when something is hidden, you want to see it, which gives censorship meaning?

Maeda: I would say so. Also, if artists have to draw genitals, that takes a certain amount of energy. Which means most of the energy required for manga would plummet. So, if you want to see genitals, it makes more sense to show them in another way.

—*Especially since you can see tons of genitals on the internet now.*

Maeda: Which is why I think that you don't really need to demand that genitals be in manga, right?

Even with eromanga, at first there was a story, and while there were erotic scenes, because sex scenes are more popular, the amount of story-telling in current works has decreased. In many cases, it's all only erotic scenes now, period. Of course, there's regular manga, too, but we've gotten into this polarizing place where erotic stuff is erotic, and basic stuff is basic, and there really is not much of an in-between. But how is that adult entertainment? That's what I think.

We do have artists that create stories with themes that only adults can understand, and I understand that erotic content is one of those themes, but I just wonder about taking those [erotic] scenes and just having them lined up back to back from beginning to end. I'm not saying we should completely deny people those scenes, because I think it's okay to have some of it. But I question expanding sex scenes to that degree.

Basically, I would like to see other adult manga. Perhaps I'm telling people to read more manga that's of the *Big Comics* magazine (Shogakukan) variety. Or maybe not. For example, I personally want to see more stories with incubi or succubi in manga.

—*Originally,* Manga Erotopia *was that kind of magazine. I always got the sense that it was less about the erotic content, even though it was the place where eros became the heart of gekiga. And ultimately, gekiga faded away.*

I'd like to ask you your thoughts now on this period where there was this turning point of manga as a whole moving away from gekiga and instead turning to bishojo comics. During this period, what kind of changes did you feel were needed within manga?

Maeda: I felt that any of those changes would be pointless at the time. I'd made my preferences clearly known, which is to say, *kashihon* (rental comics). They were full of darkness and gloom, and I liked that culture where I had to hide them from my parents and read them in secret. I wanted to draw things like that. I could say, "While I love Tezuka's work, I still read *kashihon* from time to time." I feel the same about foreign media as well, so to me, content about love, peace, and *moé*—that isn't manga.

"My activities abroad now."

Maeda: So now I've more or less retired from the manga publishing world and instead participate in manga drawing contests. (laughs)

—While it's embarrassing for me to admit this, I only found out about the events you've participated in worldwide about two years ago. What was the impetus behind you participating in these events?

Maeda: Oh, don't worry about it. I only started doing all that stuff about a couple years ago. I think you already know why I've been doing those events, but have you noticed how medium and smaller presses have been just absolutely crushed lately? Especially those that haven't been able to switch to digital publishing. Around that time, my manuscript fees started to plummet. Like one time, I was offered only 7,000 Yen.

—Per page of work?

Maeda: Yes. At that time, I was ready to throw in the towel altogether.

—You mean, of continuing your career as an artist?

Maeda: Yes. Of course, there was nothing I could do. But if the total manuscript fee only ended up being 5,000 or 6,000 Yen per page, what would I do? That's what I thought. Around the same time, the passion of drawing manga on paper started to fade, so everything became rather slipshod, and I thought that it would be rather lonely for those pages to end their lives that way. And that's when I quit manga. That was about four or five years ago.

But when I quit, I wondered how I was going to live from that point on. After some research, I found out that around the world there are various manga competitions that are held. Because I was blessed enough in the past to be able to sell my material to be made into anime, I thought I'd be able to go abroad and be okay financially. But then the next question came up: what was I going to do about learning English? One of my hobbies is watching movies, so I watched foreign films, American TV series, and the like, and I thought my level of English would be okay.

—What?! Just by watching movies and TV shows?

Maeda: That's how I found out that my English was actually pretty adequate.

—So you're telling me that you learned English not by studying but just by watching your favorite foreign movies and TV series and absorbing the language?

Maeda: I didn't really have any issues otherwise. I was in a motorbike accident about four years ago, and I really couldn't do much then. I had a lot of spare time, so I would watch lots of movies. And because I'm from Kansai, I thought I would be fine when it came to talking. (laughs)

Of course, it was rather half-baked. But when I had to speak, I didn't have any issues with it. So I'm pretty thankful I was born in Kansai. That's when I started doing international events, and someone once told me that if I could speak English that well, I should do a talk show. When I tried doing one, I thought, "Oh, I can do one of these after all!" (laughs)

—That's just too cool.

Maeda: So I've been increasingly asked to do talk shows and panels ever since. They're usually about an hour or an hour and a half long, I think? Mainly I tell dirty jokes, though. Because these events are usually limited to people age 18 and up, I get to tell dirty jokes, share insider tales about the manga world, and stories about women from the position of being the *Tentacle Master.* (laughs)

—You mean you talk about the relationships between tentacles and women?!

Maeda: Because people abroad have an interest in both Japanese manga and women, I would mix both stories and jokes about both together and they were pretty happy to hear them.

(Compiled October 2015)

Censorship Births New Expressions

As Toshio Maeda said in his interview, tentacle rape as an expression was born to evade regulation and censorship, and we've been able to establish that Maeda drew vivid insertion scenes to that end. Within the rules of how genitals are censored in Japanese pornographic media, it's difficult to draw portrayals of those unions without getting censored. So in the place of male genitals touching those women, tentacles were invented as a substitute, becoming like an honorary secondary type of male genitalia.

In the next chapter, we'll talk about how this became the origin of the *cross-section view* expression. One couldn't draw a direct depiction of sex acts with genitals, and however much one couldn't change that disposition, readers instead got excited and aroused by this expression's conveyed libido. Maeda's creative originality helped birth this expression.

In reality, we also got testimony from the editor in Maeda's vignette. The editor that accepted the various works of manga that featured things that "didn't exist" according to Maeda was documented in the book that chased after that story, ***Kesareta Manga,*** under the chapter "Evidence 5: Asking Mr. Ichirou Hashimoto." Hashimoto ran publications like *Shonen King*, *Young Comic*, *Bessatsu Young Comic*, and others. Below is a snippet from his testimony in that book:

> *I was sucked in by Toshio Maeda's manga. I got a call from the police and told them, "I understand, I'll issue a letter of apology." When I was about to go home, I heard someone shouting, "What the hell happened with Maeda's most recent manga?!" It was a short called "SEX Tearing," where an alien rapes a female Tokyo University student inside of a mountain. It has long, octopus-like tentacles that it can move independently, and they wrap around the girl. And that's not a human having sex with a woman, right? (laughs)*

> *—Because expressions that depicted skin-to-skin contact were off-limits, right?*

That was the debut of tentacles. And the Tokyo Metropolitan Police? They couldn't really figure out if Maeda's manga was depicting sex or not. It became a whole thing. Even now, I think it's a really funny story.

–*Kesareta Manga (Yuichi Akata & Barboa 2016, Saizusha)*

In this way we see the strategy of Toshio Maeda and the editor's crime of conscience, and how those behind censorship enforcement were thoroughly confused by Maeda's work. At the very least, "SEX Tearing" didn't go against regulation, and the creative side's idea succeeded. But here we see the brilliance of Maeda's tentacle rape expression. It wasn't created in desperation or as a last resort, and it blended the *gekiga* style along with elements of violence and the story well.

Precisely because it was a tentacle meant that it could help create such a daring composition, and its position in eromanga meant that it would spread. As a result, it was because there was regulation that this expression was born. But because artists are beholden to follow their editor's orders, fans' ideas, and deadlines, it is also a creation that happened because of those things, too. It is because there is a rebellious will to create that I believe that new expressions will continue to be born from them.

I've been able to determine that the first time Maeda used the tentacle expression was in 1976, and I have not been able to find a work that portrays sex between women in tentacles in manga that occurred any earlier than that.

Which means that Toshio Maeda currently holds the title of being the progenitor of the tentacle rape expression. He's the central figure that introduced the whole world to tentacle memes. His title of *Tentacle Master* isn't just him showing off.

I will be covering Maeda's overseas popularity in a forthcoming chapter about foreign eromanga expressions, but in the shadow of *Urotsukidouji*, there was a pedigree of different tentacle depiction expressions that stretched out its tendrils into eromanga culture. And that pedigree would emerge due to the rise of *bishojo* comics in the 1980s.

The Beginning of Tentacle Diversification

Toshio Maeda's style of drawing was exaggerated, with an affinity for blending sex and violence quite well. But because of the overwhelming impact of his skill, people started to equate his name with tentacle porn. That impression was strong, and no other gekiga artists followed in his footsteps. If anything, his achievements within the anime world of the 1980s and the influence it had on artists after was larger. Since the adaptation of *Urotsukidouji* became a huge hit, sequels, spin-offs, and other works that resembled it were being churned out one after the other, and it seemed that any and every subsequent work that came out at that time had tentacle rape in it. The many anime that had tentacle rape in them no doubt helped to awaken many fans of the trope, also.

At the beginning of the '80s, *bishojo* comics, which evolved from post-ero-gekiga, had a high affinity to the sci-fi and fantasy genres that started to push tentacle rape in their material. In reality, from the '80s to the '90s, the tentacles that appeared in *bishojo* comics had a higher level of freedom in their movement, and a bigger range of variation compared to the tentacle material of today.

The type of tentacle monster that Hideo Azuma favored was a "freely transforming lifeform with tentacles." Ryu Hurricane had more orthodox "octopus-type tentacles" (3-15). This type of tentacle, from the earliest period until now, is one of the standards in the genre. They were since used by Wataru Watanabe, Rei Nekoshima, and other popular creators, who aggressively inserted this tentacle in their work (3-16).

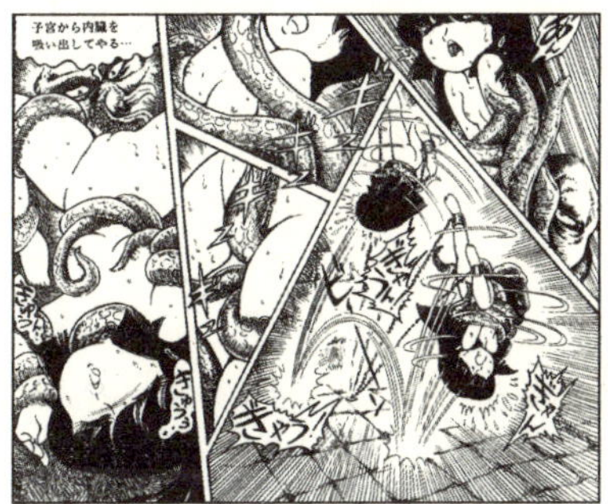

3-15: "Gekisatsu! Uchuken" (Ryu Hurricane 1982, AMATORIA)

Then there's the now rarely seen "mechanical tentacles," which were a characteristic of their time. Speaking of machines, *fucking machines* have their own genre, but, in terms of shape and looks—being long, narrow, relatively freely moving—they have a similar tone to tentacles (3-17, 18). Moriwo Chimi drew robots who gave girls thorough physical exams with tentacles, usually featuring the gentle and virtuous girl naked and a mad scientist wearing an armored exoskeleton with extended robotic tentacles attached.

In the case of mad scientists, I'm not sure if this counts as more machines, but there's also the technique where it looks like a girl is being crept up upon. In Juzo Minazuki's "Yakan" (1992, France Shobo), a mysterious lifeform named Tentacle Unit 01 makes its debut (3-19).

Adjacent to the mechanical tentacle is the "wire tentacle" trope, where wires wrap around a girl like tentacles (3-20). Then there is the "thorn tentacle" trope, where a mysterious plant's stalk, roots, or vines entwine around their victim and then rape them (3-21). Yui Toshiki excelled at the fairy tale-like "mysterious tentacle lifeform" that took place within fantasy worlds (3-22, 23). A reincarnated high school girl is forced to fight while

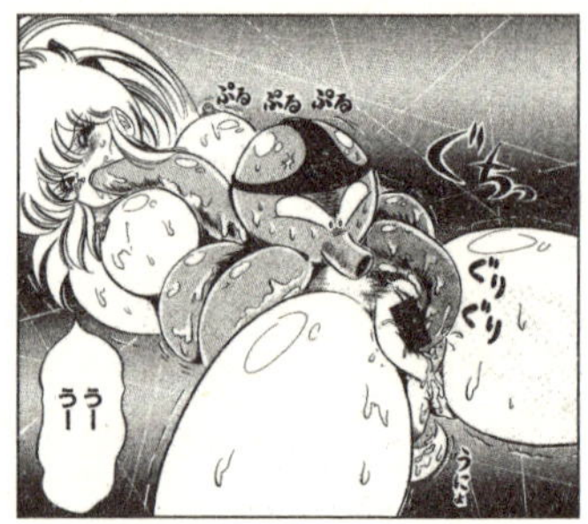

3-16: ***Dokkin ♥ Minako-sensei***, Vol. 2 (Wataru Watanabe 1987, Byakuya-Shobo)

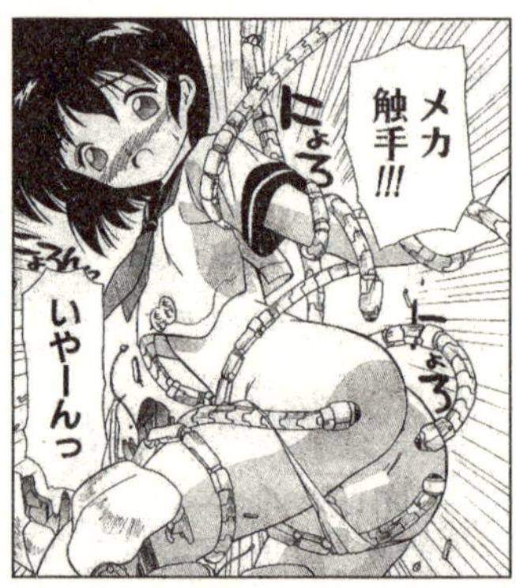

3-17: "Oedo Ankokugai" (Irumakamiri 1998, France Shoin)

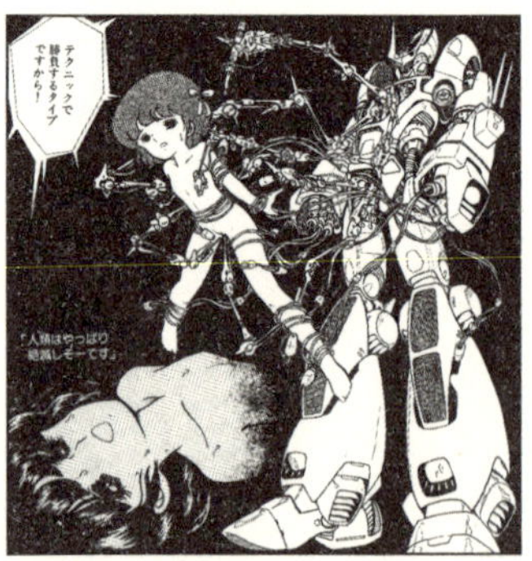

3-18: "Ashita naki Sekai, ♂ naki Jinrui" (Moriwo Chimi 1983, AMATORIA)

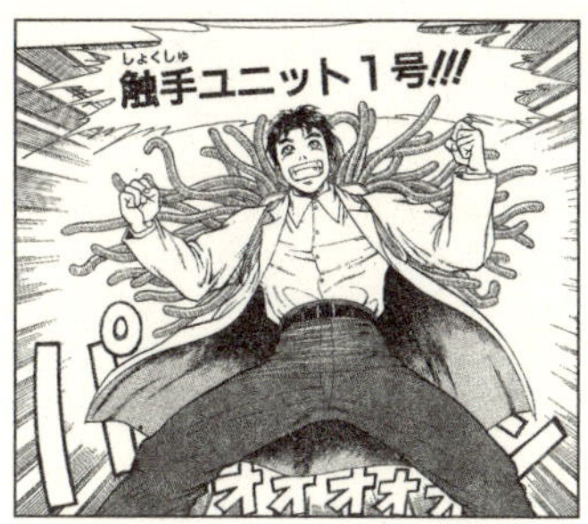

3-19: "Yakan" (Juzo Minazuki 1992, France Shoin)

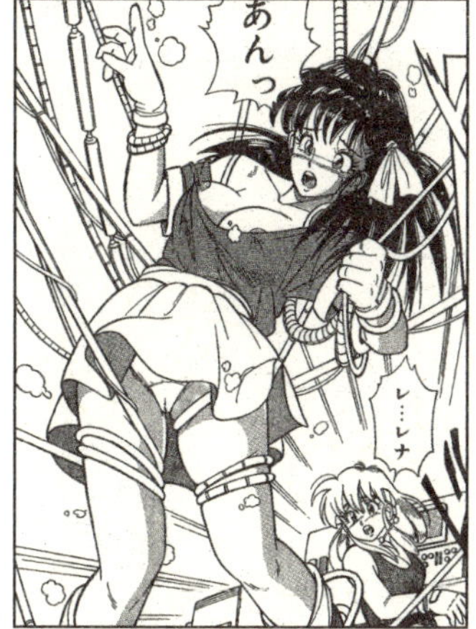

3-20: "Valis" (Ikuo Dodonpa 1991, Tatsumi Publishing)

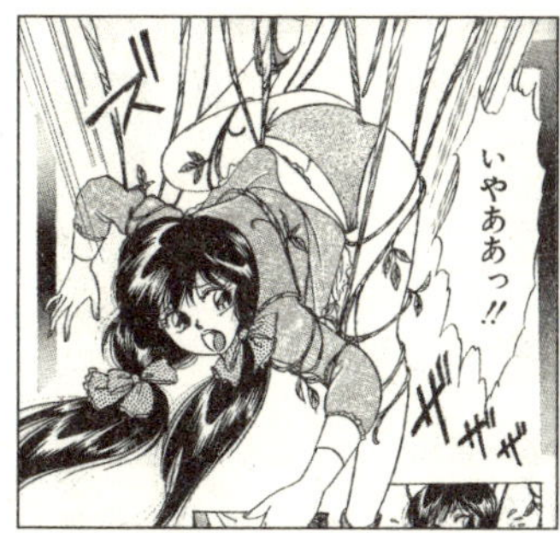

3-21: "Haru ga Kita!" (Momo Nakafusa 1989, Tokyo Sanseisha)

being treated horribly in ***Slave Warrior Maya*** (*Dorei Senshi Maya* 1989, Fujimi Publishing), featuring the "mysterious tentacle monster" trope (3-24). Even in the case of Tou Moriyama, who hadn't really drawn tentacles before, drew the "tentacle worm" trope in his work (3-25).

The "tentacle creature" trope that Maeda cultivated, with the "tentacle worm" that did not waste its mother's body and devoured it, soon became the noble path that others took in order to develop their own tentacle expressions.

But what was rare was work like Ikkou Sahara's "Angel Heat" (1990, Taiyou Tosho), which rendered a hard steel frame that gets softened by magic, and then attacks a female character, creating the "steel frame tentacle" (3-26). And in a perhaps more literal look at the word "tentacles," Masaki Kamitou's "Fairy Saber" ("Seirei Tokusou"; 1993, Tatsumi Publishing) features his "tentacle hand" (3-27).

Another expression, though I'm not sure it counts as one about tentacles, can be found in the shocking Taro Nakayama's ***Naizo Lady*** (1988, Kubo Shoten). The protagonist, a special investigator, Mio Kiritou (and her alias, Naizo Lady) splits open her stomach and her intestines (as tentacles) elongate to defeat her enemies.

Because the condition of "tormenting girls" isn't met here, it can't properly be labeled as a *tentacle rape* meme but instead, simply, can only be called tentacles. But as she transforms, she shouts, "Abdominal hernia!", which is almost too severe for the settings drawn by the artist (3-28).

As you can see, in the dawn of the new *bishojo* comic age, various new types of tentacles were created, though it is important to note that they were not mature enough to undergo the encoding process. Most likely because this was a period when a section of artists were busily engaged in creating their own tentacle expressions through trial and error. In contrast, Maeda's violent tentacles influenced regular seinen genre romantic violent works like Makoto Ogino's ***Spirit Warrior*** (*Kujaku O*, 1985-89, Shueisha), but, thanks to a quick turn of events, underwent encoding and cementing. Ever since, that development has been visibly clear.

When one sees the genealogy and spread of tentacles, the spread that grew out of *bishojo* comics, while lukewarm, went further than that of the spread of the Maeda's visuals. Content from the '70s, like that of Go

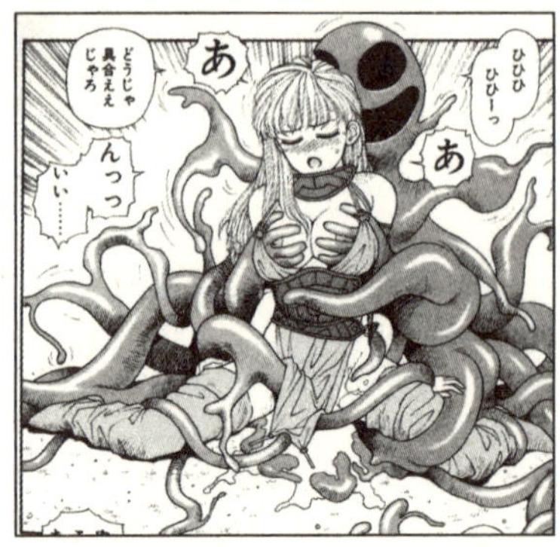

3-22: ***Princess Quest Saga*** (Yui Toshiki 1994, Fujimi Publishing)

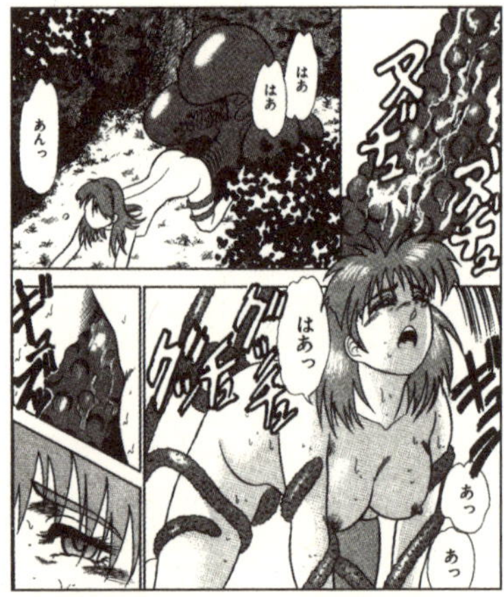

3-23: "Gody Britt" (Yu Tomiaki 1993, Tokyo Sanseisha)

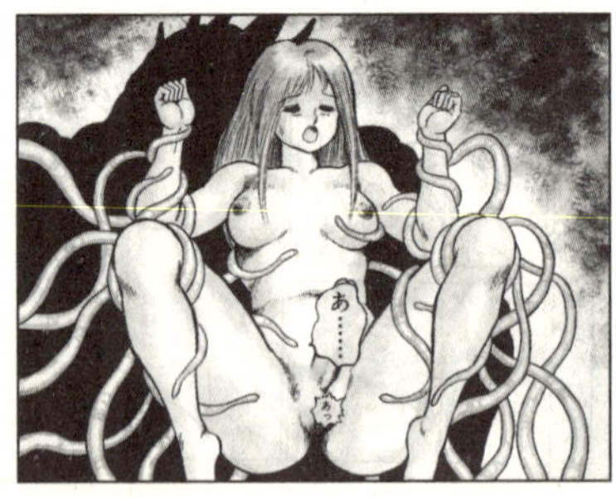

3-24: "Slave Warrior Maya" (*Dorei Senshi Maya*; Conodonts 1989, Fujimi Publishing)

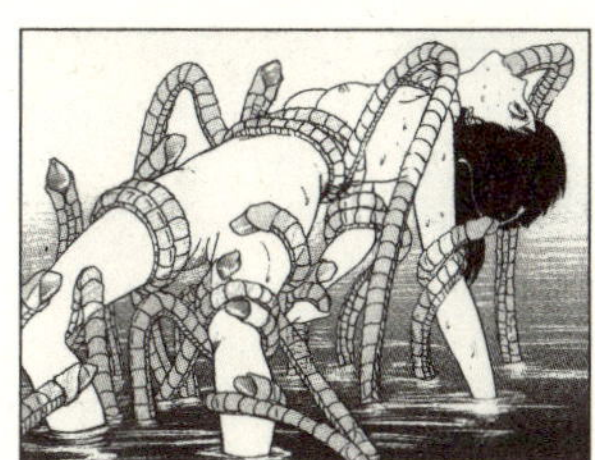

3-25: ***Rough & Ready*** (Tou Moriyama 1986, Tatsumi Publishing)

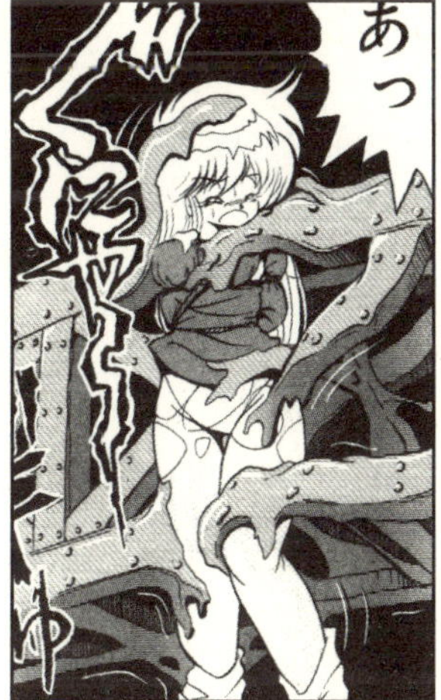

3-26: "Angel Heat" (Ikkou Sahara 1990, Taiyou Tosho)

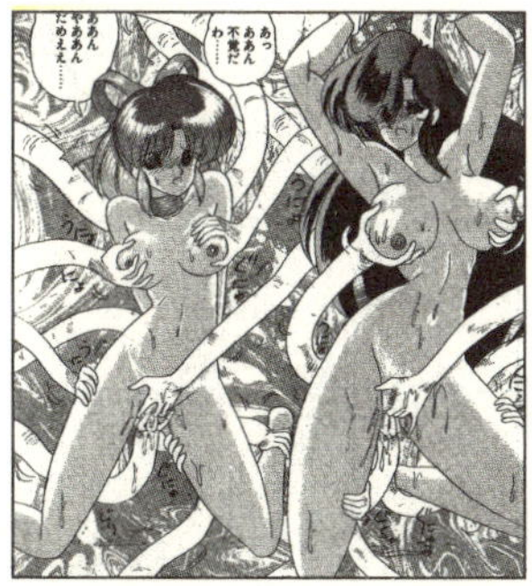

3-27: "Fairy Saber" (*Seirei Tokusou*; Masaki Kamitou 1993, Tatsumi Publishing)

Nagai and Hideo Azuma, as well as shonen and seinen comedic content drew expressions where girls had things that looked like tentacles doing perverted things to them.

To be certain, Toshio Maeda's work was the first such work that had sexual intercourse drawn out in it, and as the *bishojo* type of tentacles started to spread, because they were so different compared to Maeda's tentacles to fans, the origin points for the evolution of both are separate and different. It was thought that until the latter half of the 1980s when the anime version of *Urotsukidouji* became popular that the two family trees of tentacles merged. In the early half of the decade, before *Urotsukidouji*'s magazine serialization, content of girls having sex with tentacle rape expressions was already being published within the world of *bishojo* comics.

In one of the first *bishojo-style* adult anime during that early period, there were works like ***Cream Lemon Part 3: Super-Dimension Legend Rall*** *(Cream Lemon PART3 SF・Cho-jigen Densetsu RALL,* 1984, Fairy Dust, 3-29*),* and a porn company-backed galactic adventure, ***The Legend of Lyon Flare*** *(Lyon Densetsu Flare*, 1986), whose anime adaptation with tentacle rape debuted earlier than those in *Urotsukidouji*'s anime adaptation. However, because of how the *bishojo-style* adult (anime) genre was still seen as a niche at this point in time, the influence of it only spread within the genre itself and wasn't able to really develop any further than that. Whereas with *Urotsukidouji*, which had a very strong impact on many regular readers not into anime, made the world recognize the tentacle genre. At the same time, tentacles were seeping into other genres, and continued to evolve.

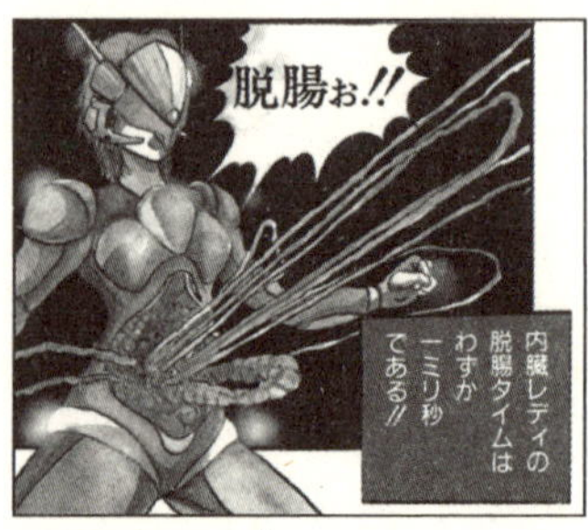

3-28: ***Naizo Lady*** (Taro Nakayama 1988, Kubo Shoten) – Abdominal Hernia.

Or so they should have been.

Transmission is the first step of the encoding process and is a needed component in generalizing them. But all of a sudden, the speed at which those expressions were evolving suddenly slowed to a crawl. A paradigm shift occurred within the eromanga world's release environment, and the tentacle genre experienced a slow period on the same level of dinosaurs going extinct.

The Tentacle Recession

While there wasn't a huge tide change within the 1980s, the tentacle rape expression, which had blossomed within the world of eromanga, found itself being gradually but unavoidably reduced in the 1990s. It was presumed that from its evolution, that change with such freedom of ideas would continue to spread and increase in number. But its frequency of use declined by the mid-'90s and entered into a period of stagnation. And I can't help but wonder if that

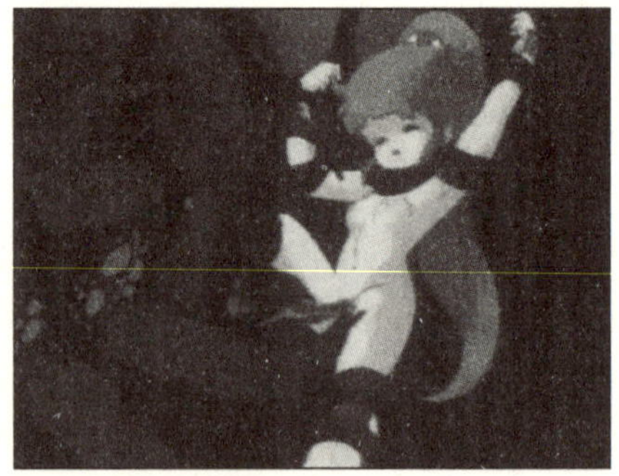
3-29: ***Cream Lemon Part 3: Super-Dimension Legend Rall*** (*Cream Lemon PART3 SF・Cho-jigen Densetsu RALL*; 1984, Fairy Dust)

will end up being the only fad that featured tentacle rape.

While I cannot definitively say that there wasn't an influence due to the sudden uproar over harmful comics, when it comes to tentacle rape, I think there is another larger reason as to why it declined.

The second half of the '80s was the golden age for swords, magic, and fantasy, and during that time, one can see that many eromanga works were set in fantasy worlds which had tentacles within them. While originally, tentacle rape was an expression born out of a flight from censorship, in this period, instead, it's been thought that it was heavily regulated most of the time. However, when the fantasy boom settled down, and after eromanga entered its bubble period in 1994, tentacles became seen as extreme.

1991 saw the introduction of the self-inflicted *adult mark* within the industry, which became the trigger of eromanga becoming more developed as a key genre than *bishojo* comics. At the same time, the demand for erotic scenes jumped higher than it ever had. It was also the same period where fantasy and sci-fi, which were responsible for the separation of the narrative and world views, were kept at arm's length. Consequently, there were indications within those works that editors were trying to ward off or dodge such stories.

Instead of scenes that would've aroused fans in the parallel land that eromanga shared with regular comics, eromanga readers were starting to ask for works that only had erotic content, and as a result, the demand for tentacles fell. Even though magazines were not welcoming to tentacle content, it managed to stubbornly survive as a niche genre.

In 1996, a tentacle rape-themed anthology, ***COMIC INDEEP Inju Collection***, Vol.9 (Toen Shobou) was published. Then in 1998, another title that called attention to the genre as well, the simply titled ***TENTACLES*** (Kazumasa Ichikawa, Tsukasa Shobo) was also released (3-30). The afterwords for both books said something to the

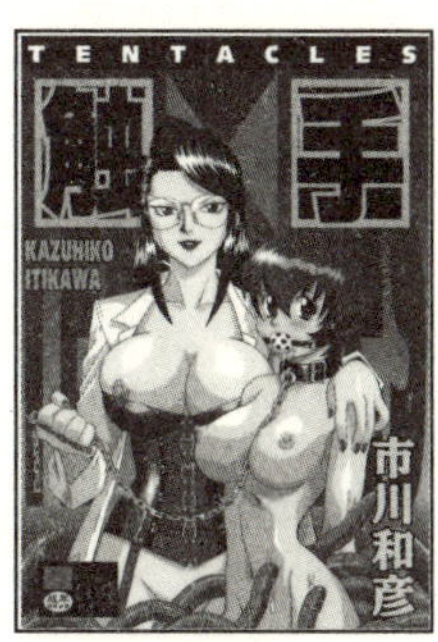

3-30: ***TENTACLES***
(Kazumasa Ichikawa 1998, Tsukasa Shobo)

effect of, "The flames of the tentacle rape genre seemed like they've been running low, so we decided to draw some tentacles." Clearly, a listless comment from some artists who thought little of the tentacle rape genre.

However, in 2000 we would see a roaring leap from the low-burning flame of the tentacle rape genre.

The Revival and Encoding of Tentacle Rape

Truthfully, what happened in 2000 wasn't the only time that the tentacle rape genre managed to revive itself since its decline. After 1994, *bishojo* comics underwent its erotic change and in 1998, it became hardcore, which enabled a greater spread of the expression. Up until that point, one magazine would publish content with various types of eromanga, but one by one, magazines started to split off and only publish certain sub-genres—*loli*, rape, consensual sex, and so forth—which brought more attention to niche genres like tentacle rape and *futanari*. As a result, comic anthologies with niche topics increased.

The eromanga genre expanded, as did the number of sub-genres which were tied to publishers' marketing strategies. In 2002, in order to appeal to the group of male readers highly influenced by the sexual content from the fantasy boom, Tokyo-based publisher Kill Time Communication launched *2D Dream Magazine*. This magazine was a combination of erotic fantasy novels and manga, fusing fantasy novels and erotic content together into one package where female knights are often sexually assaulted. These new ideals included tentacle rape as well, contributing greatly to the revival of both the tentacle rape and fantasy genres. Manga, by way of light novels and anime, also made a comeback in a sudden reversal of fortune.

Both the *nipple afterimage* and *cross-section view*, as well as other eromanga expressions, have been seen within regular manga but overwhelmingly, have a history of evolving and developing within the confines of the eromanga world. However, the tentacle genre is different from these two other expressions, as it passed through many forms of media, comprehensively evolving, and spreading. Even during the "Tentacle Recession," tentacle expressions were a stubbornly persistent phenomenon within eromanga, taking their time to slowly develop into one genre. The violent, erotic tentacles that began in *Urotsukidouji* had become a long-form video series and influenced other mediums outside of anime.

In the erotic comedies of shonen comic magazines, squid and octopus-like tentacles were active in stories in the name of the age-old shonen goal to violate female characters, and in this way, tentacles were accepted by a readership that didn't read eromanga.

I spoke a bit before about the stagnation that happened in the '90s, but it seems that unconsciously tentacles became ordinary. Perhaps we'd all been brainwashed. Readers had the seeds of literacy planted within them during this time, though perhaps it had come to the surface as times changed.

After 2005, tentacle rape anthologies became published in greater numbers, which meant that there was a degree of familiarity out there now on behalf of the readership. Expansion was connected to a growing number of fans. At some point, when eromanga readers heard the word "tentacles," they remembered the erotic context that had become linked to the term. It was to the point where whenever tentacles were involved, there was a growing belief that it had to be connected to something erotic.

It seemed that the presence of tentacles as well as their expressions and everything else in between had well and truly become encoded.

Tentacles' Charm vs. Their Regulation

Because the encoding process of non-gekiga style tentacles never reached critical mass in the 1980s, there were many different variations of the expression. Now it is divided into three main types: the squid and octopus suction cup style of tentacles, the insect-type tentacles, and the small, pleated anemone-type tentacles. Because tentacles tend to constrict their victims quite intimately, readers understood that behavioral principle almost immediately upon seeing them. Of course, while it's possible to categorize the type of tip and mucus excreted, whether singular or plural in number, whether or not it is manipulated, or even other factors more minute in detail, because this book's goal is not to biologically classify tentacles, you'll have to forgive me for leaving a few things out. For those looking for a biological classification approach, I recommend looking into ***True Theory: A Guide of Tentacles*** *(Shinsetsu Shokushu-gaku Nyumon;* Dojin Sakai 2012, Sogo Kagaku Shuppan).

The original charm of tentacle rape as a meme was that a woman would know pleasure beyond human intellect, which would easily feed the reader's imagination. In many such scenes in them, there were symbolic lines like, "I'll make you feel pleasure like you've never had before!" By using tentacles, a woman would be violated both on the inside and outside, and much like the *afterimage* or *cross-section view*, it enabled an artist to show a kind of sexual play that was impossible for humans to achieve. Readers felt a sense of co-ownership with the antagonist, now being able to show a woman that kind of pleasure, and that excited them.

It made the simultaneous rape of a woman's mouth, anus, genitals, breasts, and nipples possible. More extreme depictions, like having the tentacle, after being inserted anally, traveling up through her organs only to fly out of her mouth were able to be seen. Freely transforming tentacles would cause her to blush, caressing her body all over, while raping her on the inside.

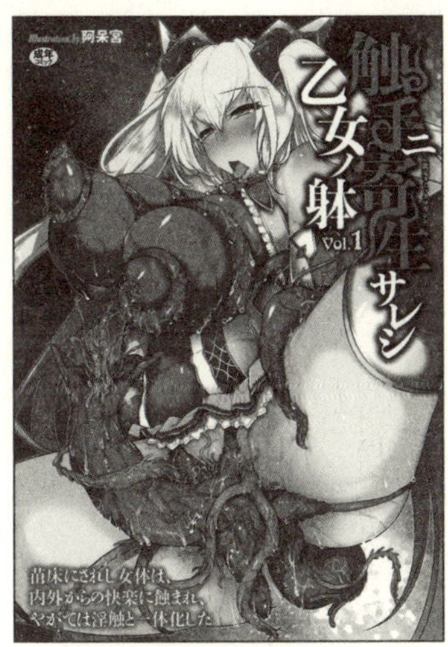

3-31: ***Shokushu ni Kisei-sareshi Otome no Katachi*** (2017, Kill Time Communication)

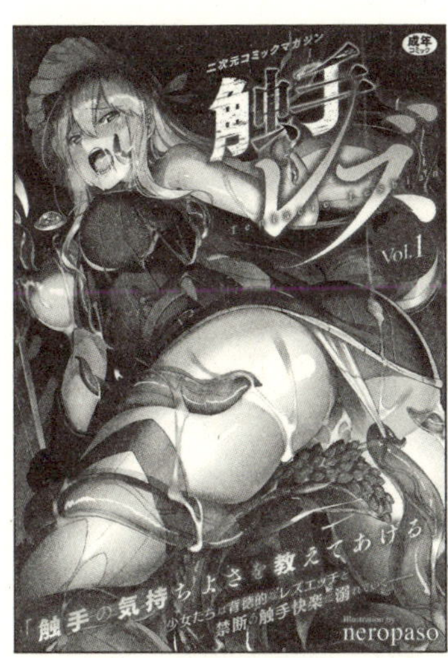

3-32: ***Tentacle Lesbians*** (*Shokushu Lez*; 2017, Kill Time Communication)

Recent tentacle genre material has become increasingly complex and radical. Instead of becoming fixed, the amount of different rape variations has evolved further than that of those that existed in the '80s. In the tentacle rape realm that existed from the 1980s to 2000, the owner of those tentacles made the best use of their special characteristics. They could decide how best to rape the victim, or if they wanted to torment them all while maintaining sight on their target. However, because of the current iterations of the expression, the shape, movement, and role of tentacles have all been encoded to a certain extent, and able to see the future development of those expressions.

The flag-bearer of the newly reborn tentacle genre, Kill Time Communication, presents cutting edge examples of those so-called "tentacle situations" in their many anthologies. Works like ***Shokushu ni Kisei-sareshi Otome no Katachi*** (2017, 3-31), ***Tentacle Lesbians*** *(Shokushu Lez;* 2017, 3-32), ***Marunomi Haramase Akume!*** (2017, 3-33) and others, it seems that nearly all of the scenes featured are striking and original.

The "marunomi" (vore) genre is secretly quite popular. The swallowed whole genre isn't strictly only tentacles, but also gets close to categories like sexual bondage, restriction, and desperate situations. This genre features situations where the target, usually swallowed whole by a mysterious lifeform or monster, is restrained and unable to resist, and then raped (3-33).

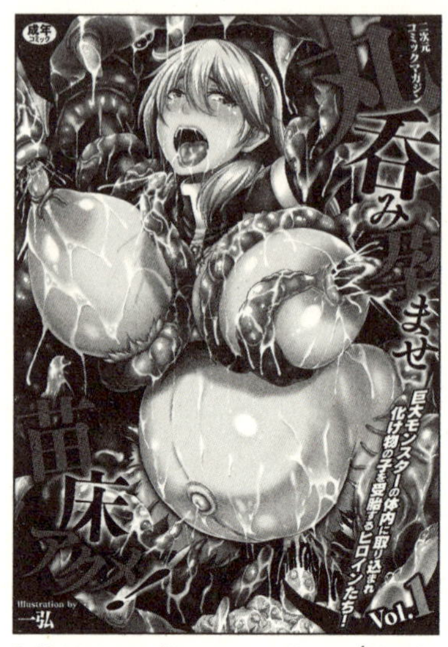

3-33: ***Marunomi Haramase Akume!*** (2017, Kill Time Communication)

In this way, because tentacle rape has been encoded to a certain degree as an expression, it's been easier to include more complex, niche situations and scenes within it.

Tentacle rape was an expression born from regulation evasion, but those involved with regulation probably never imagined that it would get to this point where it can include such charming and erotic expressions within it so freely. Toshio Maeda, who thought if tentacles were used that his work wouldn't need to be amended for censorship by specifically drawing tentacles that were meant to replace male genitalia. His work did escape censorship but that brought about new problems. If not human, what human male genitalia lookalike shape should be used, and how should it be drawn?

No one knows the answer to that question. Regulators clearly weren't prepared, and explanations differed by publishing company and date. In Sanpei Kamirenjaku's ***Moho Love*** (2009, Akaneshinsha), a scene where a boy gets assaulted by a tentacle-shaped genital debuted. In this book, the boy's genitals should've been censored. But

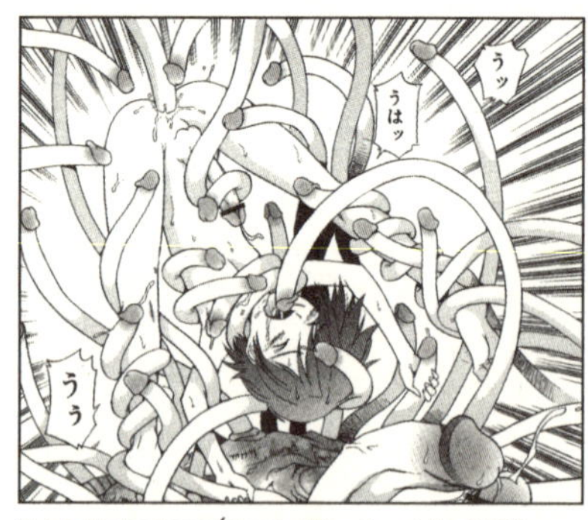

3-34: ***Moho Love*** (Sanpei Kamirenjaku 2009, Akaneshinsha)

instead, the tentacles shaped like male genitalia weren't censored at all (3-34). The shape of both the tentacles and the boy's genitals were exactly the same. There was the theory that because the tentacles "weren't" male genitals (even though they were shaped like them) the book was able to escape censorship. But some had concerns, namely: if this happened, then what's the point of censorship?

In many publishing companies' censorship rulebook, the standards said that if a book had tentacles whose tips looked like male genitalia, then they were to be censored as actual male genitalia. While obscene concepts were difficult to deal with, at this point in time, there was no precedent on how to deal with tentacles that looked like male genitals. Were they obscene, or not? I would love to hear those behind the administration of justice's take on this one.

Furthermore, to the point of being complementary, *shunga* like Hokusai's *Fisherman's Wife*—the origin point for the octopus-style tentacle—existed before Hokusai created that painting. In 1771, Shunsho Katsukawa drew a monster-genre *shunga* piece, ***Tale of 100 Vaginas*** (*Hyaku Bobo-katari*), which featured a monster that had eight legs named Yamara no Orochi, which were male genitals (3-35). While it's closer to parody than to tentacles, one could say that tentacles and male genitalia have had an affinity since ancient times.

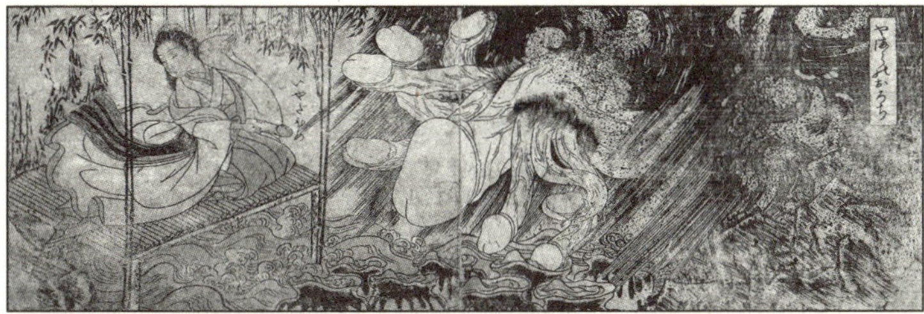

3-35: ***Tale of 100 Vaginas*** (*Hyaku Bobo-katari*; Shunsho Katsukawa, 1771)

The Reconciliation of Man and Tentacle

Now that tentacle rape had undergone encoding as an expression, it was known to be one where tentacles could hold down and rape women and allow them to lapse into a degeneracy towards pleasure in a single chain of events. But the evolution of the expression did not stop there.

Tentacle's basic form had come to represent the image of the rape of an unwilling partner. At first, that partner had been a woman rejoicing over sex, and while there was the development for that for those that wanted it, tentacles had debuted as a symbol of fear, with a woman being the target of an assault. However, from the beginning, there had also been works that debuted of the friendly monster, or the creature with tentacles, paying a human back for a favor, bringing about the reconciliation of man and tentacle.

This was the debut of consensual tentacle rape.

Of course, seeing as how it was a genre targeted towards men, it wasn't that there wasn't any consensual tentacle sex, but it was still exceedingly rare. But tentacles, which had been encoded, overcame the framework of male-targeted eromanga, and recently, is making debuts in genres like *BL,* and *TL* (teens' love). While not everything became consensual in terms of content, the depictions were the exact opposite of that of male-targeted content.

TL had stories where boyfriends have tentacles, and love was cultivated, where tentacles become the go-betweens between men and women, and when it came time for sex, the tentacles assisted in the act. Love itself took on a new shape when drawn.

Similarly, *BL* has romances with men who had the power of tentacles and the like, drawn in them most of the time. In Kitsune Miyashita's ***I Got Married to the Tentacle*** (*Shokushu na Kare to Konnin shimashita*; 2016, Kaiohsha), there is story about a marriage proposal from a non-human

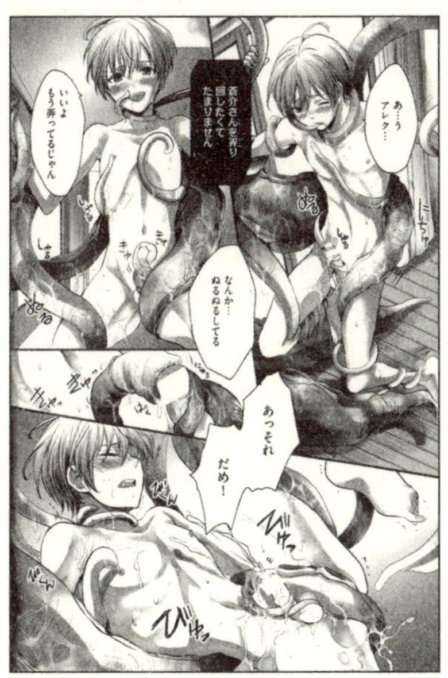

3-36: ***I Got Married to the Tentacle*** (*Shokushu na Kare to Konnin shimashita*; Kitsune Miyashita 2016, Kaiohsha)

tentacle lifeform (3-36). The mysterious lifeform is usually in the form of a human (probably biologically male as well), but because it's two men, of course the partner proposed to can't accept his offer. The tentacle being feels kindness towards the man he proposed to, and also self-hatred towards his natural form (as a tentacle lifeform), carries around anxiety because of it. Surprisingly, even though they are both men, and one of them isn't even human, the human partner accepts the being's earnest feelings for him. Overcoming the difficulties of an existence called "tentacle," the story is drawn with a stronger type of love that binds the characters closer together after this event. The presence of unrestricted sex helped bring about a new expression in *BL.*

In the tentacle anthology ***ManiaEx Special Issue: Tentacles*** (2015, Kaiohsha), one can see a lot of BL tentacle scenes. There's an S&M expression that can be seen in this one also, where most of the book is full of "consensual tentacle" stories. While there are scenes where tentacles are violating characters, there are also men that rescue the people being violated who fall in love with each other in a series of developments. In other words, there is a lack of pleasure during these tentacle assault scenes.

However, the sci-fi *BL* series ***Perfect Planet*** (Iimo, 2016, Julian Publishing) is slightly different in nature. Harvesting and researching extraterrestrial life, a spaceship continues its probe of a planet that bears a strong resemblance to Earth. The tentacle creatures in the story go berserk on the ship. There are many components taken from the film ***Alien***, with

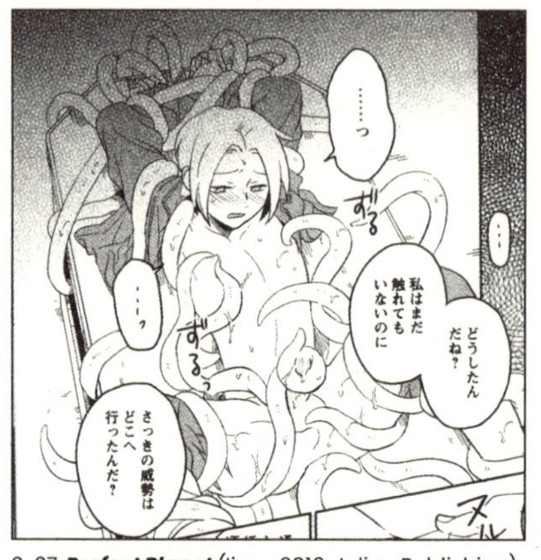

3-37: ***Perfect Planet*** (Iimo, 2016, Julian Publishing)

men onboard the ship who fight, betray, and ultimately, fall in love, that are drawn. As a human drama, it has a lot of charming plot developments, and the tentacle creatures blend well into the story…until those creatures start raping and forcing obedience out of the men on the ship (3-37). At this point in time, the consensual tentacle rape genre is at the center of the female-targeted tentacle genre. But in the future, yet another new genre will emerge and inevitably spread.

Not stopping at the second dimension, the history of tentacles in AV is older than I thought. From 2007 on it suddenly grew until it became a whole genre unto itself within the AV world. ***Shokushu Akume!*** (Soft On Demand) is an AV with special effects made in 2007 and features a female nurse, a female doctor, and a female high school student, all raped one after the other (3-38). Even if it is technically in the *tokusatsu* (special effects) genre, the scenes where the women get raped by the tentacle creatures are frequent, and as a result, a new AV genre was born. As tentacles can be a symbol in so many genres, this awareness cleared the way to help it become its own genre.

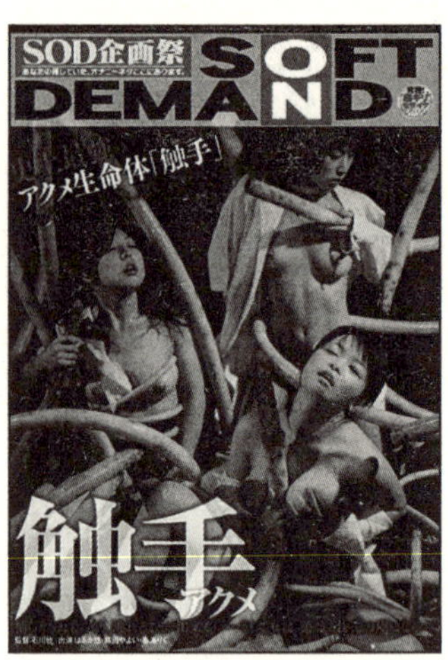

3-38: ***Shokushu Akume!*** (Soft On Demand, 2009; video)

We Are the Offspring of Tentacle Expressions

As I mentioned before, I think that directly connecting *shunga* with current eromanga expressions is rather reckless. But in recent years, the reason why tentacle rape expressions continue to spread is because of a massive re-appraisal of Hokusai's *Fisherman's Wife*. Since 2005 or so, mainly on internet aggregate sites, under the context of, "Look! Ancient people were just as perverted as we are today!", many *shunga* pieces have been reproduced and distributed. But whenever *Fisherman's Wife* is present, people startled by the fact that tentacle rape has been around since the Edo period usually write extensive comments about it.

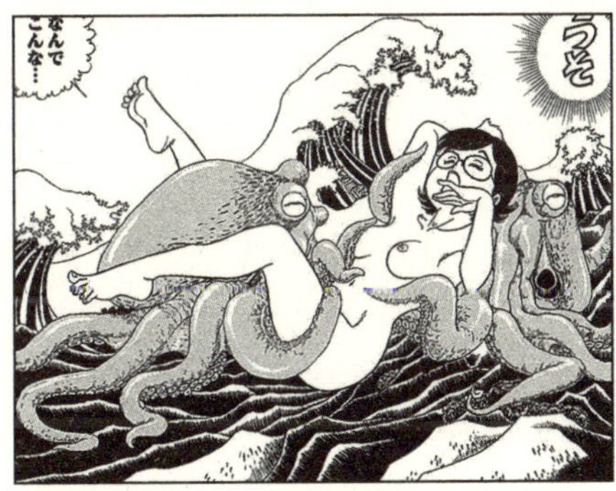

3-39: ***Amai Seikatsu***, Vol. 7 (Hikaru Yuzuki 2015, Shueisha)

As evidence, in 2015, Eisei Bunko opened its first *shunga* exhibition in Tokyo, which ended up attracting over 220,000 people. This popularity wasn't just due to tentacles, but also because of Japanese sex culture, and perhaps a re-evaluation of the prints on a larger scale. It was also possibly because many eromanga creators dropped by to visit the exhibit for themselves. The exhibition may have become both a shot in the arm, and perhaps, lead many to be proud to be

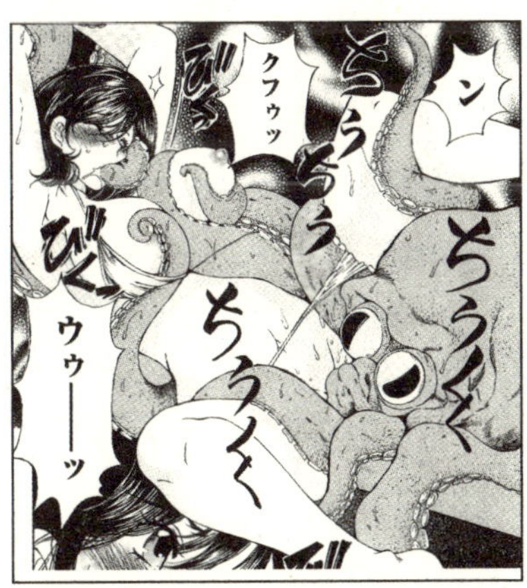

3-40: "Tonight, My Wife Will..." (*Koyoi, Tsuma ga.*; Takashi Sano 2016, Nihon Bungeisha)

the great expressionists' grandchildren. So, I also believe that the homages in manga to Hokusai are proof of that (3-39~41).

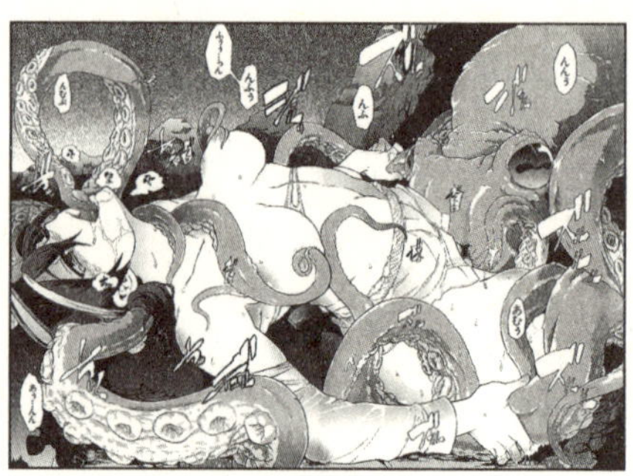

3-41: ***ShindoL's Cultural Anthropology*** (*ShindoL no Bunka Jinruigaku*; ShindoL 2016, TI NET)

Just as many people know Hokusai didn't only draw *shunga,* he was a master of *ukiyo-e* as well. His drawing of Mt. Fuji, ***Thirty-Six Views of Mount Fuji*** (*Fugaku Sanjuurokkei*, 1830-32), is his most famous non-eros work. He is considered a top-class painter that went from landscapes to *shunga,* leaving behind works beyond expressions that are wonderful.

In modern day Japan, where regular manga is first-class, the erotic is third-class. While the thought that first-class artists will not create erotic work isn't very common, even Masamune Shirow, creator of the international cyberpunk hit ***Ghost in the Shell*** (1989, Kodansha), has themes in his art that appear to be tentacles (3-42).

Since the end of the '60s, the tentacle rape expression that Toshio Maeda strongly attacked readers with remains. In eromanga, it has many different forms that have come about as developments from artists looking for solutions. For a time, it simmered low, but now the expression that represents the genre has a great deal of diversity coming out of its evolution. While there are no depictions of sex, the DNA of the tentacle rape expression that eromanga helped develop can be seen in regular manga

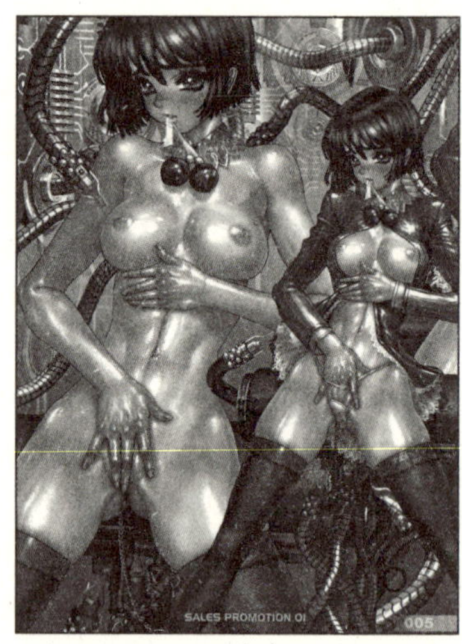

3-42: ***GREASEBERRIES*** (Masamune Shirow 2014, GOT)

like the *To LOVE Ru* Series (3-43) and ***Monster Musume*** (*Monster Musume no Iru Nichijo*; Oyakado, 2012, Tokuma Shoten/Seven Seas Ent., 3-44) which is clearly inherited.

The genes of the tentacle expression, which have overcome the framework of eromanga, will most likely continue to spread throughout the world. ✿

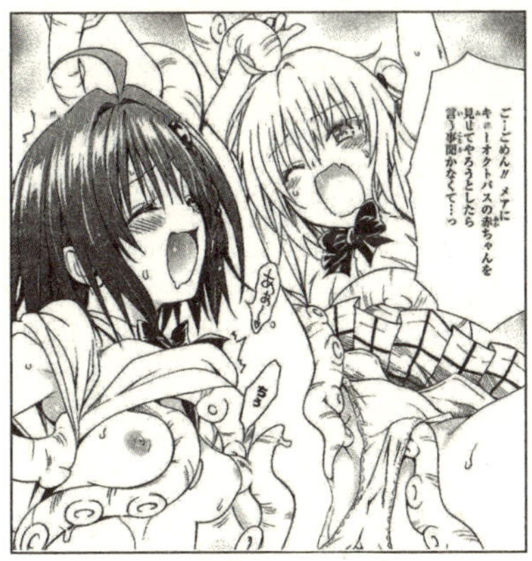

3-43: ***To LOVE Ru: Darkness***, Vol. 14 (Kentaro Yabuki & Saki Hasemi 2015, Shueisha/Seven Seas Ent.)

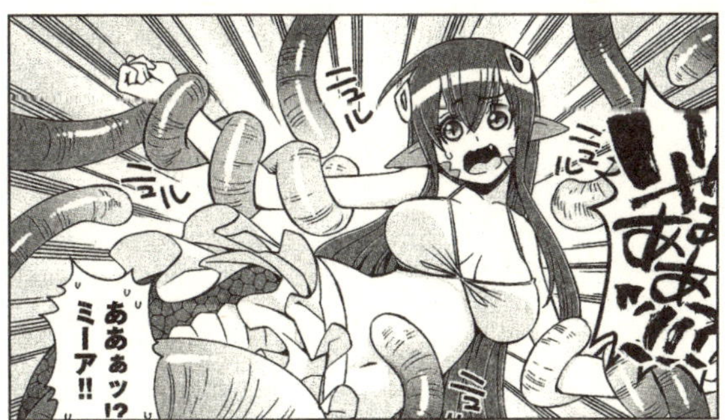

3-44: ***Monster Musume***, Vol. 9 (*Monster Musume no Iru Nichijo*; Oyakado, 2016, Tokuma Shoten/Seven Seas Ent.)

The History of Hentai Manga

CHAPTER FOUR

The Evolution of the Cross-Section View

What Does the Sexual Intercourse Cross-Section View Explain?

While it's rare, there are several types of visual expressions one can only see in eromanga and nowhere else. These are expressions that independently evolve within the purview of the genre. As we just saw with the *nipple afterimage,* there is one more expression that is unique to eromanga that has become a default expression: the "sexual intercourse cross-section view."

The *cross-section view* is an imaginary view in the form of an MRI captured at the moment penetrative sex between male and female genitalia takes place and is closer to something like an anatomical drawing more than anything else. It's a unique meme that depicts how things change during and after the moment of insertion.

However, it should be noted that in situations where that moment of insertion isn't between a male and female set of genitalia; more specifically, in situations like anal penetration and oral penetration. Another commonly seen off-shoot of this expression is the "transparent view," when emphasis of the picture is not one piece of a round slice of internal organs, or when the organs alone are only depicted.

But for the sake of this book, when guts are depicted as if they were transparent Japanese rice fish with long tube shapes floating inside of internal female sexual organs, we will call that the "cross-section view"(*danmenzu*; 4-1,2).

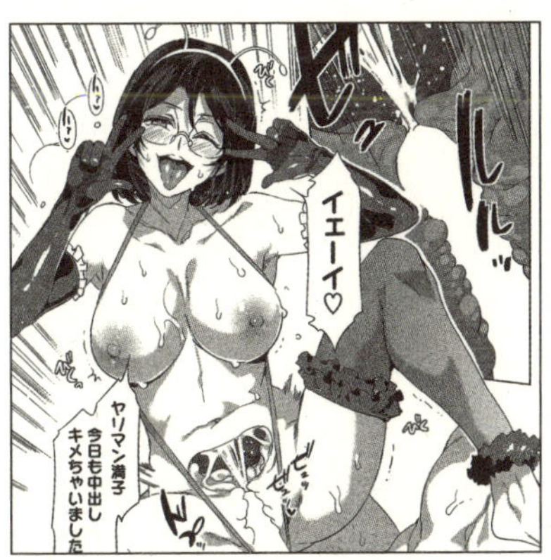

4-1: "Souma Kurumi no Hahaoya" (Kei Mizuryu 2016, Core Magazine)

While Japanese rice fish may be able to see their own insides, if not via a violent murder or a sci-fi plot device, those engaging in sex aren't able to see their own insides. And precisely because we aren't able to see our own insides, being able to express that you're able to do so is a very uniquely *manga* idea.

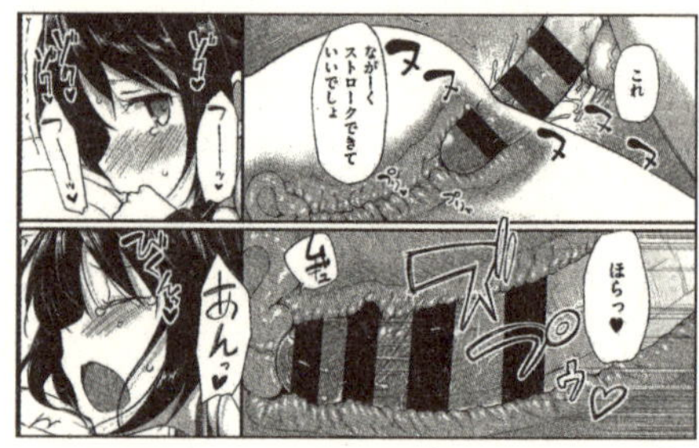

4-2: "DokiDoki ★ Community Life" (TakayaKi 2017, GOT)

The *cross-section view* is a manga technique developed to convey information to the reader, more than anything else. And it has become indispensable to today's eromanga. But before we go any further, I suppose an explanation of why the *cross-section view* of two people's conjoined parts is so important is in order. And to do so, we need to look at the relationship between pornographic media, and how it excites its various readerships.

What does the *cross-section view* explain, and how does it excite and arouse its readers? The roots of those two things are directly connected to the entire history of manga expressions as well as the history of the policing of (other) pornographic media, which is entangled messily with the unique fetishism of eromanga.

In this chapter we'll be looking at the history of the *cross-section view,* the role of how this expression was designed, and how it has changed, spread, and followed the other steps in the encoding process.

The Desire to Know What's Going on Inside

Generally speaking, this expression is a drawing where a body is cross-sectioned in its point of view. For example, in order to get a better understanding of how an engine works in a car, it's effective to take a cross-section view of the structure of the engine in slices to do so. In the 1960s, in order to figure out more about *kaiju* monsters, there were many drawings of cross-sections of various *kaiju* organs, from their mouths to the gas they breathed out. The technique became a quite popular part of the study of sci-fi creatures at the time.

In reality, if we could use the *cross-section view,* it would be easier to understand things by seeing them on display. But when we put it that way, when we learn about the earth's crust and its mantle via the *cross-section view,* we get enough data from these materials to draw our own conclusions.

While at its core the function of the *cross-section view* is to help overcome the reader's intellectual desire by providing an illustration of a situation, in manga there are many cases of the *cross-section view* being but one tool in the toolbox when presenting a story. In violent manga, in order to render the sharpness of a sword, or excellent bladework, it comes in handy when trying to fully convey the cruelty of the swordsman. As such, that use of this perspective has become essential to the storytelling process of manga.

In a sci-fi title touched by the nipple afterimage, Hiroya Oku's *GANTZ,* the *cross-section view* is used to illustrate how humans move through time in that title's universe (4-3). This expression is used to enhance the impact of these panels. The *sexual intercourse cross-section view* in eromanga also once had the same goals. Because the readers couldn't see into the body, they wanted to know what was going on inside of it.

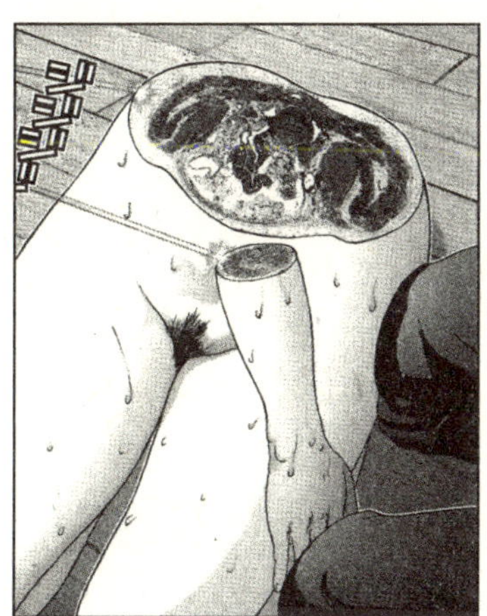

4-3: ***GANTZ***, Vol. 1 (Hiroya Oku 2000, Shueisha/Dark Horse)

While this expression was most likely originally born out of these curiosities, the *cross-section view* has become one of the most indispensable direction techniques for a story.

So, who invented the *cross-section view,* and when did it become the standard expression used within the eromanga genre?

The First Cross-Section View

To be truthful, it has been difficult trying to suss out who was the original inventor of the cross-section view. For the *nipple afterimage,* I was able to figure out that Hiroya Oku and Hiroyuki Utatane had invented it at the same time. But that incident is an extremely rare type of discovery. If we're talking about discovering the original cross-section view, there's also the possibility that perhaps someone in antiquity had used it in a fresco or mural. If that's the case, then trying to determine who invented the very first cross-section view is a hopeless undertaking.

But what about the first *sexual intercourse cross-section view?*

Here, we have the luck of finding a picture left behind by someone famous. Leonardo Da Vinci, creator of the ***Mona Lisa*** (1452-1512), is a great figure who seemingly dabbled in a bit of everything from the arts to all of the sciences, music, and medicine. But his huge drawings have been left behind in a series of collections. In the Windsor Collection, found in the British Royal Family's Windsor Castle, there is a sketch using the cross-section in a depiction of sex between a man and a woman (4-4). It was drawn roughly around 1493, and amongst researchers it's known as the oldest depiction of the sexual intercourse cross-section view.

However, it's also been acknowledged by those same researchers that the sketch is completely anatomically incorrect. Its positioning of organs and connections to intestines are all over the place. It's more a representation of imagination than actual accurate anatomical portrayal.

Da Vinci's motives for producing such a sketch are unclear to this day,

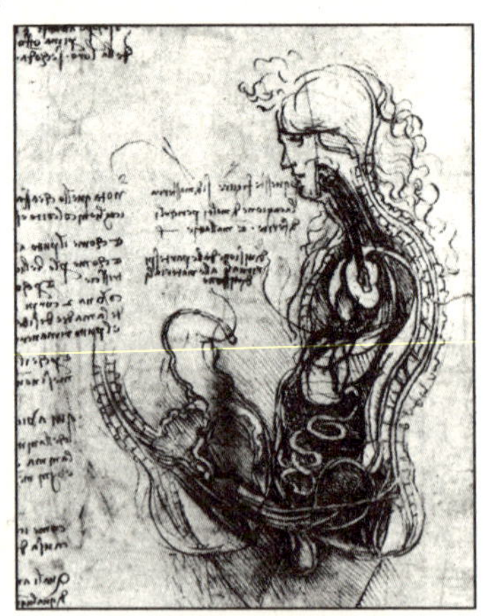

4-4: ***Coition of a Hemisected Man and Woman*** (Leonardo Da Vinci, 1492)

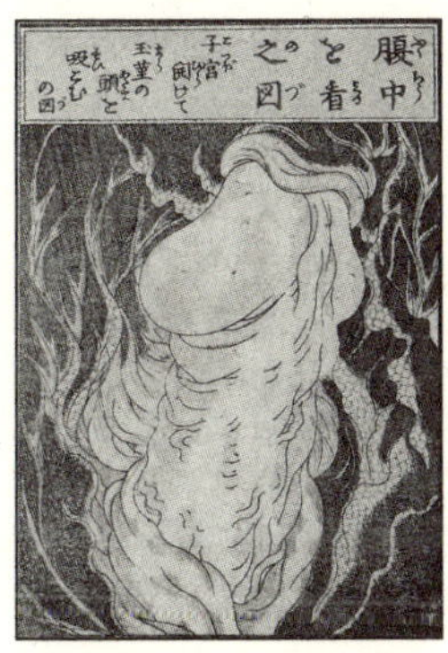

4-5: ***News from the Bedroom: The Pillow Library*** (*Keichu Kibun Makura Bunko*; Eisen Keisai 1823)

but it could be that he had drawn it out of a curiosity or fascination with how organs played their roles during intercourse.

Shifting to Japan, I said before that prior to manga, there was no historic usage of the sexual intercourse cross-section as an expression. However, in the *shunga* pictures from the Edo period, I did see a usage of it. Speaking of *shunga,* just as Hokusai's famous *Fisherman's Wife* became the possible origin point of the tentacle expression, in *shunga* we also see Edo period mannerisms, eros, and other elements in various forms. In those pieces we can also see consensual intercourse, rape, loli/shota content, BL, lesbians, group sex, peeping, cuckolding, hermaphrodites, bestiality, incest, and many of the other current genres of eromanga.

Yet again, I would caution against making a statement like *shunga* and modern eromanga are directly connected to each other, but seeing as the sexual intercourse cross-section view exists within *shunga,* I'd like to go ahead and introduce a few of those to you all now.

As a member of the Utagawa school that pumped out many famous *ukiyo-e* works, Kunisada Utagawa drew his ***Azuma Genji*** book of illustrations beginning in 1844, published in 1857. In *Azuma Genji,* there's a splendid representation of the sexual intercourse cross-section view. It contains a closeup of the moment of insertion of male genitals into female genitals, as well as a precise depiction of the moment of intravaginal ejaculation, with fluids and all. In Eisen Keisai's ***News from the Bedroom: The Pillow Library*** (*Keichu Kibun Makura Bunko*), the moment of insertion has happened, and the male genitals are wrapped up within the female's. It's drawn incredibly well (4-5).

The cross-section views within these pieces were meant to function in a pornographic capacity, as well as a sexually educational one, even in a comedic capacity as well. There are many different theories, but there's also the element of the unseen being depicted; a sort of primordial desire.

Is the Cross-Section View Used to Deceive?

I wonder, what was the first cross-section view to appear in manga?

I haven't clearly identified this yet, either, but I do believe that it was around during the dawn of the manga age.

A cross-section of genitalia has been used for the purpose of sexual education for a long time, too. But in terms of modern manga and the sexual intercourse cross-section view connected to it, this expression did not really appear until the 1970s. Out of those usages, I have been able to confirm an especially older point of origin for the sexual intercourse cross-section view, which was, of all things, found in sci-fi genre manga.

Known for their popular children's manga ***Doraemon*** (Shogakukan), Fujiko F. Fujio also created a lesser-known adult-targeted short with an intercourse cross-section view, "Uchuujin Report: Sample A to B" (1977, Tokuma Shoten). This work was short and unique, with Fujio writing the manuscript and a shoujo manga artist, Mami Komori, drawing the panels. The plot has aliens descending to earth, keeping mankind under surveillance. In an homage to classic sci-fi, the ultimate goal of these aliens is to create a report about humans to send back to their home world. The aliens label the subject of their reports (a man and a woman) A and B, and, as if they were some new product about to hit the market, coldly test

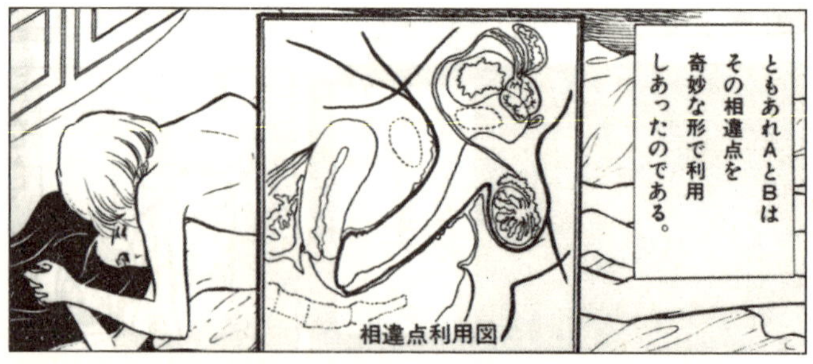

4-6: "Uchuujin Report: Sample A to B" (Mami Komori & Fujiko F. Fujio, 1977 Tokuma Shoten)

them this way and that to collect data. It is during the part of the plot when these aliens are studying A and B's activities when the sexual intercourse cross-section view is used (4-6).

From the beginning of in this work, in order to understand how humans are constructed on a systemic level, we see cross-section views of ears and eyes. Most likely, this was done for the reader to get the full, cold, almost robotic flavor of this surveillance these aliens are conducting. Considering the age of the readers for this work, it might have even been a parody of the sexual education films made by the Ministry of Science, Education, and Culture about birth control in the 1950s. To that end, the scenes of intercourse aren't erotic nor excite any kind of arousal response, but rather are made with a cold, scientific eye.

Aside from erotic works, the cross-section view also appeared in comedic works as well. Hideo Azuma's ***Yakekuso Tenshi*** (1978, Akita Shoten) shows a scene of what looks to be intravaginal ejaculation along with a sort of "transparent cross-section view," as well as an intercourse cross-section view shown with a woman from the back (4-7, 8). Azuma came from shonen magazines, but *Play Comics* was read by working adult men, and often features a lot of erotic, sex-depicting slapstick comedies.

In "Seishun Sanmyaku," a short story from Tatsuhiko Yamagami, known for ***Gaki-Deka*** (1982, Futabasha), a more anatomically correct version of the intercourse cross-section view was used (4-9). Here the author seems to be poking a bit of fun at a series from the 1950s, ***Igaguri-kun***

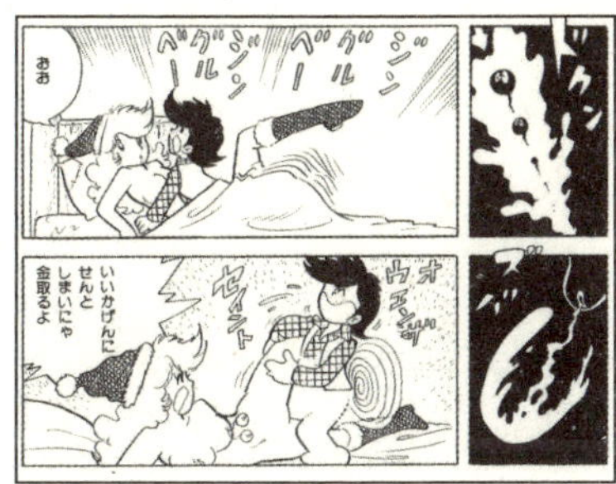

4-7: ***Yakekuso Tenshi***, Chpt. 48 (Hideo Azuma 1976, Akita Shoten)

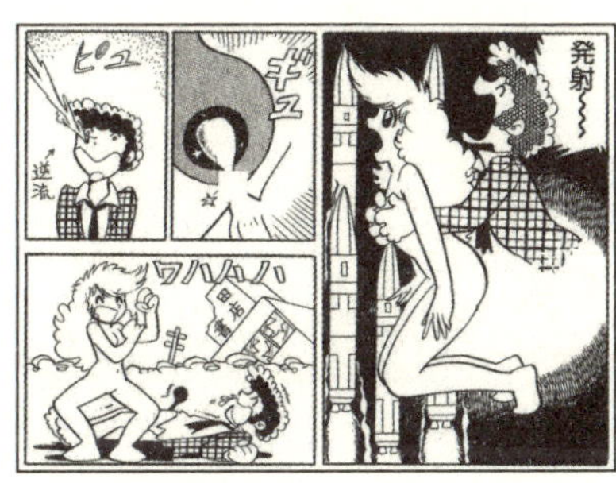

4-8: ***Yakekuso Tenshi***, Chpt. 77 (Hideo Azuma 1978, Akita Shoten)

by Eiichi Fukui, with his protagonist, Iboguri-kun. Iboguri throws a rock at a girl, who loses consciousness. He proceeds to rape her and also goes on to do other unexplained, mysterious sociopathic things, ending the story with a surreal "Ah, that felt great!"

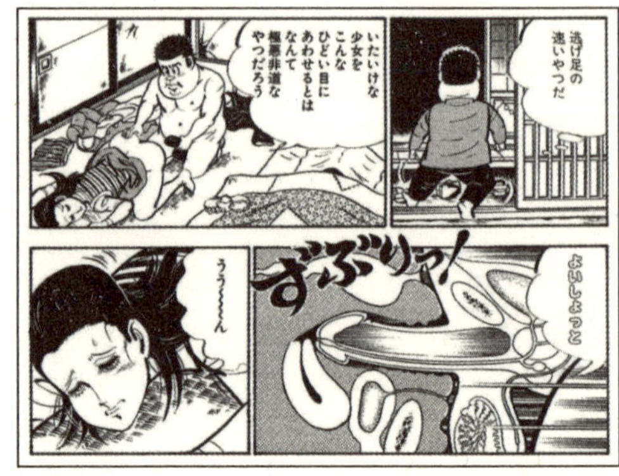

4-9: "Seishun Sanmyaku" (Tatsuhiko Yamagami 1982, Futabasha)

The original was one of complete and utter deviance in its extreme depictions of sex and violence, but was also one that was highly praised, and helped open up a new realm of gag manga. The parody is also a gag manga; a work that is high comedy. While it has erotic elements, it could not really draw depictions of genitalia, so it pulled even more comedy out of an anatomical version of the cross-section view.

At this point in time, it wasn't legally possible to draw a representation of the intercourse cross-section view outside of the realm of educational content. The cross-section view as an expression pivoted to an anatomical likeness at this time in order to comply with that, but also managed to subvert a negative like censorship and turn into a positive with regard to its potential for comedy in stories. Some believe that was the intention behind the expression during this time.

However, when you turn it inside out, calling the cross-section view obscene doesn't really work because of its anatomical projection. I wonder if this was a position that artists and editors might've held.

But getting back to manga expressions. Because genitalia could not be drawn, one of the most common arrestable offenses under the penal code was violating Japan's Article 157, the "circulation and distribution of obscene materials." However, it should be noted that the wording of this law did not include "drawing genitalia." Because there was already a precedence on the books stating that depictions of genitalia were obscene, regular magazines, even shonen manga magazines, were actively censored. However, in *Uchuujin Report* and works like it that used the cross-section view in a scientific or educational way, were not considered obscene and thus, were acceptable to be run in magazines.

That is how the cross-section view became shorthand for the depiction of intercourse for when one couldn't draw it. Thus, it is thought to have become one of the obscener manga expressions that outran the law. Because if one suddenly found a work that was somehow off, or had an overly comical depiction of sex, the offending scenes in question could be easily removed. So even as the world headed into the '90s, we saw more use of the cross-section view in erotic comedies within regular manga rather than eromanga titles.

If the woman's partner was a male virgin, one could imbue a story of sex not going very well by using the cross-section view and showing both partners' faces and how they change through the act comedically (4-10). In regular manga with light erotic themes, the artists behind them understand how to use the cross-section view very well as an expression.

Speaking of regular seinen manga that are relevant to this topic, one absolutely cannot forget about ***Manga Sutra*** (Futari Ecchi; 1997~, Hakusensha/Tokyopop) by Katsu Aki.

When the cross-section view is used in regular manga series, its role is largely a comedic one most of the time. But in the case of *Manga Sutra*, while this is still the case, it also has a very strong sex education tone. In this manga, the comic seemed to have switched places with a sex manual, and brand new heterosexual sex positions appeared in every chapter. However, as a protective measure, when it came time for

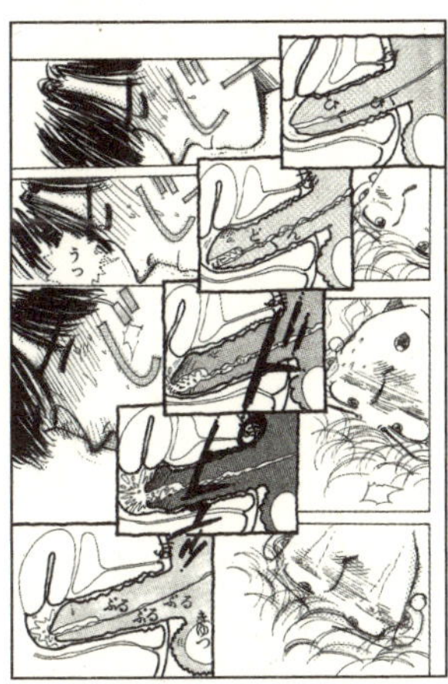

4-10: ***Ecstasy off Limits***, Vol. 1 (*Genkai ni Ecstasy*; Ai Shiraishi 1990, Shogakukan)

depictions of sex, the so-called "banana" expression was used instead of actual male genitalia. Yet, after the moment of insertion, the cross-section view was used to illustrate the situation thereafter (4-11, 12).

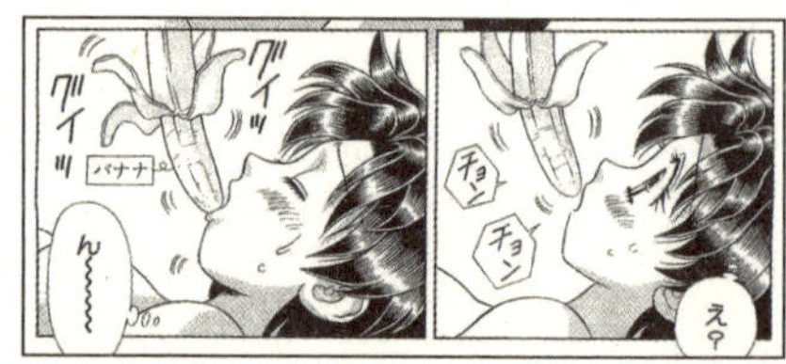

4-11: ***Manga Sutra***, Vol. 25 (Futari Ecchi; Katsu Aki 2004, Hakusensha)

However, because this work was serialized in a regular manga magazine, it should be noted that the version of the cross-section view used here was not the same one that popped up in eromanga. It was different both in how male genitals were depicted, and given how it was used in both of these elements, one can confirm the existence of the male urethra.

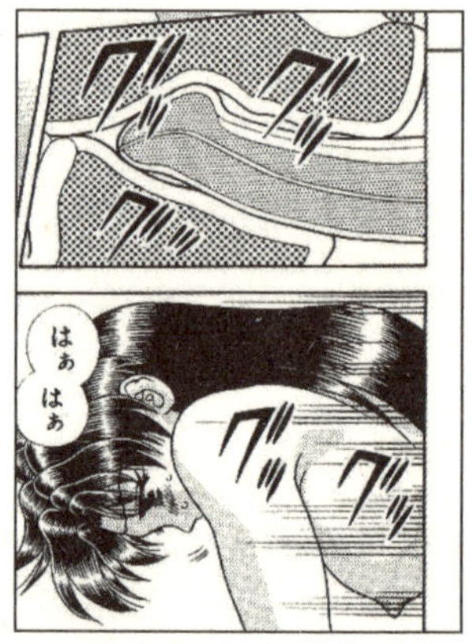

4-12: ***Manga Sutra***, Vol. 22 (Futari Ecchi; Katsu Aki 2004, Hakusensha)

As of 2017, *Manga Sutra* has been serialized for twenty years and counting. It continues to have both sex scenes and uses of the cross-section view with every new chapter. While this hasn't been precisely counted, it is now thought that this series may have the most uses of the intercourse cross-section view within it (to the point where it may want to talk to the Guinness World Records people about it getting an award).

Now that we've talked about the sexual intercourse cross-section view and its use in regular manga, let's move to how it's been used in eromanga next.

Cross-Section Views That Debuted in Ero-Gekiga and Bishojo Comics

The cross-section view as it's used today within the world of eromanga has a fair number of variations. But I can't help wondering how it was used in *ero-gekiga* previously.

Ero-gekiga had its heyday in the early 1970s, and during its peak in 1978, it had roughly one hundred different magazine titles catering to it each month in publication. However, because the number of samples of these works I have at hand are so small, I cannot really allude to how this expression spread throughout all of eromanga. So instead, I shall discuss examples of the unique characteristics of this expression by introducing some of them.

In Shigeru Tomita's "Inmitsu Honeymoon" (1981, Tatsumi Publishing) the cross-section view is used to show the process of how an egg vibrator is inserted into the vagina (4-13). It's a depiction meant to explain that particular process by dividing the panels and carefully drawing what's happening. By doing so, the artist got the eros of the situation across to the audience.

In Fumio Nakajima's "Yukishoujo Densetsu" (1982, Sun Publishing), an intercourse cross-section view is used, but both the male and female genitals are gradated, and the depiction is closer to a perspective drawing (4-14). Because it depicts a hymen being penetrated, blood is drawn near the male genitalia. This work is unique because the artist is trying to explain this situation by using it.

Even in Toshio Maeda's ***Eden no Kaze*** (1990, Koike Shoin), one can see an identical expression in terms of how a hymen is being penetrated (4-15). In Maeda's use of it, we also have sexual

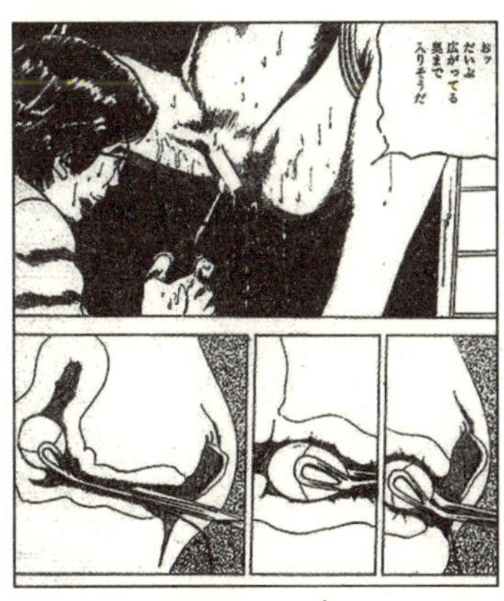

4-13: "Inmitsu Honeymoon" (Shigeru Tomita 1981, Tatsumi Publishing)

fluids within the woman's vagina, so the reader can easily understand what is happening.

Within the genealogy of gekiga, Tou Moriyama also uses the cross-section view in his work. However, his approach to it is a bit different; instead of cross-sectioning things horizontally, he uses the three-dimensional "transparent cross-section view" version instead. He used it fairly early on within his work, usually during a creampie scene. In ***Penguin in Bondage*** (*Toraware Penguin*; 1986, Tatsumi Publishing), the transparent cross-section view is used in concert with sound effects like "dokkun!" (*splurt*) at the moment of ejaculation within the vagina (4-16).

So as you can see, within the early period of eromanga, this expression is used in an informative capacity (in terms of what's happening between both partners' bodies), but is also used a fair bit of the time as a way to telegraph the situation at hand, as well as its changes, to the audience. It has been thought that this was used as an expression to show both partners' sexually related emotions in order to arouse the audience.

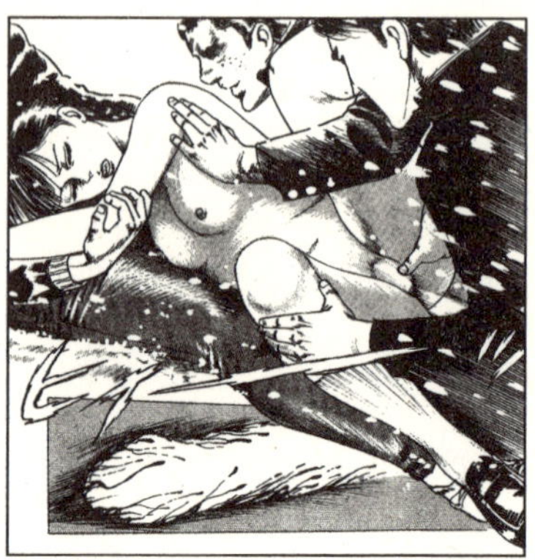

4-14: "Yukishoujo Densetsu" (Fumio Nakajima 1982, Sun Publishing)

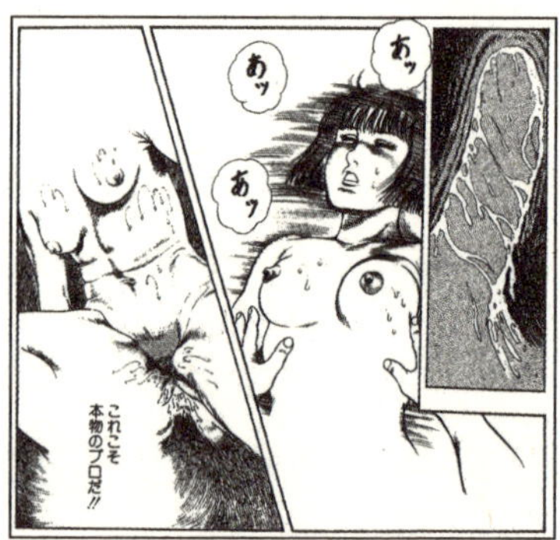

4-15: ***Eden no Kaze*** (Toshio Maeda 1990, Koike Shoin)

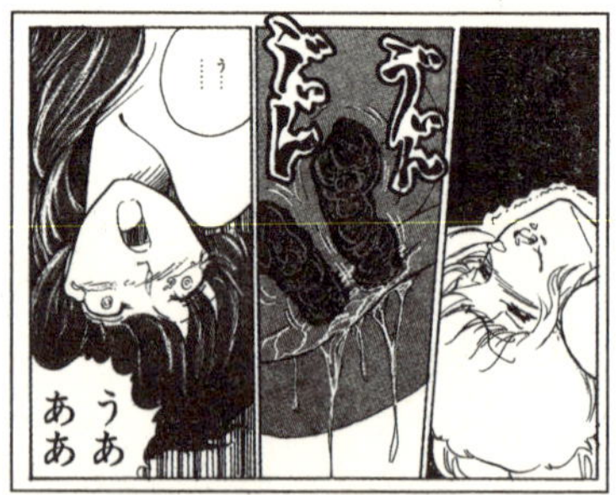

4-16: ***Penguin in Bondage*** (*Toraware Penguin*; Tou Moriyama 1986, Tatsumi Publishing)

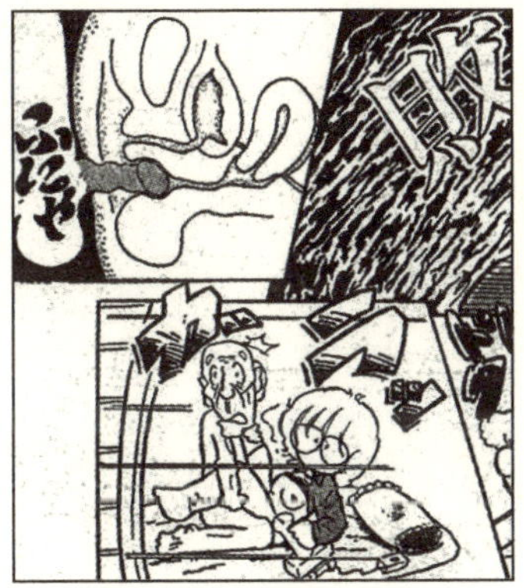

4-17: "Android wa Denkikokeshi no Yume wo Miruka?" (Kasumi Goto 1983, Byakuya-Shobo)

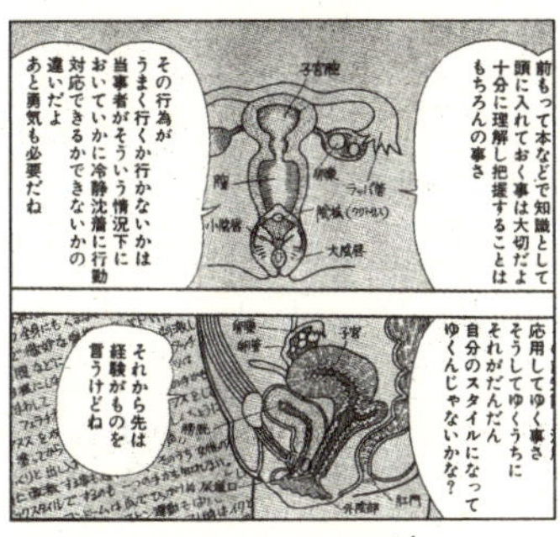

4-18: "Tadaima Benkyouchuu" (Juzo Minazuki 1991, Fujimi Publishing)

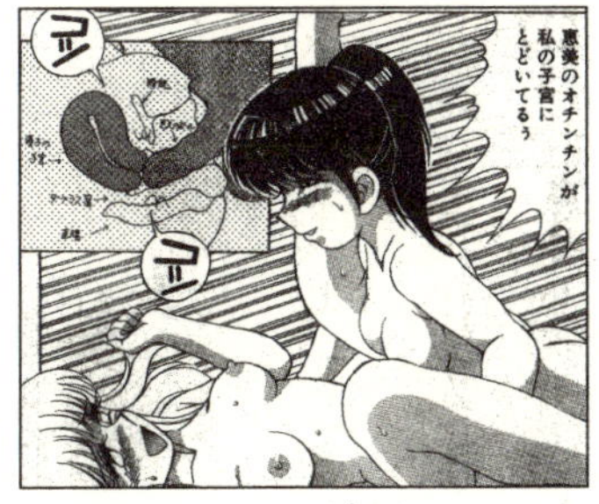

4-19: "Happy-ning Star" (Mizu-Youkan 1991, Tatsumi Shobo)

However, because the general use of the expression itself in eromanga is quite scarce, it didn't really undergo a general encoding process.

It was the same in the world of regular manga, too. There were many works out there like Kasumi Goto's that used this expression to show the humor in situations like this (4-17). Or take Juzo Minazuki's, where it was used in an educational capacity (4-18). But even if I could find more of them, the ones I found were mostly like Mizu-Youkan's (4-19) and HindenBURG's (4-20), where a comparatively simpler form of the cross-section view was used.

Entering the '80s, the lone artist who began aggressively using the cross-section view was Yui Toshiki; specifically in in his work ***Mermaid ♥ Junction*** (1987, Byakuya-Shobo). It may be appropriate to say that Toshiki's version is the closest to the one used today (4-21). I also think that out of everything I found while researching, *Mermaid ♥ Junction* was perhaps the one example of the cross-section view where, at the moment of insertion, the male genitals were left uncensored. I can't help but wonder if this was a purposeful stylistic choice. If penises are left uncensored, then it does bring a stronger sense of reality to the situation being explained this way.

However, because not many artists used this expression, it wasn't one that made much progress, and instead, it required many more months and years in order to fully mature for all to use.

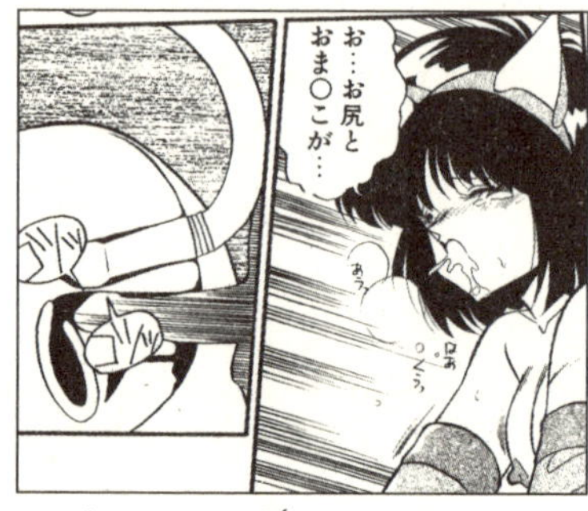

4-20: "Utamai-chau" (HindenBURG 1991, Taiyou Tosho)

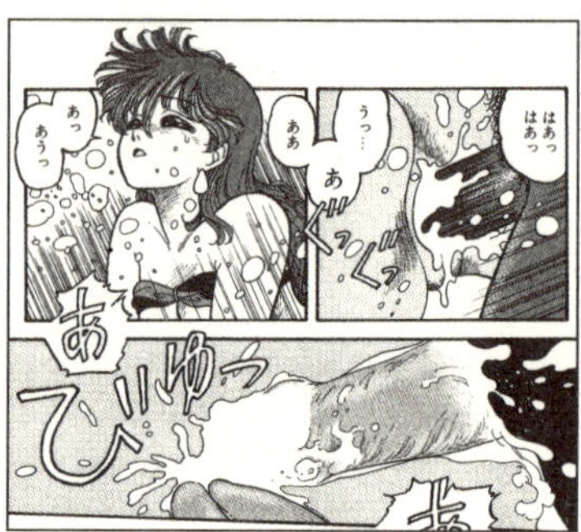

4-21: ***Mermaid ♥ Junction*** (Yui Toshiki 1987, Byakuya-Shobo)

The Cross-Section View Depression

Much like the *nipple afterimage,* the cross-section view did not catch on immediately as a fad with authors and artists.

I'm not sure if it was just a matter of how eromanga developed, but different expressions needed a fixed time to develop, as it were, as its expressions seemed to have slumps during their growing process.

To be clear, there is no definitive promise that all expressions, whether they be hard-won fruits of their creators' labor or they just accidentally came into being, would spread shortly after their birth, as many expressions have disappeared over the years. After all, what is vogue is a backdrop to specific eras, and manga that are recognized are what become hits. Other external causes of fads tend to pile up in a complicated way, and their accidental yields are something of a phenomenon.

As a result, as I've related before, the version of the cross-section view that appears within eromanga didn't really take off until around the year 2000, after which it spread like wildfire. No one really hit the pause button to stop the development of the cross-section view as an expression, but there had been a slump within eromanga until then, when eromanga artists went crazy creating new versions. I can't help but wonder why the cross-section view lived in obscurity for such a long time.

I can think of many reasons why, but perhaps the largest is that regulation and censorship was quickly growing during this era. Even in the case of the nipple afterimage, there was a bit of a break during the *eromanga ice age* with regard to its use and development.

While the cross-section view was an expression born of evading censorship, during the early '90s there was a hard crackdown on comics that were considered "harmful." This regulation was so strict, it was to the point where one wasn't able to depict anything below the hips, and because of this, there was no room, no chance for anyone to use the cross-section view. As a result, it failed to charge ahead at full strength into its development and went dormant for a time.

But then in 1998, the tide turned, and suddenly, the eromanga world became fertile soil for the development of the cross-section view.

And thus, the curtains rose on age of hardcore eromanga.

The *More* Hardcore Eromanga

Eromanga became *hardcore* in 1998, and thus censorship and revision began to decline.

As these expressions became more and more extreme, depictions of sex below the waist became more finely detailed, and more extreme as well. Eromanga is a world where, riding on the back of *doujinshi* (fanzines), has a quality known as *gakuyaochi* (inside jokes). *Doujinshi* fans and creators make up this inner circle in the world of eromanga, which dictate how the eromanga world functions in every way. So, they would consider whether to draw anything erotic, and what to draw next that is also erotic, and the like. It is clear that many editors have also asked these questions, and in response, allowed all of eromanga's content to roam free-range without interference.

Insider content was strong, but there was also actual comedy. There were sex scenes, but without depicting the actual unison of biological parts. There was also a great deal of content without any erotic scenes as well. Taking all of this into account, all of this particular content sold well, as there was high demand for it. However, in the mid-'90s, the doujinshi marketplace became laden with rivalries, and as a result, the market became oversaturated. Sales fell, and there was a shoring up of content.

In response, content became more hardcore, more radical. At this point in time, magazines that self-enforced censorship had "adult only" marks placed on their publications, which helped isolate eromanga expressions. Instead of content becoming softer due to censorship, content depicting sexual intercourse became ever more radical, and the responsibilities placed on editors and artists grew.

I would like to assert that this was the moment whereas an expression, the cross-section view, was rediscovered. Of course, before this point, because depicting the actual union of genitalia was disdained, the affinity of the cross-section view wasn't very good.

However, with the beginning of the hardcore era, with content becoming more sexually explicit (one could call it a reinforcement of depictions), people began to see the cross-section view in a new light, and thus, the cross-section view took center stage at last.

Just as the *nipple afterimage* rode the waves of the *kyounyu* boom and developed by keeping pace with it, the cross-section view rode the waves of the hardening of eromanga, finally bringing its slow start to a close.

The Cross-Section View and Guro Have an Affinity for Each Other

Even amongst seasoned eromanga readers, there are a great deal many that are uncomfortable when it comes to the cross-section view. These readers tend to agree that its use is very *guro* (grotesque), and it makes them feel sick.

There may be some people out there that when they see an anatomical picture, they may get turned on by it. Originally, anatomical pictures are grotesque in nature, but the erotic components of them that have been strengthening from the '90s onward, helped make the cross-section view a standard within eromanga. Even within bishojo comics and anime, it was thought that the affinity between the two (the erotic and the grotesque) wasn't very good at all.

Nevertheless, there is indeed a genre of manga where the erotic and grotesque have great chemistry with each other—*eroguro.* It is a horror genre, with content in the spirit of the so-called 1980s "splatter boom." But even though eromanga went through a hardening, initially readers were still reluctant to dive into the blend of *ero* and *guro.*

What brought about the heightening of eromanga readers' cross-section view literacy was a group of artists and creators that had a taste for horror, and a tolerance for the cross-section view. Of that group, one creator stands out as the "Cross-Section View Master" or the "Cross-Section View Noble." He is known for drawing out the maximum charm of the cross-section view in his work, and also for helping to make the cross-section view a standard expression within the genre.

His name is John. K Pe-ta.

As one can tell from how he converted famous splatter film director John Carpenter's name into a Japanese pen name, he helped to assert the erotic qualities of the cross-section view.

How did he marry the cross-section view to the erotic, I wonder? And what possibilities did he see within this expression?

I decided to go straight to the source to find out.

A
B
C

INTERVIEW WITH
JOHN K. PE-TA

"I think that the cross-section view is fantasy."

PROFILE

His name is hard to get past. Debuted in *Bessatsu Young Magazine* (Kodansha), he has contributed to Core Magazine's *Manga Bangaichi* and Toen Shobou's *Comic Jumbo*. He caught an editor's eye and became an eromanga creator. He used bold examples of the cross-section view to the point of being called the "Cross-Section View Master" and "Cross-Section View Noble." His expressions depict humans as if made of rubber, utilizing comedy often in his work. He is also considered the founding father of the new "honwaka ryoujoku" (comfy humiliation) genre, which has come to possess some of eromanga's most cult-like fans. A former assistant to Harold Sakuishi (***BECK*** and ***Seven Shakespeares***); his hobbies include participating in airsoft games.

A: ***Geki!! Monzetsu Operation*** (2005, Toen Shobou)
Large panel cross-section view from his early days.

B: ***Tokimeki Monzetsu Vulcan!!*** (2008, Core Magazine)
She's vomiting because a big penis is punishing her insides.

C: ***Super Monzetsu Megabitch*** (2010, Core Magazine)
Her stomach is bulging after insertion

“From my debut onward, it’s been all about the cross-section view.”

—In your career, you’ve drawn many a cross-section view expression. But I’ve been able to determine that you did so even in your eromanga debut (4-22)!

John K. Pe-ta (JKP): Oh, you’re right. They haven’t been moderate or reserved in the least, either.

—And why was that?

JKP: It didn’t meet certain requirements. Well, more like, it didn’t have enough pages. (laughs)

Apparently, an editor-in-chief at the time said, “Because you haven’t fulfilled these requirements, you can’t participate.” But the editor in charge of the project said that my project was “interesting enough,” so he overrode the other person, and because of that I was able to make my debut. I’m still grateful for that.

4-22: ***JKP’s World*** (*John K. Pe-ta no Sekai*; 2005, Toen Shobou)
His first eromanga contribution to Core Magazine, entitled “Jet Kentauros.”

—And at that time, did you know about the cross-section view expression?

JKP: I did, but I didn’t really think it was very erotic. I thought it was an expression used to tie things together and explain them, and nothing more than that.

I think it was around 2002 when I finally got how erotic it could be, thanks to Type.90’s work released at that time (4-23)! I think it was a collection of their early works, but I had this sense of solidarity with the way they drew uteruses and other innards. The way they drew breasts and female genitals in a way that could excite men, and then tie it all together with the cross-section view... When I saw that, I was like, "This is amazing!" I think it only had one panel with it, too, but regardless, I read it and fell in love with it. I remember doing that with reckless abandon. That page alone probably divided the book into two pieces. (laughs)

—Wow, it must've been a thunderclap out of the blue. As if you had awakened to a new sense of eros.

JKP: It was quite the jolt. But at that time, there weren't many creators drawing things with the cross-section view as of yet. I really wanted to see more of the content I liked, so I started to draw my own stuff.

—Aside from Type.90, what other creators and artists have influenced you?

4-23: ***Juice of Girl*** (*Shojo Jiru*; Type.90 2002, Shobunkan)

4-24: ***Freshness Abnormal*** (*Sawayaka Abnormal*; Henmaru Machino 2007, Toen Shobou)

JKP: Henmaru Machino is definitely a big one. His was the first eromanga I ever bought, so there's definitely a big influence from him on my work (4-24). When I debuted, I held a wish deep in my heart. I hoped I could become an eromanga artist with extreme content like Henmaru.

"When you think of it that way, what's inside of us isn't real, and precisely because of that reason, it's very valuable."

—The cross-section view existed way before then, but since you started putting out your work, the use of it has exploded within the genre.

JKP: It definitely is erotic, and no one else was doing it. I thought that if I drew the cross-section view as if it were a large panel, that my work would stand out that way. Perhaps that was a bit of a wicked motivation. I always loved splatter-type horror from the '80s, and I wanted to draw a manga like that, and that's exactly why I entered this industry. And thinking about it, I thought that the cross-section view was a good fit with my work. I wasn't able to make my debut a horror title, but when you really think about it, eromanga is a genre where anything is possible. I figured because it's a genre where anything is possible, I could draw whatever I wanted, including innards. (laughs)

—So, the affinity between the cross-section view and with how it handles organs is strong after all. It works well with the horror genre. I know this because your pen name is taken from a splatter era director. (laughs)

JKP: Yes, my name is a parody of John Carpenter's name. Other contenders were a parody of director Lucio Felci's name, which would have been turned into Lucio Furuchi. Mix up the syllables and Sam Raimi's name would have been turned into Misa Murai. As you can tell, I had horror on the brain back then. (laughs)

But going back to the cross-section view for a moment… Female genitalia are inside of the body, and it looks really slick inside, doesn't it? But the way organs are arranged in there is more complex than people know. I'm aware this is grotesque but there's a certain eroticism in that.

—I think that one's reaction to the cross-section view depends on the person looking at it, and their boundaries are dependent on one's sense of reality. The way you've drawn sex scenes, where arms are thrust both into the body and we get to see how our organs look inside, has a sense of the fantastic to it. I saw a movie about the human body recently, so I feel that the way you draw your sex scenes is incredibly erotic.

JKP: Ah, when I saw those scenes, I was surprised too. When you think of it that way, what's inside of us isn't real, and precisely because of that reason, it's very valuable. But what's inside of us is really pretty wild.

—Mentally, were you disappointed by that?

JKP: No, not at all. I was pretty aroused by it. I was able to see what I'd been wanting to see. But when I went to go draw manga after seeing it, I wondered if there was value in drawing it. It was a very strange, complicated feeling.

—Just to confirm, the reason why you started drawing manga like this wasn't because you were influenced by real life movies, but rather, because the content wasn't out there? Life caught up to you at last, in other words.

JKP: Yes, of course. It was a half happy, half disappointed feeling. Eromanga allows sex to be portrayed realistically but throw the cross-section view in the mix and it takes on a sense of the fantastic. So, I think that the artist has some true freedom to use when they draw. When life does come at you fast like that, then it's even more important to add the element of the fantastic to your work. But if you're going to go that far, then there's the question of if it's even still erotic at all.

I myself love the cross-section view, and because I've drawn so much of it, I've had to start being careful about it. At the same time, when you work with such niche content, you get stubborn and bullheaded and you start to escalate things. After a certain point, I lost track of what was erotic, and what was grotesque. (laughs)

—That's definitely a condition all mangaka suffer, I think. Your sense of the erotic becomes paralyzed.

JKP: In my case, I was worried about something a bit different, but I think that's about when I hit a slump.

"The sphere of what is considered 'erotic' is expanding."

—A special characteristic of your work is how you draw your cross-section view in large round slices, or as you call it, a "large panel." It's quite a beautiful form of the expression.

JKP: Nah, I think all the youngsters out there are better. In my case, in my early career, I drew all of the organs myself. Uterus, large intestine, small intestine, so on and so forth. But then I decided it would be a bad thing to draw too much, you know? So now when I draw this expression, for female genitalia, I now just draw a uterus, and for the anus, I draw the colon. That's the attitude I'm taking so that I don't overdraw things. But when you insert something in a body that has a big capacity [for holding things], it's more convincing to draw the whole body. (laughs)

—As is custom within the eromanga world, external genitalia usually need

censorship, whereas internal genitalia have been left alone. And though there hasn't been any political controversy, I think that, as custom, most folks have decided that internal genitalia aren't erotic. However, because the cross-section view is so in vogue right now, there's the issue of joint ownership of that feeling that it is erotic...

JKP: I do think that there's always the possibility that those organs will be censored one day. So I'm a bit concerned about that, as it's kind of a scary idea. If it does happen, it might become a bit of a strange game of cat and mouse with enforcement.

In my early career, I drew uteruses because I thought they were erotic, of course. But in the last five years, me and a few others have been drawing content with the goal of making ovaries erotic, and I think there's a general awareness out there that the sphere of what is considered erotic is expanding. And of course, it's within the realm of fantasy, but now there's content coming out where there's people orgasming from the act of ovulation.

—The recent development of the cross-section view as an expression really has been quite considerable.

JKP: The girls drawn with it have been really cute, while the cross-section views used have been erotic; it's really kind of troubling. (laughs)

I never really wanted to draw content that only used this expression, but I did want to draw the expansion of female genitalia. Bodies that have genitalia like that should also have hollow stomachs, right? But that's hard to portray on the outside without an expression, and the cross-section view is able to utilize a way to reveal what is happening properly.

—Ah, I see. You mean that using the cross-section view shows what's going on inside the body effectively?

JKP: In people's scripts, they always say, "I'm going deep inside of you." But by only saying it, it's amorphous and hard to understand. When you use the cross-section view in that situation, everything becomes super simple to the reader.

When I draw the insertion process with a big penis, it tends to kind of oppress the female organs, so I use vomiting to express how that process has affected the girl in question. But when you use the cross-section in that way, I think that it's really quite effective. When you see how a big dick puts pressure on the stomach, it's no wonder why the girl is vomiting (pg. 195-B). Because when you think about it physics-wise, when you insert something with a lot of mass, of course it's gonna push something else out. That's how I'm using eromanga mechanics, I guess. (laughs)

—Ah yes, the law of the conservation of mass as it relates to the female body. (laughs)

JKP: I got a bit mad recently because I've been thinking about the cross-section view and organs. People need to stop using other expressions. Recently I was told that I needed to "think more about using sound effects and other elements" and that pissed me off. (laughs)

—Ordinary eromanga creators have different emphases they pursue in their work. Another special characteristic of your work is that you tend to use the "large panel" version of the cross-section view, and that makes it very bewitching to behold.

JKP: I figured out years ago that if I have twenty pages to draw, I'm going to spend five of them using the "large panel method." Doing things that way tends to make my work more eye-catching.

—You call it large panel, but what you're basically doing is using one whole page for a version of the cross-section view, right? I think that method of use for this expression really shows me your true worth to the genre.

JKP: I am aware of that. Why won't others use the expression this way? If they won't, I will. (laughs)

—In your case, you tend to mainly use the cross-section view from the side, right?

JKP: Using it that way is more fun because you can bisect the whole body that way. One of the biggest pains in the ass is doing diagonal composition. Depicting organs that way is tough. (laughs)

—Do you think a certain paranoia will develop if people start wondering if the cross-section view used in eromanga is proper?

JKP: Sometimes when I work, I recheck old medical textbooks, but then someone takes a stance on how it's impossible to draw [body] parts correctly, so I've decided to draw things in a more deformed style. Of course, I draw erotic content, but I mostly want to shock my readers. So that's why I draw insane types of sex and weird insertions. In that way, *Comic Jumbo* (Toen Shobou) has really let me do whatever I wanted in my time with them.

"The cross-section view and organs escape from the protagonist."

—Speaking of which, the pace at which you produce books is quite fast. If there were a word that would describe your work, I think it would be "monzetsu" (comfy agony).

JKP: Use of it has definitely increased, but when I debuted, no one really used that in their titles. Out of all of my work, the only book that doesn't have *monzetsu* in the title is ***Kiseki no Ana.*** At that time, editors told me not to use it in the title, and it was during the time when I'd hit a bit of a slump. I thought that it wouldn't really suffer without that word in the title.

—So, in terms of content, were you in a deadlock in your manga?

JKP: Up until 2012, most of my content was organs and the cross-section view, and my female protagonists were nothing but cyphers. That brought me to a dead-end, and I knew I couldn't continue like that. But it made me study a lot of really skilled creators' manga, and I realized that with female characters, using other versions of the cross-section view was the only way for me to go. That only took me fifteen years to figure out. (laughs)

—If anything, I thought that using simple female characters was your policy. Instead of giving them names, you always used pronouns like "her" or "she."

JKP: It's not a policy so much as I had no emotional attachment to those characters. I drew the depiction of those characters as optional extras in a script. When you have a twenty-page manga, it's kind of a pain to give every one of those characters a name.

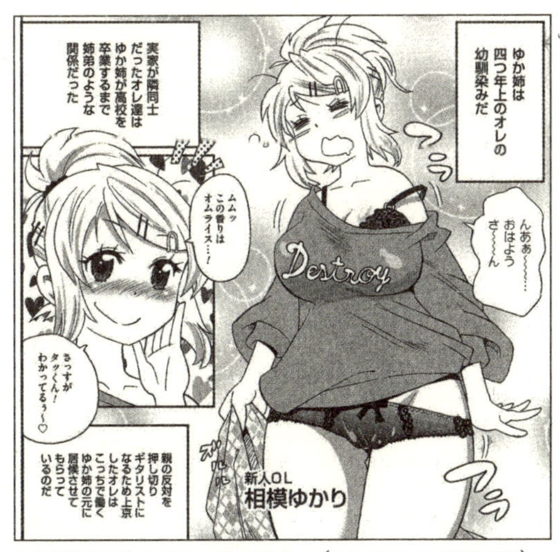

4-25: ***Waku Waku Monzetsu Maison*** (John K. Pe-ta 2015, GOT)

Recently I realized that in order to make my female characters really cute, I had to put a lot more effort in during the development stage. So now I name my female characters when I draw them (4-25).

—Admittedly, that shocked me a bit, too. When I read one of your recent books, even though the trends your stories follow haven't changed much, your characters really do stand out more now. Even the sisters of your characters have names now!

JKP: Before I entered my slump, all I ever watched was anime or stuff with robots in it. But recently I've started watching *moé* anime, and I've found myself having thoughts like, "Maybe having characters like this within 2D art is actually pretty good."

At a recent drinking party with other manga creators, I was talking with K-sensei (whose works I've been a huge fan of for some time). We were talking about falling in love with our own characters and somehow hearing those words were a huge shock. I realized I had to start doing that with my own characters and that conversation kind of woke me up to that way of thinking.

—So would you say that shock was enough to get you out of your slump?

JKP: An eromanga creator's job, in one way, is to draw cute naked girls. But in my case, I entered this world because I wanted to draw organs. It's taken me fifteen years to wake up to that fact, and I've taken many detours on the way. (laughs)

—But you've held on to your popularity, and you've been able to continue drawing organs all this time. So, I think you clearly have some talent there. (laughs)

JKP: I believe that the cross-section view is the ultimate component of the *eroguro* (erotic grotesque) aesthetic, and because of that, I only want to draw more of it. I think that there are more angles from which I can draw it, and maybe other organs that can be considered erotic, too!

—Like the spleen?

JKP: Possibly. Because the world of the cross-section view is a world full of fantasy, I'd love to see more artists drawing it. (laughs)

(Compiled August 2016)

The Encoding Process of the Cross-Section View

The cross-section view that appears within the eromanga genre puts an emphasis on the eros of intercourse itself and awakens the reader's voyeuristic fetishism of the act by explaining its unseen details. But it has thus far been used as nothing but a means to an end to spice up the act itself and has long been stuck in that role.

However, just as John K. Pe-ta said, since 2000, the cross-section view itself became erotic, heralding a new age of erotic literacy along with a new crop of creators. Herewith, one layer of the development of the cross-section view technique unfolded, and as a result, it underwent an encoding process as a meme.

Just as when people became conditioned to believe that a neck massager could be used as a sex toy, the cross-section view had the same phenomenon happen as well. It was as if the synapses in the brain connected the two in both cases (cross-section view and neck massager = erotic), and its use guaranteed the eroticism of any work it appeared in. However, this still required some scheming on behalf of the creator.

Just as we saw with the *nipple afterimage*, when an expression undergoes the encoding process, it isn't a stretch to emphasize how explosive its use and spread becomes shortly thereafter.

Now that I've explained the modern iteration of the cross-section view, next I'll go into a step-by-step explanation of how the expression has spread and evolved.

The Relationship Between the Creampie and Cross-Section View

When a penis is inserted into a vagina, what happens? And how does one relate that information?

While the cross-section view has helped provide answers to this problem, the way that it's been used for depictions of sex are not uniformly the same. As to why the expression evolved so quickly, there were many reasons—the hardening of eromanga, the relaxation of censorship rules, the rise of manga containing pornographic content like John K. Pe-ta's (where internal genitals were not subject to censorship). But I think there's one more big reason: the visualizing of the *nakadashi* (creampie; literally "shot inside") meme.

The *Creampie* is the act of male ejaculation during coitus, and when this big finish of sorts became a meme in eromanga it often results with the receiving partner reaching orgasm at the time of ejaculation. In scenes where the cross-section view is not used, those receiving would often cramp or spasm wildly as they are overwhelmed by the ejaculator. However, with the informative power of the cross-section view, it became a way to directly show the act of ejaculation within the body.

The *creampie* expression could explain, at the time of orgasm, the force, amount, time it takes, and other such factors in the ejaculation process. At the same time, it increased the amount of visual information transmitted, which added to its sense of realism. It transformed the work into a multifaceted sensual entity akin to a movie theater equipped with IMAX and 3D or 4DX Dolby Digital sound.

In the porn industry, a *bukkake* (facial) would be used to create the big finish as a means of strengthening the visual information to the audience, and that too began to develop as a meme. In a way, a *bukkake* would be a "sotodashi" (shot outside). And eromanga has a track record of borrowing things from that particular industry, so this case was no different.

As a result, the *creampie* meme developed the concepts of force, frankly unrealistic amounts of ejaculate, and the effect of strange sound effects in eromanga. But the evolution of the cross-section view easily obliterated it. After 2000, popular hardcore artists like Jogi Tsukino (4-26), Sessyu Takemura (4-27), Kinohitoshi (4-28), DISTANCE (4-29), Shiwasu no Okina (4-30), Kengo Yonekura (4-31), and Fuusen Club (4-32), whom all have exceptional art skills and are all great examples of proof of how the influence of the cross-section view on eromanga at the time was only increasing.

The current iteration of the expression, though, has the following pattern... In the act of intercourse, after the penis is inserted in the vagina, the penis expands, and the process of the phallus invading the female genitalia is portrayed, it visually transmits the information to the reader as to how the vaginal walls and muscles have clamped down onto it. Piston movements and rhythm are then portrayed, followed by ejaculation into the uterus. This pattern is known as the "righteous approach."

In many cases, the cross-section view itself is used in concert with portrayal of female expressions and sexual positions, as well as showing movement both inside and outside of the genitals. The so-called round slices used with the cross-section view are strong, but recently, the "penetration expression" where both the vagina and uterus are floating in the panel is a broader interpretation of the cross-section.

This *penetration expression* is a more developed version of the expression used by Tou Moriyama in his early works. As a stronger feeling of tone developed, it evolved to show the delicacy of internal organs, and this expression is shown as flooding the uterus with semen.

The common classic version of the cross-section view shows a horizontal view like an MRI, concentrating only on the genitals that are being inserted (4-33, 34). When artists want to emphasize the depth of penetration by the penis, you could say this was one of the most effective expressions to use in order to transmit that information. Some outright showed how the vagina was clamping onto the penis, but no matter how you slice it, the uterus becomes the protagonist (4-35~37). The male genitalia reach the uterus, but the versions of the cross-section view that are perhaps the best at strongly relaying this information tend to draw the endeavor of the moment of ejaculation directly into the uterus.

The *penetration expression* is widely used in case of different sexual positions, like riding in a sitting position or in cowgirl, but its use in concert with showing how the penis is invading a character's insides is perhaps the most effective method to render these scenes (4-38, 39).

However, it should be noted that the version of the cross-section view where the artist focuses the female partner's facial expressions at the moment of orgasm is a separate, uterine-focused cross-section view expression.

The deployment of the "ejaculation into the uterus view" tends to separate the woman's face from her uterus, with her face usually floating nearby. This version tends to synchronize well when the artist centers the focus to what is being felt by the protagonist's uterus (4-40, 41).

This "synchronization rate" increases even more, as does its degree of artistry when everything else of and about the woman in a work is in the background but the uterus, once again focusing on the uterus. When one sees this sort of artistic direction and design, you don't get a sense of anything else but sex and sexuality, and thus helps the cross-section view to evolve (4-42, 43).

The part that ejaculation plays with the cross-section view can be effective by helping make the process of sex itself easier to understand. RAYMON has portrayed anal sex by showing the intestines full of semen after ejaculation (4-44).

In Mitsuka Hattori's case, she further uses the cross-section view with

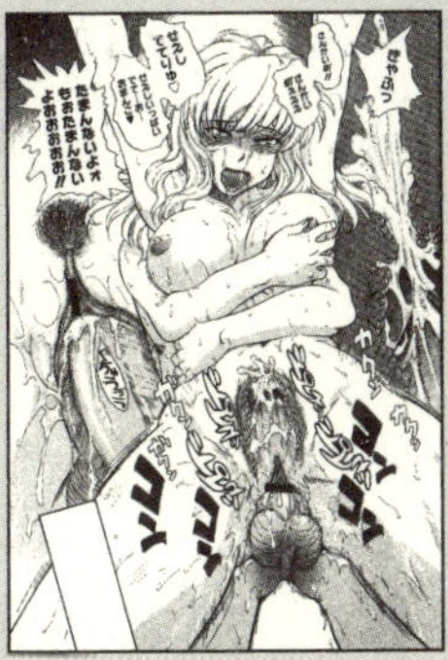

4-26: ***B-Flat 38'C Loveberry Twins*** (Jogi Tsukino 2004, Core Magazine)

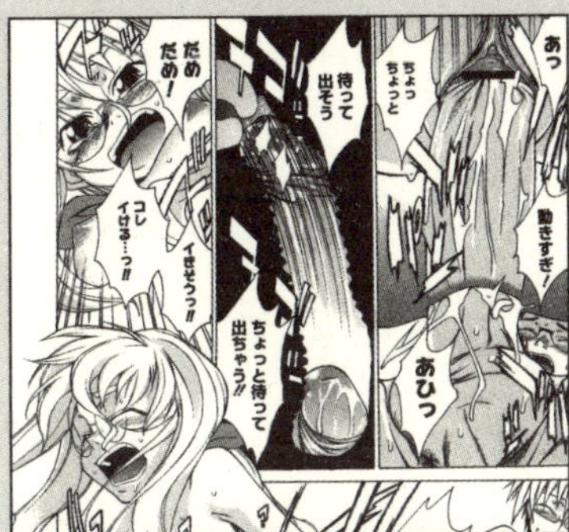

4-27: ***Domin-8 Me!*** (*TAKE ON ME*; Soccyu Takemura 2004, Core Magazine/ Fantagraphics)

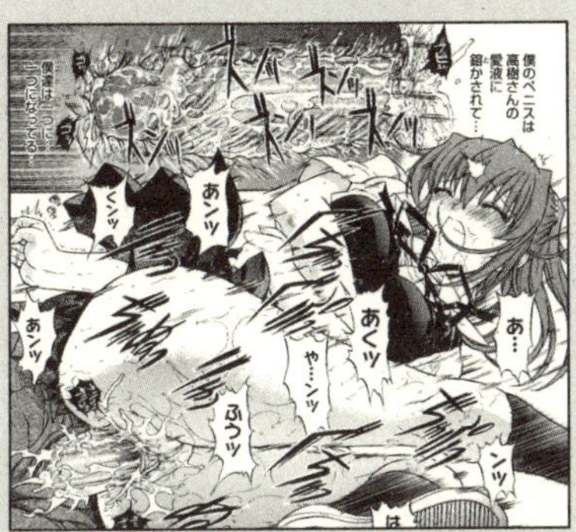

4-28: ***KinshinSoukan*** (Kinohitoshi 2004, Core Magazine)

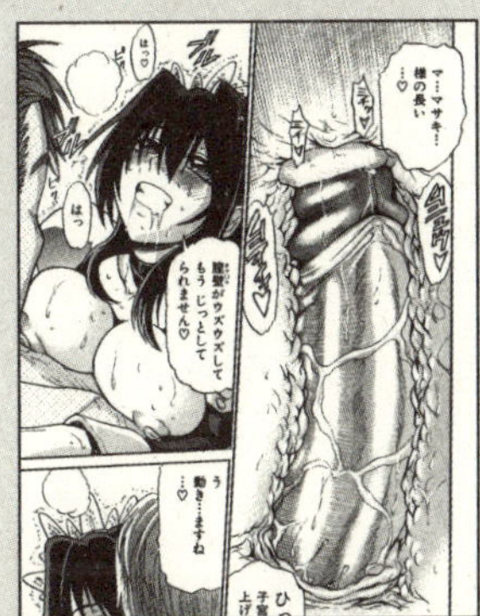

4-29: ***MySlave*** (DISTANCE 2004, JC Publishing)

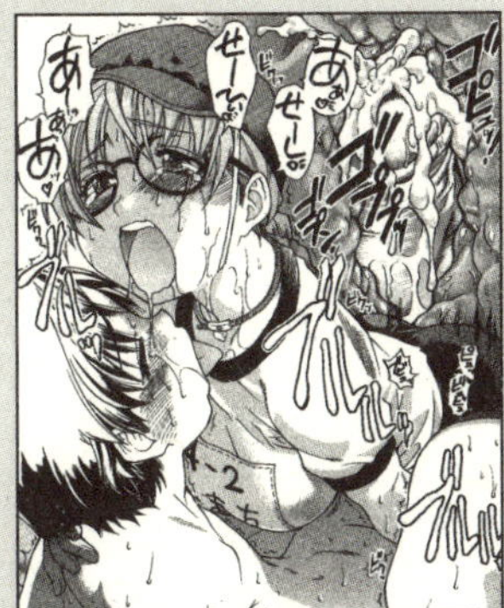

4-30: ***SEISO TSUI DANSHA*** (Shiwasu no Okina 2003, Hit Publishing)

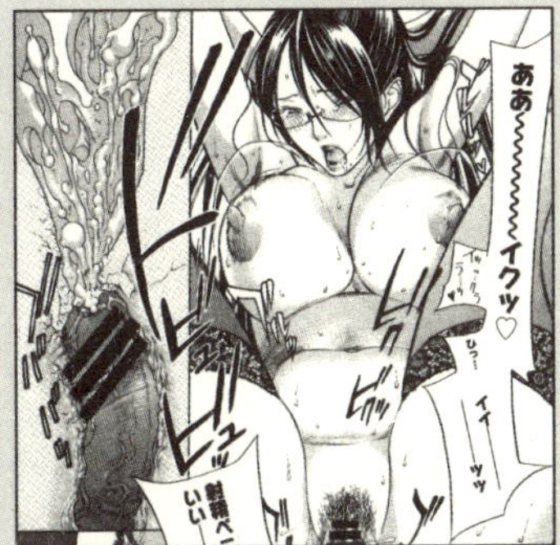

4-31: "Suzuki-kun no Juunan" (Kengo Yonekura 2005, Core Magazine)

4-32: "Kairaku-G" (Fuusen Club 2004, TI NET)

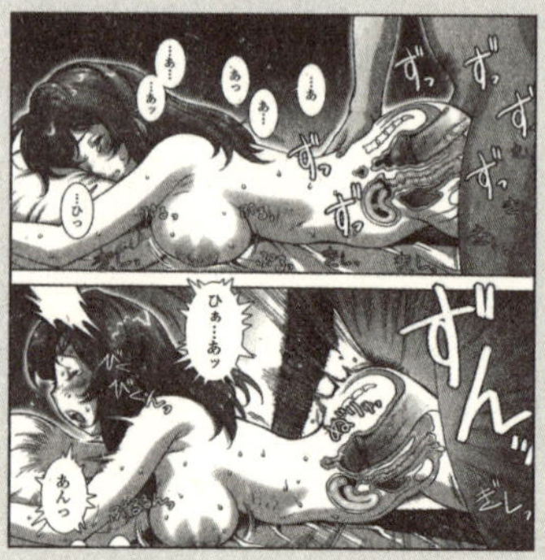

4-33: ***PRETTY COOL*** (Sengoku-kun 2009, Akaneshinsha)

4-34: ***Netorare New Heroine*** (Kon-Kit 2013, Issuisha/FAKKU)

4-35: ***Cheerful Eros Project*** (*Akarui Eros Keikaku*; Yuzuki N-Dash 2007, Akaneshinsha/Icarus)

4-36: "Sexgiving Day" (*Onii-chan Kansha-sai*; Knuckle Curve 2015, Wanimagazine)

4-37: "Natsu no NokoriKa" (Amayumi 2016, Fujimi Publishing)

the uterus itself in order to later show it full of semen after ejaculation. In doing so, she invented the "double layer cross-section view" (4-45). When compared with the regular cross-section view, making more cuts of it advanced the difficulty of the technique.

Speaking of skill, using 3D modeling and CAD software when drawing this expression lends the cross-section view a very delicate, exquisite air (4-46).

The intended targets for use with the cross-section view aren't limited to just the anus or vagina. Instances of fellatio with the cross-section view have been portrayed in many works. The artist GESUNDHEIT drew the cross-section view of an oral ejaculation with enough force that it passed down the throat, through the stomach, into the small intestine (4-47). You can tell by looking at those panels that there is a strong sense of "Pe-ta-ism" that can be felt throughout the work. It would be appropriate to say that it was a bold use of the expression.

There followed a cross-section perspective of anything a man could insert his penis into. Recently, it seems that the process leading up to ejaculation itself has become an expression. This expression has been in use roughly since 2010 when it started to see an increase in use, to the point where a process of a man ejaculating without resting was portrayed.

This technique uses the cross-section view by featuring semen gradually rushing up the urethra, as if it were magma rising from deep within the earth to the surface, showing an eruption of semen in terms of force. I think its name is something to the effect of the "rising magma view," but it isn't just about the flow of semen, but also the moment of ejaculation itself, capturing the cross-section view. To that end, the magma that Shindou draws shows the widening of the urethra, as though the "magma" here is quite thick, which tangibly seems to exert pressure on the testicles themselves (4-48).

And in this way, with the process of reaching ejaculation drawn in many different ways, the cross-section view has evolved. From the testicles to the testicular epithelium to the ejaculatory duct; the prostate to the urethra, to the ultimate destination of the urethra, where semen floods into the uterus... The journey that we take with the cross-section view is a great journey indeed. It is a great struggle for existence, drawing throbbing sperm, making contact with eggs as if in a dream.

Past that, images become part of the spiritual or psychological world (4-49~53). When it gets to this point, it goes past the realm of the erotic, to where one can only feel moved by the mystery of life itself. While medically, there are many points where there is suspicion as to whether or not this information is scientifically correct, it proves that using manga in the role of sex education is difficult.

Moreover, if we return upstream to the '70s, we find that Osamu Tezuka wanted to draw a sex-ed manga, which resulted in ***Yakeppachi's Maria*** (1970, Akita Shoten, 4-54). Go Nagai's ***Harenchi Gakuen*** (1978, Shueisha) had extreme sexual expressions, which I can say resisted causing a controversy at the time. However, in this particular work, there is a depiction of an expression close to the cross-section view. It simply explains the journey of the sperm to the uterus while using a scene in the penis to do so. While this depiction might have had a fixed design aimed towards sex appeal, it has been thought that throughout this manga's run, its primary purpose was to transmit sexual knowledge to the audience and it paid close attention to that.

After bouncing from one place to another, I did not think that this particular depiction would end up resurfacing in the current eromanga era. While it is unclear as to whether Nagai was influenced by Tezuka's work, the expression evolved from a piece of sexual education to part of the eromanga canon. Paradoxically, if it presents the fact that one can understand the mysteries of life by enjoying erotic things, then the will of Tezuka has surpassed the genre. While I think he is possibly, ceaselessly, passing on the baton here, there is no possible way to confirm this theory. Which is really quite a shame. If he were still alive, though, Tezuka might say that he could "draw an even better eromanga."

In this way, this endlessly spreading expression depicting internal genitals has helped construct an entirely new world of fantasy. A special trait of the cross-section view in eromanga is how it's an all-knowing mirror reflecting both internal and external genitalia in synch producing new

4-38: "Moso no Saki made…" (Edara 2013, Issuisha)

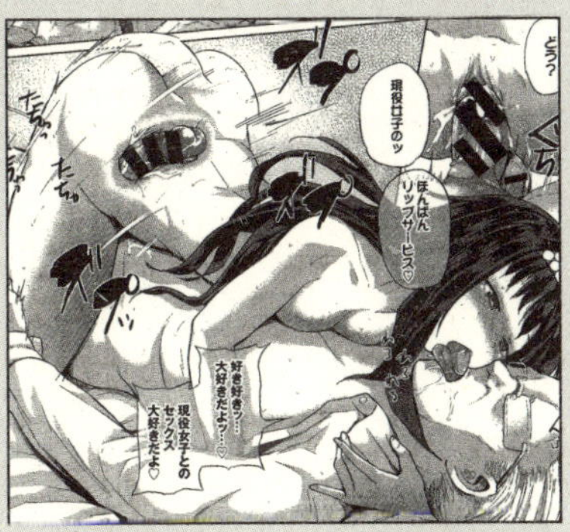

4-39: "Under Lip Service" (Yumenotanuki 2015, Bunendo)

4-40: "12-ji made Matenai!" (Isonogi 2016, GOT)

4-41: "Renai-gokko" (Hiryu Tawara 2016, Akaneshinsha)

4-42: "Ongaeshi no Tsuraoka-kun TS: Sakata" (Kei Narusawa 2016, Hit Publishing)

4-43: "Onee-chan Book Camp!" (Rei Yuki 2016, Sanwa Publishing)

4-44: "Sono Toko, Gakkou de", #1 (RAYMON 2006, Core Magazine)

4-45: "Hito de Nashi no Koi" (Mitsuka Hattori 2015, Issuisha)

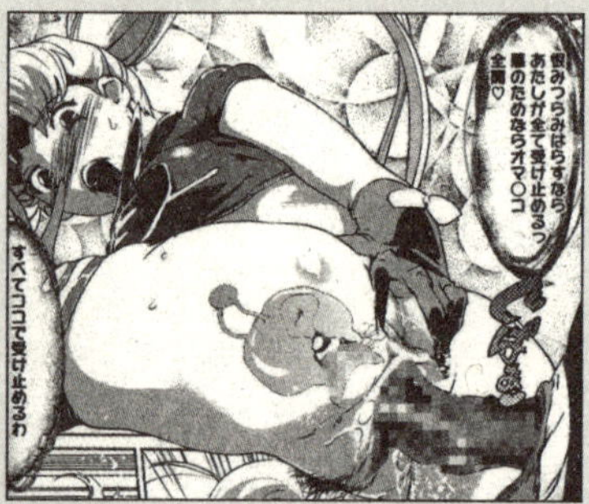

4-46: "Niku Maho no Okite" (CLONE Ningen 2014, Core Magazine)

4-47: "Inchou vs The World" (GESUNDHEIT 2016, LEED Publishing)

4-48: "Sisters Conflict" (Shindou 2014, Core Magazine)

4-49: "Futari no Tenkosei" (Takashi Shiran 2010, TI NET)

stories strictly within the limited worlds of genitals. Therefore, vaginas have become their own cosmos where new stories may start to unfold.

The Cross-Section View Creates a New Narrative

The act of sex is designed to show the love between men and women. However, apart from the affection between men and women, the cross-section view is also where both sets of genitals are drawn independently of each other. Both sets of genitals begin to carry their own will, creating yet another world.

I appointed artist F4U to tackle the expression in this book. F4U's work ***Sikorsky Tonight*** (*Konya no Sikorsky;* 2009, Core Magazine) depicts a world where genitals have their own will (4-55, 56). It is as if the female genitalia—when the male genitalia have been inserted—possess a will all their own, and the uterus speaks. It does that by opening the os uteri (or cervical os), and at times, as if strongly answering the penis, it sticks to the glans.

This is the story of love.

When the pleasure brought by the moment of orgasm hits the medulla oblongata, the cross-section view is used on the brain to emphasize how the character has taken a blow to the head.

Perhaps it would be appropriate to say that this is a surrealist use of the cross-section view (a *galaxy brain* of sorts).

All of the female organs—the uterus, the ovaries, the fallopian tubes, and so on—have sound effects, as if to show their pleasure at this moment and all have the cross-section view used. At times it seems even the heart itself shows its pleasure, and all the internal organs seem to carry their own facial expressions.

Recently, in a similar pattern of sex organs becoming characters, male genitals knock at the door to the womb, the os uteri, and one can even say that they kiss it in what is most likely the birth of a new type of love expression. LOW has depicted and rendered this story of love between two sets of genitals in their book and has proposed that this situation is the "kind cross-section view" (4-57, 58).

Kousuke has fixed the uterus as a reflection for the receiving female partner in his work; at times with it having a completely different, separate will than its owner, speaking through sound effects, thus creating another expression (4-59). In this way, the cross-section view has possibly evolved to become a new technique to create a new world of fantasy out of visualizing the (usually) unseen.

The Evolution and Spread of the Cross-Section View

The cross-section view has existed from the early days of manga, but its explosive growth did not happen until 2000 by way of evolving to become a delicate, subtle expression. It also evolved to become an indispensable meme for eromanga as a technique. It would not be inappropriate to say that it is not a simple explanatory device, but instead relies on a shared awareness on behalf of both the artist and the audience in order to undergo the encoding process.

Even if the cross-section view that the reader sees is not an intercourse version, as long as they think it's erotic, then that particular symbol will become stenciled upon their unconscious. Those feelings have helped fix this expression in place, which aided in overcoming the limits of the genre and allowed it to continue to develop.

Hentai anime, which handles the same type of sexual imagery as eromanga does, has also had the cross-section view established. Many recent hentai anime titles have taken advantage of 3D modeling during the production process, using the cross-section view to create a human model, which is fairly easy to do. If VR technology continues to evolve as it has been, you might be able to see your favorite angle of the sexual intercourse cross-section view sometime soon.

The cross-section view has been used in *BL,* as well. While anal sex is

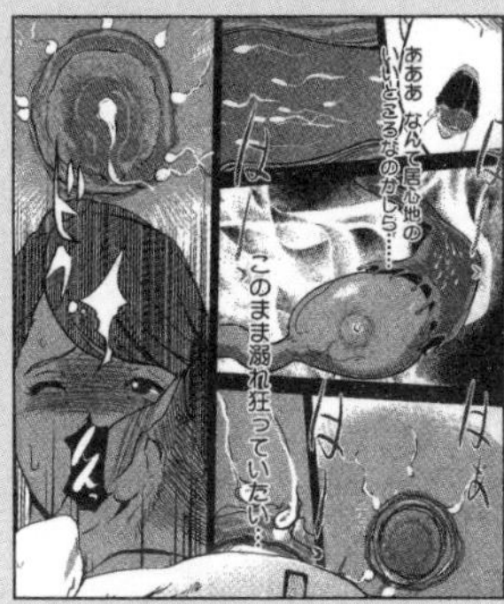

4-50: ***Confession de Miel Mére*** (*Mitsubo no Kokuhaku*; CLONE Ningen 2015, Core Magazine)

4-51: ***Jyusei Ganbou*** (Meet Sido 2015, Sanwa Publishing)

4-52: ***Jinro Kyoshitsu*** (Kyotaro Suzuki 2016, Hit Publishing)

4-53: "OPEN THE GIRL" (Hidari Ogawa 2016, Akaneshinsha)

4-54: ***Yakeppachi's Maria*** (Osamu Tezuka 1996, Akita Shoten; pocket edition)

4-55: ***Sikorsky Tonight*** (*Konya no Sikorsky*; F4U 2009, Core Magazine)

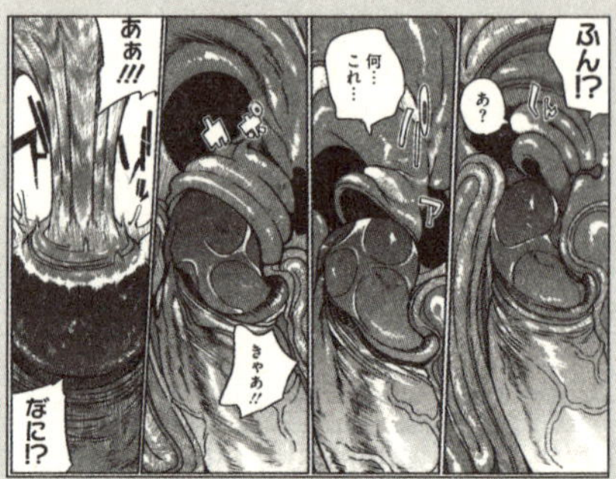

4-56: ***Sikorsky Tonight*** (*Konya no Sikorsky*; F4U 2009, Core Magazine)

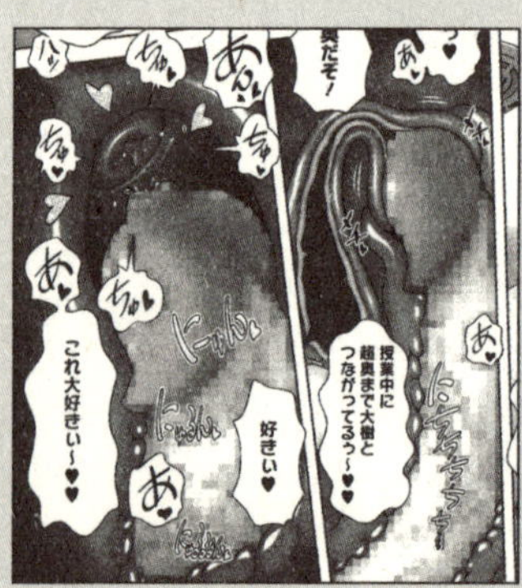

4-57: ***Chibitch Bitch*** (LOW 2014, Core Magazine)

4-58: "Hajimete no Hatsujo-ki" (LOW 2008, Core Magazine)

4-59: "Akumakko ♥ Sakyura" (Kousuke 2016, GOT)

the main type of penetrative sex within *BL,* the cross-section view is also used with organs not in the female body such as the prostate. The colon takes the place of the os uteri in this situation, reframing the male body in a frankly unthinkable way. Other ways of using the expression for male genitalia have included showing urethra torture and other such acts, but in recent years in male-targeted eromanga, masochistic play has become a focus in some stories. So, the amount of incidents where urethra torture has been depicted using the cross-section view has increased (4-60).

4-60: ***Punishment to Peeing Boy!*** (*Shoben Kozo no Oshioki!*; Ryo Sakurai 2014, Libre)

In recent years in the *otokonoko* (femboys) genre, there are similar themes much like I just described within standard BL, but because it is a male-targeted genre, there are many incidences of cute boys visually coded as girls that are drawn having anal sex. Even if it is still anal sex, one can see the schemes showing how the cross-section view has been incorporated into these cute *otokonoko* (4-61).

Within the encoding process, there is merit in how an expression compresses the information of the situation or condition that is happening and efficiently transmits it to the reader. The information that the artist compressed into the expression is kept alive by it, and independently updates itself and appends that information into yet another new expression. But to readers not versed in the literacy of sexual imagery, this is a double-edged sword. Because the cross-section

4-61: ***Chin ☆ COMPLETE*** (Chinzurena 2014, Mediax)

view carries a very strong visual image, to the readers who cannot understand the information compressed by it, it becomes a strongly repugnant expression to them. Or to say it conversely, as those failures become buried, and when new iterations and versions of the cross-section view are reclaimed and cultivated from that wasteland, new worlds should come into existence one after the other.

4-62: "3-nengo mo Koibito de Itai nodesu" (Ayato Sasakura 2017, Akaneshinsha)

Even in shojo manga there may be a possible use for the cross-section view, by showing a pounding heart during a love confession scene.

Finally, this is not a use of the cross-section view within eromanga that evokes arousal, but please allow me to introduce it anyway.

In eromanga, there is a technique used where the male body is not depicted but is nonetheless implied to be present called the "invisible man" or "minimalist man" (*danshari*; 4-62). In this situation there is the emphasis on the limbs of a cute girl, so the male body is not needed. However, the information that he is there nonetheless must be transmitted somehow. The male form is instead shown as half-transparent or fully transparent. And in its reverse, only the man's body is shown whereas the female body is shown through cuts (4-63). I think you can understand the reasoning here, and I myself think that depiction has a comedic sense to it and is rather funny. ✿

4-63: "Passion Tsushin" (IZAYOI 1999, Shinyusha)

The History of Hentai Manga

CHAPTER FIVE

The Genealogy of Ahegao

The Climax Is Eromanga's Platonic Ideal

In eromanga the most encoded element leading to the moment of climax (ejaculation and/or orgasm) is quite possibly the story that builds up to it.

In recent years, in terms of putting an emphasis on its immediate effectiveness as a pornographic medium, there has been a general trend that has led to the abridgment of foreplay to diversify what leads to climax and orgasm. This never-ceasing range of diversity is truly eromanga's ideal, and its pure identity.

Many artists have depicted the climax in various ways and with various schemes and stories. With regard to ejaculation, the use of expressions like the *cross-section view* have led to the development of a new range of expressions, such as the "creampie." These new changes include things like spewing semen at the moment of orgasm, using heavy breathing as a device, and many other variations of expressions we already know. But the most important meme of them all is the facial expression that is made at the moment of orgasm.

The facial expression made by female partners at the moment of orgasm has many names. For example, there is the *ikigao* (cumming face) and *acmegao* (acmé-face, from the French loanword "*acmé*," or orgasm). The moment the body rejoices in that pleasurable anguish, there is the *yogarigao* (satisfaction face). When the artist exerts their creativity and combines different expressions together along with plot devices and stories, a new expression is born.

The field of research centered around the *ikigao* is incredibly deep, but I would like to go into how in recent years, uses of the *ahegao* and its variations have spread at an explosive rate.

So how has this expression been used as a plot device, and how has it been universalized? I looked into it and found that the way it became accepted was completely different from that of the *nipple afterimage* or the *cross-section view*. It was more of a result of the various artists and creators' originality acting as an external influence than anything else.

What Is the Ahegao?

The *ahegao* is a trope mainly seen within eromanga, *eroge* (Japanese adult video games), and hentai anime. It is a pattern of facial expressions identifying the moment of the female partner's climax (the *ikigao*).

It is important to note here that a formal definition of this term has not yet been fixed within the genre (as of the original Japanese publication of this book). However, the following three traits have generally been recognized by many as its special characteristics:

1. **The whites of the eyes are visible or are close to becoming visible. The focus of the eyes is not fixed, nor are they "rape eyes," where the eyes are rolled up into the head and the pupils are not visible.**
2. **The mouth is open and the tongue is sticking out.**
3. **Saliva, mucus, sweat, and other bodily fluids are often present.**

The above three conditions are the major components of the *ahegao*. They do not necessarily need to be grouped together, but instead the strength of each individual factor helps raise that of the *ahegao's*. The recognition of the strength of those individual conditions has been turned into public knowledge.

If you look at the sample images provided (5-1~3), I think you'll get a general understanding as to what the *ahegao* looks like. When drawn properly, the facial expressions of the girls absolutely must not only show their pleasure and joy during the act of intercourse, but at the same time present how their appetites have been sated.

Chronologically, the *ahegao* was seen in doujinshi zines and hardcore eromanga since 2000. However, as eromanga became increasingly hardcore, the proper spread of the three conditions did not really begin until 2007. And in its present form, eromanga readers commonly use and understand the term *ahegao* for this visual expression.

Outside of the facial expression, the other concept is that of a "mind break," or a breakdown of the female partner's mental condition; where she goes mad from pleasure and acts as if she is a fool. Instead of an *ahegao*, the mind break variation of the expression is closer to a *hengao* (strange face). By adding that element of comedy and playing with the use of the *hengao* along with the *ikigao*, the impact of these new expressions becomes quite interesting indeed.

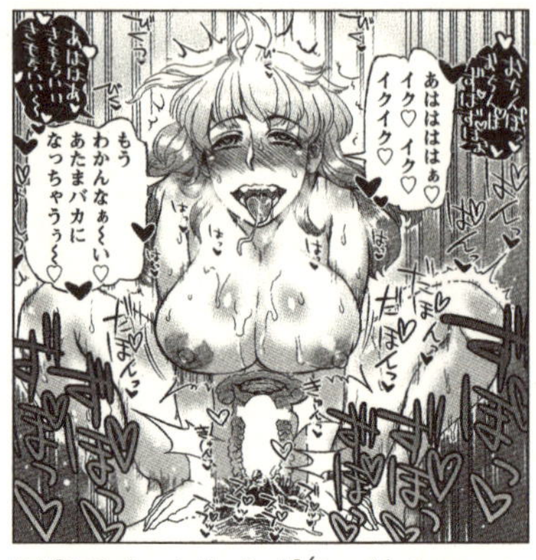

5-1: "Patissiere in the Dark" (Denshin Ameyama 2016, Angel Publishing)

Consequently, there is a visual impact from this expression. So, in recent years, this expression has evolved and undergone the encoding process within eromanga.

As I said earlier, there is still no standardized definition of *ahegao*, but according to the *Jitsuyou Nihongo Hyougen Jiten* (a Japanese web dictionary; http://www.weblio.jp), the *ahegao* is "a visual expression that shows someone immersed in ecstasy, having lost all their energy yet still physically struggling. An *acmegao*."

In terms of an explanation, instead of strictly enforcing the three conditions I covered previously, the most important quality is that the character is in ecstasy. However, for this book, I would like to fix the *ahegao's* main three conditions as an axis and proceed from there.

5-2: ***Kanyo Shojo*** (Ippon Nagare 2015, Hit Publishing)

There are many theories as to what the "ahe" in ahegao means, including the theory that the etymology comes from the sound of heavy breathing ("ahe ahe") when the character is really feeling what her

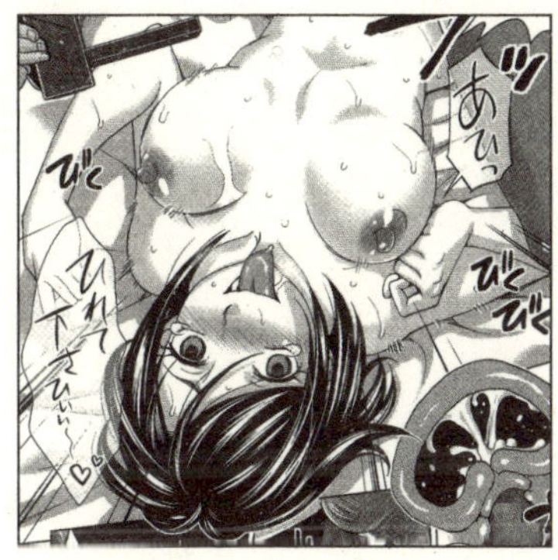

5-3: "Bijin OL Hame Hajime!" (Clock Asakura 2015, Issuisha)

partner is giving them. It has been said that this is also the etymology of the Japanese verb *aheru*, the act of a sex partner making an *ahegao* facial expression during sex.

We can see the spread of this term begin in 2006. While it is a word where the degree of familiarity with it (within eromanga) has risen considerably, it turns out this word has actually been around since the 1990s, mostly used in pornographic publications. However, the meaning of the word at that time has evolved, as it previously was used as a frame of reference within magazines at the time. It also was not the almost comical-looking *ikigao* we see today, but instead was a facial expression of ecstasy, as if women were losing consciousness. Therefore, it tended to leave a far simpler impression on the reader.

In the February 1994 issue of the erotic pin-up magazine *Muscat Note* (Taiyou Tosho), there is a special article called the "SPERMA Ahegao Bijin GALLERY." In that piece, the model's facial expression does not fulfill the requirements as presented by the three *ahegao* conditions of today (5-4). It may be the case that because it is a feature focusing on *bukkake*, the *ahegao* featured is one combined with facial ejaculation, to which there may not have been much of a meaning to the way *ahegao* was used here at all. During this time, though there were many erotic pin up magazines in publication that focused on the topic (even

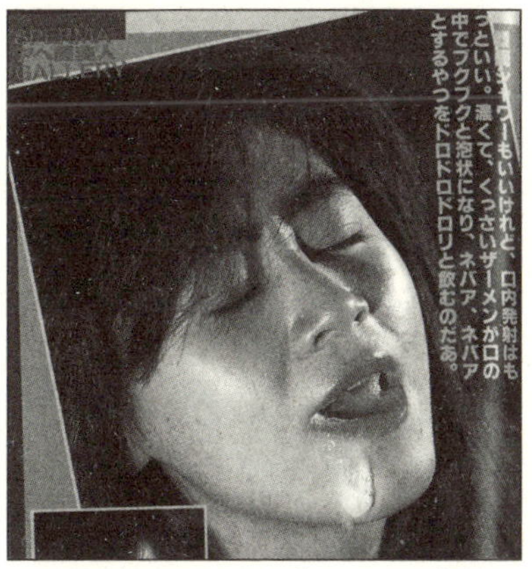

5-4: *Muscat Note*, Feb 1994 (Taiyou Tosho) Photo of a woman with a "sperm ahegao."

devoting special issues to it), there was no uniformity as to how it was visually represented. The facial expression being represented was one of ecstasy but had no formal name. The publications were seemingly more concerned with the task of adding that nuance to the expression and just used it that way.

Accordingly, it would be natural to think that the continuity of the modern *ahegao* used in eromanga has a loose connection to this predecessor indeed. For the word that, up until that point, had such infrequent depictions within the eromanga industry, a new definition was appended. I happen to think that this development only happened within eromanga.

If this indeed is the case, then there is a second point of ignition: a second impact, if you will. But when and how did it happen? I'll go into those details soon. First, I would like to expound upon the connotation of the meaning of the term, as well as the different facial expressions and other details of this phrase.

The Reasoning Behind the Ahegao

If someone not familiar with eromanga were to see the ahegao, they would be more likely to get the impression that it is a funny, eccentric expression before recognizing that it is a depiction of ecstasy. But even amongst eromanga readers, quite a lot of them are uncomfortable with it, want the expression removed, or feel it is too extreme for them. And even amongst eromanga creators, there are those that do not want to put it in their work; with some using any other expression but the ahegao. That is how much of an impact this facial expression has made. It is clear, the ahegao definitely leaves an impact on those that have seen it, perhaps nothing but an impact after the fact.

Regardless, eromanga is also a story-telling medium. In order to use this expression, there must be a reason to do so. I listed the three conditions that make up the major components of the expression, but there is many a variation in the expressions related to the situation, emotions, and

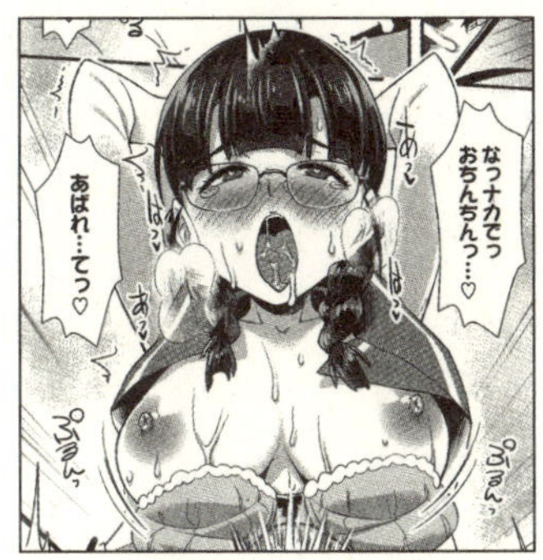

5-5: "Hokago Nymphomania" (Shimon Tomomimi 2016, Bunendo)

pleasure this expression represents.

I also said before that the ahegao is a subspecies of the *ikigao*, but there are times that it has been used other than the moment of climax (finishing). In that sense, it is not a strict subset of the *ikigao,* but instead, one could say that it is but one version of the facial expressions that are used by artists when drawing sex scenes. So above all, a composite or combination of those three emotion-related expressions must exist.

The first emotion-related expression is one that reflects pleasure, ecstasy, and rapture; three of the more major emotion-related expressions used in depictions of sex. Because it is supposed to be pleasure beyond one's imagination, symptoms like the following are all included: mental haziness, a chaotic mental state, loss of energy and body control, having their holes become wet, mental breakdown, and in many cases, the receiving partner acting foolishly (5-5~7).

Now, the most important thing at this juncture is how the artist will render pleasure and enjoyment. As an answer, it is thought that a very extreme version of the ahegao evolved to fill this need. In ShindoL's debut work, ***Sarashi-Ai*** (2010, TI NET), at the moment of orgasm, the character has become mentally hazy and has had her energy sapped. He has the character secreting tears, nasal mucus, sweat, and vaginal fluids in what is a magnificently drawn ahegao (5-8).

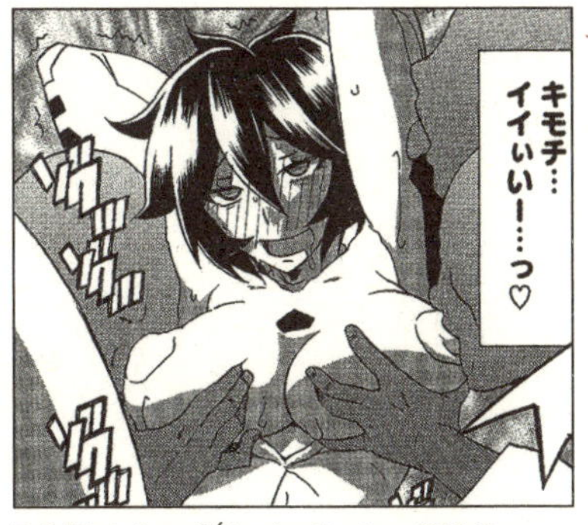

5-6: "Elekutorea" (Kyoden Sanbun 2013, Core Magazine)

In current depictions of the ahegao, to illustrate the difference between facial expressions the popular approach has been to illustrate the depth of pleasure the character is undergoing. This approach is the one that perhaps has the highest degree of recognition.

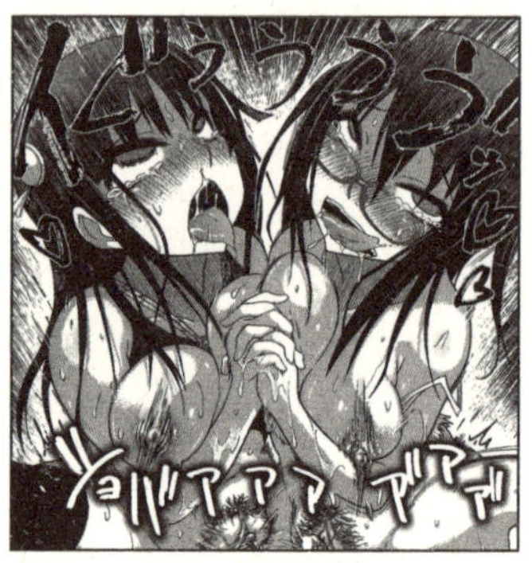

5-7: ***Yutosei no MuchiMuchi Chigoku*** (Marukidou 2013, TI NET)

The second emotion-related expression is one that shows reluctance, fear, and despair; or in other words, one that shows the negative emotional components. This version of the expression is the one used the most as a plot device to develop the story within humiliation stories. It is also the one used the most in stories with rape, where the victim displays an ahegao during the act. This version shows how the act is pushed upon them as well as the fear and panic they experience as they are disgraced. In order to increase the strength of this expression, there is an even more extreme facial expression that was developed.

However, in order to justify the male-leaning "circumstances doctrine" excuse of "this act was pushed on me but I'm enjoying it," there have been many cases where positive emotional components like pleasure are combined with the negative ones in order to do so. The cases where this does not happen has created a growing trend where this function changes the pornographic elements to violent ones within the story.

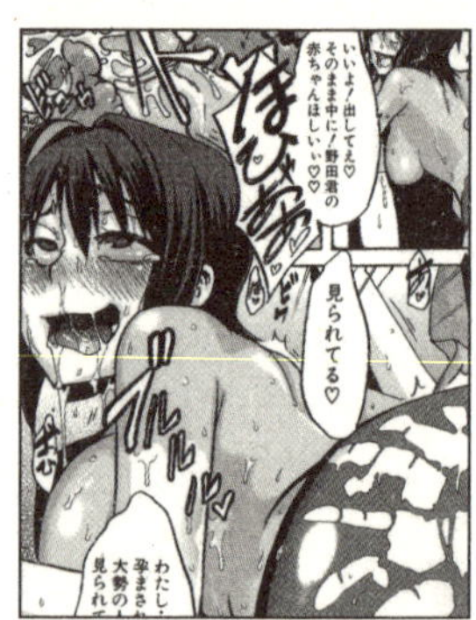

5-8: ***Sarashi-Ai*** (ShindoL 2010, TI NET)

In the humiliation comics that Hirohisa Onikubo specializes in, the audience feels the resistance and fear that the girls being gang raped feel, all the while receiving a sense of "it was pushed on me, but I'm enjoying it" since they all have ahegao (5-9). The savage humiliation eromanga that artist OYSTER creates feature a similar case of the victim's facial expression of despair turning to that of an ahegao as the scenes progress (5-10). While she is being both mentally and physically tortured, her mental state begins to break down as she weeps. So as her tongue hangs out, one can also see how her dignity has been broken down as well.

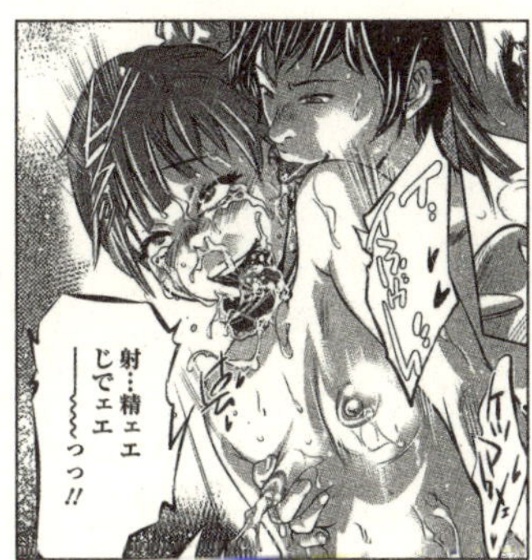

5-9: ***Chikusha no Nushi*** (Hirohisa Onikubo 2011, Angel Publishing)

These scenes in these two examples differ, but both have a build-up that leads to the use of the ahegao. The "negative emotion leading to ahegao" pattern is one of the oldest ones with regard to the history of the expression, and one that has been in use since the days of *ero-gekiga.* It is also a traditional *ikigao.*

The third emotion-related version is one that includes domination, submission, and loyalty. As a basic rule, this expression is an extension of the humiliation genre, and initially, the feeling of resistance on behalf of the victim is broken. In order to transmit to the reader the difference between the before and after of the victim giving in to feelings of pleasure after their will to resist has been broken down, a stronger version of the ahegao is used.

At first, the victim hates what is happening to them. They try to put up with it and attempt to endure until the end, but those feelings give way to one of pleasure. As a sign of proof of the transformation of those feelings, the artist will use the ahegao. In a similar vein, many works with masochistic themes, as a sign of loyalty to the male partner, the female partner will make an ahegao.

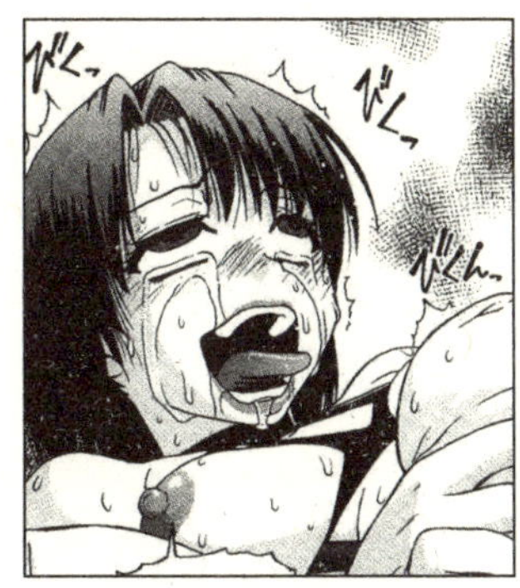

5-10: ***Miru mo Muzan*** (OYSTER 2011, Issuisha)

There are also many stories that do not follow the S&M template, but show women as molesters. In these stories, these women sometimes plead with their victims for forgiveness and to not be exposed to the public with an ahegao. The pleading female molester trope is one most famously used by artist Hiromitsu Takeda, as we occasionally see these situations in his work.

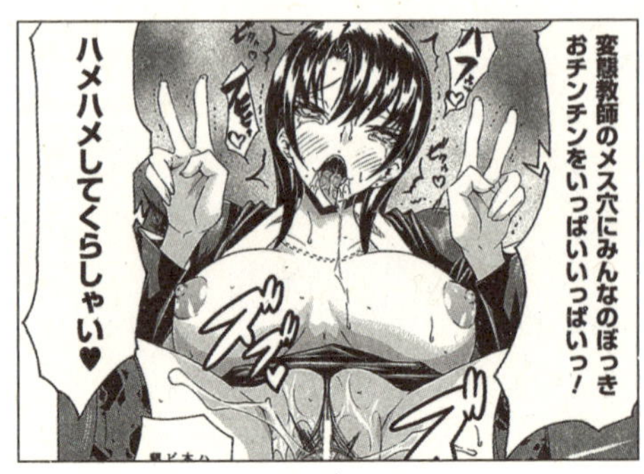

5-11: "Abareta Onna Kyoushi" (Tokisana 2012, Kill Time Communication)

From there, the women acting foolishly trope became an expression of its own and evolved into a stronger version of the ahegao—the "double peace sign ahegao."

In this expression, a woman who has fallen to pleasure wishes to show her emotional loyalty to her partner and strikes a pose that shows her submission to said partner. Usually a commemorative picture is taken, combining a double-peace sign while making an ahegao (5-11, 12). Originally this version was usually used after gang rape, breaking the female victim's spirit by training her, or as a final process in a humiliation scene. But because it was so limiting, the cases where it was used as a joke more than anything else are those greater in number than the original use.

The reason why the *double-peace ahegao* became a subject on its own is due to its readers, but it's been said that the real reason is due to the popularity of the self-published adult video game that Nankotsu Misakura helped introduce, ***Futa Letter*** (*FutaL-eta*; 2010 Harthnir). The content of which is explained by its subtitle, but the main character's girlfriend is

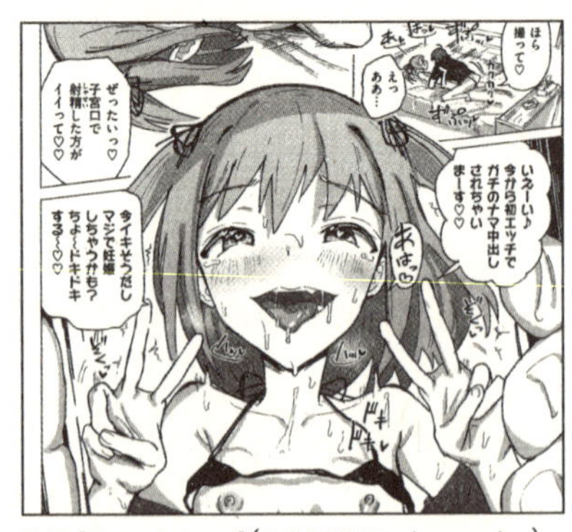

5-12: "Kinen Satsuei" (Noji 2017, Wanimagazine)

thoroughly broken by his uncle, and the proof of the end of that breaking—or training—is her double-peace sign ahegao video sent to her boyfriend. It's a tale that fuses cuckolding (*netorare*) with breaking and training story elements (5-13). While the fusion of the ahegao and double-peace sign existed before this game was released, the fusion of the terms themselves had not. The point-blank impact became propagated as a joke, and faster than one could blink, the expression went through the encoding process.

As a subset of the *ikigao*, the ahegao has evolved in a particularly unique way, thanks to eromanga, adult video games, and hentai anime. This strong expression transmits an even stronger sense of pleasure, despair, and obedience to the reader, and next I would like to go back upstream a bit to where and when this expression of excess that one cannot see in real life first appeared in the wild, how it was developed, and the ignition point for the boom that followed.

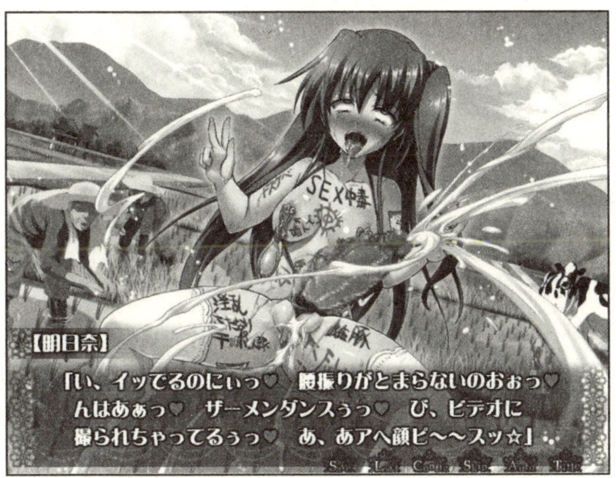

5-13: ***Futa Letter*** (*FutaLeta: Shinjite Okuridashita Futanari Kanojo ga Noka no Oji-san no Hentai Chokyo ni Domarishite Ahegao Peace Video Letter wo Okuttekuru nante;* 2010, Harthnir; video game)

Where Was the Ahegao Born?

First, which artist redefined the three components of the ahegao?

In eromanga, from the year 2000, those three components of the ahegao, which the *ikigao* carried within it, started to increase, until it hit critical mass and exploded in use in 2006. However, it is hard to definitively declare 2000 as its year of origin. And that is due to how it had already thoroughly been fixed in use within Japanese pornography far before that point. On the other hand, it was also because there was already a similar facial expression to the ahegao within eromanga since its early days.

At this juncture, I would like to link this other expression that had already existed within eromanga to the ahegao's three main conditions, and while asserting these three conditions do make the ahegao what it is, introduce a new general idea into the mix when it gained prominence in 2000. Even if an artist were to surface now claiming that they invented the ahegao expression, because we can go further into history to take a look at the symbol itself, it has become unclear as to the identity of the inventor of the expression.

Instead, what is far more important are those three conditions, as well as the awareness of the artist during the production process as to what the ahegao is. Or it should be, at least, but the reality is that designating that third person is incredibly difficult. Because that manga drawn by that creator was not drawn with the ardor needed for the ahegao in mind.

In that case, then, who is the first artist that drew the ahegao within the confines of commercial eromanga?

Speaking of which, within eromanga magazines published from 2000 to part of 2008, the word "ahegao" does not appear within them at all. Instead, it is said that the honor of the first appearance of the word goes to Hiromitsu Takeda, whose 2008 short "Ai ♥ Scraper" was published in *Comic Megastore H* magazine (Core Magazine; 5-14).

In this comic, the situation is as follows: a mother is speaking to her daughter from a window, while their neighbor (the daughter's lifelong friend and schoolmate) torments the daughter's anus from the back. Up until now, the girl did not know what pleasure like this was like, and she tries to bear it, but in the end she is unable to as her facial expression begins to contort, and morphs into an ahegao. Her eyes are unfocused, her tongue is sticking out and saliva coats her face…satisfying all three conditions for the expression. Commenting on her facial expression, the boy says, "If she were to see your stupid ahegao, she'd probably figure out what was going on here," as a way to explain the situation.

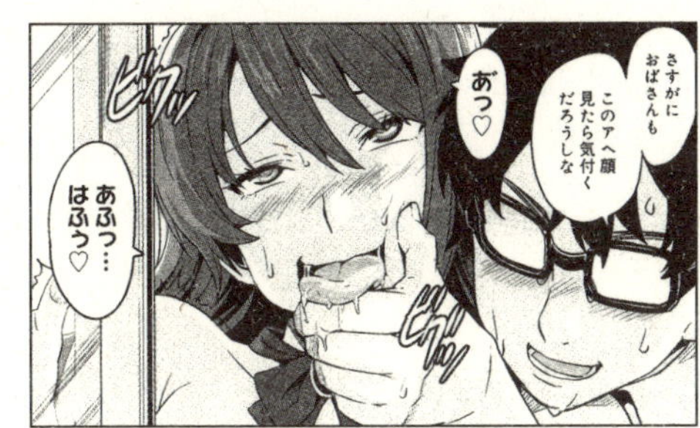

5-14: "Ai ♥ Scraper" (Hiromitsu Takeda 2008, Core Magazine)

From this point on, due to this particular panel, both the characters and the audience have a shared recognition of the ahegao. Takeda made his debut in 2006, and was subsequently popular because he used the ahegao, but he did not use the actual word in either the titles of his work nor within the stories themselves (outside of the panel I've described previously in 2008). So as a symbol, the ahegao already existed within eromanga, but there had been no word to describe it up until that point. I suspect that even if there had been one, it would have been nonsensical.

It has been thought that he used the term "ahegao" in 2008 because both in the doujinshi scene and on the internet at the time the term had a degree of shared recognition as slang, which both editors and artists already knew about.

In 2008, right as the ahegao became the talk of the town, there were already fevered discussions online trying to unearth the "founder" or "progenitor" of the expression. There are still discussions about it today, but one can spot components of the expression in any time period, people are still constantly running into trouble trying to find an origin point. And even now, an answer has not yet surfaced.

However, it's important we also explore how the ahegao is one of the offspring of the *ikigao* within eromanga. While partial, I would like to turn to this lineage and take a closer look at it.

The Ahegao Is an Offspring of the Ikigao

One particular theory to the origins of the ahegao is linked to Mitsuru Bangaichi. Bangaichi was particularly active in the mid-'80s within the just-emerging *lolicon* genre. His early works do not satisfy the three conditions, but a similar facial expression is used on his girls quite a bit (5-15). As early as 1995 do we see the one condition of the tongue hanging out in his work, and it does look as if it is an ahegao. However, because of when it occurs—immediately post-male facial ejaculation, where the character is lapping the semen off her own face—it's a very weak satisfaction of one of the conditions.

When asked about being a trailblazer in a previous interview I had with Bangaichi, he answered, "While the facial expression looks similar, the situation it occurs in is quite different. So you can feel that something is off." He continued, "Much of the time when you see those similarities in my work, the situation is different. It's basically just me shoving a fat dick into this girl, and her fainting because of it. So, it's obviously a different setup." He further clarified things by saying, "While it might've met the requirements of today's ahegao, I didn't draw it specifically with that in mind."

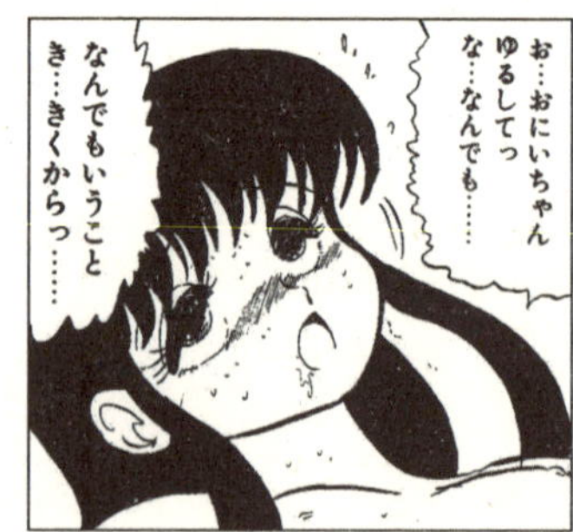

5-15: ***Lolikko Kiss*** (Mitsuru Bangaichi 1986, Nippon Shuppansha)

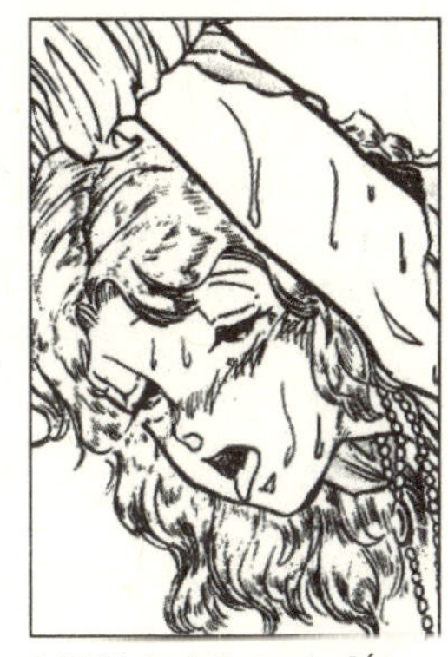

5-16: "Hatsujo Densetsu" (Tou Moriyama 1985, Shobunkan)

In the end, there was an expression that was close, but there was no definition for the word itself, and the artist of those works wasn't explicitly aiming for that expression during the creative process.

But there is another artist and work with ahegao elements older than that of Bangaichi, which would be Tou Moriyama's "Hatsujo Densetsu" (Shobunkan, 5-16), originally drawn in 1984. In this work, we also see a facial expression close to that of the ahegao used on a young girl. The plot is a girl gets raped by a horse, and instead of enjoying it, one can tell by her facial expression that she's exhausted by it. And though this expression looks extremely close to that of the ahegao, it's hard to entirely rule out whether her expression is not one of pleasure, but possibly of something else.

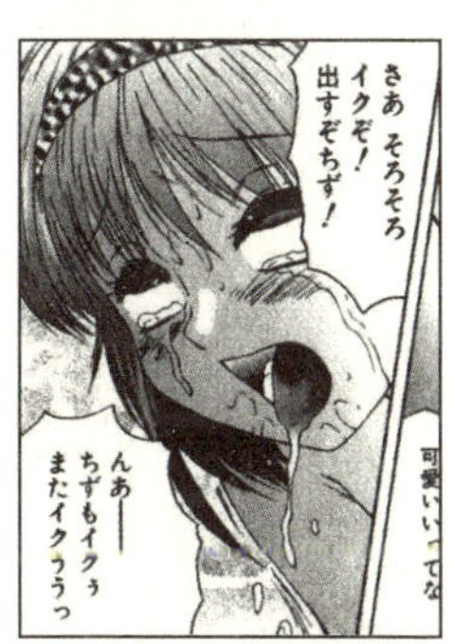

5-17: ***Orgasm King*** (*Zeccho Ou*; Fuusen Club 1998, Tosho Shobo)

In Fuusen Club's hardcore sex and humiliation-filled title ***Orgasm King*** (*Zeccho Ou;* 1998, Outo Shobo, 5-17) the ahegao appears as an *ikigao.* But if one rereads the text, the girl feels pleasure and does reach orgasm, so it's hard to tell whether her expression is one of agony or one of pleasure.

If one searches Fuusen Club's name online, then one will see that at one point, people thought that they were the progenitor of the ahegao. I asked the artist on *twitter* about this, and they flatly denied it.

> *"Who first invented the cross-section view and the ahegao expressions? Thanks to someone's copying and pasting, they thought that Fuusen Club was behind both. But I replied once, and I'll continue to reply with my answer, which is: it wasn't me."*

"While I think there were many memes I used, I've forgotten how many that was. Even if people think and feel that I was behind them, to have someone say that I was the first person to use these expressions hurts."

(Both tweets from the artist's twitter, *dated March 2016.)*

From this remark, we can tell that this expression is one that has been around for a long time and has been recognized as such (5-18).

I haven't been able to get a hold of the precise numbers, but up until 2000, these ahegao lookalike expressions were used a great deal within humiliation stories. However, after 2000, uses of the "pleasured" ahegao expression increased. The more Jogi Tsukino's heroines desperately tried to put up with a feeling of pleasure, the more charming they became. We see this in 2002 with their work *B-flat 37°C* (2002, Core Magazine, 5-19). So as the heroine tried to put up with feelings of pleasure, the harder she tried to hold on to her ego. But when she finally degenerated and hit her limit, the facial expression that resulted is very much a special characteristic of the artist's work. It became the establishment of Tsukino's own *ikigao* expression. There are fairly comical elements to this story, leaving an impression close to the one that the ahegao tends to leave today.

Haijme Okano, a friend of Tsukino's, is also an eromanga artist. Okano states that his friend drew that ahegao-like expression for a precise reason. When I interviewed Okano in 2009, here's how he explained it to me:

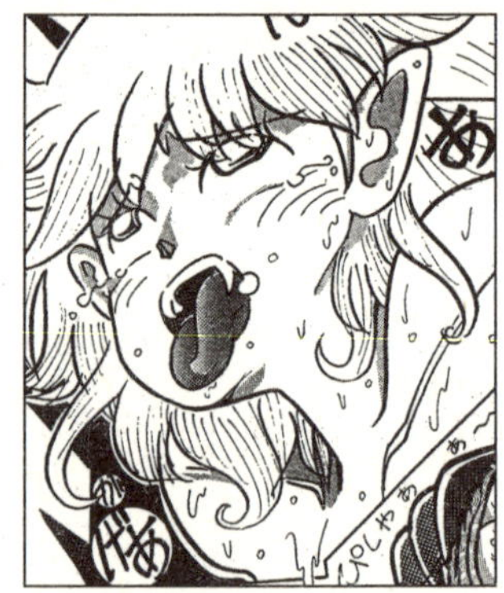

5-18: "Pla-Ude Sunlight: Kouhen" (Araya Shiki 1993, Tsukasa Shobo)

"I think there was one reason why [Tsukino did that]. Mr. Tsukino is an eromanga artist that is quite thorough and fussy about his storyboards. He leaves the ahegao until the very, very end of a story, when the heroine is always close to passing out from the act,

as she says her lines about trying to retain her sense of reason. Therefore, he hasn't betrayed or disappointed that expectation [on behalf of the audience]."

In other words, Tsukino doesn't rush the heroine into the process of pleasure, not using the expression until the end, when she's so desperately trying to cling to her sense of reason. As a result, she degenerates, and lapses into an ahegao-like expression.

So now you can see how this lookalike expression fits into the *ikigao*'s lineage, even if in reality, there were many different ways it was used in works at the time. In this way, the artists' originality helped create variations within the *ikigao* expression.

But at this juncture it is important to note that at this point in time, the artists I have introduced were not aware of the ahegao as it had not yet undergone acceptance, and instead only chose to create expressions that had the special characteristics of the ahegao expression and were close to it, but were not it. In a very real sense, one can call this time period the "prehistory" of the ahegao. But out of the many variations of the *ikigao*, why did the ahegao alone get a name attached to it, and why did it explosively spread throughout the genre?

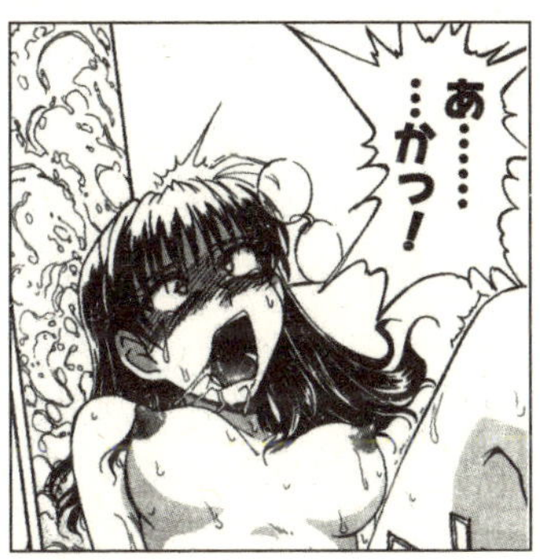

5-19: ***B-flat 37°C*** (Jogi Tsukino 2002, Core Magazine)

Here, I would like to talk a bit about another absolutely separate starting point for its spread.

The Power Difference the Ahegao Created

Before its name became fixed as the "ahegao," many used this expression anyway. But the term has widely been used in media outside of eromanga, having overcome the framework of the genre to the point where one can see its relationship of influences.

We see this in animation, particularly in the contributions of erotic anime director Teruaki Murakami, whose work is quite important to the genre. The special characteristics of his animation is depicting fast piston-like thrusts during the intercourse, close-ups, and scene cuts he uses, where he often focuses on humiliation elements as part of his stories. Murakami often uses visual clues in his works, and as a result, he has had an entirely different worldview develop. In this particular story, Mina, the girl who is being raped, lapses into a degenerate ahegao during the act in an ideal way, which is unique to Murakami's world (5-20).

It's unclear how many of Murakami's works have become smash hits, and he continues to produce many series to this day. I happen to think that with his fans' support, he has influenced many artists in a latent way. There are reports that the Murakami movement gained steam just as use of the ahegao in *eroge* began to increase. One can see how anime, manga, and games all had co-ownership over the expressions they used.

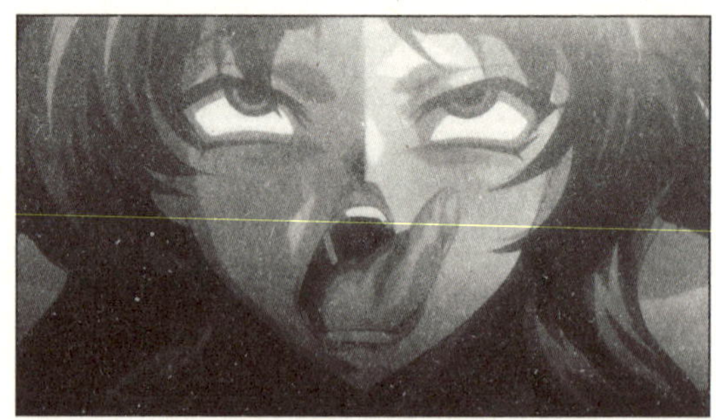

5-20: ***Taimanin Asagi***, Vol. 1 (PIXY - Lilith Soft 2007; directed by Teruaki Murakami, anime)

After 2000, many genres were beginning to widely recognize this expression after repeated simultaneous uses of it, and the ahegao became something that was commonly recognized. Because of the wide recognition it received, the three conditions of what makes an ahegao narrowed. At that point, in order to be properly accepted, the expression needed a name. Possibly because one name already existed, it could be that its use in the eromanga genre was the reason why it became renamed. Perhaps the term "ahe ahe suru" (to breathe deeply) was used in order to reflect some of the comedy elements within these stories. Perhaps the affinity between the nuance of the term and the subject matter was just good. Though it is important to note that at this time (using) the term did not turn into a big craze.

As a result, there was one more incidence of chance that happened with regard to the ahegao, and that was the existence of online message boards where one could upload pictures and art. On these boards one could anonymously upload images or write text, and for the sake of comparison, I present to you one of the longer standing boards of its time, *Futaba Channel*, or as it has come to be called, *2-chan*. It was a place where one could post parody works, or post their art, or talk about their hobbies. Shortly thereafter a similar community illustration contribution site named *pixiv* went online.

The origin story of the ahegao online on these message boards goes like this...

A user named Yukiman uploaded a picture of Patchouli, a character from the underground cult hit shooter game ***Touhou Project*** with an ahegao expression (5-21).

(It is important to note here that the original joke about ahegao Patchouli appeared on *2-chan*, but as Suiseiseki, a character from the manga series ***Rozen Maiden***.)

Ahegao Patchouli did satisfy the three conditions of the ahegao (though there wasn't much sweat and so it just squeaked by in satisfying those conditions), had hengao's strange face elements, and it was thought that this image was obviously supposed to be a collage made to shock people.

This manipulated photo was obviously created as part of an inside joke, and other members of the message board were encouraged to continue posting manipulated pictures of different characters as well as their own, all featuring an ahegao.

Much of the ahegao material at this point in time was coming from these message boards, to the point where a flash point for the ignition of the ahegao boom explosion occurred, complete with a "create-your-own-ahegao" template (5-22).

Furthermore, genres like that of the *Touhou Project* were exploding on their own, easily diffusing and spreading throughout. Around 2007, with the aforementioned ahegao picture was a caption that read, "Once you are infected with ahegao germs, you'll make a hengao like this." Though this was part of the joke that went on with derivative works, this was the first time the term "ahegao" was tied to the image of one in this way, and many became popular enough to spread to other message boards. I happen to think that in this way, the term ahegao and the three conditions of the expression finally became linked and it was all thanks to one photoshopped joke image.

On images from eromanga and hentai anime, you'll often see a description by the artist to the tune of "I wanted to mess around and give this character a strange facial expression," but as a result of the neighborhood of derivative works spreading as they did, it's natural to think that people made comments like "oh, so that strange face is called an 'ahegao,'" as it was becoming a widely acknowledged expression.

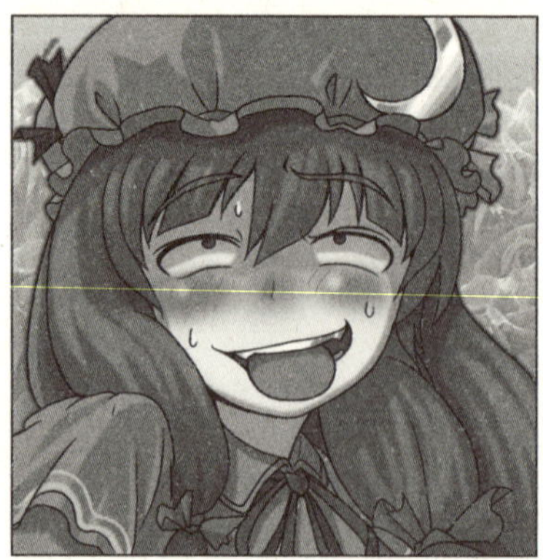

5-21: "Ahegao Patchouli" (Yukiman, illustration on *pixiv*)

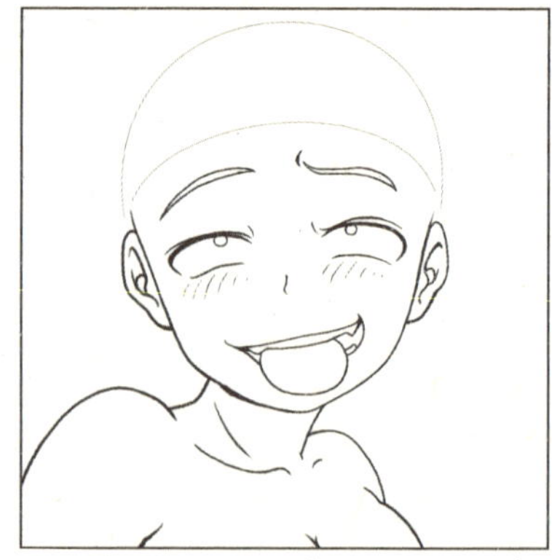

5-22: "Ahegao template" (circa July 22, 2008)

So that made for a big open space for conjecture. I happen to think that after this book, research in this area will continue to happen. But the last act in the encoding phenomenon that took place on the popular creative social sites of that time was actually quite interesting. Of course, this could not have happened in a time without the internet.

From the Third Dimension to the Second, the First, and Back Again

The ahegao had gone public, underwent the encoding process as it was shared as a meme, and it might be correct to say that 2008 was the 2nd Year of the Ahegao Era. This may show how much of a fad it had become, but the lynchpin came in the form of doujinshi, ahegao-only content, and the illustration zine that fused the two: ***A-H-E Ahegao Hybrid Expression*** (2008, A-H-E Production Committee; 5-23).

Trade paperbacks were beginning to carry the term ahegao within it, publishing titles with the prefix "ahe" in them, and those books and anthologies steadily continued to sell. Books like ***Ahegao Anthology Comics*** (2010, Kill Time Communication), SINK's ***Ahekan!*** (2011, TI NET), Morris' ***Mix Ahenomics*** *(Hitsozuma Ahenomics*; 2013, Sanwa Publishing), Torajiro Sanagi's ***Ecstasy at 3seconds.*** (*Aheochi ♥ Sanbyoumae*; 2013, Fujimi Publishing, 5-24), Naoto Fukuyama's ***AheColle*** (2014, Sanwa Publishing, 5-25), and others, are still being seen made today.

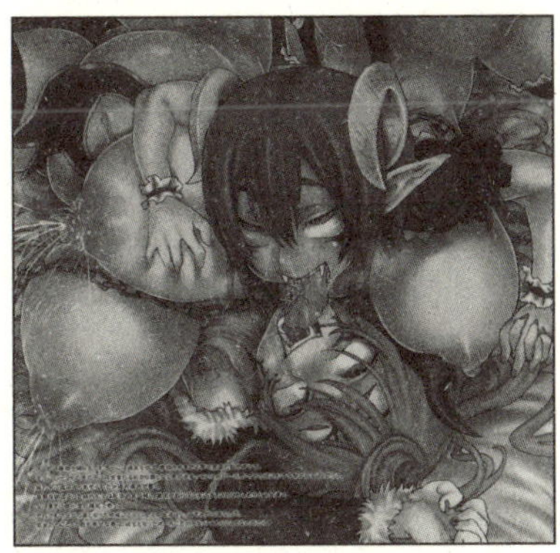

5-23: ***A-H-E Ahegao Hybrid Expression*** (Alice no Takarabako 2008, A-H-E Production Committee; Illustration by Asanagi)

The ahegao has mainly been used on women, but rarely, men occasionally make an appearance in the genre as the ones making them. Even in genres targeted towards men like *shota* (young boys), *otokonoko,* or works with masochistic attributes, ahegao content has increased. In Chinzurena's *otokonoko* work, all of the feminine boys have been given ahegao as well (5-26). In Bu-chan's "oneshota" work (where a boy is paired with an older girl/woman), in order to coerce ejaculation, the boy makes an ahegao (5-27).

The ahegao that doesn't seem to choose between genders isn't just an expression within male-targeted work only. In recent years, the world of *boys' love* has begun to venture into the genre with anthologies like *b-Boy Love*'s ***Ahegao and Torogao*** (2016, Libre Publishing). The *torogao* is another species of ikigao that isn't quite as funny-looking as the ahegao. Here the victim's pleasure breaks out across their entire face as a smile that also shows the relaxing of muscles. The term is in reference to the feeling of their body melting (coming from the word "torotoro," or to melt).

Within that anthology was Ryou Sakurai's "ToketeMite wa Ikaga Desu?", where the protagonist does not know the meaning of either of the terms ahegao nor *torogao*, and asks his partner about them, only to have him dodge the question. The protagonist is drawn into sex with his partner, and when he orgasms, his partner takes a picture of him (5-28, 29). Afterwards, his partner shows him the picture, lightly teases him and says, "This is the face you were asking about."

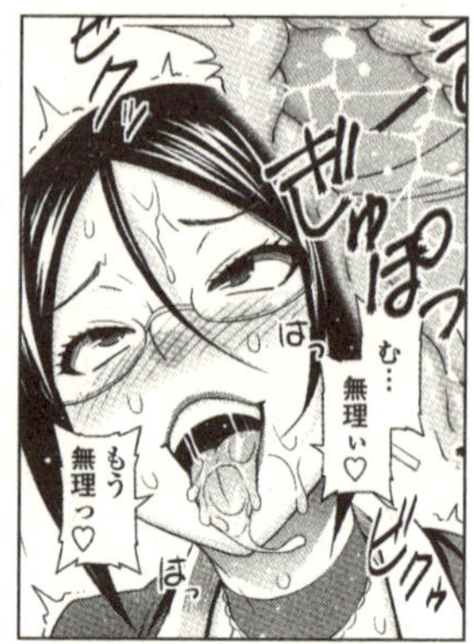

5-24: ***Ecstasy at 3seconds.*** (*Aheochi* ♥ *Sanbyoumae*; Torajiro Sanagi 2013, Fujimi Publishing)

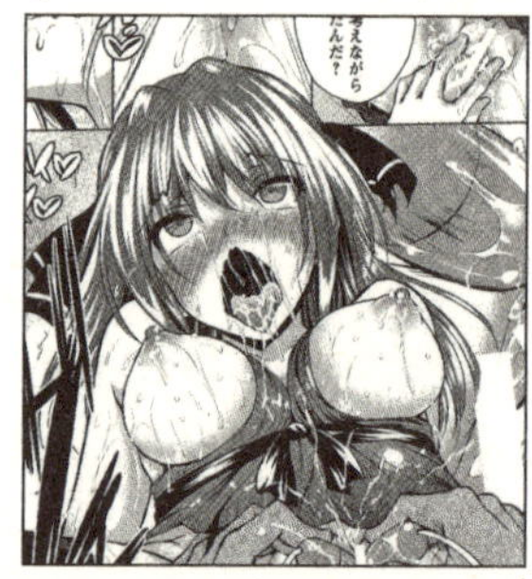
5-25: ***AheColle*** (Naoto Fukuyama 2014, Sanwa Publishing)

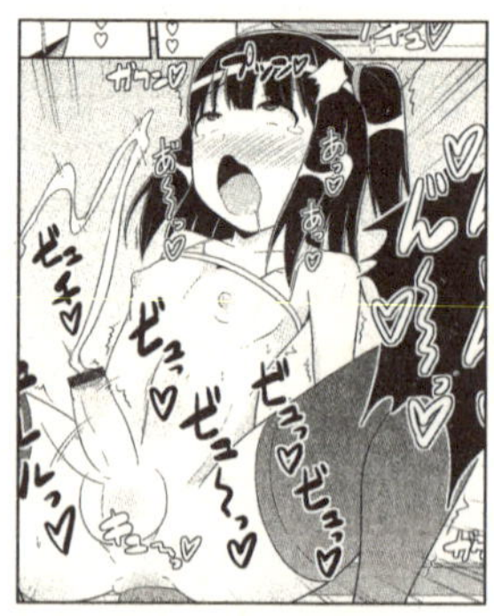
5-26: ***Chin ☆ COMPLETE*** (Chinzurena 2014, Mediax)

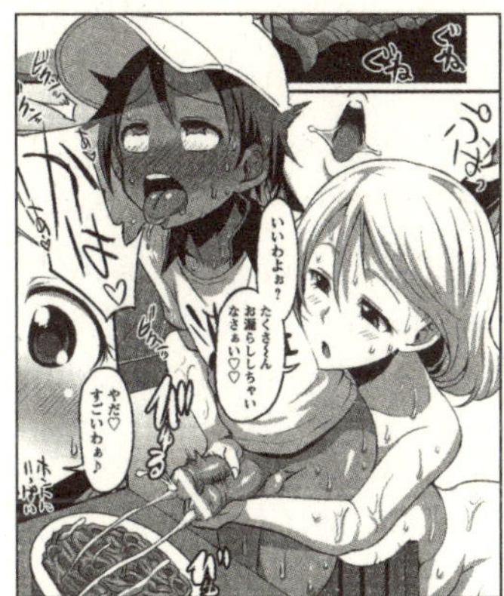

5-27: "Aru Natsu no Hiwai de Kirei de Yokoshima na One-san" (Bu-chan 2016, Angel Publishing)

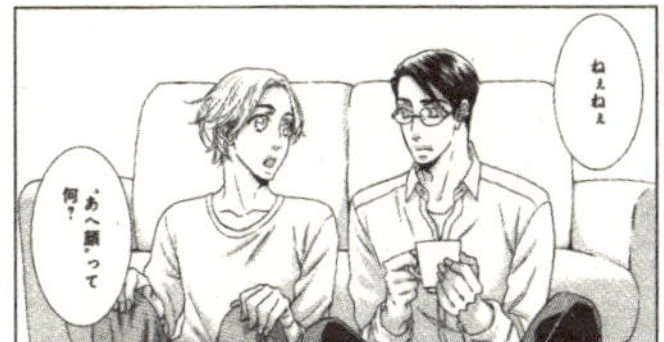

5-28: "ToketeMite wa Ikaga Desu?" (Ryo Sakurai 2016, Libre Publishing)

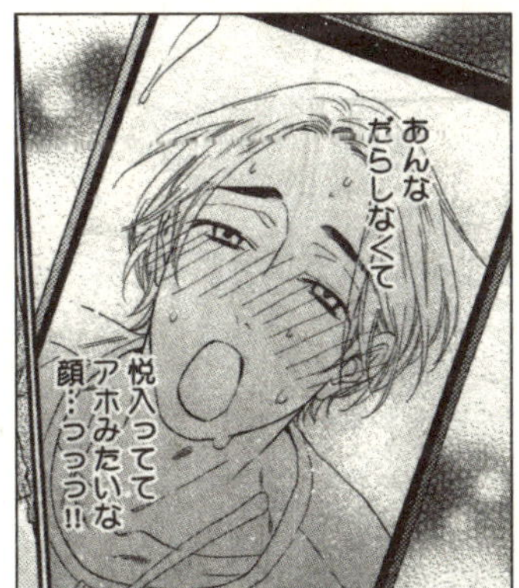

5-29: "ToketeMite wa Ikaga Desu?" (Ryo Sakurai 2016, Libre Publishing)

The protagonist is so embarrassed that he made such an undignified expression during sex that his face turns red, which gets his partner angry, after which they apologize and make up. In this development, the ahegao itself is shameful, and this is the special characteristic of this particular work. Though here the ahegao is not used directly to show the pleasure of the target, something different than what is in male-targeted media.

Because the ahegao has so many variations, it has been thought that it was an expression limited to the world of visuals. However, even though it's not expressed through words, the ahegao recently debuted in adult light novels.

In Shin Takahane's ***Ahegao Minaide!*** (2010, France Shobo), a new female teacher at the protagonist's school has an obscene innate (physical) predisposition that allows her to purify evil during sexual intercourse. The protagonist, knowing this, makes it his mission to save his teacher from becoming a slut.

Which begs the question… How does one render an ahegao with only words?

Interestingly enough, the protagonist by chance finds a column in an erotic magazine that covers the ahegao in it. So, through his exposition, the audience are told what the ahegao is. Moreover, it is established that the teacher can only be reformed if brought to an extreme orgasm, with the "kind of sex that would make her make an ahegao."

The chapter politely starts off by explaining what kind of facial expression the ahegao is, then establishes the concept of intense sex as the way to reform the teacher. Of course, as it is a light novel, there are also illustrations of what the ahegao looks like (5-30). But within the chapter itself, there is a brief explanation of how the ahegao has its origins in eromanga. So it lives on as a shared idea.

Originally, the term ahegao came from the porn industry and was used by adjacent media, but it has since been bestowed with extra meaning coming from the 2D world of eromanga, and after further evolving, has seeped into the 1D world of light novels.

What's even more interesting is that the new interpretation of the term that happened because of eromanga was a countercurrent of the one used within porn, and the one used within the eromanga genre was a rewrote/superscripted one used within porn and adjacent media.

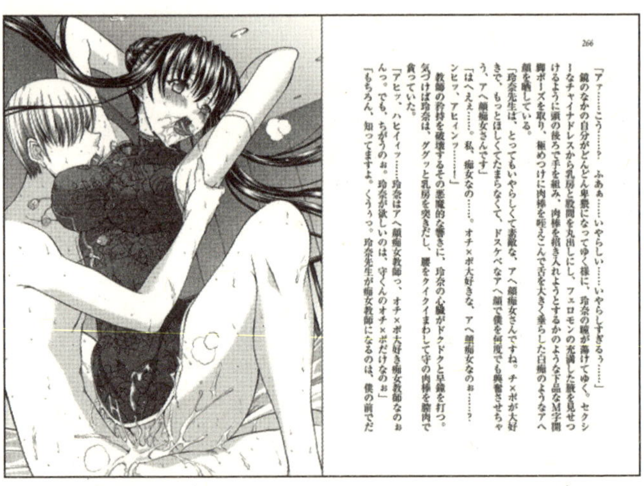

266

「アァ……こう……？　ふあぁ……いやらしい……いやらしすぎるぅ……」
鏡のなかの自分がどんどん卑猥になってゆく様に、玲奈の瞳が蕩けてゆく。セクシーなチャイナドレスから乳房と股間を丸出しにし、フェロモンの充満した腋を見せつけるように頭の後ろで手を組み、肉棒を招き入れようとするかのような下品なM字開脚ポーズを取り、極めつけに肉棒を咥えこんで舌を大きく垂らした白痴のようなアヘ顔を晒している。
「玲奈先生は、とってもいやらしくて素敵な、アヘ顔痴女さんですね。チ×ポが大好きで、もっとほしくてたまらなくて、ドスケベなアヘ顔で僕を何度でも興奮させちゃう、アヘ顔痴女さんです」
「はへぇえ……。私、痴女なの……。オチ×ポ大好きな、アヘ顔痴女なのぉ……？　ンヒッ、アヒィンッ……！」
教師の矜持を破壊するその悪魔的な響きに、玲奈の心臓がドクドクと早鐘を打つ。気づけば玲奈は、ググッと乳房を突きだし、腰をクイクイまわして守の肉棒を膣肉で貪っていた。
「アヒッ、ハヒイィッ……玲奈はアヘ顔痴女教師っ、オチ×ポ大好き痴女教師なのぉんっ。でも、ちがうのぉ。玲奈が欲しいのは、守くんのオチ×ポだけなのぉ」
「もちろん、知ってますよ。くうぅっ。玲奈先生が痴女教師になるのは、僕の前でだ

5-30: ***Ahegao Minaide!*** (Shin Takahane & Kinohitoshi 2010, France Shobo)

In 2015, a *JAV* movie that parodies the three conditions of the ahegao, ***Eromanga Mitai na Ahegao wo Sarashita Onna-tachi*** (2015, Moodys; 5-31). It tosses away the genre's original idea of what the ahegao was, and rewrites the definition as established in manga. It's a very rare example of how this expression has gone from 3D to 2D and back again.

In recent years, the worlds of Japanese adult video and eromanga have enjoyed a mutual sphere of influence with elements like tentacles, hermaphrodites, and other fantasy elements that one could never see in real life being aggressively developed within the world of video pornography. Seemingly the use of delusional erotic expressions has become even more seamless (5-32).

And as a result of each medium continuing to challenge greed and avarice, I can't help but wonder what genre, or even industry, will find itself going "ahe" next. ❁

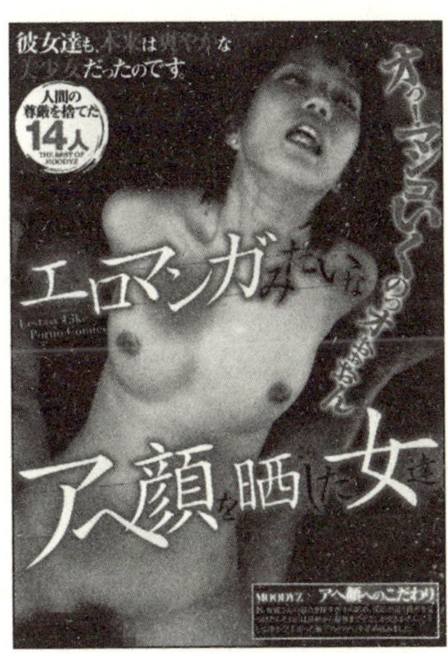

5-31: ***Eromanga Mitai na Ahegao wo Sarashita Onna-tachi*** (2015, Moodys; video)

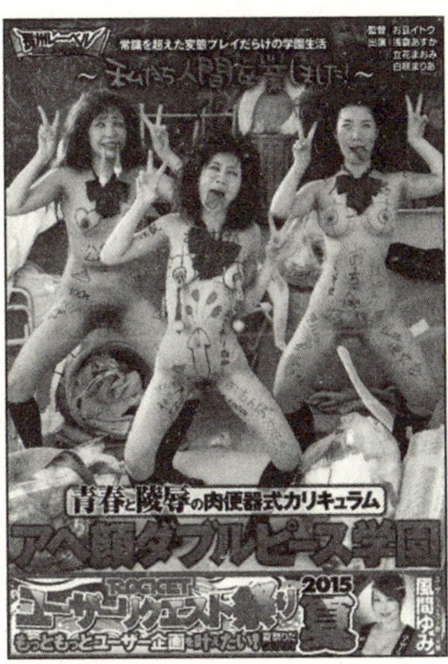

5-32: ***Ahegao Double Peace Gakuen*** (2015, Rocket; video)

The History of Hentai Manga

CHAPTER SIX

The History of the "Kupaa" and "Ramee" Sound Effects

Phenomimes, Mimesis, Onomatopoeias, and the Erotic

A great deal of phenomimes (onomatopes) and mimetic words exist within the Japanese language. Phenomimes are words that are made by onomatopoeias like "bark," "meow," or in simpler terms, words that mimic the sounds made by living creatures. Comparatively, mimetic words encompass emotions, movements, sounds made by non-living creatures, and states of being.

In the following, the italicized words are referred to as onomatopoeias within the English manga community: "*Bursting* into pale flames" and "the girl's heart *squeezed* tight."

Compared to Western languages, a great many more onomatopes exist in Japanese, which have been rendered in many ways within manga. The lines of dialogue in a speech bubble within a panel of manga do not just include typed memetic terms with different meanings but may also use hand-drawn lettering to accompany them. If an artist draws something with emphasis, they can get the impact and force of what's happening across within the panel to the audience by drawing a large sound effect. Or if they choose to do so in a weaker way, the lack of size or a softer font may minimize the impact of the contents of a manga panel emphasizing loneliness or misery to make an impression. To say it more simply, using sound effects is another tool used by artists that utilizes words/sounds as visual cues explaining the situation within a panel.

This is also used when the "meaning" of the words themselves is not considered sufficient, or when those words aren't subtle enough. Onomatopes can hide the artist's true meanings or motives, so it's possible that manga expressions can have stratified structures to them.

Within the history of manga, the history of visual expressions is quite old, but over time more diverse manga expressions have been invented and evolved. Because of that, the importance of onomatopes that occur within manga is incredibly critical. Just within the scope of manga research people have analyzed their symbolism, researched how they've changed, and submitted them for text analysis. And looking at them from a genre perspective, many have compared their sociological elements within manga.

So, it's obvious that even within eromanga, onomatopes are very important tools used to advance stories. Unfortunately, not much research into these sound effect expressions has really advanced within manga research.

That said, I have come to believe that the amount of onomatopes in eromanga are far more in number than of those in other genres. For example, depictions of intense intercourse where bodies collide, breasts shake, and bodily fluids dance through space—each of those scenes when rendered have their own unique sets of sound effects.

In order to properly present those scenes, and the movement within them many onomatopes were invented to create a unique sense of nuance and sound that cannot be found in live filmed material.

For example, when male genitalia are forcefully inserted into female genitalia, there's a "zubu" sound. When there's a fast, pistoning motion of the hips, there is a "paanpaan" sound of a smacking impact. And when sexual fluids are added in, sounds of contact like "nucha," "kucha," or "shubu" are used to express sounds like slip, slurp, or glop. When a male reaches his climax, an ejaculation sound like "dokun" is used, followed by something like "dopyu" or "byururururu," which are similar to the sounds made when shooting finger guns and a balloon deflating. When a woman reaches orgasm, and her body stiffens with a jolt, that is "bikun" in eromanga. And if that orgasm would reverberate through her body and makes her tremble, a quivering "gakugaku" would be used.

Just like martial arts, when bodies make violent physical contact during sex, the sounds involved in that process are many, as are the situations in which they are used. So, the types of sound effects that artists use can show their individuality and creativity.

As you can see, the great amount of diversity in approaches taken with onomatopes all have different origins and reasonings. The new onomatopes and their related research that have appeared in recent years I will have to entrust to other researchers hereafter. In this chapter I would like to probe into the ones that are appearing in regular manga magazines, as well as two very unique eromanga expressions that have undergone the encoding process: "kupaa" and "ramee."

Is "Kupaa" a Phenomime or Mimetic Word?

I know we just looked at some of the examples of phenomimes related to the act of intercourse, but there are many other mimetic words that are particular to the eromanga genre. Compared to phenomimes, there has been a general trend where mimetic words have been encoded more easily, and in order to make a scene easier to understand for the audience, they are more frequently used than their phenomime counterparts.

When breasts move, they jiggle with "purupuru" and "purunpurun" sounds (the latter being a heavier tone). When a man masturbates, the fricative stroking sound is "shikoshiko." When a man's large flaccid penis is pulled out of pants or underwear, it flops heavily with a "boron" (6-1~4). "Boron" resembles the sound of a classical harp or other string instrument, and as such has been used in a very limited way, but I wonder if anyone ever imagined that it would become one of the mimetic words of choice within an erotic genre?

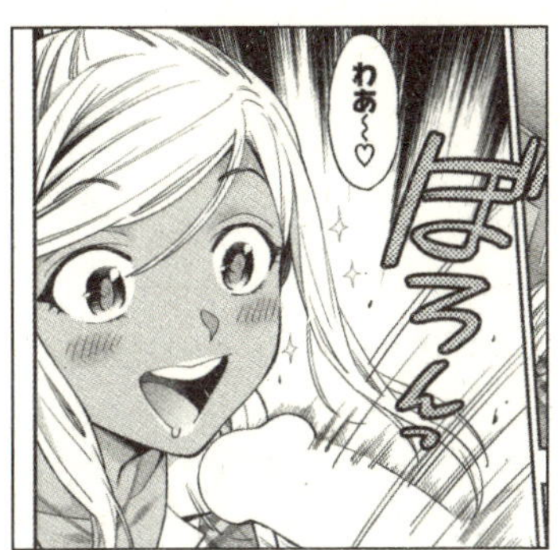

6-1: "Zangyou~Keibiin wa Mita!" (Tesshin Azuma 2017, Wanimagazine)

After male genitalia are inserted into female genitalia, if the uterus squeezes around the penis in joy, that sound is a "kyuun" or "kyun." "Kyuun" is the sound effect of choice for artist Yoshiharu Makita, and thus kyuun's nickname has become "makita-on" (literally Makita's sound) (6-5, 6).

In the midst of all of this, we have two other onomatopes that are used in very specific situations with some degree of familiarity. These are "kupaa" and "ramee."

"Kupaa" (sometimes written "kupa") is a mimetic word that has been used quite a bit in the situation where a woman spreads her legs. Specifically, it is the sound made when the labia minora part and her sex partner can see inside of her vagina. It can also be used for the situation where a female takes her index and middle fingers (and occasionally, her ring finger) and spreads her vagina with her fingers as she invites her partner inside her. It has also been used in situations where women are shamefully coerced into sex.

This onomatope has been in use since 2000, and comparatively, its use has slowly increased until it's become recognizable. In the grand scheme of things, this is a relatively new sound effect that's come into use fairly recently. But in 2006, it experienced rapid growth and spread (6-7~9).

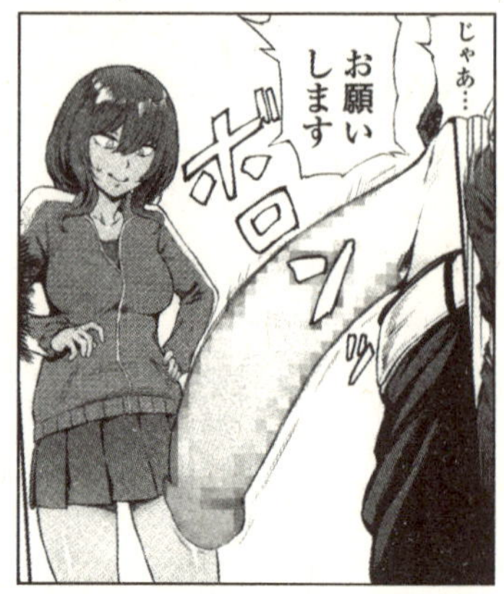

6-2: "Ippatsu Kaiketsu Onayami Soudan" (Kuroitsu Tsuruga 2017, Akaneshinsha)

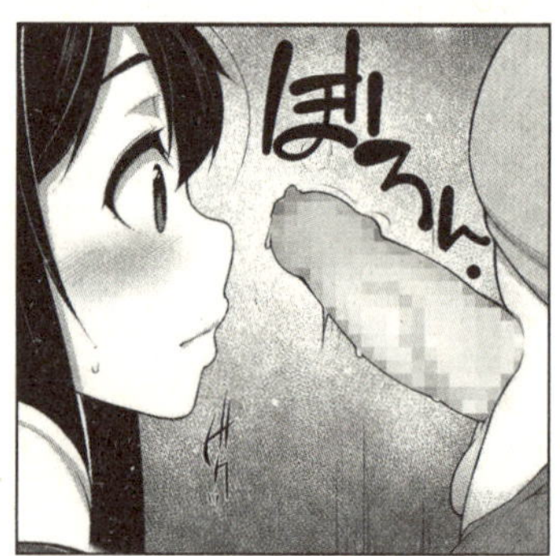

6-3: "Manga Mitai ni" (Sakamata Nerimono 2017, Issuisha)

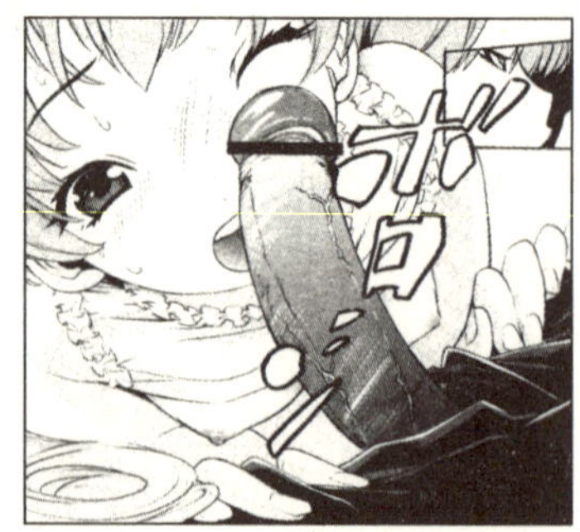

6-4: "Peeping Mom" (D.P 2004, France Shoin)

6-5: ***Radical ☆ Temptation*** (Yoshiharu Makita 2005, Akaneshinsha)

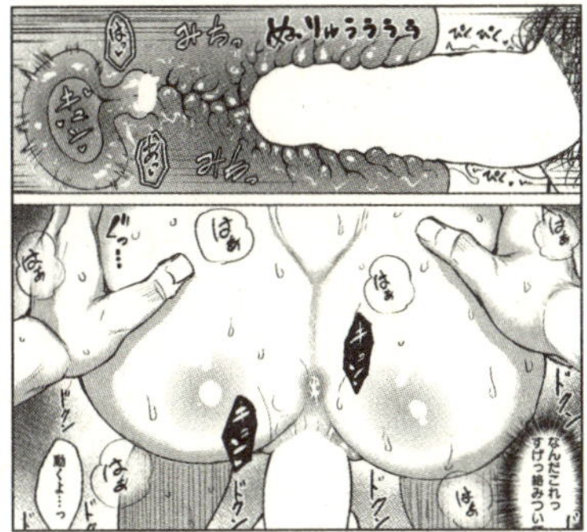

6-6: "Kagero" (Coupe 2017, Wanimagazine)

6-7: "RinRin Ecchi" (Doku Denpa 2017, GOT)

And the reason why it suddenly exploded into use? That can be attributed to Akazawa RED.

He added "kupaa" to the title of most of his books: ***Kupaa Resort*** (2006, Shinyusha), ***Jealoussic Park*** (2009, MAX), ***Loli-Pako: BrakKUPAA-ruzu!*** (2014, Akaneshinsha). And as a result, readers recognized its existence as an expression (6-10~12).

Its main use is overwhelmingly paired with sexual fluids dripping from female genitalia, but it also has been used in situations where it's used to refer to the viscosity of the fluids sticking to the genitalia. It is also seen in situations where the genitalia are like a forbidden treasure not to be seen by anyone and yet it looks as if it's about to burst open; in what is an absolutely magnificent way to allow the audience to imagine things.

The "ku" part of the term is also seen in sucking and slurping terms like "kuchu," "kucha," and other mimetic words that have a degree of viscosity to them.

The "pa" part is an explosive sound, like "pop," with a hard "P" to reflect the suggestiveness of the expression.

Akazawa RED has commented on this phenomenon online.

> *"The reason why I used* hiragana *instead of* katakana *for 'kupa' (クパ) was because the temptation it presents somehow seems cuter, right? And that's why it's now written as 'kupaa.'"*
>
> *(From Akazawa RED's* twitter *account, June 12, 2013)*

6-8: "Osanajimi no Eroge Seiyuu Motivation" (Fujishima Seiichigou 2015, Akaneshinsha)

6-9: "Tissue Story" (Shikkarimono no Takeshi-kun 2016, Wanimagazine)

In terms of the written orthographic characters, *hiragana* was always the better choice because it seemed more appropriate in order to transmit information about this gesture the character uses. That also works for for "ramee," but we'll go into that later.

Up until now we've been talking about mimetic words, but with regard to "kupaa," there have been different opinions on the topic.

Mimetic words are actually different from other sounds. Most agree about the idea that its purpose is to describe a situation being its most appropriate use. It has been defined already, but for example, when you think about a giant ball splitting down the middle, it would make a "pa" sound, which is close to a pop. There are some people that think that in this situation, instead of a mimetic word, it would be a phenomime due to what it is explaining.

6-10: ***Kupaa Resort*** (Akazawa RED 2006, Shinyusha)

Of course, even without such limited conditions, one still wouldn't be able to hear that exploding sound, and it's the same with "kupaa" as well. There's no way one would be able to hear that kind of delicate sound in real life, and so this expression is a delusion, a gift to the audience.

6-11: ***Jealoussic Park*** (Akazawa RED 2009, MAX)

Female genitalia aside, in scenes with masochistic elements and the receiving partner opens their otherwise closed legs, "kupaa" is used when that partner spreads their anus, inviting the other partner in. But chiefly, this expression is used overwhelmingly in situations where female genitalia are being spread open. Or to put it conversely, "kupaa" is an onomatope where if you use it, the reader will already know what situation is happening inside of the story with this girl, allowing them to naturally imagine it in their own minds.

6-12: ***Loli-Pako: BrakKUPAA-ruzu!*** (Akazawa RED 2014, Akanoshinsha)

It's important to note that with the use of "kupaa," it is formally not bound as such. It is widely known that by combining gestures or movements with words and using sound effects like this tends to leave a very deep impression on the audience, allowing the expression to undergo a particularly vivid encoding process.

6-13: ***Dekinboy*** (Shin Tamura 1978, Shogakukan)

6-14: ***Urusei Yatsura***, Vol. 17 (Rumiko Takahashi 1983, Shogakukan)

This isn't a similar onomatope, as it isn't erotic per se, but "chudoon" was used when a character is shot/slammed into space, and they disappear into the horizon or explode.

It has been widely acknow-ledged that Rumiko Takahashi (***Ranma ½, Urusei Yatsura***) used it quite a bit in her early work. In Shin Tamura's ***Dekinboy*** (1978, Shogakukan; 6-13), where the correct spelling of this written sound effect appears as "chudon." However, Rumiko Takahashi's "chudoon" differs in that it has a unique visual cue attached to it. In this case the character's ring and middle fingers are bent (leaving their pinkies, index fingers and thumbs sticking out) while their legs are in the shape of the Japanese katakana character "KU" as they fly through the air (6-14). Once could say that this is an ideal expression and when used in concert with a pose, it could take the nuance that the onomatope carries and etch it into the minds of the audience.

Aside from "kupaa," Akazawa RED pairs other onomatopes really well throughout his work, which had the effect of drawing out the maximum amount of charm out of the sound; ultimately culminating in a rather inflammatory sound effect as a result.

Now to our next question… Is Akazawa RED the inventor of the "kupaa" expression?

6-15: "Nii-chan to Issho" (Akazawa RED 2004, Shinyusha)

No, of course he is not. In RED's earliest works, "kupaa" was originally a cuter word "kupa." Like many other onomatopes throughout his early works, "kupa" had not fully matured yet (6-15).

Now, how was "kupaa" fixed in its current spelling as an expression? What is the history behind it, as well as the process? Let's take a look.

"Kupaa" Becomes Regulated and the Change of Gender Roles Is Born

If we're talking about a simple, clear use of "kupaa," then I would be remiss if I didn't talk about shonen manga artist Kazuhiro Fujita and his series, ***Ushio and Tora*** (1991, Shogakukan, 6-16). In this situation, "kupaa" is the onomatope used for when a ghost opens its mouth, but even with this usage, there is still the aural sense of viscosity attached to this sound (since it's a mouth that's opening). But just like in eromanga, however, use of this expression even in this context is to grab the audience's attention. This is the only appearance of this expression within *Ushio and Tora*, but because it was not used incessantly by the artist in his work it did not gain recognition or popularity with readers to undergo the encoding process.

Going back to its use in eromanga, in the 1998 doujinshi drawn by Hormone Koijiro and MARCY Dog ***Please Teach Me*** (Chodokukan, 1998), "kupaa" is used for the anus. Their next work, ***KupaaBon*** (Chodokukan, 2004; 6-17, 18) which eventually became a series, was released before Akazawa RED started using the expression often. One can understand that this was drawn with a clear, conscious intention on behalf of the artists to use it.

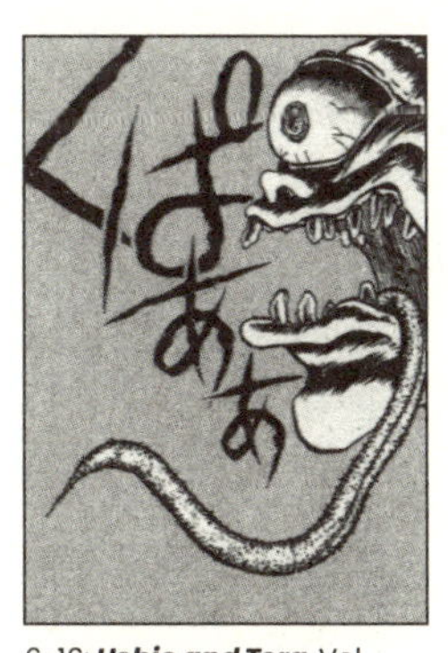

6-16: ***Ushio and Tora***, Vol. 4 (Kazuhiro Fujita 1991, Shogakukan)

The "kupaa" sound effect already existed in magazines before *KupaaBon*. In Aoi Makia's "Kaori Monogatari" (1993, Byakuya-Shobo), which was in *Manga Hot Milk*, "kupaa" was used when female genitals are being opened (6-19). This time, a voiced consonant adds a fair amount of power to the sound effect to create "gupaa," but that force is attached to the situation where the heroine is being forced to do so.

In 1997, Rei Hidiri wrote "kupaa" in katakana orthography (クパァ) within issues of *Comic Natural High* (Fujimi Publishing; 6-20). In the doujin magazine *Comic Potpourri Club* (Shinyusha), Katsupiko Fuji wrote the term as "kupa" (くぱっ), with an emphasis at the end of the second syllable, but he also sometimes used "kupaa" (くぱぁ) as well (6-21).

On the other hand, there is a history of other onomatopes used for spreading legs and the like. In *gekiga* master Toshio Maeda's ***Dance of Desire*** (*Yokubo no Rinbu*; 1983, Ichibankan), he uses the onomatope "nunu" when one of the characters pulls apart her own labia minora, impressively demonstrating the auditory existence of the mucous membrane by attaching this mimetic word to the situation (6-22).

The next onomatope was not used the same way, but the first *lolicon bishojo* manga artist, Aki Uchiyama, has been using the strange and distinctive visual effect "man" from the '80s onward to

6-17: ***Please Teach Me*** (Chokudokan 1998, self-published)

6-18: ***KupaaBon*** (Chokudokan 2004, self-published)

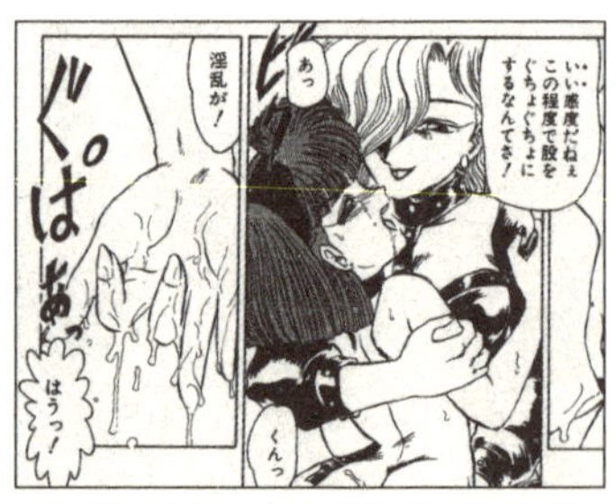

6-19: "Kaori Monogatari" (Aoi Makita 1993, Byakuya-Shobo)

denote when vaginas are exposed (ed.: "man" being slang for vagina; 6-23). In eromanga from the '90s on, one can see a great deal many onomatopes like "nunyu" or "gunyu" used for plunging and inserting. "Paka" and "pira/piro" denote opening sounds, with the first being more of a pop and the latter two having a peeling tone. "Munyo" is another peeling sound but it's a lot slower. While "kyuu", which we hinted at the start of this chapter, is a pinching or clenching sound (6-24~28).

It's rare to have an artist use the same onomatopes repeatedly, as scenes and situations change depending on how the artist must draw them for the audience to understand the plot. Furthermore, the situations in which onomatopes were used pre- and post-2000 "kupaa" were completely different. Up until the '90s, scenes where female genitalia and thighs spread open were exceedingly rare, as through the mid-'90s manga was still softcore. Leg and genitalia spreading scenes were considered hardcore, so there was also the issue of such scenes being uncensored.

At the height of censorship in manga, the scope of genitals that were revised or censored was extremely wide. Accordingly, there was a risk that a depiction of a girl spreading her genitalia would be meaningless. Because artists knew this, there was no point in drawing the "kupaa" at that time.

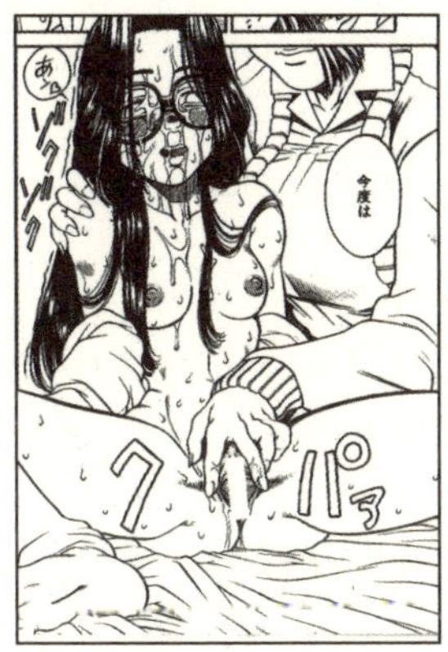

6-20: "A Slave" (Rei Hidiri 1997, Fujimi Publishing)

6-21: "Hisho no Himegoto" (Katsupiko Fuji 1997, Shinyusha)

6-22: ***Dance of Desire*** (*Yokubou no Rinbu;* Toshio Maeda 1983, Ichibankan Shobo)

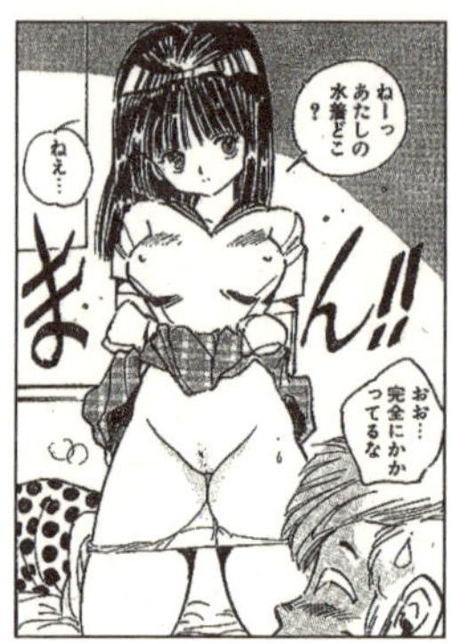

6-23: "Sonna Hiromi wa Damasarete!" (Aki Uchiyama 1995, Sun Publishing)

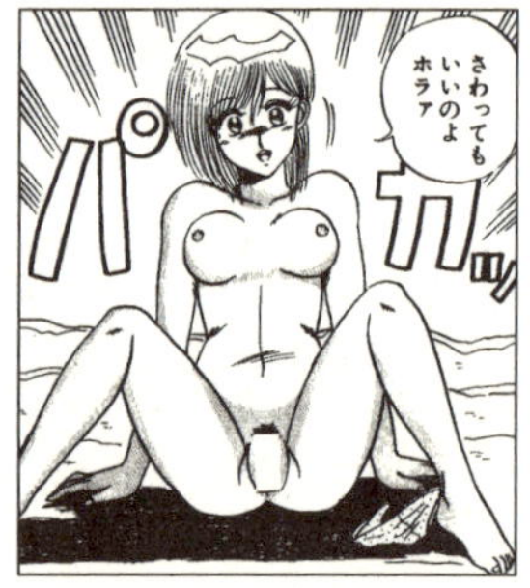

6-24: "Go-nenme no Natsu ni" (Shinkukan 1988, Tsukasa Shobo)

Another reason was due to a change in gender roles (men were *seme* (tops) and women were *uke* (bottoms)).

Up until the '90s, there were many male dominant situations and scenes. It was men who were peeking into embarrassed girls' genitalia, sometimes by force. However, after 2000, there were many cases in manga where women were inviting men to look inside of them, or even opening themselves up by choice. There was a shift from mainly male dominant scenes to female dominant scenes in storytelling. And women were assertively, at times aggressively, inviting men to take part in intercourse, so there was a need for a softer, cuter onomatope expression like "kupaa."

But this shift between male and female sex scenes wasn't limited to eromanga. Porn researcher Rio Yasuda discussed it in her book ***Chijo no Tanjo*** (2016, Ohta Publishing):

> *"In the end, in pornographic films, the orthodox school of porn actresses were requested to do vanilla movies. Should they willingly use obscene language, joyfully torment their male part ners, or adopt a (sexually) aggressive position, they were to be given a wider berth in the industry. ...In recent years, the female image has changed quite a bit. Women as molesters that aggressively seek out sex with their male partners are now seen as an affirmative thing."*

Ever since the '90s, the power balance between men and women has shifted, and the roles that each take within sex have been reconsidered. Preferences for porn viewers and eromanga readers both shifted towards content with sexually aggressive women seeking out men. At the same time, the tide turned towards a migration in the direction of hardcore content. Censorship loosened up as well, and one could even start drawing details of female genitalia if they so wished. The reason why usage of "kupaa" increased was due to the fact that within pornographic media of various sorts (including eromanga), the change in awareness of the idea of women becoming molesters was now approved by consumers. And as eromanga became more hardcore, I happen to think there are two main causes why.

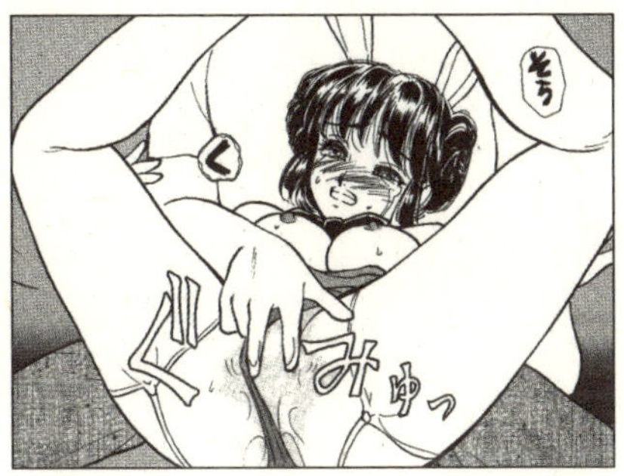

6-25: "Up-Name DANGER Miss Bunny!!" ("*Tottemo DANGER Bunny-chan*"; Mitsune Ayasaku 1992, Tsukasa Shobo)

The Versatility of "Kupaa" Is High

In many cases, numerous eromanga expressions that became fads soon after would come to influence seinen works, but in the case of "kupaa," it was hard to use outside of situations with girls opening their genitals. However, in shonen works, the expression was used for violent situations.

You may be thinking, "Oh no, not this again," but let me once more reference Kentaro Yabuki's *To LOVE Ru: Darkness* here. Even before comic regulation and policing, there have always been works holding a position about girls opening their "secret place." Go Nagai, Nonki Miyasu, and Masatoshi Kawabara helped start the trend, but a great

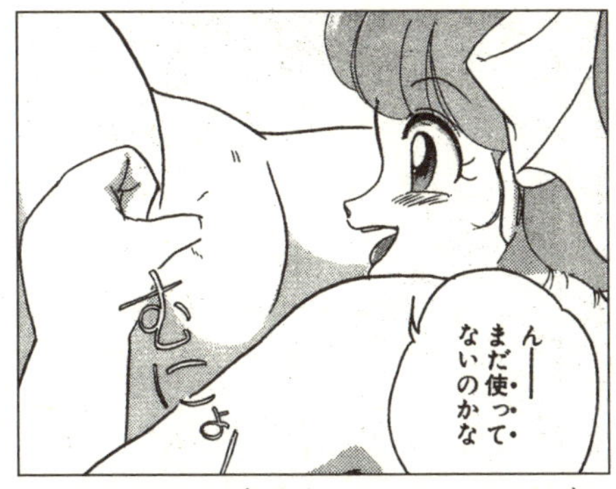

6-26: "Sweet Candy" (Tamano Tamaki 1989, Amikaru)

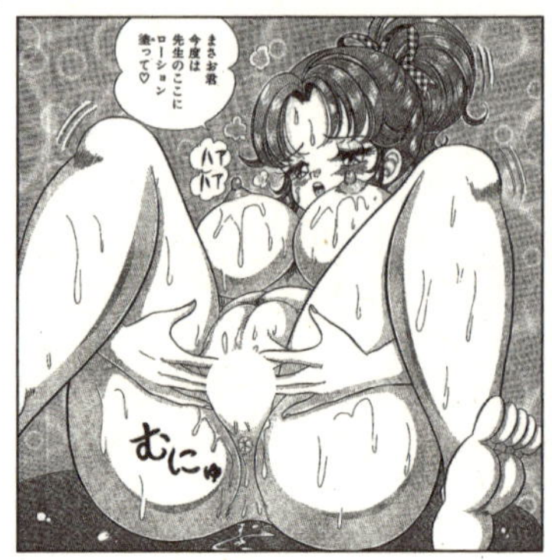

6-27: "Pururun ♥ Otome Hakusho" (Wataru Watanabe 1995, Cybele Publishing)

many of works with this theme can be seen in manga. However, since the advent of stricter regulation, if you asked anyone now, they would say putting references to this in shonen manga and having it survive revision is impossible.

But Kentaro Yabuki challenged this convention. More than anything, he wanted to place the first eromanga expression within shonen content, and with the aid of his extraordinary, creative originality, made the impossible possible with his *Jump Square* serialized series, *To LOVE Ru: Darkness. (Darkness* may appear to be a seinen title to the average reader, but this series is still considered a *Weekly Shonen Jump* property as it started off in that magazine.)

The "unforeseen accident" (AKA lucky pervert) trope in use here, with the heroine being flipped upside down into a piledriver position where she is face to face with her partner and by coincidence the protragonist just happens to hang over her. The protagonist then spreads her "secret place" apart, in an established pattern found in erotic comedies. But here is the height of Kentaro Yabuki's skills being shown to the audience. The "kupaa" onomatope isn't there, but the rest of the expression is. Yabuki placed a speech bubble and shaped it so it falls right over the heroine's gaping genitals (6-29). The dialogue fits perfectly in the bubble, while the heroine looks like she can't believe they're about to talk about her "secret place" and is thoroughly embarrassed by it. The protagonist's fingers are repositioned for

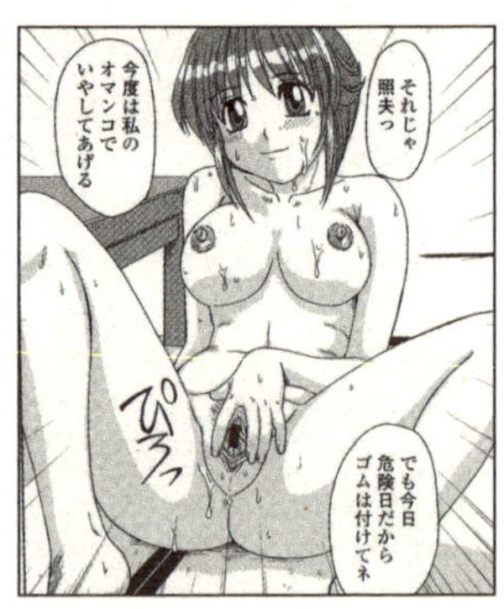

6-28: "Stamina Ryori" (Morris 2002, Fujimi Publishing)

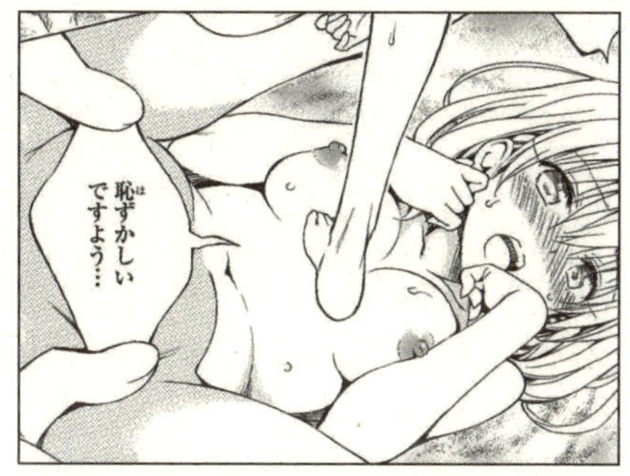

6-29: ***To LOVE Ru: Darkness***, Vol. 15 (Saki Hasemi & Kentaro Yabuki 2016, Shueisha/Seven Seas Ent.)

shonen readers, but otherwise it is a complete homage to the "kupaa" found in eromanga. I hope that with how far he went with this homage, that it lifts Yabuki's spirits.

Just as we saw with the *ahegao*, in a recent trend, the "kupaa" has migrated to the land of 3D, recycled as an element in porn movies. In those movies, just as with the *ahegao,* the usage frequency of the "kupaa" is high, and because this expression existed visually within porn before this point, the use of it has been good. Eventually the actresses whose genitals are being spread with the "kupaa" on packaging grew more eye-catching. And if you search with the keyword "kupaa," you'll get over eighty search results from major porn companies and their streaming services. The oldest *JAV* movies with this expression were made in 2009, when the "kupaa" was a fad in eromanga magazines. It rode the wave created by the fad back to the porn world in a moment of redundancy and duplication.

Even now, current pornographic films have been heavily influenced by eromanga, and we know that by how quickly the pool of users is duplicating and growing.

The reason why the "kupaa" is so heavily popular is because even though its usage is very limited in eromanga, that doesn't stop people from using it anyway. The moment that those fingers open up genitalia, the versatility of use as an onomatope makes the "kupaa" quite rich.

For example, when one wants to enhance the magnification of a photo on a smartphone, in IT jargon, it's called "pinching out" or "pinching open," which is quite frankly, rather confusing. But if you change this to "making your smartphone kupaa," eromanga readers would understand and make this spread at an insane rate, to the point where it would reach the zeitgeist. Just as with the *ahegao,* this universalization of the expression started after 2000, and the power that the internet holds as a medium helped to spread this special use expression.

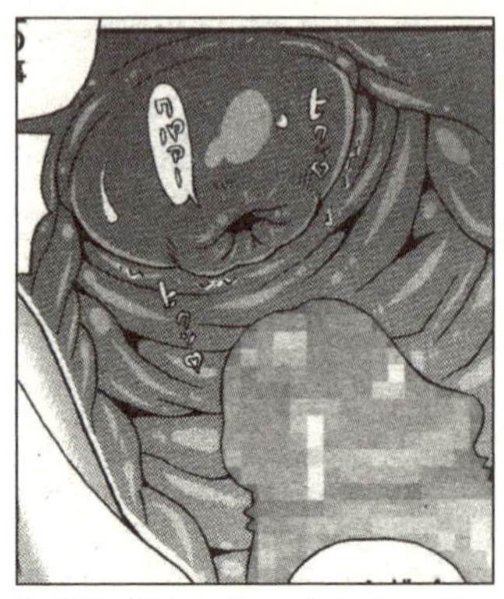

6-30: "Yoshida to Mesu-buta Senpai" (John K. Pe-ta 2016, Core Magazine)

Be that as it may, Akazawa RED aided in the packaging of the "kupaa" as situational use expression, and in order to become encoded, it had to be able to make a strong impression on its audience. And had it not been able to do so, it most likely wouldn't have become as popular as it has. But it's also a result of the many components of the issue, as well as just plain old luck.

Of course, sound effects continue evolve in their birthplace… eromanga.

In master of the *cross-section view* John K. Pe-ta's recent works, when the os uteri opens, it does so with a "kupaa." When a cotton swab is inserted in a naval and spreads it, the fetish factor for this content goes up as it also makes a "kupa" sound (6-30, 31).

As an eromanga technique, "kupaa" has become its own pronoun thanks to the efforts of Akazawa RED, even if he himself does not believe he is the inventor. But it is clear that he loved it to such a degree that he included it in the title of his works. So, he probably does carry a degree of pride that because of his use it spread as an expression. And that is why many fans probably link Akazawa RED to the onomatope in their heads.

However, because of how things happened, and because of the love that this unique symbol-like sound effect received from both readers and artists alike, one should keep in mind that this

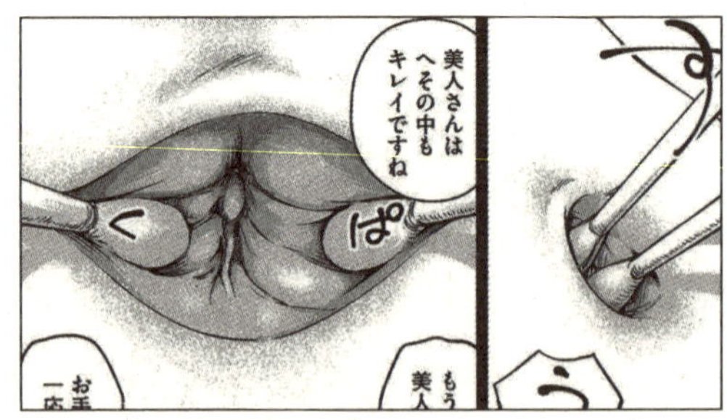

6-31: "Sokai no HESO Kaizoku" (Hirodi Ishikawa 2017, GOT)

may be a rare case when it comes to the history of eromanga expressions. Mostly because in situations like these, unrelated to both the wills of the inventor and the artist that made it spread, the interpretation of said expression has taken on a life of its own.

So, let's go into a more detailed explanation of that in the next section.

"Ramee!" and Misakura-Go

Of the two big eromanga onomatopes that I'm presenting to you within this chapter, the second is "ramee" (らめぇ). In this case, "ramee" here means "don't touch me there," and it is sourced from the word "dame" (don't). Though "dame" becomes substituted by both "ramee" and "rame" (らめ) with an orthological emphasis at the end, there are many variations where it is accompanied by an exclamation point or a heart mark, as well (6-32~36). There is even a rare type of variation which features a girl dressed up as a cat combining the latter syllable of the word with the sound that cats make (*nya*/meow) becoming "nyamee" (6-37).

Regarding its use, while it is widely used as a type of inarticulate speech (like slurring or lisping) due to both the rhythm and pleasure felt during sex, at its core, it is fundamentally a variation on dialogue. It may be different from an actual onomatope in this sense, but there are many times when its drawn form is used as a linguistic emphasis, or, in many other instances, is used as a sound of movement. For the sake of this book, I will be treating it as a sound effect; more specifically, as a type of onomatope.

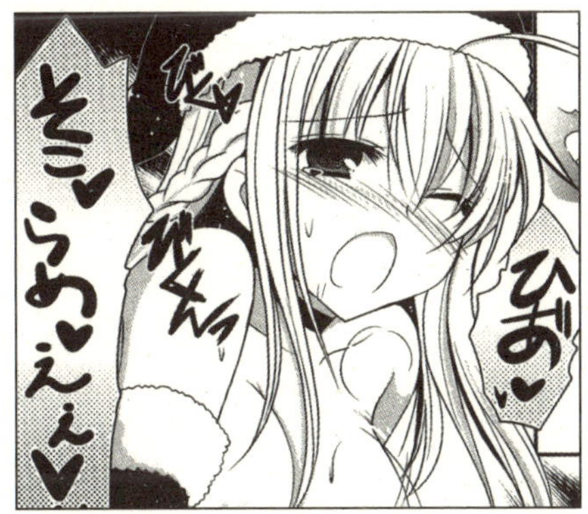

6-32: "Onedari Santa ♥" (Mari Amo 2012, MAX)

Just like "kupaa," in terms of its nuance and impact, it wasn't until after 2000 that one

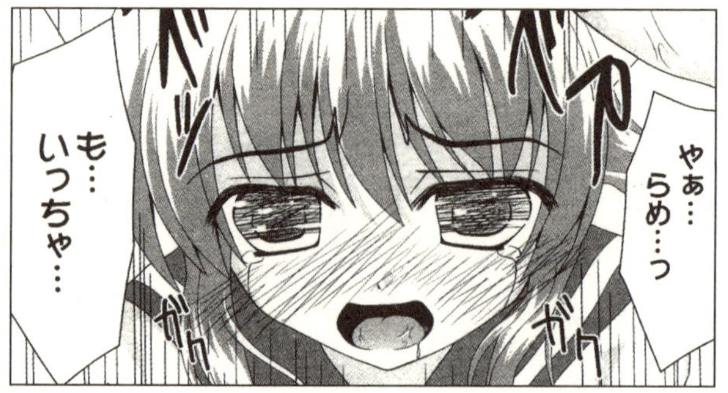

6-33: "Cosplay wa Hajimemashita" (Ke-to 2009, Core Magazine)

started seeing it in eromanga often. Due to its ease of use and practical use as slang, its spread was via the internet.

However the internet version of "ramee" was but one part of a large word organization structure of slang that was called *misakura-go* (lit. Misakura-speak). *Misakura-go* is sourced from popular manga author, illustrator, and game production creator Nankotsu Misakura. The term is a generic one from the speech patterns of his heroines, who had a peculiar phraseology when they spoke. It was not named as such by its creator, but instead was coined as such by a third party, who compiled all of the vocabulary and expressions used by Misakura and made it into a dictionary of sorts. There is impact in that alone, and in the power of these expressions, which has charmed readers, along with the power of their direction in their titles with erotic language.

In Misakura's works, in many situations a *futanari* (hermaphrodite) girl is either masturbating or having sex, and in order to cutely alter her speech when she ejaculates or in the heat of things, she uses certain words that she wouldn't otherwise use when she speaks (6-38). Phrases like "ochinpo-miruku" (dick milk), "zamen-

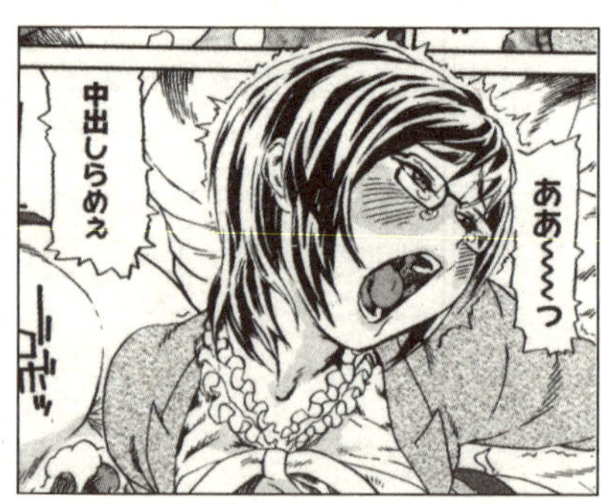

6-34: "Wakaretemo, Suki na Sensei" (Tsubura Hase 2005, Core Magazine)

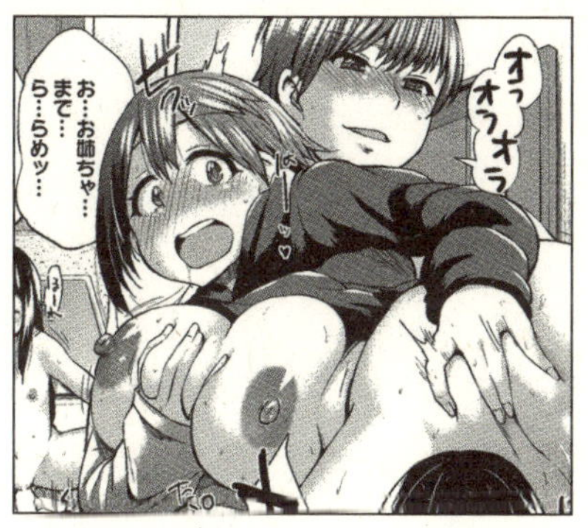

6-35: "X-Swap!" (Yume-no-Tanuki 2013, WAKOH Publishing)

miruku" (semen milk), "ecchi na torotoro-jiru" (perverse melty juice) were like magical words. In terms of other words that are frequently used in their works, the strength or weakness of the girls' voices—thick, husky, or hoarse—were all complexly jumbled together and used like a machine gun within their work.

Some examples of this would be: "Aaaaaaa!", "Nn Oooh ♥ Hot-t ♥" "My tits! Ah! My dick too! They f-feel sho good…♥", "It's hitting my pussy so deep! ♥ SHLOP! ♥ SHLOP! ♥ It's like it's stabbing me! ♥ SLURSH ♥", "I losh it ♥ I losh it so mush ♥♥" and the like.

The "i" and the "mo" syllables in the Japanese language usually do not use voiced consonants, and *misakura-go* adds voiced consonants to these syllables to get lines similar to "Feesh good" (instead of "feels good") and other sounds that sound slurred. It is important to note here that there is also dialogue used where the reader cannot figure out how to properly pronounce it in Japanese (6-39).

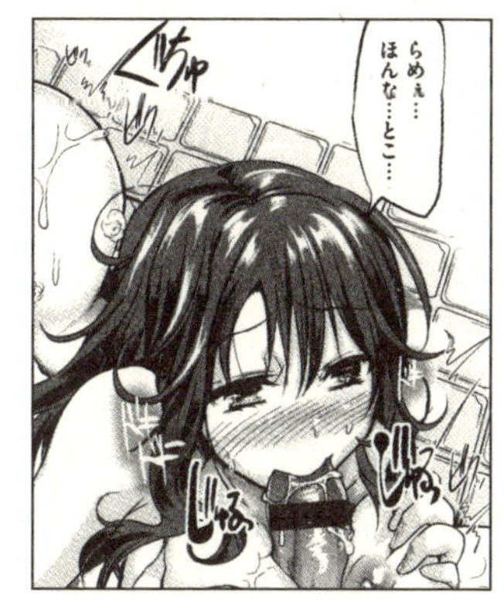

6-36: ***Don't be Hard on Me ♥*** (*Ijimecha Ramee ♥*; Shimaji 2015, Wanimagazine)

In Nankotsu Misakura's worldview, the ethical limiters have been released, and are constructed in such a way they become a broken form of art. Misakura's work became the heart of the *futanari* doujinshi fad that began in the mid-'90s, and from their early period onward had their protagonists, *futanari* girls, who often speak in uniquely lewd and verbally unusual ways. While this is not limited to eromanga, when it comes to the direction of creative works there is usually an eros related to words, attacking the target with dirty talk, as well as voicing crudely during intercourse as well. This is a technique that can be used to make a situation comprehensively erotic.

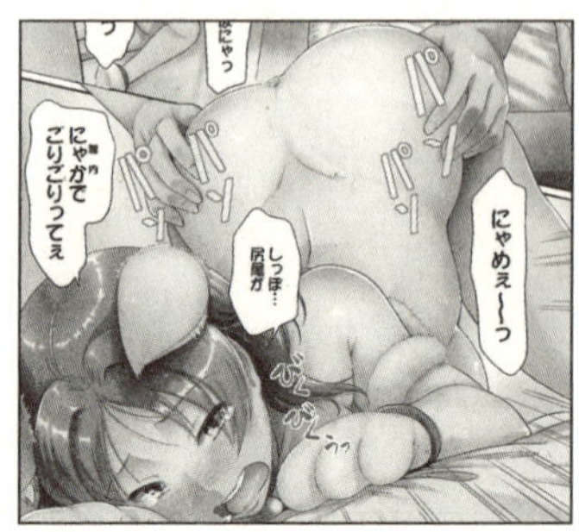

6-37: "Neko ni Saretai ♥" (Kazuki Hiro 2013, WAKOH Publishing)

Within eromanga, one often sees situations where a girl is told, "Go on, tell me what you want," a kind of guided dirty talk that allows that girl to say otherwise embarrassing things while combining a shyness on her behalf. Especially in pre-2000 eromanga, there was heavy use of these shy expressions that bordered on the unethical that were written in an enjoyable way. There might have been an awareness that when one overcame all of that character's shyness and broke it down, the eros of the situation would disappear too.

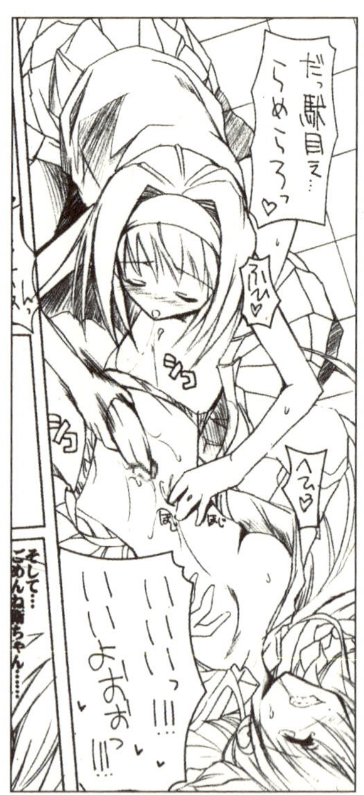

6-38: ***Binzume Imouto-tachi 2*** (HarthNir 2001, self-published)

When it came to language expressions, this is where Misakura showed everyone what they were really capable of. They cutely rendered the loosened shackles of ethics seen during intercourse and struck repeated blows to their readers with girls saying lewd things they couldn't normally say like "dick milk" that helped wreck their speech articulation ability resulting in these girls' minds breaking. These girls fell to pleasure, took it in, and *chose* to

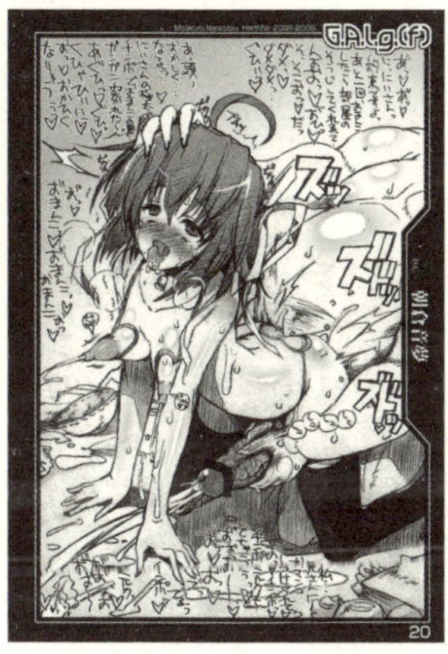

6-39: ***G.A.I.g (f)*** (HarthNir 2008, self-published)

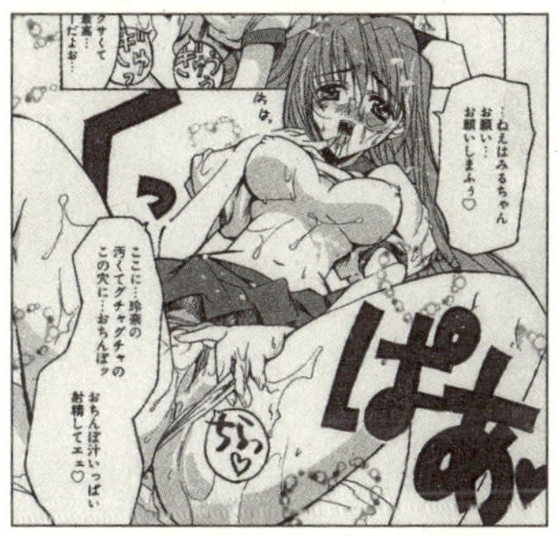

6-40: ***Gotai Choo Manzoku*** (Nankotsu Misakura 2001, Outou Shobo)

continue to speak in indecent language. Even broken down to their barest parts, these girls were a symbol of beauty, thereby reforming expressions that defied conventional wisdom (6-40).

In 2000, when Misakura's development was just getting underway, all of adult media saw the change of roles in intercourse. Where female characters were once defensive or passive during intercourse, they moved to an offensive or active role. It could be that Misakura read the room and acted upon it.

This was how *misakura-go* was born and evolved, but amongst that dictionary of Misakura's words, the term "ramee" would be the one to go viral online (6-41). But before unravelling the mystery of its spread, I would like to first look at how it came to be used in manga.

"Ramee" as Role Language

It appears that a great deal of people believe that Nankotsu Misakura is the inventor of the "ramee" sound effect. While within the *misakura-go* dictionary Misakura put an emphasis on "ramee," it was used in both regular and eromanga long before then.

Even within Osamu Tezuka's ***Black Jack***, there is a scene where Pinoko screams, "Rame!! Micha" (Don't look!!), but pleasure is not the focus of these words. Instead, it is more along the lines of baby talk (6-42). To that end, "ramee" is used here to denote Pinoko's role as a child, and so becomes one species of *role language* used in manga.

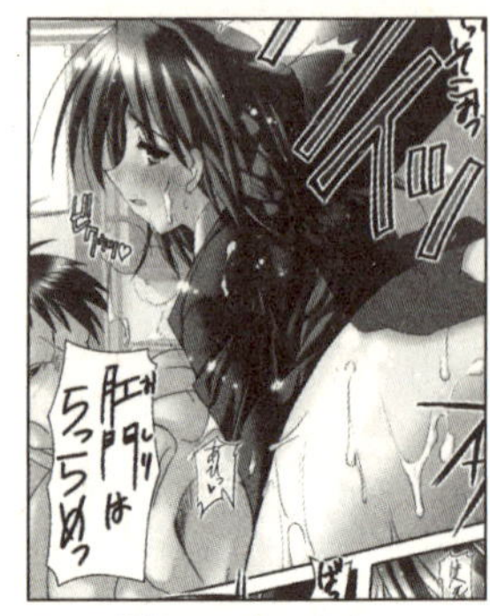

6-41: ***Hikikomori Kenkoho*** (Nankotsu Misakura 2003, Core Magazine)

Role language is used to reflect the type of character, as well as recollection of what the character has said. For example, if a character were to say "Washi wa XX Ja no~" (This old one is a XX) we would know that this is an elderly male character (because the pronoun "washi" is one that primarily older men use). There are also uses within Japanese regional dialects for role language as well, like "Ore wa Kenka Hayai jaken no~" (I ain't fixin' for a fight). In the case of a character speaking in stereotyped-Chinese, a phrase might look like "Watashi wa Ryori Umai aru ne" (I'm very good cooking, huh; with "aru" used as a Manchukuo colloquialism). For a complex *fujoshi* character ("rotten woman," a term for a female fan of boys' love), an expression like, "Onushi no Oshi Chara wa Dare de Gosaimasu ka?" (And, pray tell, which character dost thou support?) with eccentric turns of phrase including the use of the "onushi," an archaic pronoun, along with polite speech, would be best.

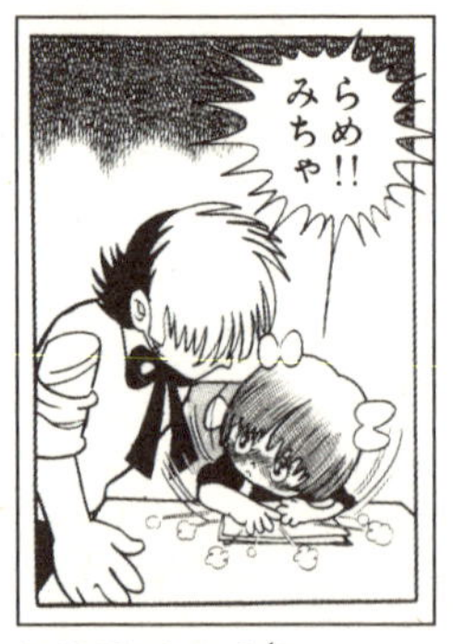

6-42: ***Black Jack*** (Osamu Tezuka 1975, Akita Shoten/ Vertical, Inc.)

Pinoko's "rame" is used as baby talk, illustrating that the age difference between her emotional age and actual age (she is a young adult whose organs were transplanted into the body of a doll). But there are many more expressions used as role language to emphasize her character. Both "ramee" and "rame" are usually used as broken inflections at the end of sentences to request the silence or repose of one's partner, but Pinoko's is the example of a speech impediment she has as a result of stunted growth. The Misakura version of "ramee" is used when the person saying it has fallen to pleasure, and thus has had their senses muddied by it. The crumbled, collapsed aspect of both words are alike, this is true, but prerequisites of their use are completely different. Therefore, one can conclude that the direct influence of Pinoko's use of the term on eromanga is weak at best.

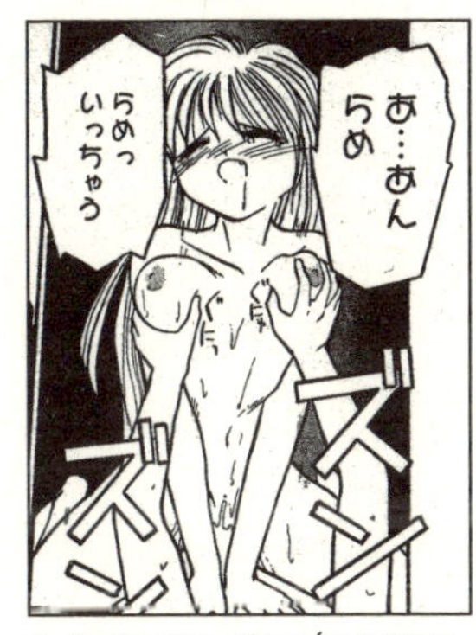

6-43: ***Any Questions*** (RaTe 1993, Tsukasa Shobo)

Let's go ahead and look at the use of this expression within eromanga. In Tsukasa Shobo's 1993 issue of *Comic Dolphin*, RaTe's manga ***Any Questions*** has a character utter "Rame, ramee icchau" (6-43). However, due to the fact that the expression is not used when the heroine is really starting to succumb to the pleasure of sex, and is instead a regular pet phrase "rametteru," it is only half-used as role language and half-used as one of the character's pet phrases.

On the other hand, in a 1998 issue of *Manga Zettai Manzoku* (Kasakura Publishing), Takashi Sano's serialized work has a heroine saying "rame" when she is trying to endure punishing pleasure at the hands of her partner (6-44).

In eromanga we can find uses of this expression prior to Misakura's, but unlike "kupaa," it makes a tiny impression. Because its use is so limited to when the character is experiencing pleasure and their consciousness is muddied (much like the "ramee" of today), one could say that it is the progenitor of the "ramee" that later appeared in *misakura-go*.

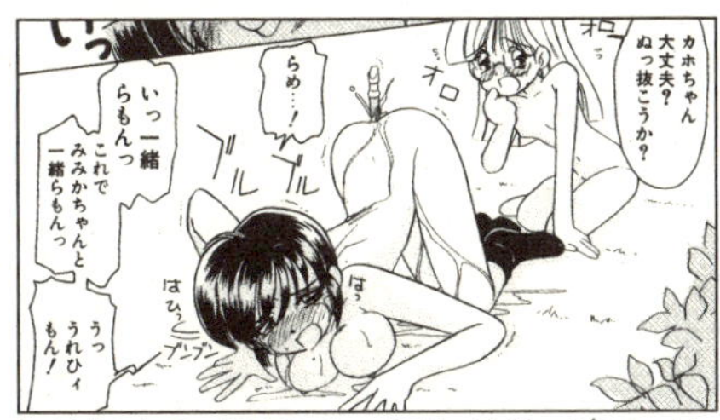

6-44: "Maka Fushigi Shukusei Shinshi Jiken" (Takashi Sano 1996, Kasakura Publishing)

"Ramee" Explodes as It Should

I wonder how recognition for the *misakura-go* "ramee" increased? I can say from my conclusion that because *misakura-go* is a linguistic expression, it overwhelmingly adds to the information load given to the audience. I believe that due to its explosive power as a neologism combined with a mixture of delusion, it made a very strong impression on readers. So, within the intense settings of once one reads a Misakura work they can't forget it. Add the lewd language that sends any sense of morals flying out the window, with the artist's tenacious obsession with all things erotic and other pieces of originality that until that point hadn't been seen within eromanga, and it carried an unforgettable energy with it. That worldview drew many people in, but these wild works often transcended common sense. Conversely, it seemed ripe with the potential for luring people in, which was probably a bet that the artist made during production.

Misakura's ideal was their written expressions, and until they were perfected, many processes, ideas, devices and schemes, as well as effort were surely required. But in reality, in Misakura's early works circa 1999, "ramee" was not one of them. Nor were there other speech patterns that indicated an inflection of crumbling words at the end of sentences like there is now. I went ahead and confirmed this, but the first time we actually saw "ramee" make its debut was in the work that Misakura began to release in 2002, specifically in ***Wakaitte Subarashii,*** which was serialized in *Comic Kikasuma Vol. 6* (Shobunkan, 6-45).

When I interviewed Misakura in 2016 about the birth of the "ramee," this is what they had to say:

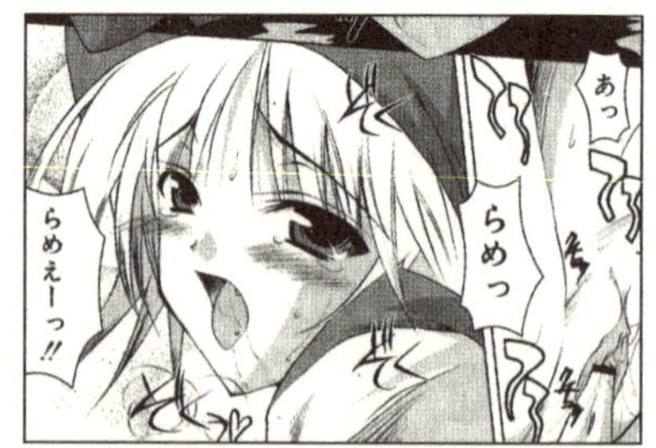

6-45: ***Wakaitte Subarashii*** (Nankotsu Misakura 2002, Shobunkan)

"The "ramee" term was an idea I had so I could show girls in a cute way."

The general concepts of both cute, used for girls, and cool, used for boys, are quite amorphous as is. So, to convey that to readers in pictures alone is actually quite difficult. In order to do this, a common technique is to have a third-party character say something in dialogue like "Oh! He's so cool!" In that way, even if the work doesn't show it in any other way, readers can still put two and two together and share a moment of recognition.

A similarly amorphous concept in eromanga would be the phrase "I can feel it!", when a character is feeling pleasure in intercourse, but it's actually quite difficult to get that across when drawn. Since these are done with attractive young female characters, in order to show that they're feeling it even more, one has to depict it in a cute way for the audience to understand. So of course, this plays out in dialogue, when a character says "I'm fweling it!" Mostly due to the fact that it's been thought that it's incredibly difficult to render this concept, Misakura's answer was to create his own language.

Just looking at the words, one can see that "I can feel it" is a bit of role language put into play, and *misakura-go* helps convey a worldview where these characters are feeling so much pleasure that it seems to be seeping into the language centers of their brains directly in a "cute" way. "Ramee" is a cute way to speak, conveying how charming and adorable the character is as they experience pleasure. They experience it until it seeps into their brain, making their words come out in *misakura-go*. This gives the audience a direct connection to the worldview, which is in no way the curveball it would seem but may be within the audience's heads that is the result of their view of *bishojo* characters.

At least, I feel that way when considering the degree of perfection of the expression.

Misakura went on, saying:

"This is only but one of my many funny ideas of phraseology within manga that I've thought of. But I do not think the idea is entirely mine. I think that I don't want my work to become a standard. I feel that would

pile up and crush me with its weight. And if that happens, I feel that I won't be able to draw manga freely anymore."

Constantly scrapping and building, always conceiving new concepts. These words give me a strong feeling that Misakura is never satisfied with the expressions they've created, taking a posture of being constantly constructive without being conceited. Misakura can speak of "ramee" as a phrase in their work, but it isn't like they're constantly using it as an expression. Instead, they are constantly groping for new solutions, coming up with new sound effects to use.

I've looked at the entire run of works that feature "ramee" and I understand its comprehensive potential within work, but I am skeptical and not quite convinced of the thought that this is what drove many people to recognize and spread Misakura's expression. Many people know about the "ramee" expression, but few realize that it's only but a part of the *misakura-go* dictionary.

Certainly, Misakura's works have created a strong impact on their readers. Not just "ramee," but parts of what we covered in the last chapter, the *ahegao* expression, as well. Misakura was one of the first to promptly introduce the "double-piece ahegao" in their work, and even now is attacking new expressions. That posture of theirs with regard to how they work has no doubt influenced others.

However, its transmission reached readers who do not read eromanga. I believe the reason it was able to develop as it has is due to the word's potential, but also due to many tailwinds that caught it as well. Just as with "kupaa," its ease of use is immense. Just by code-switching the mundane "dame" (no) with the slurred "ramee," it has yielded a ton of jokes as a result. To that end, thanks to its diffusion via social media and the internet at large, when I looked at conversations between *otaku* (fans), internet message boards and the like, of course I found many people using it that were familiar with Misakura's works. There were also many people using it that didn't know about them, and those that used it as a general joke. As I searched, the diffusion spread on and on and on.

It was easily used as a parody by voice actors and actresses when they were on the radio. On the eromanga side of things, Misakura's works have supported the females as molesters boom that's been happening in recent years. When you have a worldview that has a broken sense of morals from the jump, it was already okay.

As an onomatope, "ramee" combined latent potential with vocabulary and the internet age's power of diffusion into a turn of phrase. The interaction between the two accelerated the encoding process and developed it to the degree where the public at large didn't care if it was erotic or not in origin as it became common use.

"Ramee" Stands Alone

Originally, even *misakura-go* was only but one component of Misakura's works. But "ramee" had spread too far, separating itself from Misakura's works and began to walk on its own. A dilemma developed where the more recognizable "ramee" became, the murkier the impression of all of Misakura's works became. Misakura felt that this was becoming a problem, and when we look at their words, we understand that this wasn't their real intention at all.

In this book so far, we've seen how this has happened to many expressions. When this happens, while their sphere of influence may grow, there is a trade-off with a fading of memory of their origin. But that is an expression's predestined fate.

However, the originality of *misakura-go* was just too strong, and precisely because it was too difficult for other eromanga artists to appropriate it, I'm sure there was a dimension of the expression being absorbed into the genre. I don't think that the reality was that pessimistic, though. The fact that it had the power to charm as many people as it did, that it spread as far as it did was more than anyone ever could've imagined. It flew over eromanga and into regular manga, anime, and other forms of media.

It is here that I would, once again, like to bring up the all-expression-absorbing shonen black hole that is *To LOVE Ru*, where of course, there is an example of the "ramee." What's especially spectacular about this use of the expression is that it is not typeset dialogue, but instead it is hand-drawn like a sound effect (*To LOVE Ru: Darkness, Volume 3,* 6-46).

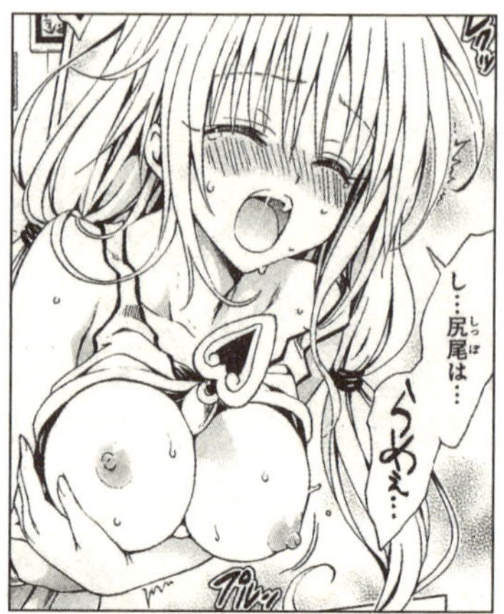

6-46: ***To LOVE Ru: Darkness***, Vol 3 (Saki Hasemi & Kentaro Yabuki 2011, Shueisha/ Seven Seas Ent.)

In the 36th volume of Kenjiro Hata's ***Hayate the Combat Butler*** *(Hayate no Gotoku;* 2004, Shogakukan/ Viz Media), it's been added to a chapter title (6-47). In this chapter, the heroine is desperately trying to make sure that Hayate, the love interest, doesn't see her doing anything embarrassing. The title encapsulates her feelings the moment when it happens anyway. In the end, the actual term is not used in the chapter's dialogue, but it still becomes a theme for the story, absorbing the expression when it denotes a girl's embarrassment and becomes the height of the term "dame."

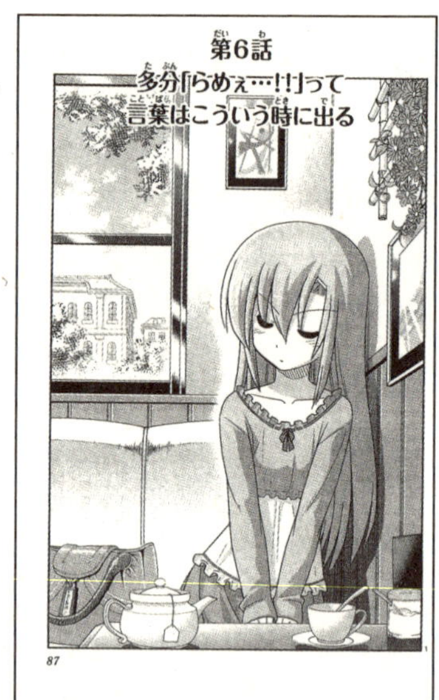

6-47: ***Hayate the Combat Butler!***, Vol. 36 (*Hayate no Gotoku!*; Kenjiro Hata 2013, Shogakukan, Viz Media)

"Ramee" has spread to many other places as well. The irregularly serialized hit from Kodansha's *Weekly Young Magazine*, Kazuyoshi Tomoki's ***Zeppin! Ramen Musume*** (2012) also features the "ramee," where it became "raamee~" just for ramen (6-48). And by the way, this is not a manga about food; it's actually an erotic comedy.

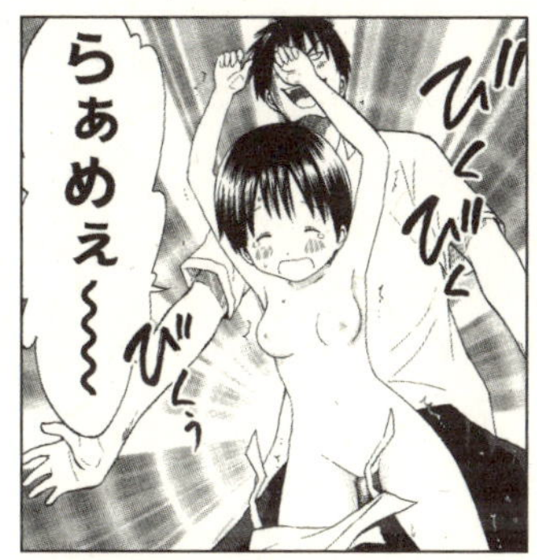

6-48: ***Zeppin! Ramen Musume***, Vol. 1 (Kazuyoshi Tomoki 2012, Kodansha)

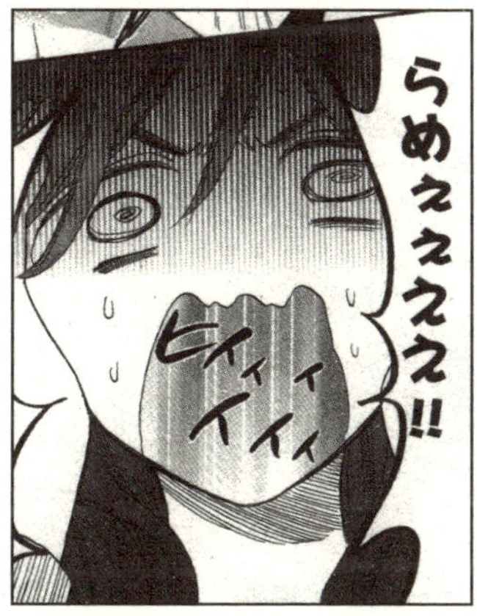

6-49: ***Kiss Him, Not Me!***, Vol. 9 *(Watashi ga Mote-te Dou Sun da;* Junko 2016, Kodansha/Kodansha USA)

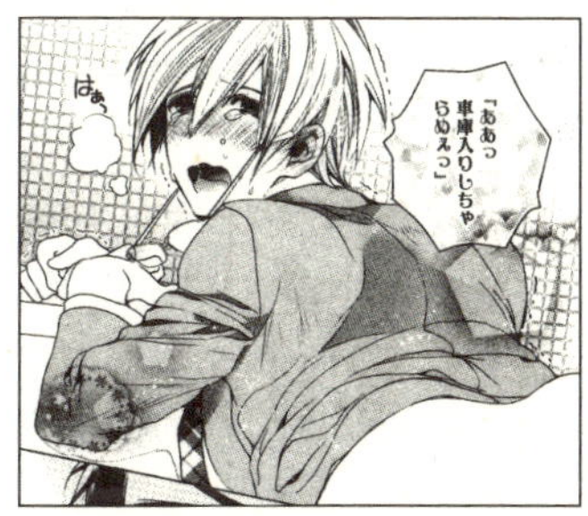

6-50: ***Kichiku, Encount*** (Owal 2014, Takeshobo)

For anime, we have ***The Tower of Druaga: The Aegis of Uruk*** (2008, GONZO) where when the heroine is being attacked by monsters, they want to hear her scream out "Rameeee" and will only stop their attack when she does so. It is used as an element of comedy, where the writers assume there is a degree of familiarity amongst the audience with the word she screams out.

In the world of shojo manga, there's Junko's ***Kiss Him, Not Me!*** *(Watashi ga Mote-te Dou Sun da;* 2013, Kodansha/Kodansha USA), where the *fujoshi* protagonist screams out "Rameeee" in a moment of panic in scene that leaves quite the impression (6-49). Here once again we see the context of the female nerd with the protagonist, where the artist assumes that if the audience is also nerdy, they will understand it as an idiom and mark of education.

For *BL*, we have Owal's ***Kichiku, Encount*** (2014, Takeshobo), where we can see a bit of a different form for "ramee." When one of the characters, a bottom who likes pornography, is inviting his top partner into anal sex, he yelps out the "ramee" he's heard in the porn movies he watches (6-50). What we should pay attention to is that "ramee" is a term used in male-targeted media, so here we have a portrayal where porn is obviously influencing the character. And of course, "ramee" is used in actual porn titles. But it's in titles like ***Oni-chan Rameeee!*** (Momotarou AV), where, in this case, it's a younger girl and multiple older men. One can see this in more than a few *JAV* titles, and while I wasn't able to confirm whether or not the actress actually says "ramee," I would like to.

In this way we see Misakura's work separating from its original meaning and intent, and with "ramee" and *misakura-go* starting to stand on their own, I fear that its ruin may be nigh. In reality, while it is an expression that sticks in people's minds, just like cooking with durian, I fear that's difficult to handle. No doubt they'll eventually be another eromanga technique that will absorb it. Therefore, I believe that it's certain that within the next decade, we'll cease to see this expression within eromanga.

It's important to remember that its ingredients are still alive and kicking even now. Because so many people love this expression, we have seen it propagate to different forms of media, which has been paired with various new interpretations of the expression. And I believe that this gives it so many different places and venues to shine.

From Encoding to Public Property

Exceedingly simple and contained in three Japanese syllables, both "ramee" and "kupaa" (*ra-me-e* and *ku-pa-a*) have potential hidden within their terms and may be overutilized depending on the delusions of their artists. And it is because they are so simple, that they are so very deep. It is also one reason why onomatope research is currently thriving in Japan.

Up until now, the other expressions we've touched upon other than the *nipple afterimage,* including tentacles, the *cross-section view,* the *ahegao,* and now "kupaa" and "ramee," all have unclear origins. What they all share in common is that someone started them, and they did not suddenly spread until after a bit of a maturation period. And like the Cambrian period for living organisms, there was suddenly a period of explosive growth.

Both tentacles and "ramee" are examples of the expressions themselves, thanks to the works that used them becoming hits. In the case of both the *cross-section view* and "kupaa," they're characteristics of changing eras, where due to the loosening of rules on censorship, the amount of their use increased. At the same time, the *ahegao,* "kupaa," and "ramee" are all post-2000 ideas that developed more due to the internet, so much so they are used as items of communication. This includes meanings that may diverge from the original, but because of that we've been able to see a wider degree of recognition.

Combining the artists' powers of delusions and creativity, they have changed the surrounding circumstances and environment of eromanga. And when further meshed with happenstance, these memes have been accepted.

Of course, within eromanga, there are probably more expressions that this book has not covered, and many more that continue to be developed. Within that lot are those expressions that never were properly encoded and disappeared thereafter. Or to put it the reverse way, the amount of accepted expressions is few indeed. Artists aren't drawing manga to invent expressions, but new symbols are constantly being invented as artists are groping for solutions to problems in their art. As a result, many people have been influenced by these expressions, which inducted these expressions into a "hall of fame" called encoding. I believe that in that sense, perhaps expressions really are an artist's fortune.

I have come to sincerely believe that the footprints of those who have faced manga are actually the public property on which the encoding process takes place. ✿

The History of Hentai Manga

CHAPTER SEVEN

The Struggle of Policing and Censorship

Censorship Is a Nuisance, but We Don't Hate It

As a form of adult media, eromanga's predestined fate has been to do battle with the powers of policing. Out of all of the genres of manga, eromanga is the only one where artists are obligated to censor their work, and the relationship between the genre and censorship is akin to two brothers bound in an unpleasant but unavoidable relationship.

What's troublesome about this is that they're exact opposites of each other, but precisely because of the fact that censorship is its own artistic process, both artists and editors alike have become skillful at using it during the revision process, and the prerequisites set to erase those revisions have become downright inflammatory as techniques to use.

Therefore, censorship and revision have become manga expressions unto themselves. The more they are regulated, the more they burn with the spirit of combativeness, and in that act, become a revolt against those very regulations. From that rebellious spirit, numerous expressions including the *cross-section view* and tentacles were developed. But as I've said before, these expressions were born out of a disdain for the censorship on behalf of both artists and readers alike.

However, when one knows about censorship's history, as well as the idiosyncrasies of the methods used to carry it out, it becomes clear that while censorship itself is annoying, it is not necessarily hated.

The reason why genitalia are censored in Japanese media originates from *Article 175*, which outlaws the distribution of obscene materials. Even if it's an illustrated image drawn in pen, if it is considered obscene, it still falls under the law and legally cannot be distributed.

As to what constitutes what is obscene, there have been many battles throughout history regarding that subject alone. It's become an important topic to those who create regular manga as well. So as long as manga exists, censorship will and must exist right alongside it.

There have been many books on manga published about this topic. For those interested on reading more about it, I suggest you take a look at ***Manga wa Naze Kisei Sareru no ka*** (Yoshiyuki Nagaoka 2010, Heibonsha) and ***Eros to "Waisetsu" no Aida*** (Hisashi Sonoda and Hiroshi Dai/2016, Asahi Shimbun Publications). But in this chapter, I thought I would focus on the particular subset of censorship as it pertains to genitalia, specifically limited to male genitalia. . . .But it turns out doing so is quite difficult.

The domain of censorship and revision of genitalia as it happens in eromanga changes its shape along with the times, much like an amoeba in fluid has evolved into mysterious creatures over time. And as censorship evolves, its effects change along with it. At times, those changes become transparent. The criterion for censorship and revision are like waves undulating, thickening and thinning themselves over and over across the ages. Accordingly, the illustrations used here from times when those standards have been so thin it was as if everything was uncensored (if we had a time like that, that is), if they were to be published again now, most likely they would be found liable. However, if we were to censor those images based on current censorship and revision standards, I'm sure we would accidentally create some kind of paradox by doing so, making them incomprehensible to people of that time.

I once asked at a Comic Market preparation meeting if we could self-publish a book that collected the history of censorship and revision [in Japan]. I was told that without censoring the images that were to be used within it, I wouldn't be able to distribute it, and that was when I abandoned all hopes in ever doing so. In order to define the history of censorship, we would have to use undefinable images, turning this into a bit of an eromanga version of the uncertainty principle, where we wouldn't be able to define censorship at all as a result.

In order to exclude those uncertain and undefinable elements, I will use schematic diagrams to explain what types of censorship and revision are used on genitalia. This will include their species, role, significance, technique, and difference based on genre.

The Standard Phallus

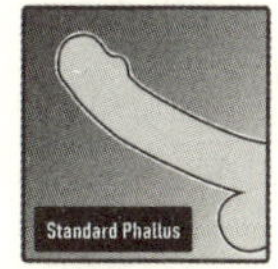

Seaweed Strip that Covers the Entire Penis

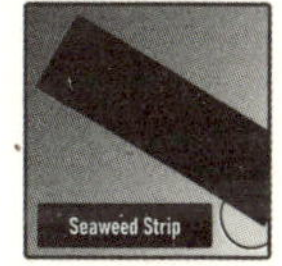

The seaweed-like strip that covers the entire penis seems like it's a relic of a bygone age, as if someone older presented it with pride [to younger people]. It is perhaps the most orthodox of censorship techniques. This technique that covers the contour of the penis is simple, and just covers the entire thing in a black rectangle; although in some cases, it is a white rectangle. At times this technique only covers the penis itself, but also sometimes hides the testicles as well (7-1, 2). This technique is used often in older eromanga, and recently has more or less completely fallen out of use. When one does see it, it's often in shonen or seinen manga titles, and more so in comedic manga.

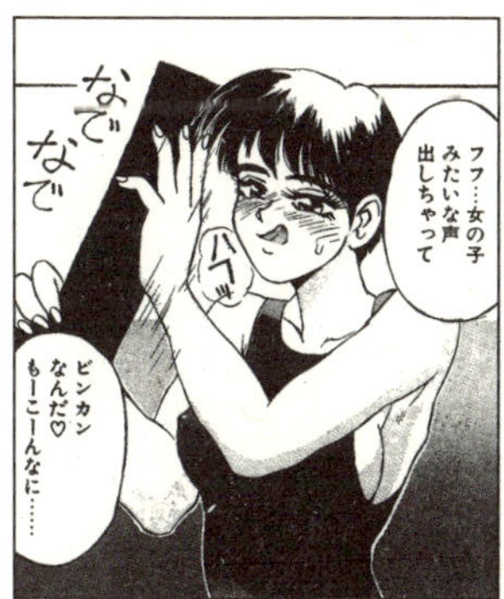

7-1: ***NeWMen*** (Go Zappa 1993, Tatsumi Publishing)

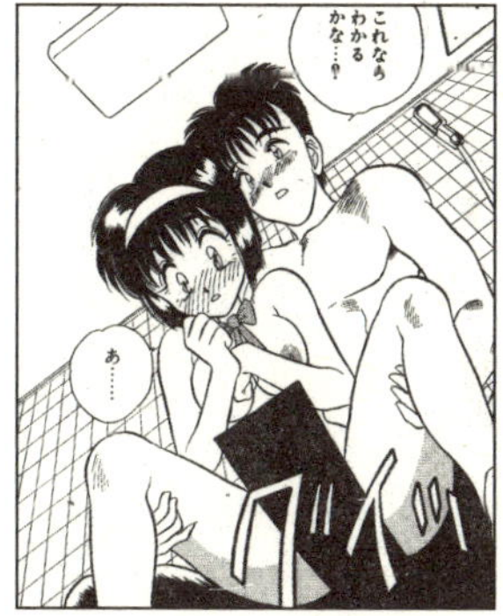

7-2: "Yura Yura Paradise" (Aura Seiji 1993, Fujimi Publishing/ Fantagraphics)

The White Rod (Lightsaber Technique)

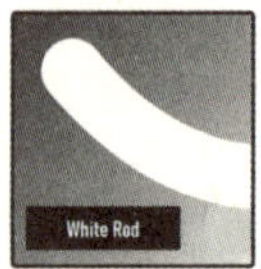

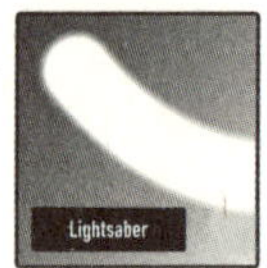

This technique does not follow the precise contours of the penis, but there are cases where the tip is on a white rod. This technique is slightly clearer than the seaweed technique, but since it doesn't depict the penis realistically, you can find this in seinen manga as well. It also can be found in *TL* and *BL* titles, and it may be the most suitable for female readers since it doesn't realistically depict a penis. Because the effect of the image looks as if it's in a shape that looks more like a lightsaber (white with gradated edges), it's been called just that (7-3).

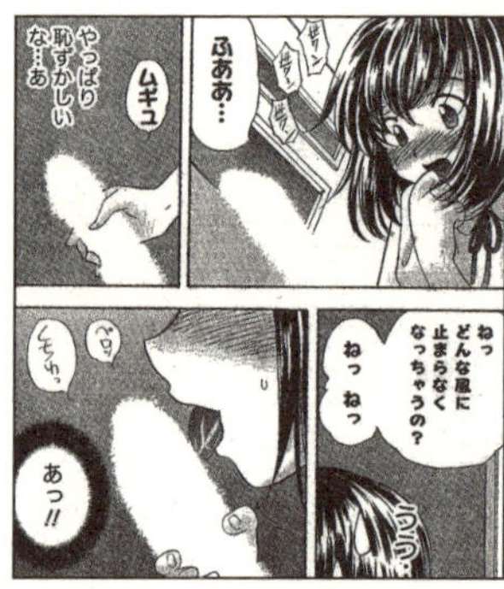

7-3: "Waitress" (Ruka Umino 2009, Takeshobo)

The White Shape

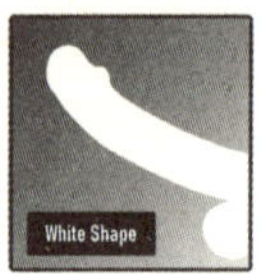

This technique is commonplace in current adult comic magazines, and it features a white contoured shape censoring the penis. Compared to the rod, this technique can show the size of the glans as well as the thickness of the shaft to the audience. There have been many ways to erase this particular method of censorship, but because this is used in magazines that are sold in convenience stores, this technique is kind of the go-to technique of choice when it comes to so-called "gray zone" magazines.

Before censorship, the genitals themselves are not drawn, but because this technique uses a contour, the artist needs to make sure there's a sense of the genitals being there regardless (7-4). Another widely seen type of this expression is one that seems to thoroughly cut out the penis, but there are also cases where this technique can have a similar visual effect to that of the lightsaber technique.

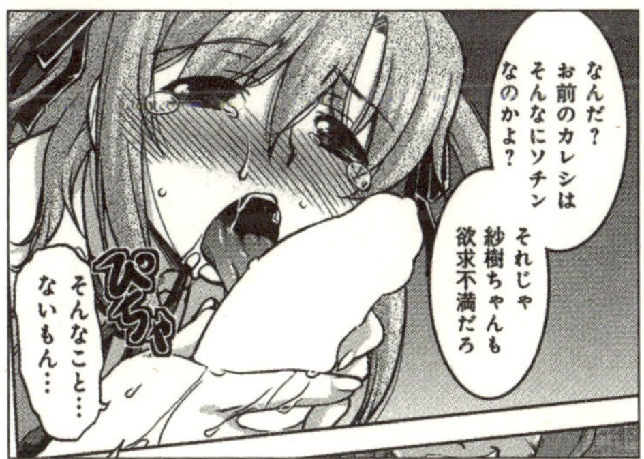

7-4: ***Chikan Yuugi,*** Play Case 2 (Harumi Shimamoto 2017, Cosmic Publishing)

The Mosaic

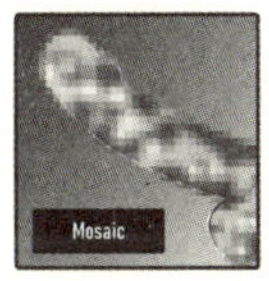

This technique does not blur the penis with a white shape, nor does it hide it with a black box, instead it uses a pixelated mosaic effect to censor. It could be said that the mosaic uses all other types of censorship on top of pixelating the actual image of the penis itself. There are only two forms of this technique: 1) where the male genitalia are censored using photo manipulation software, much like an artist's watermark, and 2) a screen-tone like mosaic that seemingly censors things randomly. The former has the same origin point as the mosaic used in porn, which creates an optical illusion where it looks as if the censorship has actually disappeared, and one can somewhat see the genitalia, thereby opening the mind's eye (7-5). The latter is much like a Showa-era bathroom, where mosaic tiles are used, and nothing more. This technique is used a lot in shonen and seinen comic magazines, but the size of the mosaic tiles/pixels tend to change during the era they're being utilized in.

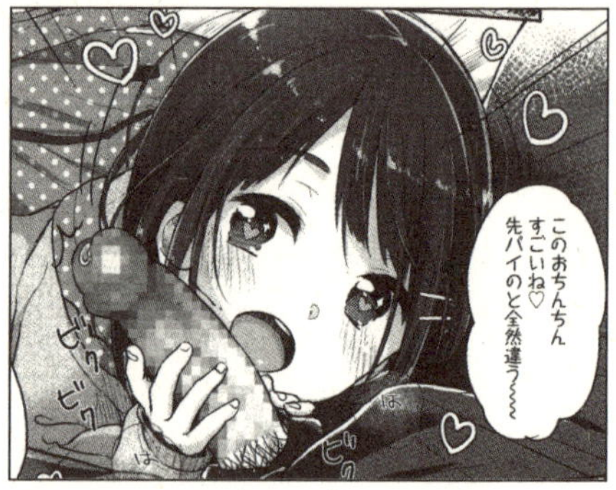

7-5: "Konnichiwa Ochinchin" (Yukiu Con 2017, Akaneshinsha)

Do the Mangaka Really Draw Everything?

One question that pops up frequently for eromanga artists is, "For the parts of the comic that will be censored, does the artist bother to draw them at all?" The answer to this question is: sometimes they do, and sometimes they don't.

In situations when the editor tells an artist that their work will be censored, they're allowed to draw the genitals in question a bit fast and rough and more messy than usual. So, there are many cases where the artist finishes their work with just contours of the genitals but nothing more. To meticulously draw genitals takes a lot of work, and there have been many examples where to reduce stress on the artists, this approach is used during production pre-revision. However, currently, it's commonplace to have most artists draw their genitals quite meticulously, and then let the editors go ahead and revise and censor their work after the fact.

But the true answer lies in the publication process of these series.

In shonen manga, the amount of censorship in general has decreased in recent years. In the manga that is serialized in shonen and seinen magazines, those chapters are compiled into volumes for release usually with less censorship. It's been theorized that only real fans will read those books, so the paper used for those releases is usually much nicer than that of the magazine they appeared in. In the minds of many editors and artists, less censorship looks better on higher paper quality. Therefore, the idea for less censorship here is more of an aesthetic one. And of course, fans will pay for this value added in what they're consuming.

While this is not the case right now, there have been times where the power balance between aesthetics and censorship have been reversed. In these cases, the serialization would have less censorship and the final books would have more. This mostly happened during the comic regulation era that began in 1991 or so, where the waves of censorship became stronger. Strict expectations on revisions on behalf of the artists and editors had to be met and ready to go before the publication of the books.

Recently, in 2013, after the editors of Core Magazine's magazines *Nyan 2-club* and *Comic Megastore* were brought up on charges of distributing obscene materials and insufficient censorship in those publications, the censorship in those magazines increased to an extreme degree compared to before. We could call this situation yet another power imbalance, but one between publishers and the government.

There Is No Solution for Censorship

The question of "Are you doing your revisions in white-out?" often comes up, but in most cases, that approach (to revise the pages directly) to revision is not really used. In the cases that have paper pages, usually a copy is created and in red pencil, the areas of revision are assigned on tracing paper, creating a separate version of the manuscript for printing with revision included. But as of late, more artists are drawing their works digitally, and in this paperless era, most revisions are done digitally.

During the height of the *ero-gekiga* era, however, it was said that revisions were done directly on the pages, which is utterly unthinkable today.

In the first volume of *ero-gekiga* master Dirty Matsumoto's ***EroDamashi!*** (2003, Oakla Publishing; 7-6), a young Dirty Matsumoto annihilates an

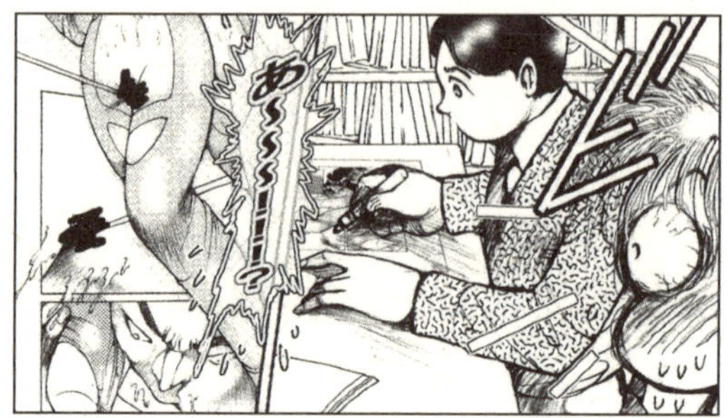

7-6: ***EroDamashi!*** (Dirty Matsumoto 2003, Oakla Publishing)

editor with his methods of revision, which occurred on the sheets he submitted. But revisions like this were allegedly happening as late as the '70s. Back then, however, it was rare that a serialized work later got collected in book form, so the general idea of preserving the artist's manuscript for the possibility of a book release wasn't well understood nor practiced. Because of that, it was common to have editors doing revisions directly onto paper.

However, this idea of a single-use manuscript wasn't isolated to just editors alone. Many artists didn't have a great idea of the value of their pages, so when they set out to draw new manuscripts, they just cut up old manuscripts and pasted new ones together. There were also events where creators sold their pages. There were even artists who just threw them away. Most likely if current artists saw that happening, they would mourn all that lost work.

While revisions are usually the domain of editors, there have been cases recently where certain artists have expressed the wish to dictate the limits of revision, and felt that if something was off, they would take it upon themselves to revise it more. The artist who opened his mouth and violated the editor's sacred land of revisions was none other than the veteran eromanga artist Ippei Ikoma. I interviewed him in 2015 and he spoke about it, saying…

> **Ikoma:** Because I'm petty, I thought about it a lot. I didn't want to erase my work completely, and I felt that the way the editors

revised my work was quite mechanical. So, I asked my editor to please, please, let me adjust my own work, and then went out and bought a bunch of white [screen] tone, and kind of stuck it all over my manuscript.

—Did you paste it directly onto the paper manuscript itself?

Ikoma: Yep, I did. I asked my editor to allow me to censor my own work on the condition that if he felt that it still wasn't enough, I would allow him to revise it further. As reference I used materials erased by Mr. Tou Moriyama that was from a long time ago. I thought the way he erased certain things was really sexy (7-7). In the end, the revisions for both the magazine serialization and the later collected volume were overwhelmingly done by me myself.

—So, by erasing things lightly, you could catch the eye with those panels.

Ikoma: At that point the term *moé* wasn't in use yet, but it has been said that the fad at the time was to draw your characters in an anime style. But I don't draw like that, so I decided to have a match of sorts between it and erotic content. I came from *gekiga* in terms of style, so I thought that was my weapon in this particular fight. And it was stupid to have so few in circulation. It seems that Fuusen Club said to an editor, "Why is Ikoma selling so well?!" To which I can only answer… Because I believed I could, I suppose.

Here, Ikoma's weapon in this fight was extreme depictions of erotic situations and content, arriving at the idea that "this would look better with a lesser amount of censorship," putting his own praxis into practice. This anecdote took place roughly around 1993, and it seems that regu-

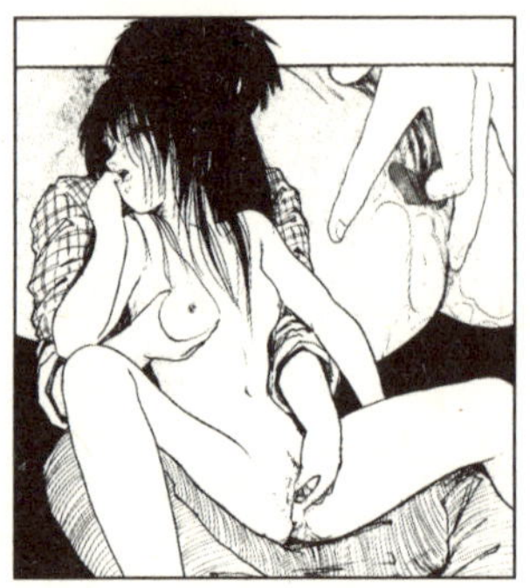
7-7: ***Towarare Penguin*** (Tou Moriyama 1986, Tatsumi Publishing)

lation was prioritizing safety (with regard to crackdowns from the police) and was still a comparatively broad idea in practice. And it could be that people linked skill with revisions to higher sales in comics at the time, because editor techniques like making the least amount of revisions (and later censored areas) possible didn't really become polished in practice until the late '90s. Therefore, Ikoma's work may have become an unpredicted hit with readers since Ikoma, who drew erotic depictions until he was able to revise them, and the latent needs of readers who wanted to read more eromanga were evenly matched. I'm not sure if Ikoma's case was the impetus here, but this perhaps might have been another reason why *bishojo* manga quickly became hardcore then.

While we are talking about the typical process of revision during this time (with artists drawing genitals and then editors censoring them), there were some cases at the time where revisions were not needed and did not happen.

This is when an artist would not draw a realistic portrayal of genitals, but instead something that mimicked them in their place. While this isn't a strict expression per se, I would still like to look at it in the framing of an expression born of trying to evade regulation.

Beastification, Materialization, Penis Transformation?

One of the most well-known techniques of censoring male genitals with "something else" is the *gijinka*, or anthropomorphization of objects and animals, or better yet, *gijuuka* (beastification), which turns humans and objects into four-legged beasts.

Beastification can be seen in Masamichi Yokoyama and Jiro Gyu's ***Yaruki Manman*** (1977-1996, Nichijou Gendai; 7-8), where a seal replaces a man's genitals. By using beastification here, this technique renders the seal's almost independent personality from the man's. This expression is probably the most fitting to use for such a story that develops by going in a sexual direction, though it has strong comedic elements to it. Originally, it uses the secret language men call their penises (like here, "son" is used) for the seal, and it gets to the point where the lower half of the protagonist's body has developed a personality all its own. Though to be honest, it's more as though the seal is representative of the man's hidden thoughts and desires.

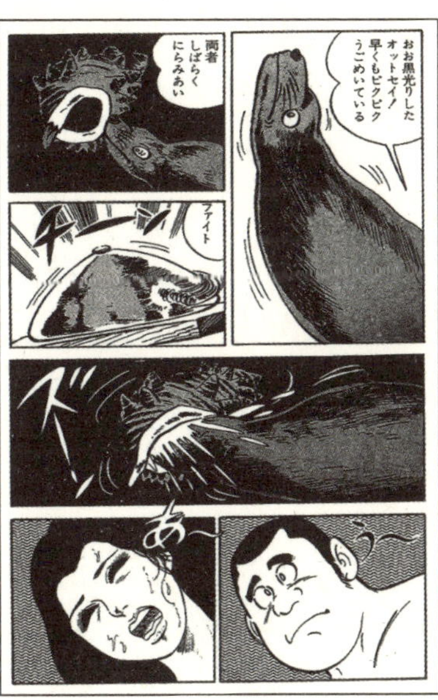

7-8: ***Yaruki Manman***, Vol. 1 (Masamichi Yokoyama & Jiro Gyu 1980, Kodansha)

A similar technique used when the main goal is not to arouse the audience per se would be one using cylinder or rod-shaped fruits like bananas. We see this in Katsu Aki's *Manga Sutra*, where a banana is used in an oral sex scene in an effort to directly circumvent regulation (7-9). This particular series has become an expert in code-switching with its audience. While it tells the reader "this is a banana" in the text (and on a very consistent basis), it has become an implicit code-switch that reinforces the idea that the banana is something more.

When one draws a realistic depiction of male genitalia, revisions will be necessary for publication. But if one uses beastification or anthropomorphization, that new "being" will become its own character, and therefore it cannot be labeled as obscene.

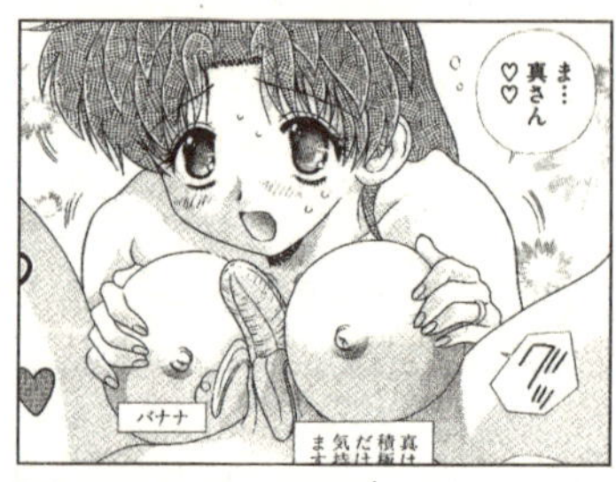

7-9: ***Manga Sutra***, Vol. 22 (*Futari Ecchi*; Katsu Aki 2003, Hakusensha/Tokyopop)

We see this in Reijiro Kato's ***Dan Kong*** (*Bokko*; 1994, Wanimagazine), where a spirit of male genitalia, Bokko, torments a woman with tentacles that seem like his own genitalia in one scene. While it's understood what this spirit is supposed to be replacing, it is also given its own character, thereby paving the way to evade censorship (7-10). It has the same origin point as Maeda's tentacle expression, but the idea of injecting comical elements into a story with this use of anthropomorphization was entirely new at the time. This is also seen in the period drama title within this same magazine, ***Heiji*** (1998, Wanimagazine). It was succeeded by ***Dan Kong Heiji***, and a more comedic and gag-based story began to unfold in *Kairakuten* magazine.

The next series I'll be talking about relies on the fact that readers know that it is custom to censor things, and that is precisely why this series has flourished. It features a meta-expression and one that argues against itself. It may be more appropriate to say that precisely because of Japan's censorship laws that this particular expression was born.

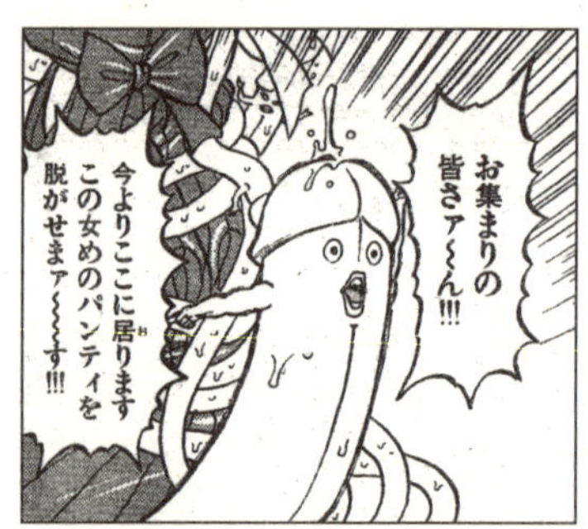

7-10: ***Dan Kong*** (*Bokko*; Reijiro Kato 1993, Wanimagazine)

Outside of anthropomorphization of penises, a new technique called "chinkaku" developed. This technique has many variations, and within *BL,* it is used in the context of a man's genitals being possessed. One might call it a "penisifcation," where it turns into a situation of "I am his [genitalia] and his genitalia is me."

In Nase Yamato's ***ChinTsubu*** (2003, Jitsugyou no Nihonsha), a man that got into a bus accident is in critical condition. He ends up spiritually possessing the genitals of the man that he yearns for. A face develops on the penis and by communicating with that man, their bond deepens. Apparently, its title comes from a portmanteau of the original term "chinko no tsubuyaki" (the murmurings of a penis). This series became much talked about due to its incredibly bizarre setting and background. The penises are rod-shaped and very puppet-like, with a cute quality to them. Because of that, they were not revised nor censored for publication (7-11). Also, because it is for *BL,* as a goal, it may be that this expression isn't necessarily used just to evade regulation, but rather as a comedic touch to show the ultimate (romantic or sexual) relationship between two men.

Either way, in recent years within *BL,* there have been many new expressions that men themselves could never have imagined being born one after the other, and in a certain sense, *BL* as a category has grown up to be far more free than those targeted towards men in terms of their originality.

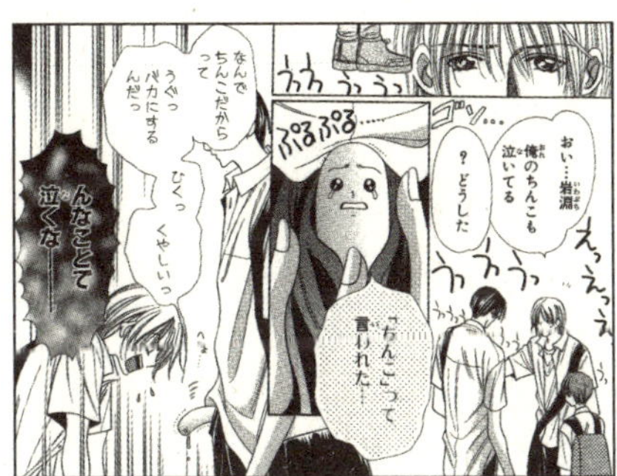

7-11: ***ChinTsubu***, Vol. 2 (Nase Yamato 2004, Jitsugyou no Nihonsha)

The Genitalia of Textbooks, Transparent Genitalia, and Other Refined Expressions

So, as you can see, there is a pattern of things used to substitute for male genitalia, outside of anthropomorphization and beastification. In the case of Koike's *Shikken Ningyo: Dummy Oscar,* the shape of the expression used here is much like that of the *white rod* revision we've looked at previously in this chapter. However, it was not added in after the fact by an editor; instead, it's an abstract stylistic choice made by the creators from the start (7-12). With this expression, its prerequisite for use hinges on those who have read the first part of the work to understand or conclude that what was being represented was male genitalia. Midway through the work, it is explicitly confirmed within the framework of the story that what is drawn is indeed a penis. At a glance, while it may not look like it, one has to look at the context and tease this from the text, like solving a puzzle. In the early days of *ero-gekiga* and *gekiga,* this technique was very heavily used.

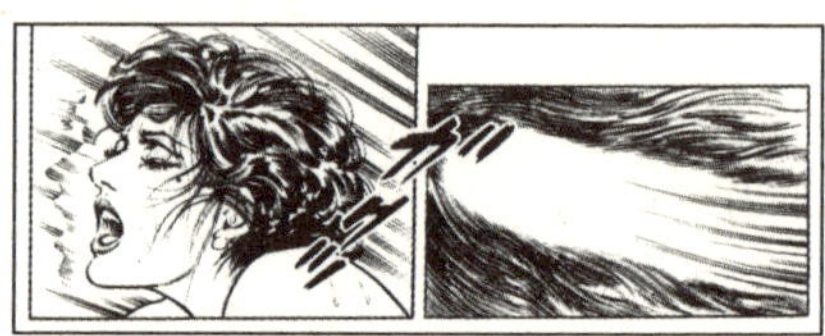

7-12: ***Shikken Ningyo: Dummy Oscar***, Vol. 3 (Seisaku Kano & Kazuo Koike 1979, Studio Ship)

Genitals that one has to imagine by teasing them out of text are the ones that the brain seizes upon and visualizes, and many genitals in eromanga have been drawn as transparent because of this from the get-go. While they may not look transparent, there is a technique to make the unseen seen. In Kojiki Ohji's ***Freesia*** (2000, Core Magazine; 7-13), the sexual fluids that coil around the male genitals are drawn with precision, thus skillfully rendering an unseen penis into something that is visible and recognizable by the audience.

You're probably wondering if an illustration this delicate would be censored, aren't you? But the main goal of drawing genitalia as transparent wasn't to evade regulation, but rather to more precisely document the moment of insertion.

We covered this expression a bit in the *cross-section view* chapter, but in order to make a female character stand out, a relationship scene might be used showing a man (or more precisely, his genitals) becoming transparent in a use of the "danshari" (invisible man). Within fruitless relationship situations, there have also been many cases where the male partner is only halfway transparent.

In this case, the male genitals are completely transparent, and by observing its surroundings, the audience is forced to recognize the genitals' existence in the panel (7-14). Much like equipment made to observe black holes, this particular technique helps the censored genitals float to the surface of the page, making them visible to the audience. To be fair, it is a bit like taking the circuitous route to get straight to the content the audience wants to see, but it is one of the other few eromanga-only expressions.

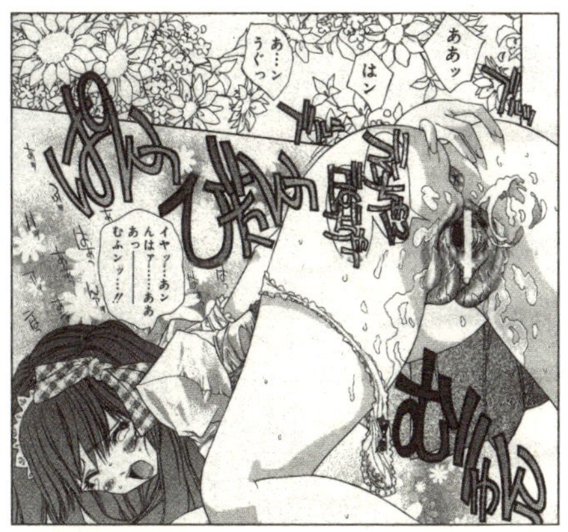

7-13: "Koton a la Mode" (Kojiki Ohji 2000, Core Magazine)

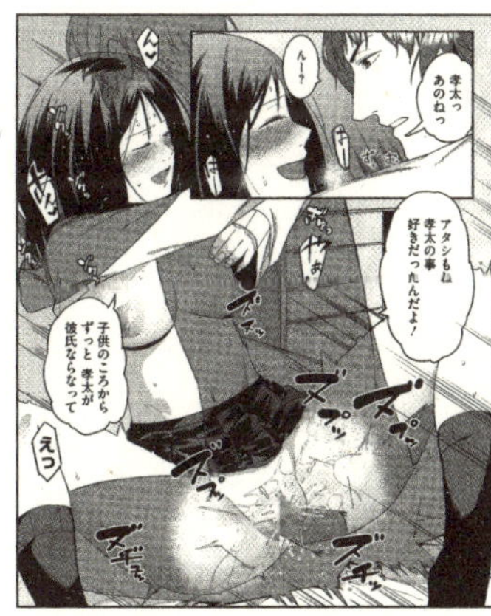

7-14: ***Watashitachi no Hajimari*** (Menea the Dog 2017, Core Magazine)

The Most Private Part?

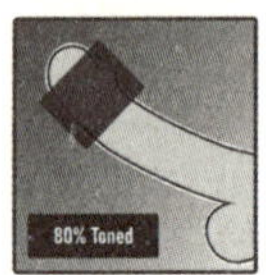

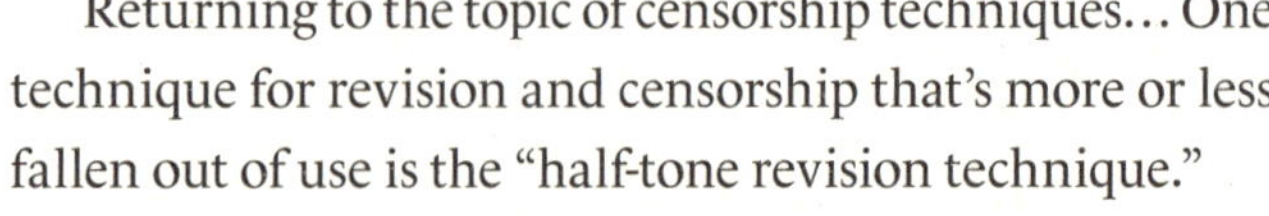

Returning to the topic of censorship techniques… One technique for revision and censorship that's more or less fallen out of use is the "half-tone revision technique."

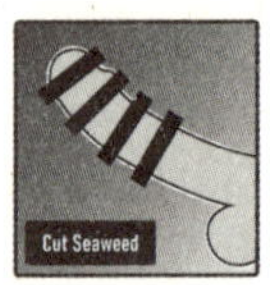

Its principle is simple; the goal is to show male genitalia like an image with screen tone covering the most detailed parts of the organ. But in reality, it isn't that there's a cut of screen tone used to create that effect, but instead it's done during the printing process where they adjust the transparency value. If transparency is at 0%, the black contact print value is at 100%, and if it's at 60% then the value is set at 40%, creating a covered but somewhat visible area.

The scope of the censored area has changed with the times in accordance with the law, widening or shrinking when needed. Changes within this expression originated from editors being pressured to widen the scope of censorship, while more subtle changes happened as the situation fluctuated.

With the next case, the censorship could be adjusted specifically as well. It is a subspecies of the *seaweed strip technique*: the "cut seaweed technique."

The *cut seaweed technique* is called such because many black bars cover the genitalia, looking like cut strips of seaweed. The number of black strips used has waxed and waned over the years, but when censorship rules were at their lightest, only one strip covered the glans of the penis. The shaft eventually had two strips, then added three more. The principle of this theory is the same as the *half-tone revision technique,* which is to say, it's easy to tweak depending on the attitudes. One can see it the most in use in so-called "convenience store magazines" (adult magazines sold at convenience stores; 7-15).

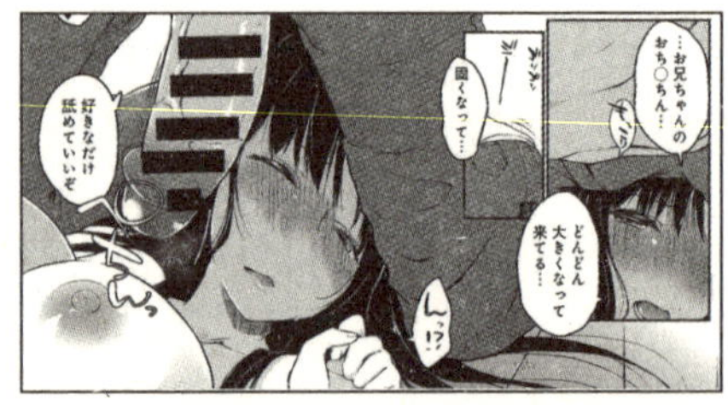

7-15: "Yamagami-san ga Kureta Yome" (Kaiduka 2017, GOT)

When censorship was at its lightest (though readers felt that it still was too much), the glans got only one strip, barely sufficient to cover the entire head. Publishers felt the heat from eromanga readers, who were displeased with how the "revisions are attacking the images." Whereas in the case of readers who didn't read eromanga, it probably caused them to ask themselves if the content was really censored at all. But editors on behalf of their publishers could not remove that one last strip of censorship from their images, as it was "proof" they were following the law.

I wondered if within the eromanga industry there was a rule where one must "defend censoring the glans at all costs." After gathering information, there was no pre-arranged rule to do that, but every editorial department would cull the use of the cut seaweed technique and naturally lower its use. What was left over from that culling was tone over the glans. It was as if editors had all conspired to do this in parallel with each other, resulting in one last standalone bit of censorship left over.

Note that this is just my reasoning at work here, but just as when a woman realizes she has been seen naked and covers up the parts of herself with her hands, men too have that same fear with regard to their genitalia. Their *most private part,* editors have decided, is the glans of the penis. But when you take into the account that this was the time that had the least amount of censorship happening, this theory may not work during the times when it was far heavier.

This type of censorship was not exclusive to *bishojo* manga. And while of course censorship was happening in *BL* as well, when compared to eromanga, the censorship happening in *BL* was art.

Is Censorship Art?

Firefly Erasure

Even within *boys' love,* which features gay sex but is written primarily for women, the depiction of sex was still a particularly important component of the story.

Compared to eromanga, there were no hard conditions, and the special characteristic for this genre is that from soft to hardcore, the amount of expressions that publishers published in magazines was, quite frankly, huge. But what's most interesting about it is that the rules for censorship vary greatly from company to company. There are techniques that are not even seen in male-targeted genres. Of these, one example would be the "firefly erasure technique."

The *firefly technique* is one that Junet, a company that puts out magazines like *Boy's Pierce*, uses frequently. It's named as such because the technique looks like a bunch of fireflies dancing around a penis (7-16). Even within *BL,* the *lightsaber, seaweed,* and other techniques I've covered are used. For the most part, they're used by publishers the same way they would be within publishers of male-targeted media, also. However, the *firefly technique* is rare and stands out in that because visually, it takes erasure to the level of art.

A technique such as this one has not happened within male-targeted media because "men don't want to see censorship." But for female readers, for whom *BL* is largely targeted, instead, publishers started to ask themselves, "how can we erase this artfully?" Their motivation to do so comes from a more artful and philosophical place. Without those publishers asking themselves that question, it could be that such

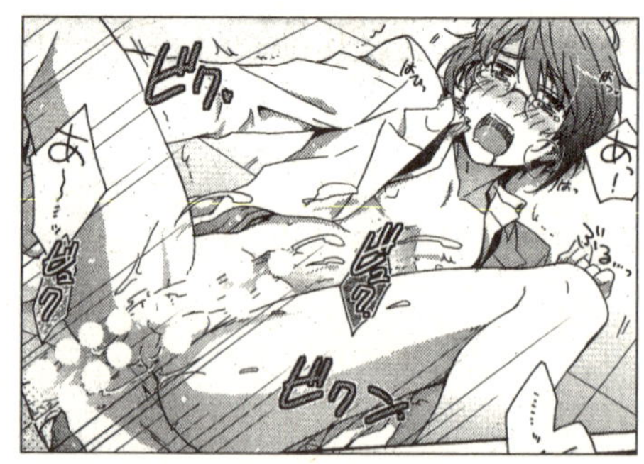

7-16: "Naisho no Shinro Soudan" (Migu Fujiyama 2013, Junet)

a novel way of censoring might never have been born at all.

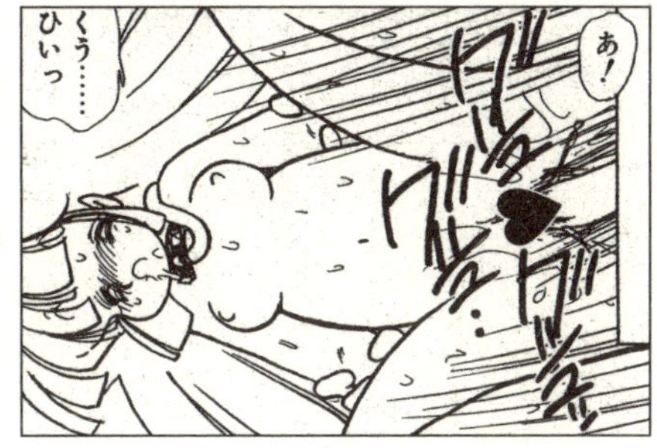

7-17: "Uchuu Keiji GALVAN" (Yuko Minami 1987, Tatsumi Publishing)

One can see a similarly novel technique used in male-targeted media for all of one moment in a 2006 issue of *Comic Dolphin* magazine. Though it is not the *firefly technique,* it is one similar in its artistry and design, as well as its use of large swaths of white screen tone.

Even within the realm of male-targeted doujinshi, a new, artful way of doing censorship came about much like the one seen in *BL.* Instead of just white round dots (fireflies), the censored parts were covered in small hearts. This method of revision has existed since the 1980s, but aside from one example at the time that instead used one large heart to obscure the genitalia, few examples of it have been found historically (7-17). However, in more current doujinshi works, many variations of that heart mark have been in use, steadily approaching the level of artistry employed with that of the *firefly technique* (7-18).

Within the world of doujinshi, those artists of course revised and censored their own work, though perhaps having to erase the genitalia they put their soul into drawing probably filled them with regret. In that case, it would be normal to want to at least make that erasure look beautiful. The solution to this was to come back to veteran eromanga artist Shiwasu no Okina's "heart mark technique." By using it, instead of the statement that genitalia were obscene, a new message was sent. In this case the artist was saying, "Look at this overflowing oasis of love!" with this technique.

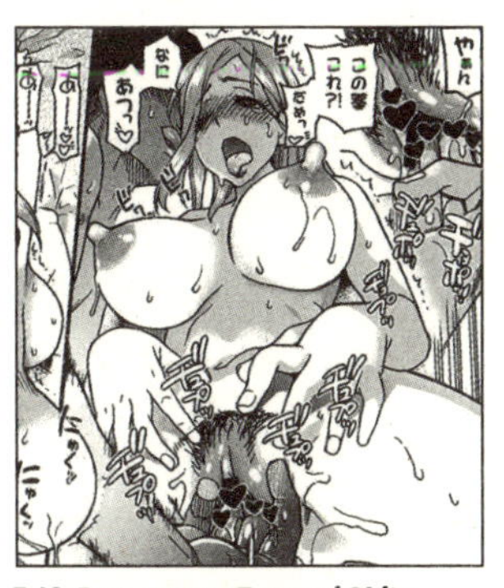
7-18: ***Daa-san no Tame ni Okita Ayako 32-sai B107*** (Okina Keikaku 2011, self-published)

Censorship techniques weren't just there to hide embarrassing things, but also became a technique to appeal to the identity of these artists using them. Throughout the revision process, this technique got the artist's feelings across to the audience, adding personality to their comic.

Within this book, I have only introduced the firefly technique out of all of the ones in the *BL* genre, but if you're so inclined, the book ***Otoko no Karada wa Kimochi Ii*** (Hiroshi Nimura, Junko Kaneda & Iku Okada 2015, Media Factory) goes a bit more in depth.

The Strength of Censorship Is Proportional to Originality

With regard to the standards of censorship, it is commonly accepted that they are constantly in flux. But what really turned up the heat within eromanga were the Miyazaki Murders, which were then bookended by a public discourse on so-called harmful comics in 1991. A more severe type of surveillance was in use for eromanga, especially when it came to creating extreme erotic content. While eromanga was still *eromanga,* it now found itself receiving the contradictory message of "protect others from erotic depictions" from their editorial departments, severely cutting down the number of books being printed at the time.

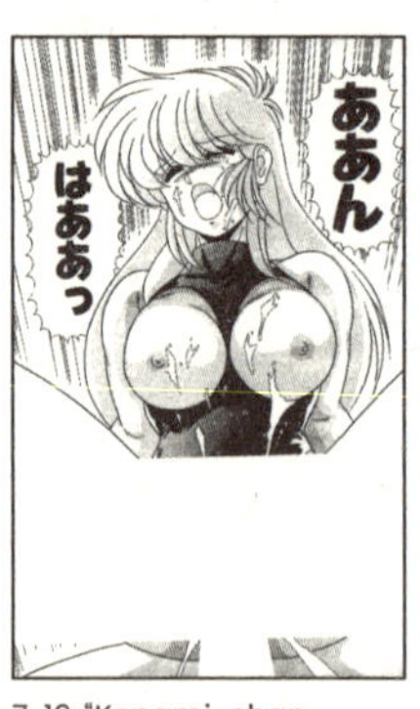

7-19: "Konami-chan Dai-Pinch" (Yoshimasa Watanabe 1992, Tatsumi Publishing)

The most pain, however, was felt at houses that specialized in extreme erotic content. Whenever they had an intercourse scene, nothing below the waist could be depicted safely without attracting the ire of the law. This resulted in a drastic increase in the amount of censorship in those books (7-19~21).

Though it's obvious for me to say, when one inserts that much erasure into things, it can cool a hot scene down quite fast, and the reader can't get aroused by it. It's at this point where we see the birth of the "speech bubble technique," a technique created to help lessen the harmful effects of censorship for the reader, while still obeying the law.

In order to still censor a scene with insertion or images of genitalia, a speech bubble is used to cover the image (7-22). Though it should be said that this technique is not something that the artists themselves used, but rather ones that editors did on their own.

Eromanga is a genre suited towards this sort of delicate handiwork, with heavy breathing and mysterious startled marks on behalf of the characters, as well as voiceless sounds (7-24, 25). The flow of these things together has been mistakenly seen as weakness, which it definitely is not. It may be better to say that it was due to the scheming and originality of editors that this technique was born.

However, due to people getting tired of it after a while, it eventually it was time to change things up and throw a curveball. In Tou Moriyama's "K no Truck," serialized in France Shoin's *COMIC PaPiPo*, the panels of the intercourse scene were purposely cut up, which has an effect on the comic itself (7-26). However, the book release does not have this scene treated the same way, showing that the severing of panels was purposeful within the serialized version to comply with censorship laws. As a result, this is one expression that was born due to the efforts of editors instead of artists.

Artists Won't Take This Lying Down

While most likely the ones most stumped by how censorship works are artists, they don't necessarily take things lying down. On the contrary, they helped create a new method of revision based on their unwillingness to just do as they were told—"message revision." This technique wasn't necessarily about how they were resisting doing revisions, but rather that there were instances when they were playing around with it instead of taking it seriously. There's no doubt that due to this particular technique, these artists helped adapt to revision and censorship. Because editors

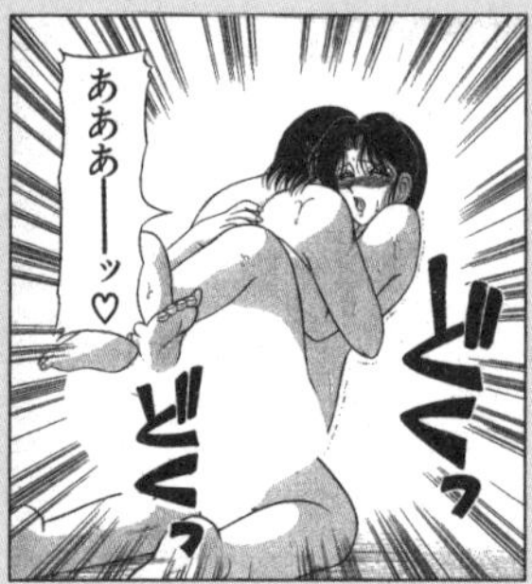

7-20: "Genki ni Narisou" (Ogami Wolf 1991, Fujimi Publishing)

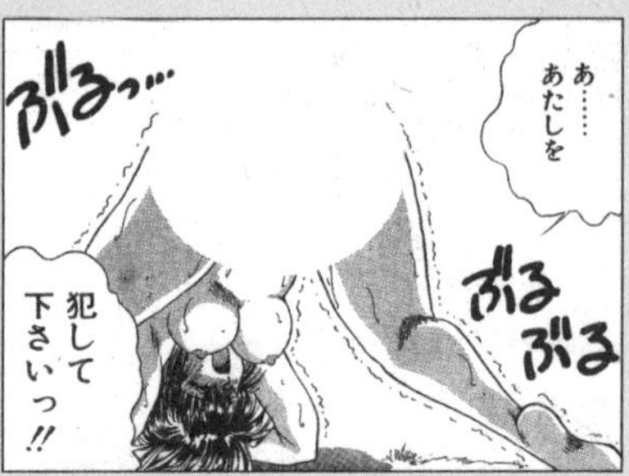

7-21: "Nene Taifu" (Chisato Takanabe 1992, Tatsumi Publishing)

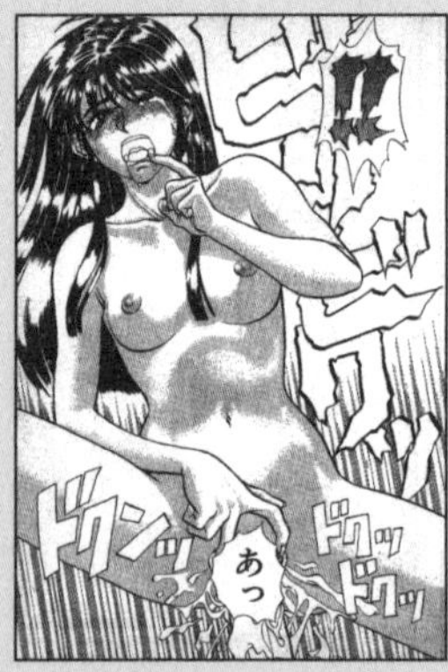

7-22: "Tadaima Benkyouchuu" (Juzo Minazuki 1991, Fujimi Publishing)

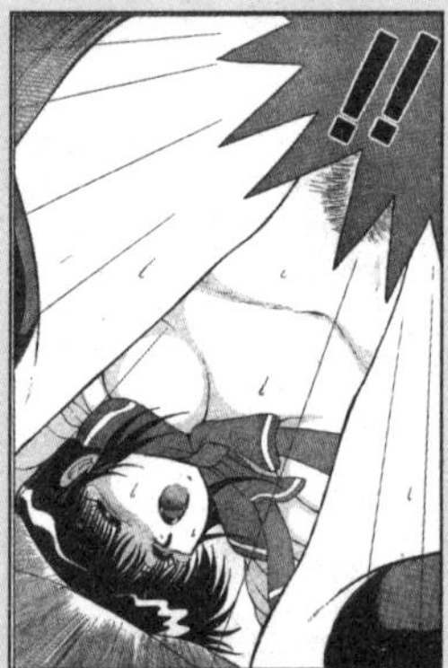

7-23: "CLUB ART PHAPSODY" (Natsuma 1991 Fujimi Publishing)

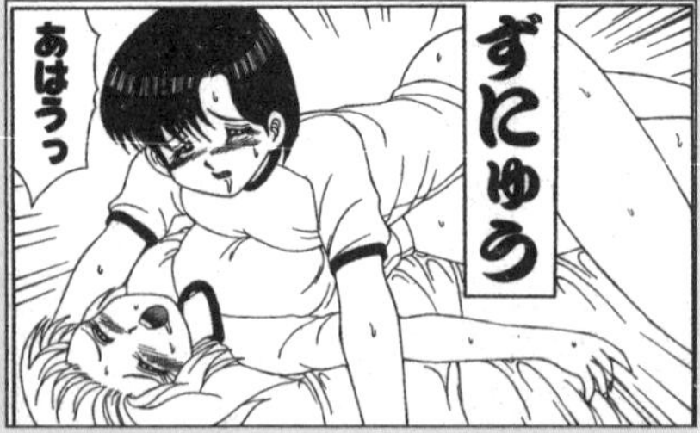

7-24: "Complex Girl" (Mizu Youkan 1993, Tatsumi Publishing)

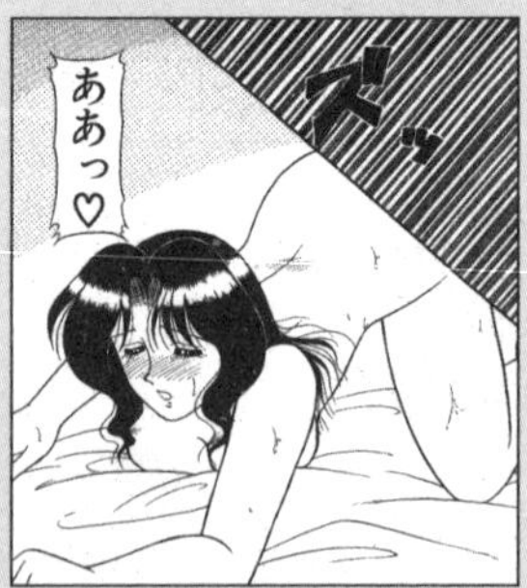

7-25: "Genki ni Narisou" (Ogami Wolf 1991, Fujimi Publishing)

would censor so-called "harmful content," the artists would respond with mildly masochistic responses, like not fully drawing things the way they should have or adding in lines to the dialogue that looked as if they were questioning the points of revision their editors raised (7-27).

Artists like Rei Shinozaki would combine male genitalia with his dialogue, creating a new sort of meme where it looked as if the genitals were a proxy for the character who was actually speaking (7-28). These sent an implicit message to the editors doing the revisions that their suggestions were little more than words from a penis, which had a sarcastic effect overall (7-29).

I'm not sure what the origin of the gap between artists and editors regarding recognition of censorship is, but let's look at an example of the rare so-called "two-layer revision." This rare technique is where the black bar is used as the first layer, and the second layer is composed of the white layer. Whenever editors felt that the black bar version of revision put in place by artists wasn't enough, they layered the white version on top of it to make sure everything was covered (7-30). I'm not sure what the chronology of events that led them to this point looks like, but what's certain is that this looks rough to the reader.

But there is an even more incomprehensible type than the *two-layer revision*—"the dot and mark technique" (7-31). At a glance, this mark looks like a road closed to traffic, another type of meta expression, however a closer look reveals that the dot layer is roughly at 80% screen tone, but the area around the glans is censored with a second white tone layer. So, in this case, after the first editor added the first black dot, the second editor decided that it wasn't enough and overlaid the second white mark to make sure everything was covered. While it may only be a case where it was an editor's judgment call to err on the side of caution, one can get a completely different implicit message from looking at it, and it catches the eye that way.

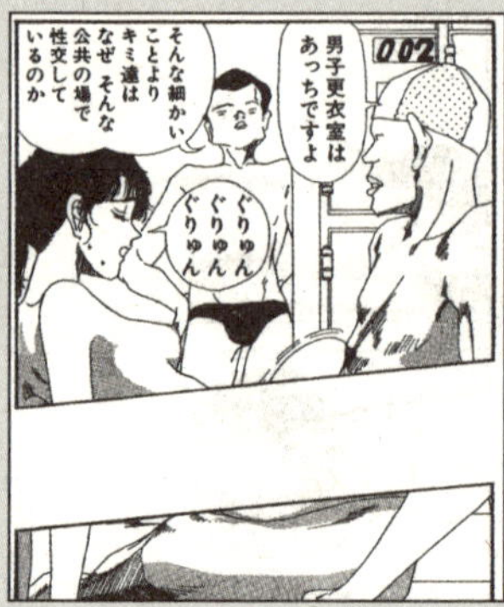

7-26: "K no Truck" (Tou Moriyama 1992, France Shoin)

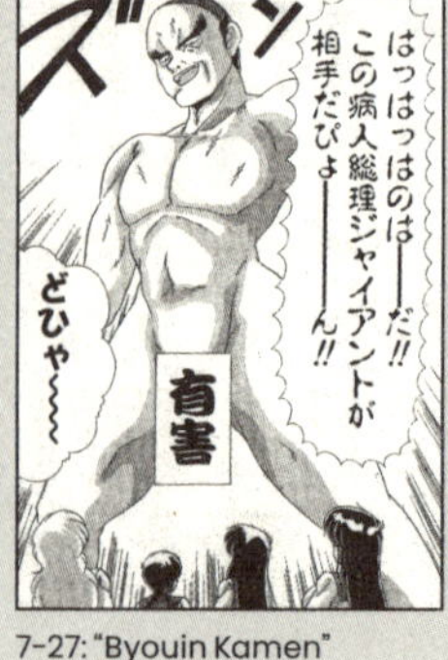

7-27: "Byouin Kamen" (Masayoshi Watanabe 1993, Tatsumi Publishing)

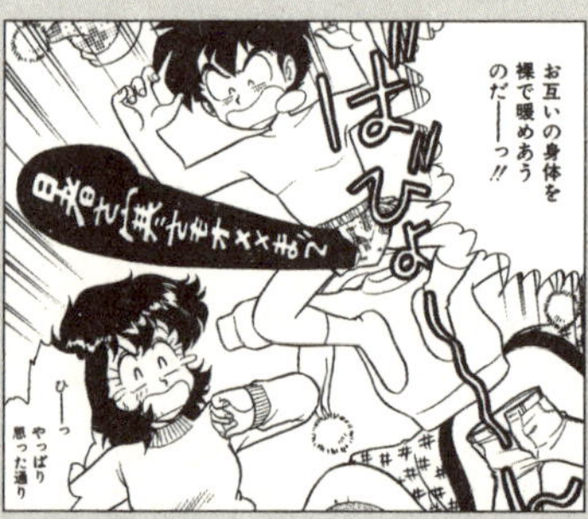

7-28: "Muchimuchi Purin" (Rei Shinozaki 1992, Tokyo Sanseisha)

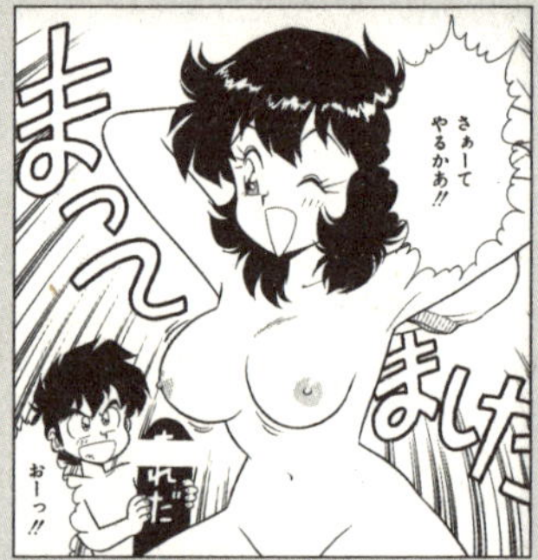

7-29: "Muchimuchi Purin" (Rei Shinozaki 1992, Tokyo Sanseisha)

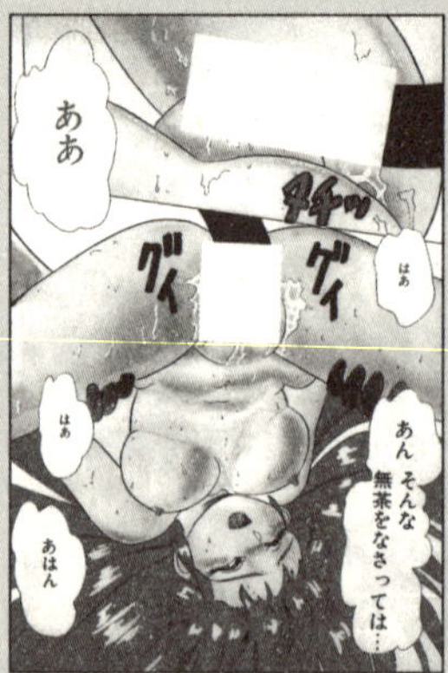

7-30: "Minerva Road" (Yu Tomiaki 1991, Tokyo Sanseisha)

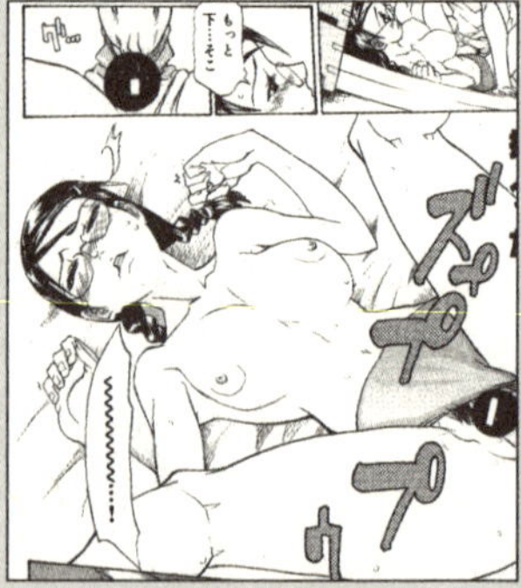

7-31: "Hurdle wo Koete" (Kanna Amazaki 2003, Tsukasa Shobo)

Who's Responsible for Censorship?

Censorship standards are always fluctuating, but in the case of magazine serializations, if there are no standards ready to go, then those projects just cannot be completed. In that situation, who decides the revisions and who confirms them?

There are cases where many production departments who look at the work after editorial departments are the ones who oversee all of the revision standards, but not all publishers operate this way. In many cases, an editor is appointed to each artist in publication, and in the case of magazine editorial departments, the department head would be the one to review all final products.

Accordingly, the buck stops with the editor-in-chief, but how does that editor-in-chief decide? In reality, they would consult releases from other publishers to see how they're enforcing their own censorship standards, and any editor-in-chief would similarly march in lockstep and make final adjustments to their own set of standards. If another publisher is only faintly censoring things, they'll think it'll be okay to lessen their own censorship as well; though the opposite thought pattern of "because everyone is censoring more, we should follow suit" happens too. Incidents where publishers are linked to obscene materials, or news that freedom of expression can be recognized a bit more are both taken into account as well. However, taking the level of revision-related erasure from 100% to 0% is something that absolutely must not be done.

Much like ripples on the surface of a lake, the change of standards of revision gently slope up and down throughout the ages, but no part of that lake goes completely dry. Accordingly, within the realm of censorship, it's been thought that it will never entirely go away. However, from 1998 to 2000, in what was quite literally a moment in time, the era of uncensored content reigned. Of course, not all publishers went through with removing censorship from their content, but it was, without a doubt, an era (albeit a short one) where the least amount of censorship and revision happened. The exact reason as to why this happened is still unknown.

In 1997, a new type of voluntary policing system was introduced for adult magazines by labeling them with a special mark to designate what they were. The eromanga magazines sold in bookstores with this mark had content that became more extreme in their depictions. Accompanying that was a softening of censorship rules, which I personally think accelerated the hardcore movement.

It was also at this time that internet culture started to permeate into regular offline everyday culture. Uncensored images made their way abroad before circling back to Japan, hastening the game of chicken, which here was about lightening censorship. Perhaps this was the reason it led to the era of "no, we can't lessen the amount of revisions anymore" period of eromanga.

Readers thought that finally, the eromanga world's dearest wish was coming to pass—no more censorship. But that was far too optimistic an outlook. While the ban on depicting pubic hair was lifted, the ban on the rest of the ideas about eromanga commonly accepted by society were not. Just as water in summer can evaporate in a moment, the water line was raised. The origin of this moment in history where (almost) uncensored manga was the norm is still unknown. It's been thought that the radical magazines of that time were periodically designated as material "unhealthy for minors" by the Tokyo Metropolitan Police Department's Security Division. But perhaps a complete uncensoring of material being nigh was a premature decision at best. As if it were a magic spell finally coming undone, the "uncensored era" had fewer restrictions than previous years, but in the end, eromanga publishing returned to the business of censoring its materials. It seemed that for a full revolution regarding censorship, it would take a bit more time for that to fully manifest.

A Sailor School Uniform Isn't Okay, but a Bra Is

The comics sold within convenience stores that were closest to magazines with adult comic content are *bishojo* magazines known as "gray zone magazines." Generally, these magazines are only sold to those eighteen and up, but that "18+" mark isn't indicated on the covers. So regular bookstores and online shops have been known to sell to those younger than eighteen. Self-regulation within the convenience store industry restricts selling gray zone magazines to those underage, but there is ambiguity associated with these magazines' content occasionally.

In situations where the content can neither be ruled as black nor white, just infinite shades of gray, there has been a considerable amount of influence on their expressions as a result. Because children may look at them accidentally, there are three main components that must not exist within the content of these magazines.

The faces of these magazines are their covers, which exert a lot of control over sales. In order to really sell erotic content, they depict girls in a *bishojo* style to draw the eye for sales. But unleashing 120% of extreme erotic content in a place where people of all ages tend to cross paths, and tend to be pretty suspicious as is, makes those convenience store companies less likely to allow pieces of that sort of content in their stores. When it comes to gray zone magazines, there's a tacit rule that exists within this self-enforced regulation that no matter how erotic content being created and sold is, a certain amount of defense and offense occurs along with it. Though, few know about that regulation.

The three components that must not be drawn on the covers of gray zone magazines are as follows: nipples, underwear, or sailor-style school uniforms. It goes without saying here that depicting genitals in these magazines would absolutely count as a violation of *Article 175*. Not even adult-targeted magazines sold in regular bookstores can show those.

So these three components are absolutely not allowed.

Note that these standards were not ones that were dictated by the convenience store industry, as it is not actually written out. Instead, they're a result of a dialogue that has happened between publishers and retailers for many years, with needs adjusted accordingly. As a tacit rule, it slowly hardened into a more solid standard, which then morphed into the so-called "gray zone."

Though it should be noted that the reason behind why these three components were selected as the forbidden components is not known. While I can see why both nipples and underwear might make the list, school uniforms as the third component is a bit questionable. If a school uniform that allowed the audience to imagine the female partner as a schoolgirl wasn't okay, I couldn't imagine that a bra would be, either. To my shock, showing a bra was perfectly fine. Similarly, underwear is not okay, but a bathing suit is. Setting the level of how strongly a situation could be considered erotic became the borderline, I can understand the difference between underwear and a swimsuit here. But the bra versus school uniform limit? I can't understand that at all. By enforcing this standard, it seems that these entities are establishing that the most erotic of all school uniforms are sailor uniforms, and instead of warning people against using them, if anything, it makes them even more erotic. It also runs the risk of making artists who use these things in their work even more stubborn by making them believe they're being attacked for doing so.

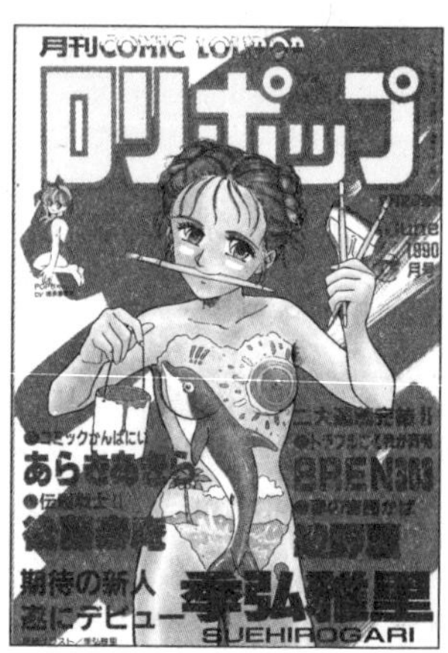

7-32: *COMIC Lolipop*, Jun 1990 (Kasakura Publishing)

Nipples have been banned in gray zone magazines since before the '80s, and not being able to draw them in these magazine covers is perhaps the oldest of the three that are banned under this code. But even so, there are still those that wish to show nipples in their work, justifying it under the excuse that their work is art, and if it's art, then surely it's okay to do so. In *COMIC Lolipop* (1990, Kasakura Publishing; 7-32), body painting is used, and nipples become the eyes of dolphins, or were stacked together as suns. And suddenly it became 100% possible to draw nipples this way without penalty.

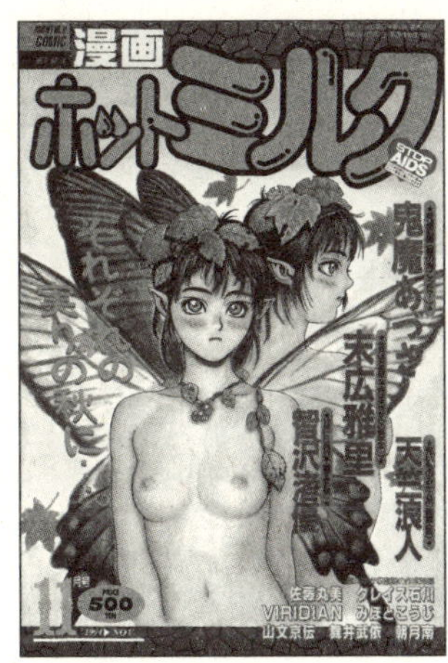

7-33: *Manga Hot Milk*, Nov 1994 (Byakuya-Shobo)

Even without intricate workmanship, *bishojo* illustrations are already art, so there's no need to hide anything. That opinion came from Jun Tsukasa, who was in charge of the covers for *Manga Hot Milk* magazine (1994, Byakuya-Shobo; 7-33). One cover allowed people to imagine encounters with fairies, and because the components of the erotic here were so watered down, a convincing cover with nipples was necessary. But in this way, by going on the offensive about the positive meaning of erotic things, it also meant going on the offensive about the negative meaning of them as well.

Comic Touhime magazine (1996, Hit Publishing; 7-34) found itself on the receiving end of no less than three continuous obscene book designations on behalf of the Tokyo Metropolitan Government and was forced to suspend publication. Possibly in an act of defiance, the publisher held a fire sale, lifting the restriction of content with nipples in it.

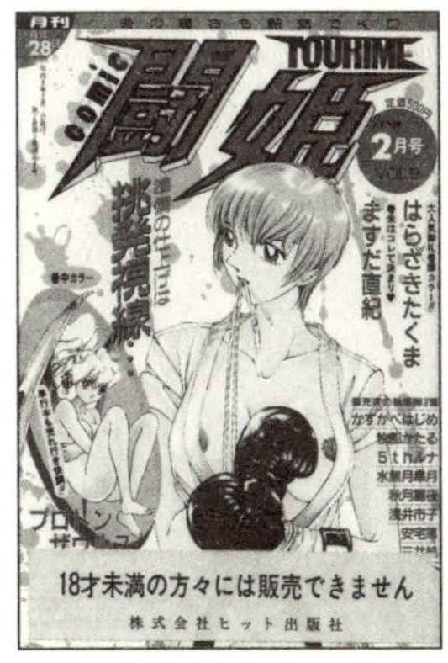

7-34: *Comic Touhime*, Feb 1996 (Hit Publishing)

It isn't very difficult to lift the ban on content with nipples in it. If one puts the adult magazine identifier mark on its cover, drawing nipples openly is a possibility, but as a result, one will lose the ability to stock and sell them in convenience stores. Precisely, it would mean that if editors were to allow extreme erotic content, it would mean having to plan for high turnover in the marketplace for purely adult magazines. Or the other side of this would be weakening the amount of erotic content, and expanding the marketplace, becoming a gray zone magazine sold at convenience stores. These were the two choices that publishers were faced with. By choosing the latter, it meant that serialization sales of series would drop, which would increase the risk of having to rely solely on collected volume sales instead. And if that happened, it meant that switching artists, and other such tactics would trigger a sea change in editorial policy.

In 1988, Toen Shobo launched the first *bishojo* magazine of its kind, *COMIC JUMBO*. It offered lighter erotic content under the guidance of Hiroshi Kawamoto, who it seemed was an embodiment of the bright, cheerful girls who adorned the pages of his magazine. However, in 2000, a recession in the publishing industry led to financial losses, forcing *JUMBO* to make a choice between becoming a gray zone magazine, or completing an about-face move to cater to hardcore material. As a result, *JUMBO* made the choice to go with the latter of the two, and the covers from that time reflect that change when they decided to finally put the adult comic magazine mark on the lower left of its cover (7-35, 36). In the August 2005 issue of the magazine, a cover shows a large-breasted girl with her nipples clearly exposed.

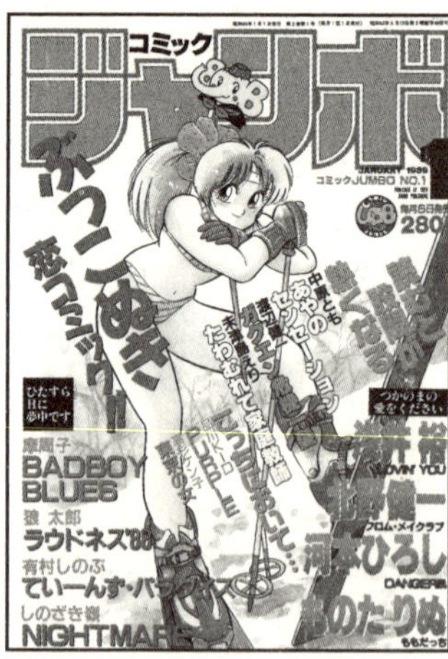

7-35: *COMIC JUMBO*, Jan 1989 (Toen Shobo)

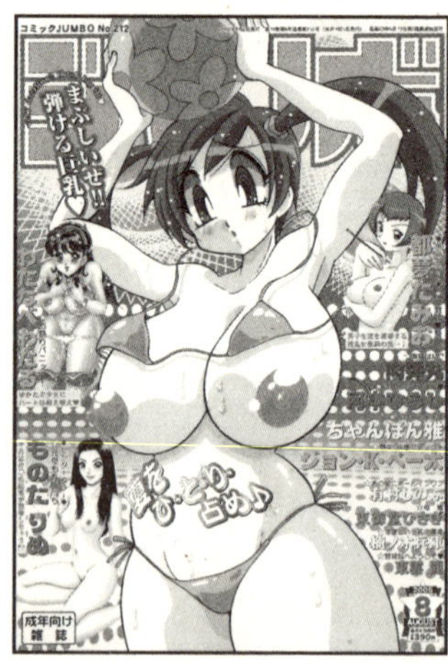

7-36: *COMIC JUMBO*, Aug 2005 (Toen Shobo)

I interviewed Kawamoto, and he confirmed that he'd given the okay to lift the nipple ban, due to popular demand on behalf of *JUMBO's* readership. By choosing to do so, it meant parting ways with convenience stores, and one could say that by doing so it effectively made a declaration that it was self-sufficient. Another way to put it, is that there was a history of covers of convenience store magazines being in a wholly separate space from that in a bookstore. So this move allowed them to maintain the dignity of their erotic content, while existing in the space between the battle of voluntary regulation and circulation numbers.

Speaking of circulation, new routes of distributing eromanga opened up after 2000, allowing not only paper magazines, but digital magazines and online publication as well. After 2008, these routes widened further, leading to online-only subscription services that curated content for their readership. The shift from Japanese cellular phones (mostly flip phones) to smartphones allowed the influence of these new routes to expand. The ability to circulate material online immediately allowed that content to bypass the final frontier of national borders, letting the material develop on its own in the wider world. But it also meant facing off against new forms of censorship.

Most of that came from figuring out global ideas of what constituted obscenity to receiving pressure from the marketplace at large. Let's look at how this content was influenced in the next section.

Encounters with New Censorship Standards

The fight about revision and censorship didn't necessarily mean that the metropolis of Tokyo or the police were the enemy within it. The individuals and groups that wouldn't leave erotic expressions alone, as well as Japan's sense of morals and ethics varied a great deal than all of those abroad, and Japan needed to be able to respond to the various pressures exerted by other countries. At a glance, the reason why there were so many calls for revision and censorship were due to morals and human rights, but in many cases, that was a public position; a market principle in the shape of taking in firm demands, but only with the intent to profit. As a result, it wasn't just a few expressions that got erased. Specifically, it was due to a movement caused by the diffusion of material via the internet, and foreign mail-order sites not seeing any point in fighting Japan on its revision and censorship norms.

Currently in Japan, within anime and manga, things like *lolicon*, humiliation, and bestiality are accepted forms of content. Even so, globally, it seems to be a rare case where there are many internet mail order sites where people need not become registered members in order to shop. Especially in *Amazon's* case, where standards about what material is not supposed to be sold are mostly decided internally, and anything that would run afoul of those standards cannot be accessed. In such events, those items are often immediately erased from the site. If it has those themes in the title or on the cover of the book, then it's taken down.

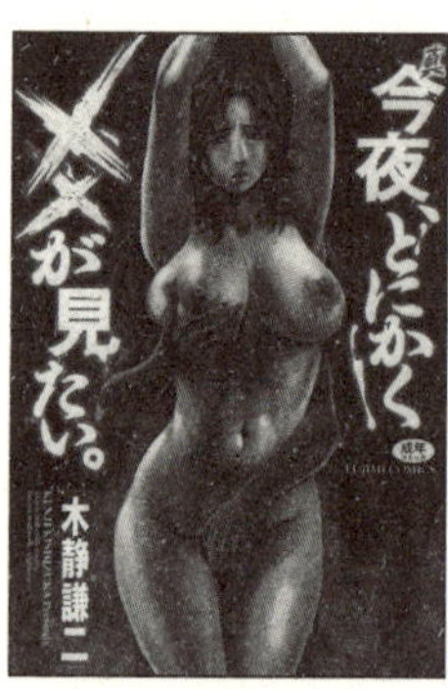

7-37: ***Konya, Tonikaku XX ga Mitai.*** (Kenji Kishizuka 2009, Fujimi Publishing)

However, there are still ambiguous areas where keywords may be triggering but not the cover. In these cases, there have been successful efforts in the past to retitle works as a way of evading regulations. This happened with Kenji Kishizuka's ***Konya, Tonikaku Ryojoku ga Mitai.*** (2002, Fujimi Publishing). Though it was published in book form in 2002, six years later in 2008, it was taken down from *Amazon* because it had the term humiliation in the title. Next year, in 2009, the title of the book was changed to ***Konya, Tonikaku XX ga Mitai.*** (2009, Fujimi Publishing) and reprinted. It was a power move that hadn't been seen before within so-called "title censorship" (7-37, 38).

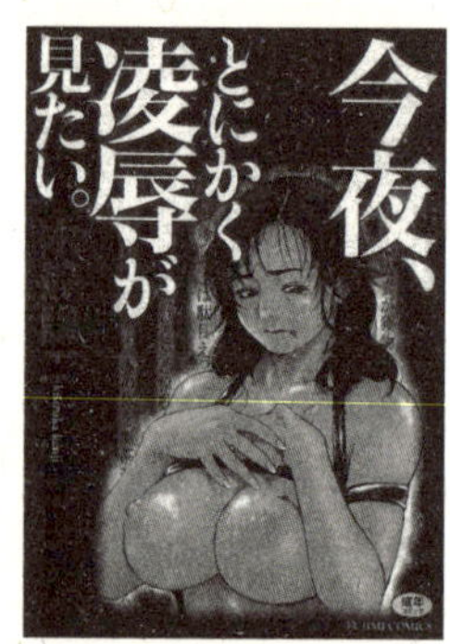

7-38: ***Konya, Tonikaku Ryoujoku ga Mitai.*** (Kenji Kishizuka 2002, Fujimi Publishing)

Public censorship norms were derived from what was obscene, and in one sense, because its claims and doctrine were consistent, it had an equivalence to that of publishers' norms, so to a certain degree they were carried out appropriately. But as a practical matter, there were far more cases where voluntary revision rules that were created independently by private companies that took on the world had difficulty with differences of culture, ideologies, and religion. Perhaps at this time, the era of "censoring genitalia alone is fine" was over and done with, and the beginning of more complicated matters of what to censor. This was since genitalia was a minor issue with regard to what these companies had to deal with.

The Mystery of the *Shonen Magazine* "Nipple Ticket"

The phenomenon of *bishojo* magazines removing the ban on nipples is also a manifestation of the Japanese belief that nipples are somehow special. The spread of which in recent years has mostly been seen within shonen manga, following an incredibly unique path of development, to the point where it's nearly become an artform. I touched upon this in the chapter about breast expressions, but from the 1970s to the 1980s, shonen magazines were overflowing with depictions of breasts. There was absolutely no hesitation in putting nipples on breasts. But by the beginning of the '90s, with the dawn of new comic regulation, shonen magazines were forced to erase any depiction of nipples.

These regulations were more commonly known as the "nipple code," a set of self-enforced rules that publishers were to abide by. There was the lingering question of whether or not the entire breast itself had to be censored, or rather if just by censoring the nipple would remove any hint of obscenity from a comic. Just as there was the issue with male genitalia and the glans of the penis being judged as the most private place on the male body, the nipple was seen as its equivalent with the female body.

The nipple is probably the one part of the body that asserts a sense of identity. As a practical matter, being able to see the nipple or not was one of the most important components for the erotic comedies that appear frequently in shonen magazines. Many people felt that if the nipple were to be censored, then 80% of the realism of the breast would disappear. That is how sensitive the Japanese are about nipples.

After the relaxed "free nipple" period of the '80s where nipples were not censored, the regulation crackdown of the '90s encouraged the practice of "flashing" to develop. This meant giving hints that the nipple was there on the breast, like the flashing of a girl's underwear.

Shonen magazines were relatively easygoing about content much like eromanga was at the time, and the instances where the *seaweed technique* were employed were few and far between. Instead, quite magnificent nipples were hidden, and the more an artist could make that act of hiding them look natural, the better in terms of technique.

However, the other side of that coin was that if the artist had hidden those nipples too perfectly, it stressed the readers out. So flashing was needed, and sometimes clever *fan service* was needed as well, though rarely there were cases where the nipple was depicted very clearly. "Realistic nipples are needed first and foremost before flashing can be employed," was a sentiment very important to people at the time. What turned the so-called "lucky nipple," into a meme was Hideo Nishimoto's ***Henachoko DaiSakusen Z*** (2002, Kodansha; 7-39). In a chapter, something that would come to be known as the "nipple ticket" stemmed from a plot point where a character was told, "If you hold this ticket, you can draw breasts freely in your own comic (however, it's limited to one ticket per set of two nipples)." In order to make sure that Nishimoto's depictions of nipples didn't become a case of

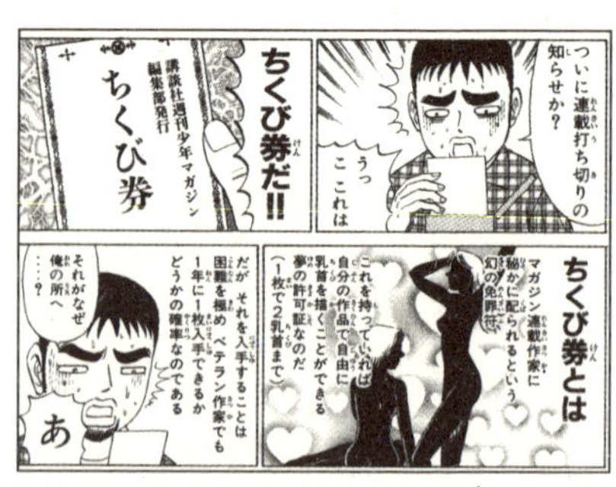

7-39: ***Henachoko DaiSakusen Z***, Vol. 11 (Hideo Nishimoto 2002, Kodansha)

friendly fire, the editor set up a guard rail that helped control the frequency of occurrence with those depictions. At the end of the day, this story was nothing more than fiction and an urban legend, but the assumption that shonen publishers were just going to go ahead and not censor nipples was pretty funny.

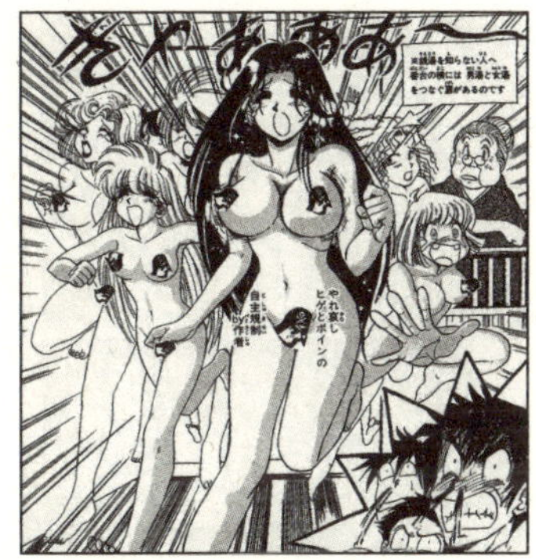

7-40: ***Hell Teacher Nube*** (*Jigoku Sensei Nube*; Takeshi Okano & Sho Makura 1994, Shueisha)

Within those shonen publications, there was a pattern of editors using the "natural hiding technique" in order to censor nipples. Within this pattern, hiding nipples behind steam, hair, small items, flashes of light, or anything else that could make the argument that originally no nipples had been depicted at all. The result was that this technique was much like a rubber ball that bounced from trope to trope, and the amount of works that used it were quite large in number. In ***Hell Teacher Nube*** *(Jigoku Sensei Nube;* Takeshi Okano & Sho Makura 1993-99, Shueisha), the artist used a *Weekly Shonen Jump* mascot in order to hide a character's nipples, which could only happen in a series that was serialized in *Jump* magazine. This was the birth of the "*Jump* erasure technique" (7-40).

Yet at the same time, depending on the time and place, hidden nipples can be reborn into uncensored nipples. During its serialization, one particular scene in Tadahiro Miura's ***Yuuna and the Haunted Hot Springs*** (*Yuragi-so no Yuuna-san*; 2016, Shueisha/Seven Seas Ent., 7-41, 42) had this happen. The image on the left is the scene used in the serialized version, the image on the right is from the book version. Nipples that had been hidden in the serialization mysteriously became uncensored in the book release. A similar incident happened in *Weekly Shonen Sunday*'s ***Keijo!!!!!!*** (Daichi Sorayomi 2013, Shogakukan). Nipples themselves have quite literally become weapons in this insane manga, and during its serialization, there are nipples drawn quite distinctly. Once again, the censored area was removed for the release of the collected volume.

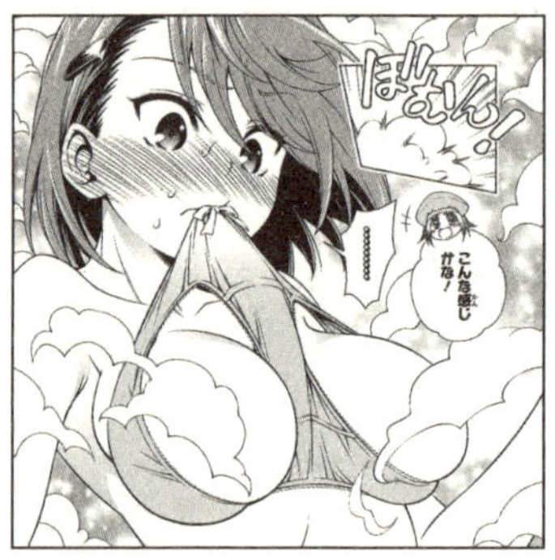

7-41: ***Yuuna and the Haunted Hot Springs*** (*Yuragi-so no Yuuna-san*; Tadahiro Miura 2016, Shueisha)

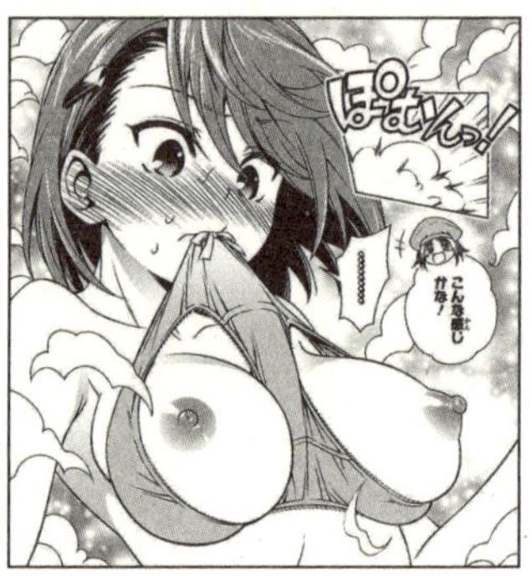

7-42: ***Yuuna and the Haunted Hot Springs***, Vol. 4 (*Yuragi-so no Yuuna-san*; Tadahiro Miura 2016, Shueisha/ Seven Seas Ent.)

This also happened in Yumi Nakata's ***My Wife is the Student Council President!*** (*Oku-san wa Seito-Kaicho!*; 2011, Ichijinsha), where, during its serialization, distinctly drawn nipples were censored by lines. On top of that, the lines were just slapped on the image, in a move known as "quick regulation" where censorship is hastily added to an image! However, once again, those lines were removed for the collected volume release, exposing the nipples within.

In recent years, we've seen a lot of so-called "nipple revivals" with uncensored book releases, but looking at the history of them, the first time that happened was with Masakazu Katsura's ***I"s*** (1997, Shueisha/Viz Media). Katsura's previous work, *Video Girl Ai* helped kick off the '90s, and didn't have any particular revisions done to censor nipples within it. But in the case of *I"s,* there was a sudden censoring of nipples in a character's swimsuit with bubbles during its magazine run, which was removed in the book release later on (7-43, 44).

However, it's important to note here that not all of the nipples in this release were censored during serialization. In a nude scene that was modeled on a rough sketch, the nipples were left untouched since it didn't give off any sense of eroticism (and thereby obscenity). That said, in the book release, the nipples were even more fully fleshed out (7-45, 46). Masakazu Katsura showed his talents not by inventing an expression

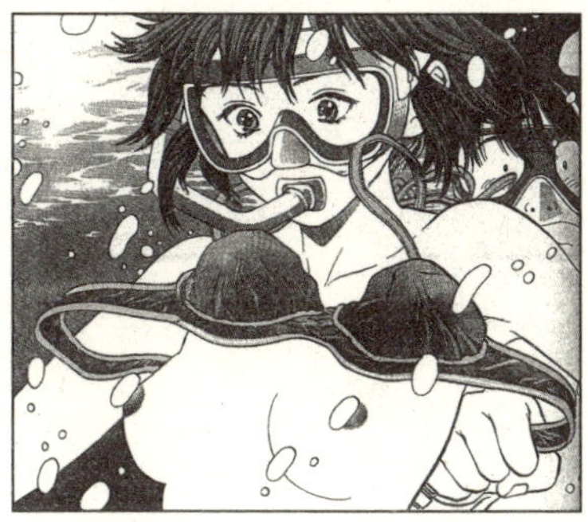

7-43: ***I"s*** (Masakazu Katsura 1997, Shueisha)

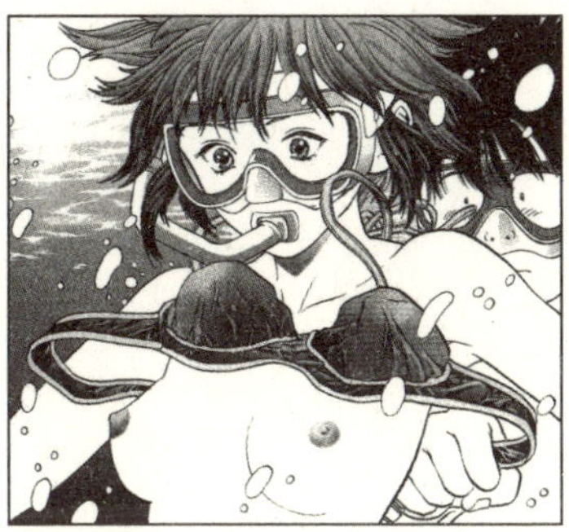

7-44: ***I"s***, Vol. 3 (Masakazu Katsura 1999, Shueisha/Viz Media)

that would allow the uncensoring of certain body parts, but by taking an already beautiful image and making it even more beautiful.

In reality, it wasn't just nipples being censored, but also the shadows on clothing and the wrinkles on underwear that were redrawn for collected volume releases, which also influenced eromanga creators as well.

No one is sure why censorship was used for serialization only and restrictions were loosened for the book release. Most likely it was due to the fact that the creators wanted their books to feel higher in quality and wanted to provide these details as tribute to the fans who would surely run out and buy them.

In the case of anime broadcasted on late night TV, sexy scenes are censored by mysterious rays of light which are removed for the DVD release later. It appears the origin point for the rays of light seem to date back to that of the *natural hiding technique,* which became a venerated sales strategy for the Japanese cult of nipples. To fans, nipples were a place that both held and delivered spiritual energy.

Not just limited to nipples, a series that elevated flashing with regard to depictions of body parts that may or may not be visible, playing with optical illusions on a deep psychological level is, once again, *To LOVE Ru*. Its relation to flashing, the series employs *trompe l'oeil* as well as concealing imagery akin to putting together a puzzle, creating a new way to enjoy manga as previously there wasn't before (7-47, 48). Though I'm not sure how far the

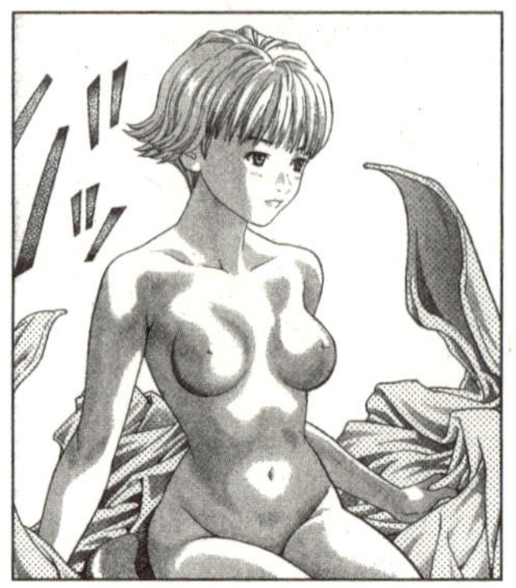

7-45: ***I"s*** (Masakazu Katsura 1998, Shueisha)

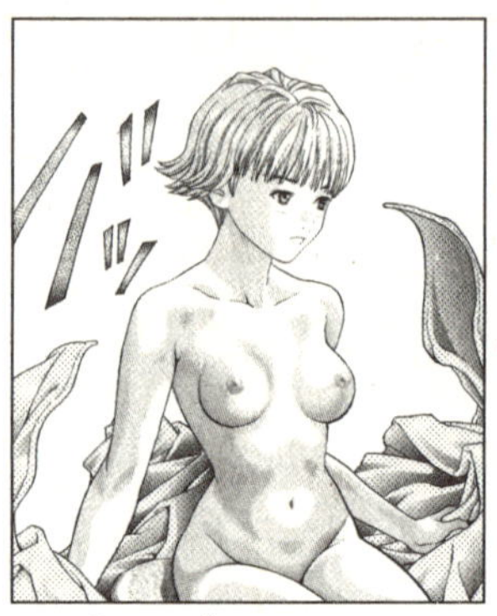

7-46: ***I"s***, Vol. 5 (Masakazu Katsura 1999, Shueisha/Viz Media)

creators' original intent ranged with this particular work, fans discovered that the space between underwear and lines of light would reflect on the back of that next page, creating a "magic muscle" of sorts that floated on the page transparently like an optical illusion. This effect was easier to achieve on the lower-grade paper used by its magazine, and something that proved to be quite difficult to look at in the book release.

Having come this far, this technique seen in shonen manga magazines has effectively become a sort of "new flashing." It also might be appropriate to call this a forbidden skill that must not be seen that reveals how much it

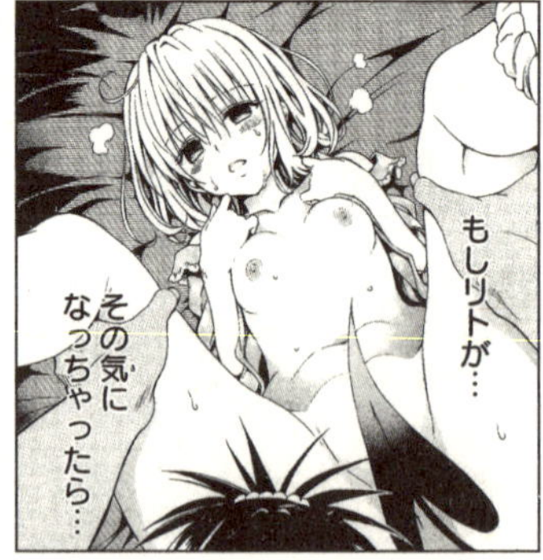

7-47: ***To LOVE Ru: Darkness***, Vol. 3 (Kentaro Yabuki & Saki Hasemi 2011, Shueisha/Seven Seas Ent.)

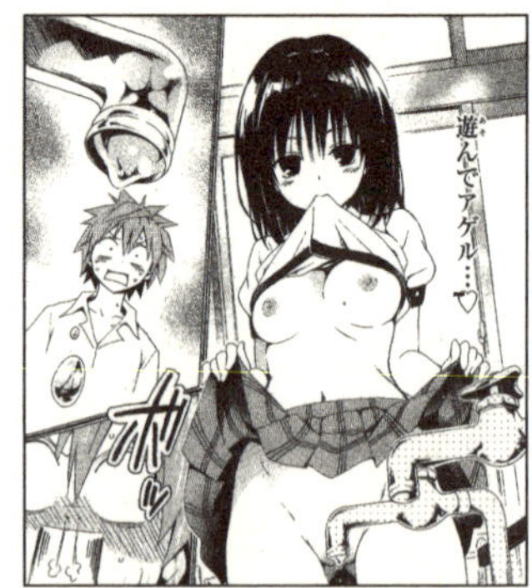

7-48: ***To LOVE Ru: Darkness***, Vol. 5 (Kentaro Yabuki & Saki Hasemi 2011, Shueisha/Seven Seas Ent.)

can be a unique piece of Japanese manga culture. Regulation itself narrows the amount of expressions that can be used successfully and tends to limit content in general. But Japanese comic artists, specifically those that create erotic content, have taken censorship under their wing thanks to the power of their imaginations allowing them to develop further.

The Mentality of Flashing

Finally, this might be me tooting my own horn a bit, but let's look at my previous book, *Eromanga no Genba*, which solved the issue of the so-called "cover problem." I asked the eromanga creator I respect the most, Naoki Yamamoto (Tou Moriyama), to handle its cover. I already had decided on the finalized design after Mr. Yamamoto set the design, but this is where a problem appeared (7-49). I was formally advised by my publisher to avoid a cover that had (uncovered) nipples on it. There was no particular industry rule against regular books having nipples on their covers, but with larger bookstore chains, there was the possibility that a live-action TV show or a book review show might be filmed at a location, and my book could show up in the background. So, they would have to move my book to a different location within the store or replace it entirely with another book. Since we didn't want to take up someone else's time by making them rearrange books, because it might inconvenience the bookstore, it would be best to have a cover without nipples on it.

In particular, if it were to be broadcast on TV, depictions of nipples or the groin would really stand out. Of course, the groin was also out of bounds, but breasts seemed to positively dance their way around prime-time airtime. However, in recent years, television has had its own set of self-enforced regulations imposed, and there has been a severe anxiety about (uncovered) breasts. When ***Thermae Romae*** (Mari Yamazaki 2008, Enterbrain/Yen Press), a time-traveling manga series about bathing that got a film adaptation later on was on a book review TV show, a red towel and a Japanese lacquered bathing pail were allegedly used to completely cover up the genitalia on the cover. The statue on its cover was censored for television broadcast, which meant that manga-style nipples were absolutely out of the question. I personally would not have revised Ms. Yamazaki's fantastic cover illustration in any way, shape, or form.

So, we all came together to try to puzzle out a solution so that wouldn't happen with my book. In the end, we figured out that to do so we needed to widen the removable belly band around the book to hide the nipples, add a seaweed strip to ensure they were completely covered, and make sure to print the band in a way where if it was removed, the nipples would still be there for the reader to see (7-50). In a way, because of *Eromanga no Genba*'s subject matter, I believe that this became a form of meta-expression in terms of the function it served, I felt that we pulled it off rather well. Even now, it's a precious personal experience of mine that deepened the meaning of the revision we had to do upon it to publish it.

That aside, the criterion of the Japanese nipple/private part binary of "is it/is it not visible?" is probably difficult to explain to those from abroad. This feeling isn't unique to manga but is also seen in the advertising and cultural spheres as well. For those that would like to pursue more knowledge about this, I suggest you look up Naoyuki Kinoshita's ***Kokan Wakashu*** and its sequel of sorts, ***Seiki no DaiMondai*** (2012 & 2017, Shinchosha). ✿

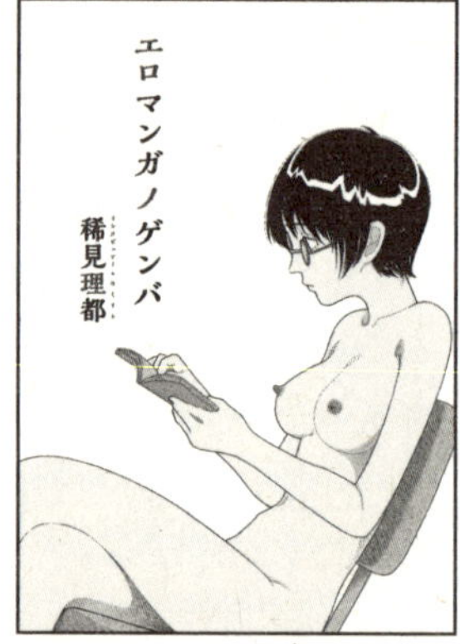

7-49: ***Eromanga no Genba*** (Kimi Rito 2016, Sansai Books)

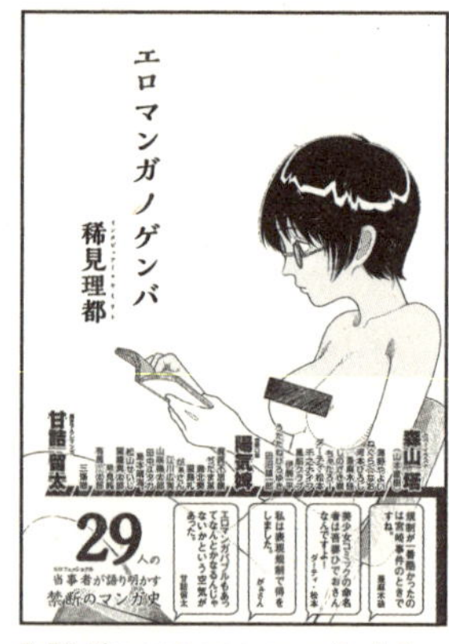

7-50: The same cover as the left but censored with a belt on it.

The History of Hentai Manga

CHAPTER EIGHT

Foreign Transmission

Eromanga Expressions Which Erode the World

In recent years, both North America and Europe have been releasing translated editions of eromanga, and its popularity is increasing by the day. I'm sure I don't need to explain why this became a phenomenon, as I'm sure everyone reading this would understand the sensation.

We are now in an age where news about Japanese releases can reach overseas fans in an instant, and where those fans can share that information, as well as stupid videos and reactions amongst themselves. Different cultures can share the same mindset, enjoying Japanese manga, games, anime, and, of course, eromanga. They fall into a frenzy about these things, and from where I'm sitting in Japan, strangely, I can understand why.

Without using the term "Cool Japan" that's been pushed on Japan by the government, one can see how these products are standing up on their own and spreading in the West with little outside help. The term "eromanga" has evolved into "hentai" in these areas (and I'll go into that a bit later in this chapter) and has flown across the globe as such.

I do not think there is another country that has an embarrassment of riches in regard to the many genres of eromanga all sorts of readers can enjoy as in Japan. Abroad, there has been a certain amount of recognition that most pornography is from an industry that is targeted towards men. Not to mention, probably many people seem to believe all pornographic comics are only targeted towards men, period.

At least in Japan, eromanga is a genre that has expressions of all sexualities and genders (and one primary consideration I would like to assert is that fixing it exclusively as a pornographic medium is a bit reckless), developing with various genres within it targeted towards both men and women. Men might like female-targeted eromanga and vice-versa, and both readers and artists can enjoy it any way they like together. This is a medium that has spread in such a diverse way, though the fact that both men and women enjoy this content surely can't be limited to Japan. And in this way, eromanga that originated there is still continuing to spread abroad via the internet.

Whether or not the content is erotic, if it's interesting to people, it will transmit and spread. And interesting manga, regardless if one is familiar with it or not, will have certain expressions that it uses, and those will surely spread as memes. At that point, I can't help but wonder how many of these changes abroad happen due to misinterpretation of the information being transmitted. Comparing cultures can yield new chances for communication, so in this chapter we'll be going back into some of these techniques and look at how those abroad have reacted to them, as well as how they've influenced others. Supplementally, I'll also go into the state of eromanga abroad.

Obviously, Tentacles Are Super Popular!

In Japan, from 2000 onward, tentacles have been reconsidered by readers at large, and has most certainly become its own genre since then. But abroad, specifically in America, fans' passion for tentacles has burned quite bright. What sparked those flames?

Some say that it was none other than the progenitor of tentacle porn and gekiga master Toshio Maeda's infamous *Urotsukidouji,* but more precisely, it was the anime adaptation of his work, *Urotsukidouji: Legend of the Overfiend* (8-1).

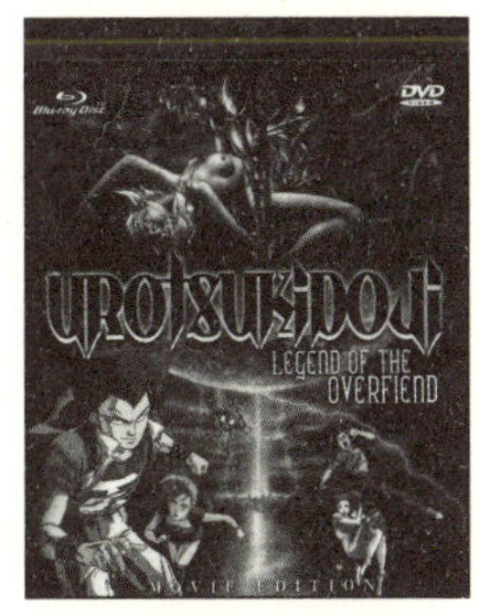

8-1: ***Urotsukidouji: Legend of the Overfiend*** (1989, Kitty Media, Blu-ray/DVD set)

I mentioned this in the tentacle chapter, but it wasn't like there weren't fans of tentacle rape before *Urotsukidouji.* The Cthulhu mythos was the progenitor of the genre, and sci-fi pulp fiction paired pretty girls with eldritch tentacle monsters long before Maeda debuted. Post-1970s, there have been many b-grade horror movies where a tentacle monster attacks a pretty girl, and sometimes there are scenes where the monster rapes the girl. However, in many of these movies, the monster only appears on screen for a few seconds, so that did not give birth to the tentacle rape genre.

In 1989, the anime adaptation of *Urotsukidouji* was made available in America and took the country by storm. Its release was mostly sold via VHS tapes, and the violent, erotic anime became a cult hit. It was an encounter with an anime filled with both sexual situations and violence, a piece of Japanese content that integrated the two effortlessly. Of course, the violence here was the tentacle monsters both tormenting and assaulting pretty girls, which surely caused *otaku* trauma amongst Americans.

Shokushu rape became known as "tentacle rape" in English. Many people propbably thought that the one special characteristic of those tentacles were that they were octopus-like in appearance. Not that there are many more variations in Japan, but to people in the States, so less used to tentacle expression principles, they probably felt the attack of this expression more. *Urotsukidouji,* which did more than just widen the genre, also helped adult anime become more recognized abroad. When the sequel to *Urotsukidouji* was released, tentacles underwent the encoding process at a rapid pace, making the genre even more popular in the US, and it was accepted almost faster than it had been in Japan.

The mix of "pretty girl and tentacle monster" tied the erotic to the genre more than just tentacles on their own, to the point where shortly thereafter, the recognition of tentacles was *only* in an erotic context. Marvel Comics distributed the ***Heroes for Hire*** series and in it was a scene where the heroines had to fight off tentacles (8-2). After its publication, there came claims of "Well, isn't this pornography?" creating a

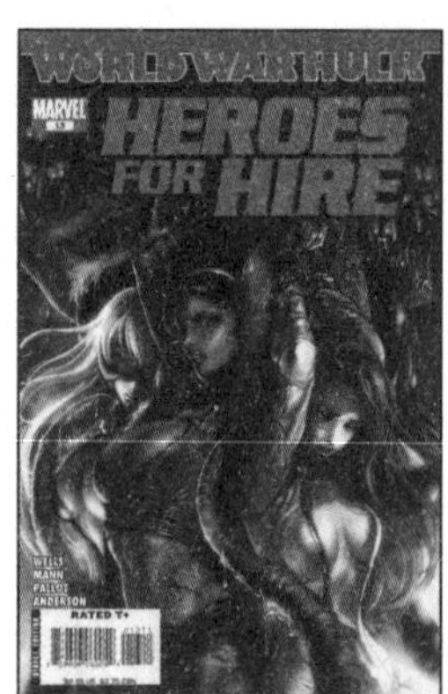

8-2: ***Heroes for Hire 2***, #13 (Sana Takeda & Fred Van Lente, Zeb Wells 2007, Marvel)

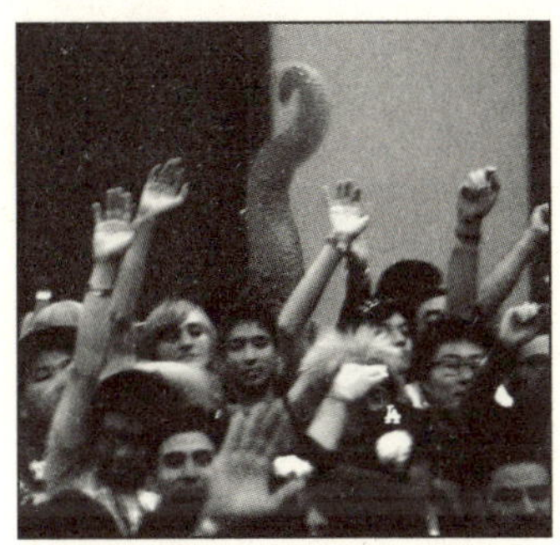

8-3: An eromanga fan with their own tentacle at Anime Expo 2016.

huge hubbub (particularly due to a lack of a rating system. From what I've been able to see, the content does look a bit erotic. But at the same time, the tentacles are not outright sexually assaulting the heroines. This anecdote may explain why people started to see tentacles as only being sexual by nature. It may be that America itself felt that it was being raped by tentacles.

In truth, at American anime events, overly enthusiastic fans occasionally bring toy tentacles with them and hold them aloft as they have fun together at panels, as tentacles continue to be spread as an item for nerds in that way, becoming its own sort of culture (8-3).

So-called "tentacle culture" began to spread throughout the world. Eventually Toshio Maeda received the name of "Tentacle Master" to reflect how many people had come to respect him as a creator. Maeda now started to enthusiastically go to more events abroad to aid in his content's diffusion worldwide.

In truth, Maeda's tentacles were not purposely drawn to look like squid or octopi's limbs, but those of an unnamed "creature." But fans began to request more octopus and squid-like tentacles from Maeda for him to draw for them at these events, so he decided to fulfill those requests as a service to those fans.

Perhaps tentacles really are the one thing that connects cultures after all.

The World Still Doesn't Know About the Nipple Afterimage

The next question I wonder about is how do Americans feel about the *nipple afterimage,* which was invented in Japan around the same point in time? It's an expression as big as tentacles are in popularity, and if Americans love eromanga, shouldn't they know what the *nipple afterimage* is? Shouldn't they recognize it when they see it?

Unfortunately, as of this point in time, it has not been accepted abroad. That said, the most famous Japanese eromanga titles that feature this expression have not yet been translated into English. So, this expression has an air of being cool but not much more than that.

Cuckolding is known as *NTR* in English as initials of the Japanese word "netorare." Hermaphrodites are known as *futanari*, similarly romanized as *netorare* has been. Lesbian content is slightly more interesting as it too has faced a similar reverse translation, becoming a written expression known as *yuri* abroad. While this isn't necessarily an auspicious omen for eromanga, female porn actresses who had their male counterparts ejaculate on their faces and bodies helped contribute to what became known as *bukkake* in the West.

Within the now world-famous eromanga genre, many terms for its expressions have been romanized into English with no further translation. I personally hold the opinion that there's no possible way people can't recognize what they are. However, in the case of the *nipple afterimage,* there has to be a lot of rough movement for that afterimage to appear, and it could be that seeing that was just too much of a shock as one can't really feel that movement just from the words alone. It also may be due to the fact that in places that didn't experience the sudden entrance of breasts as a trend into their culture in the 1980s like Japan did, and since large breasts are more common in the West, there has been little recognition of the *nipple afterimage.*

Just by looking at the words "nipple afterimage," it's true that the expression itself is not a monolith, and there is no one typical story connected to it. Bundling it together as one genre is difficult at best.

In recent years, when one looks at eromanga drawn by foreigners, one can see its use in their work as an expression. So, I wonder, wouldn't it be okay at this point to attach its name to the expression as it exists abroad? Since this is something I'd definitely like to explore more of in the future, it would be lovely if you readers out there could wait for a follow-up report.

Similarly, there are expressions out there whose types of sexual play as content are not captured by their names. The one expression that is in this situation that comes to mind is the *cross-section view.*

The Cross-Section View Is Shared Worldwide

While the *nipple afterimage* has not yet been accepted in English as of yet, there is a western term for the *cross-section view* that already exists. I thought a literal translation would call it the "sectional view," but it turns out that's not the case.

In the Anglosphere, it seems that in many cases, people call the *cross-section view* the "x-ray view." This actual term focuses less on the concept of the cross-section cuts and instead seems to conceptualize it more in the terms of roentgen (the legacy unit of measurement for x-rays) showing the gaps in the body when an x-ray is used. Furthermore, as the expression makes the invisible visible, there are some that have called it "translucent." But after doing some digging, when one gets down to the basic meaning of the term, "x-ray" seems to be the more appropriate of the two. While I'm still investigating whether or not American comics have had an x-ray sort of expression in their past, I wonder if they have something like the Japanese eromanga *cross-section view* to show the unseen insides of someone.

Both the *cross-section view* and the *nipple afterimage* are expressions where their terms do not define them as genres of sexual play, but rather as visual techniques. Does the *cross-section view* excite Americans when it's used in content at all, I wonder?

When I investigated older American pornographic comics, I didn't find any uses of this particular expression. However, when you consider the culture behind eromanga's *cross-section view,* something that exploded very suddenly and caught on like wildfire, spreading rapidly and allowing it to develop into the expression we know today (8-4). This occured because Japanese artists could not legally draw genitalia, so it was used to evade regulation, and in a sense, quite literally draw "behind the rules." Because those in foreign countries like the US did not need to go to such lengths to enjoy erotic content due to the lack of censorship laws, there was no need to invent an expression like it. However, all of this is just me speculating.

Through the development of the *cross-section view* as an expression, one can see its special characteristics. Japan's 2D culture is still firmly rooted even now. 3D's anime-like deformed 2D images serve as its base. When one compares this to European and American 3D animation, which is more realistic looking, especially adult 3D animation, one can see the moving *cross-section view* in use as an expression, and it's used quite well. If it continues to be used this well in the future, then the expression should develop further. I believe this is so because since the age of Da Vinci, humans have wanted to know what happens inside one's body, and when that is combined with a spirit of inquiry and the wild delusions of erotic material, this expression probably has become a shared desire throughout the world, a hunger to

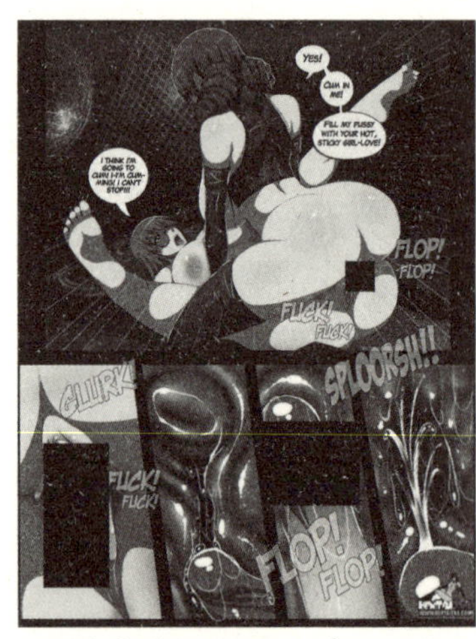

8-4: ***Alice's Nightmare,*** Part 2 (Cyberunique & ADM 2014) *Original art is uncensored.

know what is happening inside of us. (Editor's Note: The term "bisection view" has been used in the West since the mid '00s by its manga critics.)

The Ahegao Is Spreading Throughout America

Surprisingly enough, the term *ahegao* is already firmly entrenched abroad as an idiom with American eromanga fans as a necessary term everyone should know. The spelling of the romanized term is the same as it is in Japanese: "ahegao." It seems that even in the States, there's a term for the slightly silly facial expression a woman makes when she reaches orgasm: "[being] fucked silly." However, remember that without the three concrete conditions that make up the *ahegao,* a silly facial expression can possibly mean many things. Americans, who excel at everything they do, were seemingly awaiting the arrival of something with as much impact as the *ahegao.*

In Japan, the *ahegao* had a decidedly concentrated group of fans within which it was much in vogue. The internet did provide a certain amount of amplification, which aided in the expression's broader acceptance. But what many people don't know is that in America, it followed a very similar path. The concrete details about the American diffusion process are still unknown, but the process began as a "strange face" that people made circulating online. Many people took part in it, to the point where it was a meme where everyone wanted to join in.

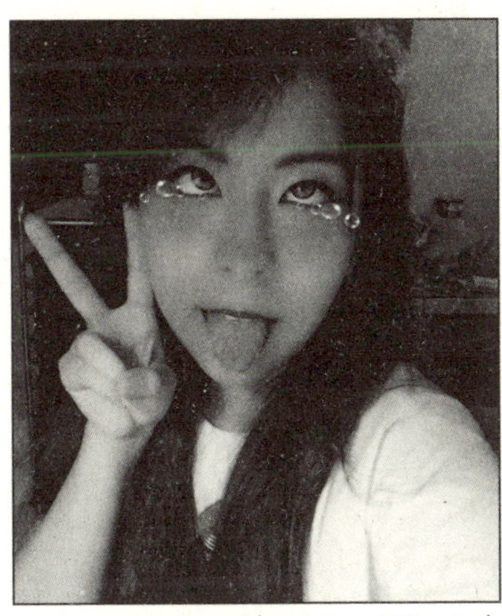

8-5: "ahegao challenge" (@oniakako 2016, *twitter*)

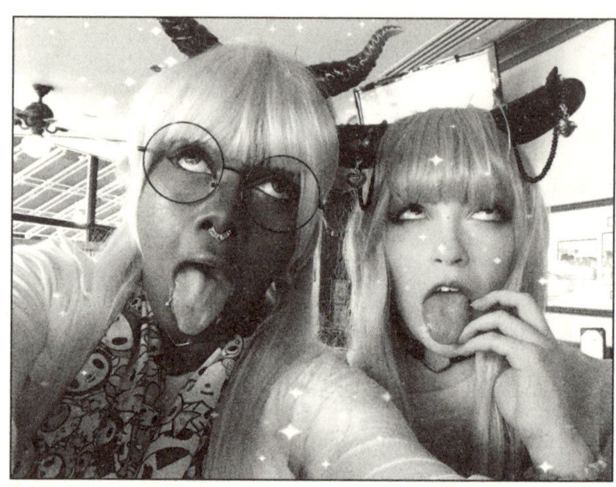

8-6: "ahegao challenge" (@DollyLoveHallyu 2016, *twitter*)

It began somewhere around September 2016, spreading via social media sites (though mostly via Instagram) as the "ahegao challenge" (8-5, 6). It spread quickly, prompting other people on social media to wonder about what that facial expression people were making was. That was the beginning of how Americans began to formally recognize the *ahegao* for what it was.

Even for Americans, this expression was very intense, and the facial expression itself was one that charmed many, becoming a template of sorts that spread through the internet in that form. The three components were a bit different, where semen wasn't required but being able to see the whites of the eyes and having the tongue stick out still stayed firmly in place as criterion.

It may be appropriate to say that in this way, the diffusion process in America was more or less identical to that of Japan's. However here it is important to note that the spread in America did not happen via fans reading eromanga, but instead spread as a meme across the internet. It might be correct to say that because of this, the *ahegao* itself became more acknowledged and recognized by Americans than *hentai* itself.

To people in the west, Japanese erotic manga and anime were grouped together and called *hentai*. Here I would like to point out that this is an area that needs some special attention, as this is not a reductive label given to the amalgamation of these two genres. So, what is *hentai*, exactly? Let's look at that more carefully in the next section.

"HENTAI" and "ECCHI" Join the English Language

Abroad, Japanese eromanga has been called *hentai*. So why was this label taken from the Japanese word for pervert? And how did it come to encompass both Japanese eromanga and ero anime?

There are more than a few theories on the topic, and there are many elements that we still do not understand about this phenomenon. One theory is that before eromanga and anime were imported officially, anime fans in America watched anime via what were called *fansubs* (illegally translated and released forms of both manga and anime) whose subtitles were translated by fans often for viewing parties. When erotic content on screen or page happened (though usually it wasn't above a brief flashing of the heroine's panties), dialogue like "Pervert!" (hentai) and "Lewd!" (ecchi) would often accompany those images in the media. At some point, all of anime and manga of this sort got mistranslated into the erroneous term "hentai" and penetrated fan culture as slang.

It is at this juncture where I wonder: during this period long ago, did American anime fans get sexually aroused by Japanese content? When the degree of eroticism was turned down, it was no longer hentai, but *ecchi*. While hentai included 18+ hardcore eromanga material, *ecchi* was more like what one sees during late-night anime slots in Japan (softcore material with sexy scenes but no actual sex), and the cases in which it was used in that context were many in number. It may be appropriate to call this Japanglish slang. The spelling for *ecchi* is the same in Japanese. But when one really thinks about it, *ecchi* is just the letter "H" pronounced in Japanese. And as that is the first letter of the word "hentai," it made the rounds to overseas *otaku* as slang.

Even though its route was circuitous and complex along with mistranslations along the way before becoming a bit of slang, I believe that the original spirit of the terms has been left intact just fine. (laughs) When one covers the sphere of [erotic] content, first one must look at the ero genre that came first. I usually say that it is akin to standing at the foot of a mountain and having that view widen itself before you. But when it comes to these slang words that have been adopted into the English language, I feel that perhaps ero-related vocabulary may spread throughout the world and become a lingua franca of sorts.

I would like to caution here that perhaps Japanese people will be hesitant when the English version of *hentai* is presented to them in conversation. When at one of these anime or manga events (like Anime Expo), and someone asks you whether you like "hentai," try not to get the wrong idea of the potential response from a Japanese native. You may not know if the person you're talking to may have a problem with that sort of material, even if it may not be an issue for you at that point.

The Three Generations of Eromanga Which Crossed the Seas to America

Eromanga has already found many readers across the globe, but I suppose it's obvious when I say that not all of that happened in one fell swoop. It turns out many people don't know that translated editions of eromanga didn't start appearing within the States until 1994 or so. The eromanga that appeared abroad was drastically different in terms of content depending on when it had been made in Japan, so let's break it down into "generations," shall we?

The eromanga translated and published in America can be broken down by time period, and there are roughly three main generations we can break it down into…

The First Generation: ***Countdown: Sex Bombs*, *Sexhibition***

At that time, the lone American publisher that was translating Japanese eromanga was Fantagraphics; under their umbrella that covered a wide range of western comics, one imprint specifically dcalt with adult comics, Eros Comix, which debuted around 1990. And it was via that imprint that eromanga was translated and released (ed.: via a sub-line called Mangerotica).

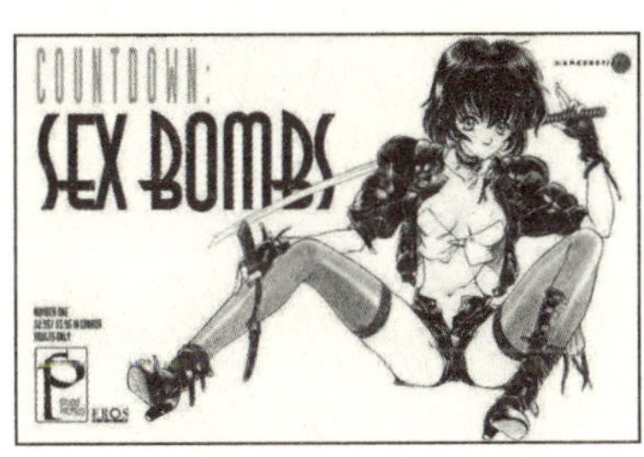

8-7: ***Countdown: Sex Bombs***, #1 (*COUNT DOWN*; Hiroyuki Utatane 1995, Fantagraphics/ Fujimi Publishing)

I'm not sure what the selection criteria was for the initial Japanese content in its earliest period released via this arm of the company, but here was the initial lineup of that content: *Countdown: Sex Bombs* (8-7), ***Princess of Darkness*** (Yuichiro Tanuma 1995, Byakuya-Shobo 8-8), ***Sexhibition*** (*Heart Ache*; Gari Suehiro 1995, Byakuya-Shobo 8-9), ***Hot Tails*** (*Mermaid ♥ Junction;* Yui Toshiki 1995, Byakuya-Shobo 8-10) and others.

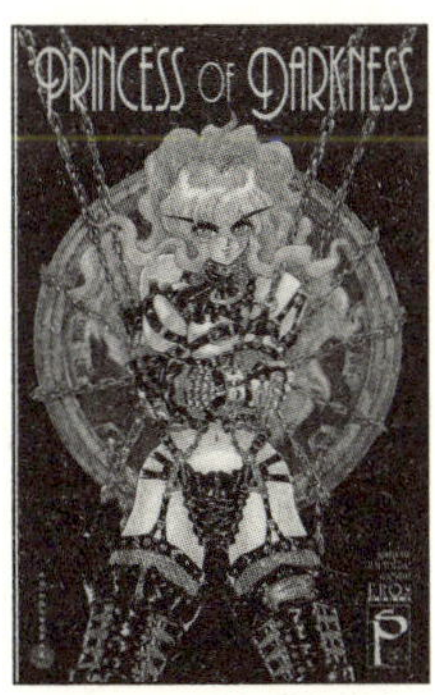

8-8: ***Princess of Darkness***, #1 (Yuichiro Tanuma 1995, Fantagraphics/Byakuya-Shobo)

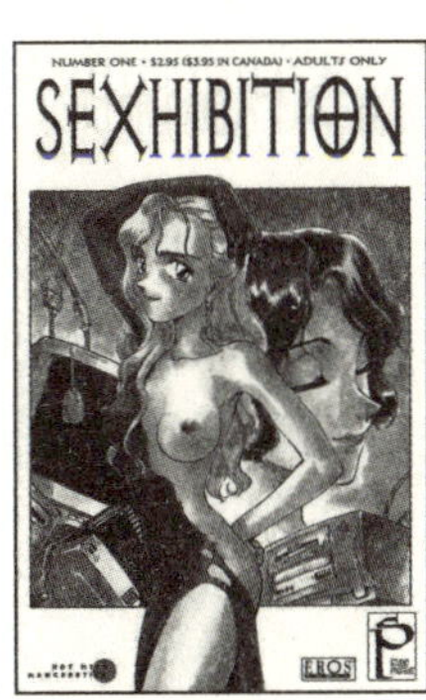

8-9: ***Sexhibition***, #1 (*Heart Ache*; Gari Suehiro 1995, Fantagraphics/Byakuya-Shobo)

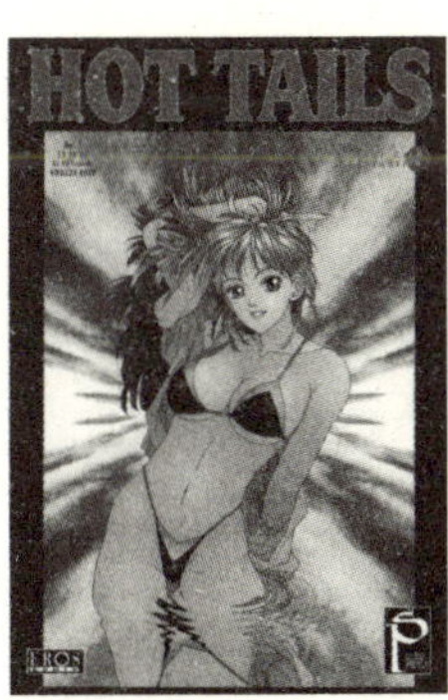

8-10: ***Hot Tails***, #1 (*Mermaid ♥ Junction;* Yui Toshiki 1996, Fantagraphics/Byakuya-Shobo)

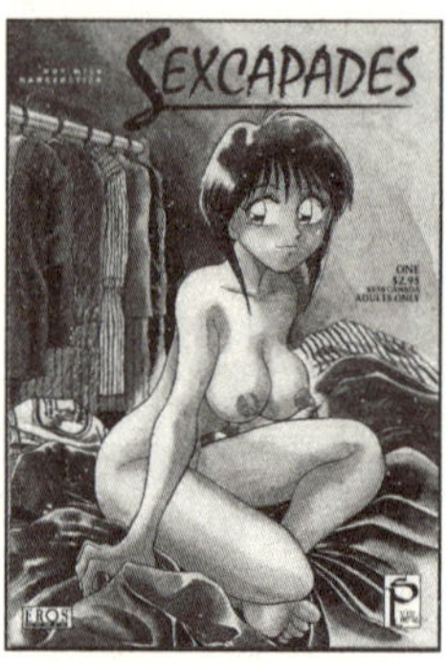

8-11: ***Sexcapades***, #1 (*Hotaru no Kibun*; Dirou Chiba's 1996, Fantagraphics/Byakuya-Shobo)

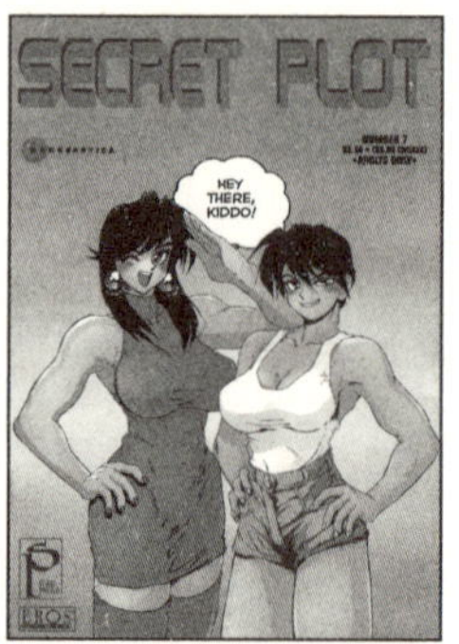

8-12: ***Secret Plot***, #7 (NeWMeN 1997, Fantagraphics/Fujimi Publishing)

The special characteristic of the titles in this first early group was that of their binding. It wasn't the Japanese style used with graphic novel style books (called "tankobon"), but instead they were released like single-issue American comics (8-11, 12). They didn't translate the material and then put it all into one big book like Japanese publishers did, but instead Eros Comix released each chapter separately as its own single issue roughly 22 to 23 pages in length in a magazine format. And these comics were sold for about three dollars per book.

Perhaps the most obvious special characteristic about these American releases was the fact that they read opposite of how books are opened in Japan, left to right instead of right to left. The whole book was reoriented and revised to do so. Manga pages are created right to left, as Japanese books are read from right to left, top to bottom (due to vertical orthography). At that time, I guess the Japanese way of doing things with regard to binding just wasn't exciting enough for American fans, which meant that everything from the ground up had to be Americanized for consumption.

But let's compare the specifics (8-13, 14). At this time, it wasn't just limited to eromanga; all Japanese manga content was being handled in a similar fashion. Because they "flipped" the pages, it meant that any protagonist that was originally right-handed became left-handed in the

American version. There were many cases during production where any Japanese signs in the comics got flipped around as well. For those in the cultural sphere that couldn't or didn't read Japanese content in Japanese, I wonder if this bothered them? Because I think that this situation would have repulsed Japanese people. However, whenever cars would show up in this flipped material, it actually might have been better after all as it meant that any left-handed drivers wouldn't have to be amended any further for the audience.

Out of all of the translated Japanese eromanga, there were cases of series that had a rather poor showing in Japan but turned out to be a big hit in the States. Even more interesting was that the most popular genre is known as "insect rape." Kondom's series ***Bondage Fairies*** (1993, Kubo Shoten/Antarctic Press; 8-15, 16) featured fairies that look like butterflies having anthropomorphized sex with bugs, earthworms, even small mammals in what turned out to be truly insane plot development.

Perhaps Japan was just too difficult a market for this series, as it didn't make much of an impression in the publishing landscape there. However, what was a surprise was how this series got its big (little) break in the American market. Much like the so-called *tentacle shock* that rocked the States years earlier, this "bug shock" was functioning in the same capacity with regard to how it surprised people abroad. So, at this point, let's take a closer look at the idiosyncrasies of both Japan and abroad to find out more.

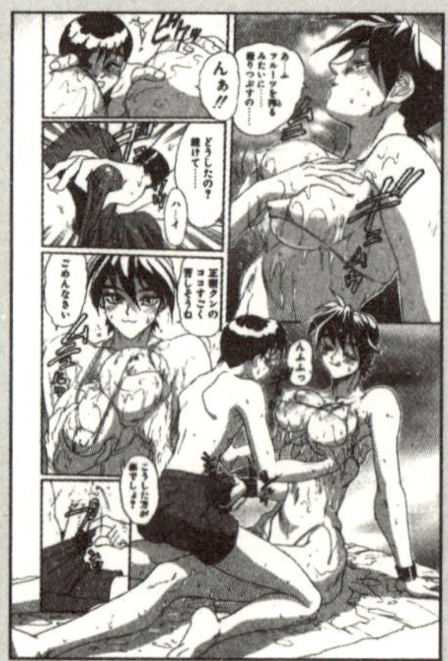

8-13: ***SECRET PLOT DEEP*** (NeWMeN 1998, Fujimi Publishing)

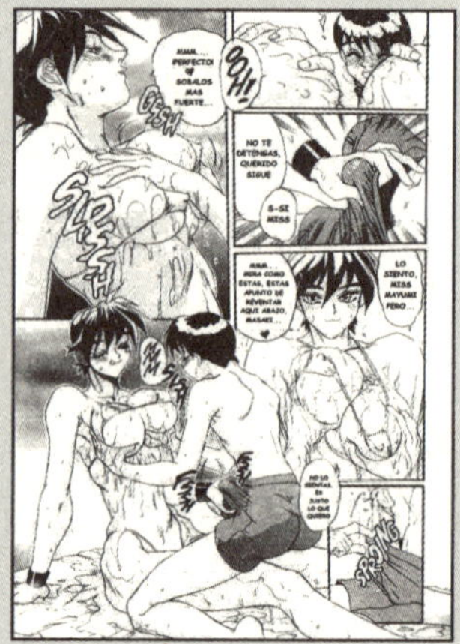

8-14: ***Secret Plot Deep***, #6 (NeWMeN 1999, Fantagraphics/Fujimi Publishing)

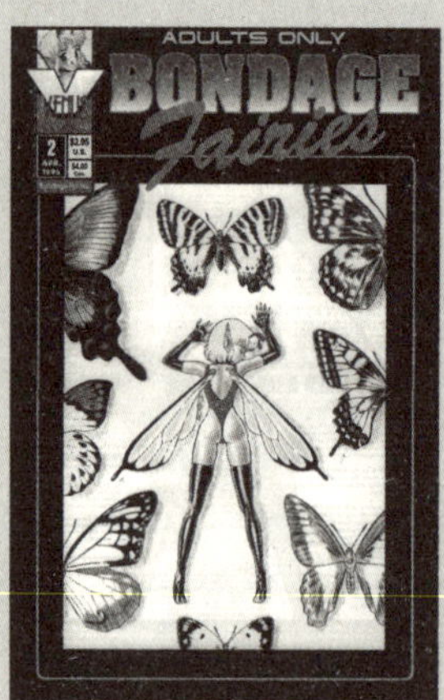

8-15: ***Bondage Fairies***, #2 (Kondom 1994, Antarctic Press/Kubo Shoten)

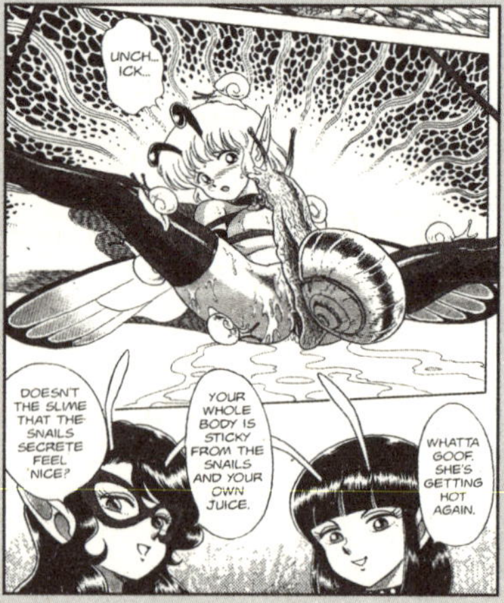

8-16: ***Bondage Fairies***, #2 (Kondom 1994, Antarctic Press/Kubo Shoten)

The Second Generation: ***Pink Sniper, Milk Mama***

The second generation of eromanga didn't wash up on American cultural shores until about 2000 or so. This wave that came to be known as the "Japanese culture boom" was due to three anime series: ***Sailor Moon***, ***Pokémon***, and ***Dragon Ball***. Both *Sailor Moon* and *Dragon Ball* had already been on the air for limited broadcast before 1998, with both ending in failures. In 1998, when a broadcast network switch happened for both, they ended up being broadcast to all of the United States. This also became the moment that the anime boom in the States truly began.

Around this time, the way that manga was translated and released in America was also changing. Prior to this time, Japanese culture had been combined with American methods, but it was at this point that we saw the change in how manga was handled during the American localization process. Within those changes, we started to see more and more eromanga creeping into the licensing landscape (8-17, 18).

First, publishers stopped using the one-chapter magazine publication strategy for their series. Instead, publishers shifted to a form that was pretty close to the way that Japanese editions are published: the trade paperback (TPB). On top of that, it was at this time that there was an increase in TPBs that reverted to Japanese right to left reading style. At this time, Eros Comix was publishing titles like ***Pink Sniper*** (Kengo Yonekura, 2005, 8-19), *Domin-8 Me!* (8-20), ***Milk Mama*** (Yuki Yanagi, 2007, Fujimi Publishing 8-21) and others. On the final page of each book, a notice to the reader saying "This is the last page of the book, please read me from the other end," basically serving as a short guide on how to read things the Japanese way to readers who may not know otherwise. This is the special characteristic of the releases from this particular generation (8-22).

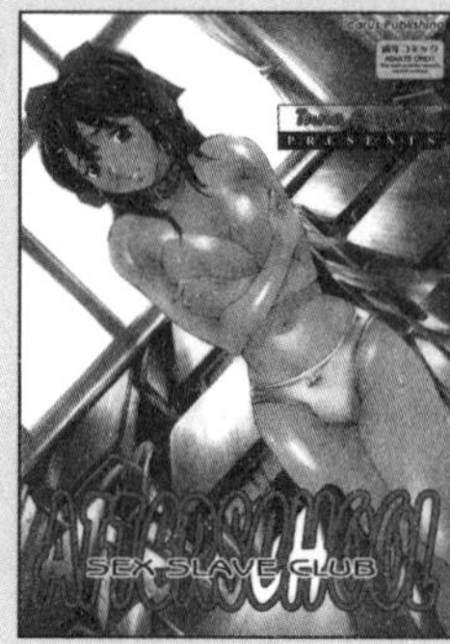

8-17: ***After School Sex Slave Club*** (*Hokago Dorei Kurabu*; Tuna Empire 2008, Icarus Publishing/Akaneshinsha)

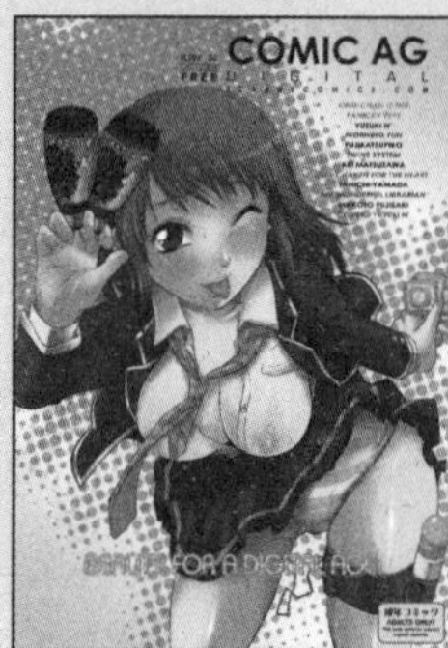

8-18: *COMIC AG Digital*, 03 (2008, Icarus Comics; anthology)

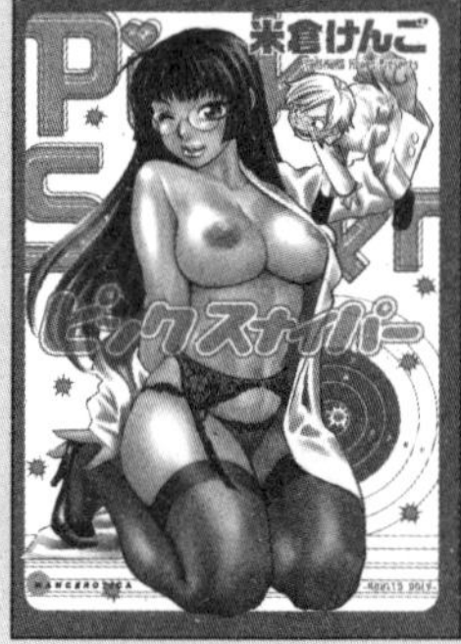

8-19: ***Pink Sniper*** (Kengo Yonekura 2006, Fantagraphics/Core Magazine)

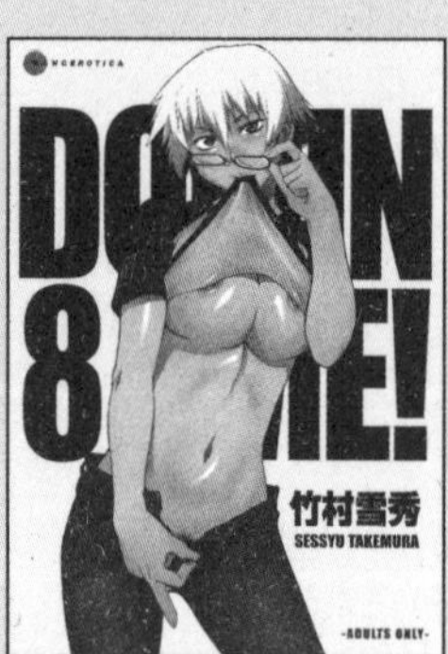

8-20: ***Domin-8 Me!*** (*TAKE ON ME*; Sessyu Takemura 2007, Fantagraphics/Core Magazine)

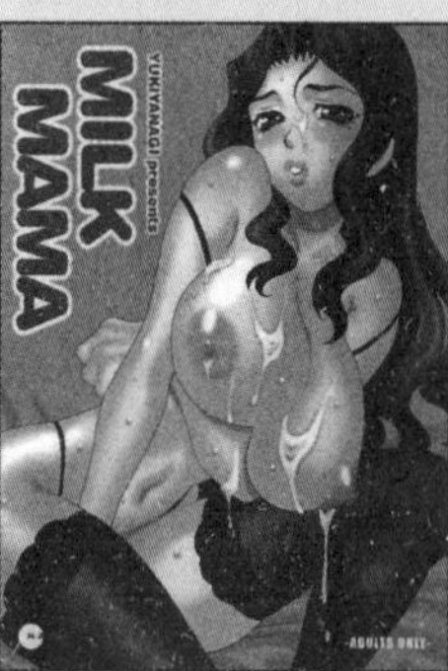

8-21: ***Milk Mama*** (Yuki Yanagi, 2007, Fantagraphics/Fujimi Publishing)

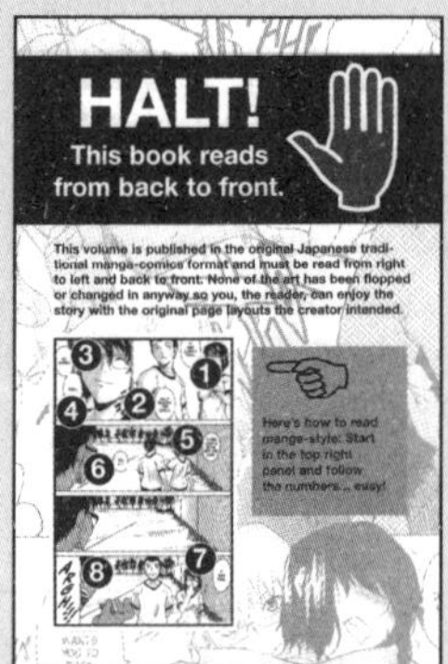

8-22: ***Domin-8 Me!*** (*TAKE ON ME*; Sessyu Takemura 2007, Fantagraphics/Core Magazine) *Reading guide on how to read it the way as done in Japan.

The Third Generation: **The Millennial Generation**

Which brings us to the current age, and the rise of a new movement (8-23, 24). Those who were born between the 1980s through the early 2000s are known as the millennial generation, the first generation that grew up entirely alongside the internet. They were also the first generation to be baptized within the Japanese culture movement by watching anime as children. This generation has started to become adults in their own right.

There's a saying that when children become adults, they have more freedom with their money (in terms of how they spend it). But here I would like to add in one more very important thing to this statement. When children become adults, they can legally access pornography. Once someone is over the age of eighteen, in most jurisdictions they can access porn. Once someone is released from age restrictions, it really frees them up. In particular, America's millennials are the one generation that have a (favorable) bias towards Japanese anime and manga. While the previous generation of Americans were asking things like "Why are their eyes so big?", "Why don't they have noses? That's weird!", "Why do these characters get nose bleeds when aroused?" and other such questions. However, the generation that grew up consuming Japanese anime and manga from a young age shrugged off any negative bias on an unconscious level. It's not as if these kids watched their beloved *Pokémon* and *Dragon Ball* because they knew it was made in Japan. They started watching those TV shows purely because of the fact that they were interest-

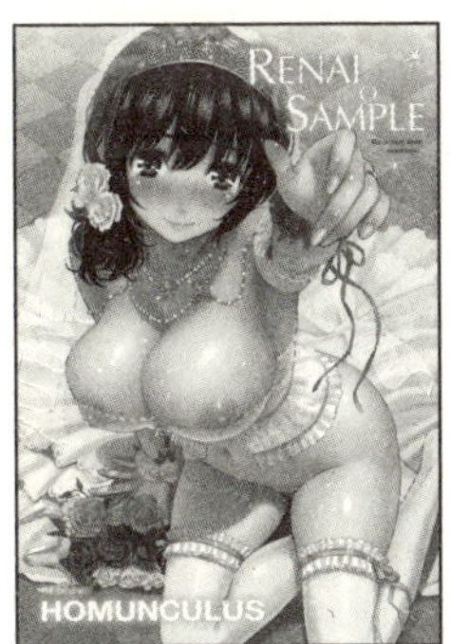

8-23: ***Renai Sample*** (Homunculus 2014, FAKKU/Wanimagazine)

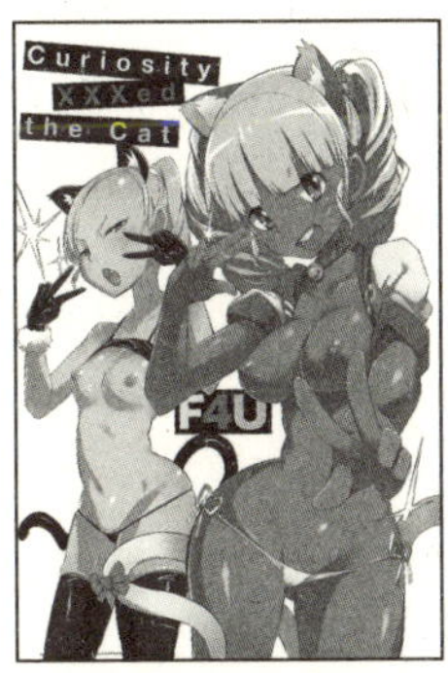

8-24: ***Curiosity XXXed the Cat*** (*Kokishin wa Neko wo mo Are Suru*; F4U 2016, FAKKU/Wanimagazine)

ing, and because of that, most likely they did not feel any sense of something being off with that content.

Furthermore, Japanese anime and manga did not forgive those who "graduated" from it, as there were tons of content made specifically for adults. It doesn't give one a timeline with which one must leave that sphere of entertainment behind, and when combined with attractive erotic content for adults, one can no longer pull away from Japanese anime and manga in general so easily, becoming a direct path for content consumption. (ed.: Very little adult material is currently officially translated into English however.)

Japan's Most Coveted Wish: No Censorship

In translated editions of Japanese material, there are different limits put on different expressions, and in many cases, many troublesome spots are further censored before publication. But there is something, quite frankly, that I am very envious of in these editions that are not in the Japanese edition. Which is to say, most Japanese eromanga releases that are published in America and Europe are uncensored, and unrevised (8-25).

In America's case, because live action pornography isn't censored for release, accordingly, other erotic mediums are not either. According to Americans, most don't understand why adult content would be censored. It's at this point where we can see different cultural ideas with regard to sex depending on country and culture start to emerge, which makes me think about the definition of obscenity once more.

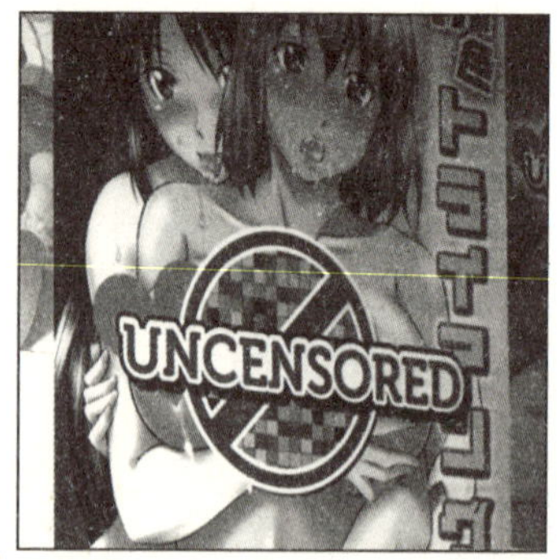

8-25: Uncensored mark (Anime Expo 2015)

Incidentally, after asking some folks who work for American publishers, I found that there are some companies that leave it all in and publish it as-is. But the real lone reason why things are uncensored is because such releases are exceedingly popular amongst American readers.

You're probably thinking, "As I thought! Keeping all the eros really is the best!", but there's actually one more reason. While there are different techniques used for censorship, it turns out that readers in America tend to be concerned with things down to the last detail of those censored parts. It seems that most eromanga pages are positively overflowing with those censored bits. To have a clean page only to be sullied with little bits of revision, which must look like garbage, has been recognized as a type of "visual pollution" or "noise" to the American reader.

I was asked by one American eromanga fan why an artist, after working so hard and spending all of their energy on drawing, would befoul it. I believe I answered them saying that Japanese eromanga fans were used to it, or something to that effect. But after this crossing of cultural spheres, it's something that I've been actively thinking about. At the same time, I was really happy that this fan realized that eromanga was its own sort of art.

Onomatopes Are the Hardest to Translate

The age of the American-born eromanga fan has come. Many wish to enjoy eromanga as it is, but it isn't easy in the least to overcome the linguistic barrier. In that sense, there's always concern on how eromanga expressions will be translated. Not all publishers abide by the same rules, but someone from one of those companies did broadly lay out the points that those in production usually keep in mind and adhere to when I asked them.

First, only include the onomatopes that are in the original script and try not to include any more than are absolutely necessary, along with leaving in the hand-lettered onomatopes that the artist inserted in the original manuscript since many Japanese onomatopes do not have a one-to-one translation into English.

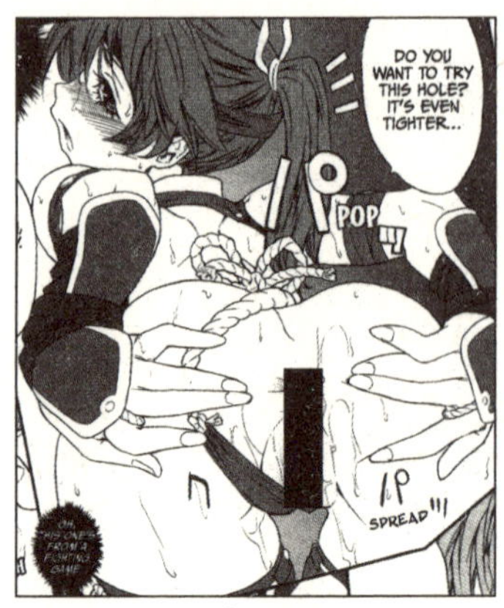

8-26: ***Power Play!*** (Yamatogawa 2012, Digital Manga/Akaneshinsha)
*This image was censored for the Japanese edition of this book.

According to many fans, even when they don't understand the onomatopes being used, they still enjoy them within that work. So this policy has become commonplace. However, in some works, there has been the subtitling of sound effects, or the insertion of translation notes to explain the situation to the American audience.

For example, "kupaa" has been translated as "spread" (8-26). An ejaculation sound, "topyuu," has been translated as "spurt" (8-27; ed.: Note that this image features a "dokunn" instead of "topyuu" but the meaning is similar, even if "dokunn" is a more emphatic onomatopea). When a woman is masturbating by rubbing her clitoris, the slang term "schlick" has been used, and when it feels so good that she cramps up a bit, "twitch" has been used. Many other terms and onomatopes have been used to subtitle for the Japanese hand-lettered sound effects along the way.

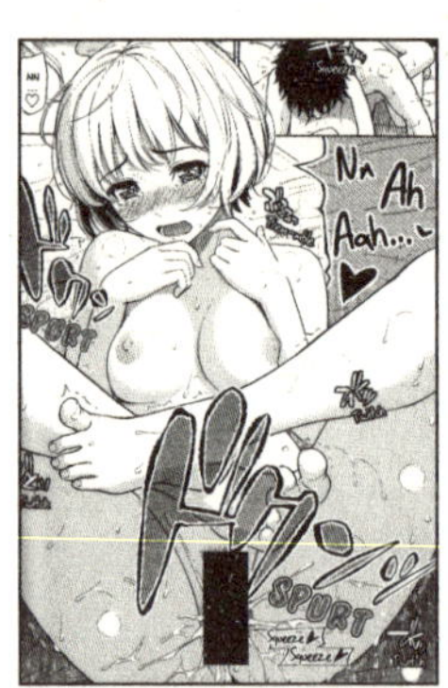

8-27: ***Renai Sample*** (Homunculus 2014, FAKKU/Wanimagazine)
*This image was censored for the Japanese edition of this book.

So, what about special-use onomatopes like "ramee"? How are those handled? If they were to leave it as "ramee" in English, then the concept wouldn't get across at all to that audience, in all probability. Japan's special turns of phrase and their nuances are even more difficult to capture in the translation process. By looking at things on a case-by-case basis, it seems we can tell how effective the translations were to capture the original spirit of these terms. Because the case of "ramee" is one that shows a bitten off end of a sentence linguistically and has been adapted to show that, just translating it to "no" in English seems out of character. In that case, if we want to keep the original spirit and function of this written expression, if we were to use "don't!", would we change it to "ron't!" for the English written expression? Though allegedly, "nooo!" has been used but changed to the English written expression of "nyooo!" instead. In this case, changing those few letters into English for its translated written expression, that strategy turns into a device used to keep the original Japanese nuance of the term.

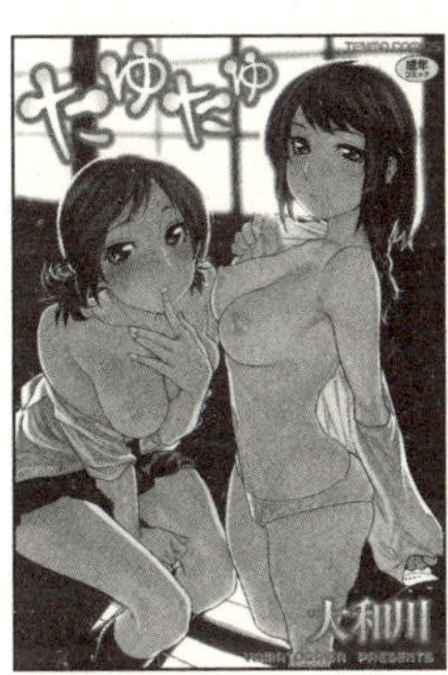

8-28: ***Tayu Tayu*** (Yamatogawa 2009, Akaneshinsha/FAKKU)

There have been many times when Japanese linguistic nuance quite literally became lost in translation. We know this because even before the age of translated manga, in marketing, when translations have had to be changed due to errors of this sort. In Yamatogawa's ***Tayu Tayu*** (Akaneshinsha; 8-28), the translation of the title of the American release of the book was tweaked by its American publisher to ***Boing Boing*** (Digital Manga; 8-29), slightly changing the nuance already there.

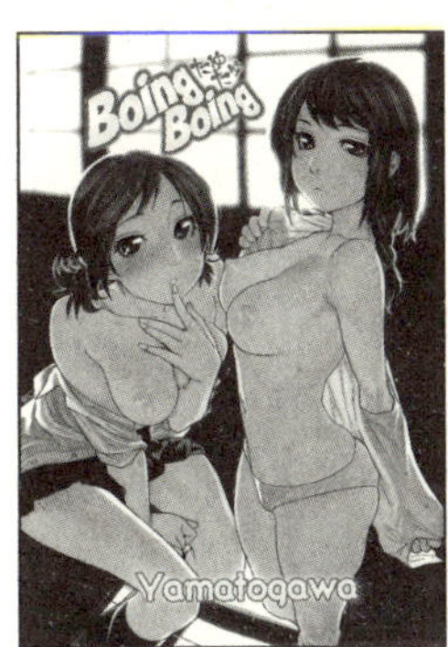

8-29: ***Boing Boing*** (*Tayu Tayu*; Yamatogawa 2013, Digital Manga/Akaneshinsha)

Originally, Yamatogawa had originally meant something closer to "tayutafu" (a gentle rocking movement), imagining a woman floating on the surface of water, gently drifting with a buoyant feeling to it. Due to the fact that there was no good corresponding term in English that captured the same feeling and imagery, the title was originally left as-is for the English release: *Tayu Tayu*. That did not last, however, due to the fact that, once again, there was no English term, the Japanese title couldn't transmit the meaning to the audience, either. After some internal debate, the publisher decided that the title for the official English release would be renamed to *Boing Boing.* This gave off the feeling that the comic was about breasts bouncing, as if they were a vine bending under the weight of its own fruit. By changing it in this way, the publisher ended up changing the nuance of the original imagery and meaning behind the Japanese title.

Healthy returns on this work were the priority, and if it did not sell, then obviously, there was no meaning to putting it out in the first place. To that end, it may be possible that there just was no helping having to change the title to something slightly different in meaning in order for it to sell. In order to reduce issues like that, I wonder if the English publisher had to append the title due to a global awareness of works like this one on behalf of their readership? (ed.: The 2020 FAKKU release of *Tayu Tayu* has been retitled *Tayu Tayu*.)

Yeah, as I Thought, Original Is Ideal!

Many of the expressions and genres we've talked about here so far including tentacles, the *cross-section view,* and the *ahegao* exist within the American publishing system, and are used as part of a tagging system for the reader. For both genders wearing the other's clothes, there's "cross-dressing"; for girls in glasses, "glasses"; and a lot of other such English terms that are slang can be seen. But in many cases, the original Japanese term is used: *futanari* for hermaphrodites, "oppai" for breasts, "tsundere" for hot-cold personalities, *NTR/netorare* for cuckolding, and "shimapan" for striped panties. The sheer amount of Japanese left as-is has shocked me, with their "made in Japan-ness" peeking through very strongly. If I were to flaunt this situation, I would say that for better or for worse, eromanga has become a big part of Japanese culture, and that one is very much aware of it.

I reject the idea that the average American knows this much about Japanese culture and eromanga. This sort of knowledge is saved for the

American eromanga fans, nay, *otaku* alone. And these *otaku* have caught up to Japanese eromanga content to the point where they're already neck and neck with those in Japan.

A long time ago, regarding the censoring of Japanese erotic media in Japan, I then thought of the Western culture sphere (that includes America and Europe) and how they uncensor erotic media. What kind countries they are to erotic media, I thought, and I yearned for that kindness. I was envious of it. But from those kind countries, I was met with the assertion that Japan, in its own way, is also quite kind to erotic content. The person that asserted this statement was someone who left the States to pursue a career in Japan specifically to become an eromanga creator.

This person is none other than ShindoL, who left America for Japan to become an eromanga creator that is, even now, amongst the top of the talents in the industry. He felt that the United States was narrowminded about erotic content and so journeyed to Japan, where the attitudes about erotic content were freer. And most certainly, he was able to achieve the "Japanese Dream."

I decided to sit down and talk with this very active and unique American artist about why he thought Japanese attitudes on erotic content are freer, as well as the differences of how Americans and Japanese people think about visual expressions.

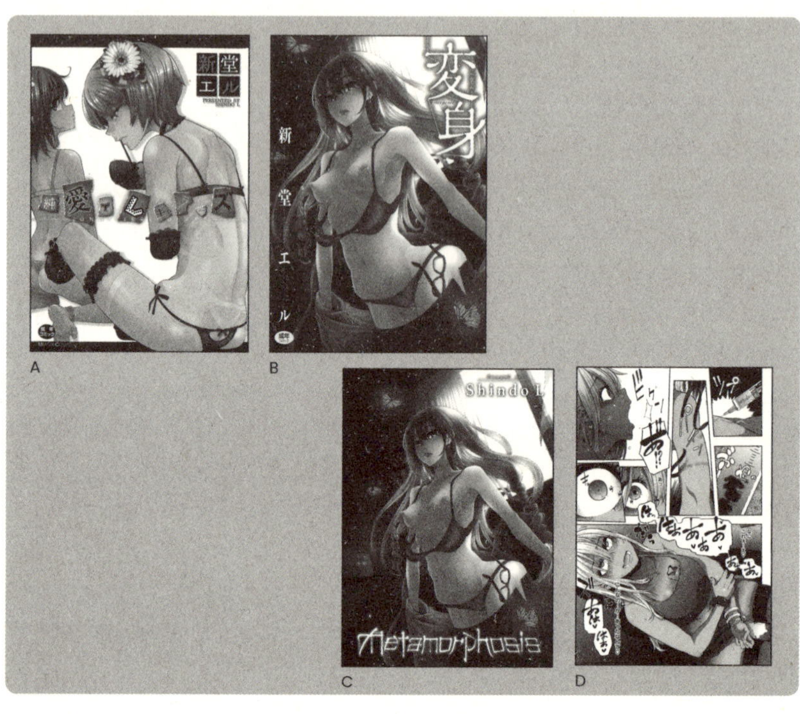

A B C D

INTERVIEW WITH **SHINDOL**

A: ***Junai Irregulars***
(2014, TI NET)
A short story collection that has immoral themes.

B: ***Henshin***
(2016, Wanimagazine)
A work inspired by realism in long form.

C: ***Metamorphosis***
(*Henshin*; 2017, FAKKU/Wanimagazine)
This is *Henshin*'s official English release.

D: ***Henshin***
(2016, Wanimagazine)
Some of the drug use depicted in this work.

"I was shocked at how abundant things were in this genre."

PROFILE

An American born in New York. After graduating from college, he moved to Japan to draw eromanga. While working part-time jobs, he participated in the doujinshi scene, and was finally scouted in 2008, debuting with his work TI NET's *BUSTER COMIC* shortly thereafter. He mostly works with themes that Japanese eromanga artists avoid, including disabled people and drugs, and draws them with a particular sensitivity. He has been criticized for his talent, which has already overcome the framework of eromanga. He is one of a few foreign eromanga artists of note. His most important works are *ShindoL's Cultural Anthropology* and *Metamorphosis*.

"I wanted to become a doujinshi creator, so I came to Japan."

—So first, I'd like to ask you... Why did you leave the States and come to Japan after you graduated college?

ShindoL: I always loved to draw, so I studied art in college, but it was also around that time when I started seeing a lot of Japanese eromanga and doujinshi online. As I started to buy doujinshi, I thought, "Oh, I can probably do that myself, too!" And as that desire to draw doujinshi grew stronger, I decided to go to Japan.

At home in the States, almost no one sold doujinshi locally, but Japan had download sites and zine events. I didn't know about the details involved back then. All I could think of was, "Well, if I get to Japan, I'll figure something out." And I did exactly that. (laughs)

—But you weren't able to become a mangaka as soon as you got to Japan, were you? Could you tell me more about how you were able to break into the industry?

ShindoL: At first, I found work with a trading company, while drawing on the side. But working at that company was starting to take up more and more of my time, and I was able to draw less and less. So, after six months I quit the company and busted open my piggy bank, and drew as much as I could.

My debut happened after my first appearance at Comiket. I'd self-published a fan comic using the theme of ***The Planet of the Apes***, and it was absolutely bonkers (8-30). (laughs) It wasn't really a proper manga, and was kind of a poor showing on my part, but because of that, my publisher, TI NET, later got in touch telling me they were interested.

—*Sounds like you went through a lot of ups and downs. Here you were, freshly arrived from a faraway country, and you even went so far as to quit your job so that you could draw doujinshi.*

What would you say your driving force at the time was?

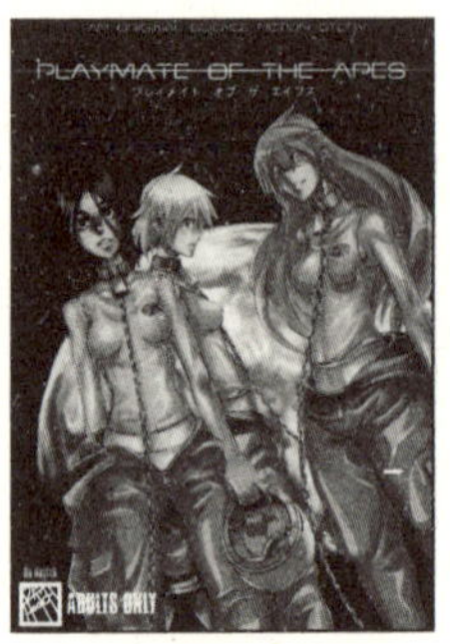

8-30: ***PLAYMATE OF THE APES*** (DA HOOTCH 2006)
ShindoL's doujinshi.

ShindoL: When I think about it now, possibly it was manga's special characteristics as a medium. It's a medium that isn't a novel or a movie and has expressions that are completely unique to it. Manga also has the potential to handle taboo topics.

—*So, you felt that it had the potential for expressions that cannot be found in, say, American comics. Is that right? In more concrete terms, could you talk a bit more about that?*

ShindoL: Personally, I was surprised at how abundant the themes and genres were within manga. Like, "Oh, it's really okay for me to handle things this way [within my own work]?" I was also taken aback by the fact that eromanga itself has so many genres within it, too.

—*What are some genres that you feel are a little hard to approach in the West?*

ShindoL: *Lolicon* and bestiality are two that easily come to mind. Japan has had those two genres for a very long time, and they've always been particularly hard to approach in the West.

—*I've actually heard that bestiality is pretty hard to handle in the West. So in its place, furries are used quite frequently.*

ShindoL: That's right. Monsters and furries are actually pretty popular as a stand-in. I think those are actually more popular in the States and Europe than Japan, to be honest. There's been a backlash against bestiality content. It's more of a knee-jerk reaction, "bestiality is bad." I feel that as a genre, bestiality collects a lot of different taboos together in the same place. As an example, it can bring together both scat and *futanari* content in the same place.

—While their shapes are slightly different, it seems to resemble the relationship between regulation and expressions in Japan. Because they're regulated, new expressions and genres have been birthed as a result.

ShindoL: You may be right insofar as both of those things are not human. For me personally, when I read eromanga, I got this sense that while both aren't human, it's okay to go this far and do things this way, you know? I was really shocked.

—Long ago in Japan, there were many people yearning towards having uncensored pornographic media like America did and how great that was, and I got this sense that the States were actually pretty welcoming towards erotic material.

ShindoL: It's like both countries envy the other's erotic content, don't they? (laughs)

—Really? You think so? I think Japanese people want one of those elements of erotic content to be completely erased, though...

ShindoL: Even if the [censored] content is so detailed you can barely see it, it's still a way of saying that something is there, under the censored area. I believe there's something sublime about that, and it can excite the reader that way. When I saw uncensored hentai anime for the first time, I remember being completely and utterly gutted because the genitalia were drawn perfectly. But when you have mosaic censorship, you don't know what's underneath. So yeah, that's definitely erotic.

"The amount of sound effects in Japanese are abundant."

—I think one of my favorites of your work is ShindoL's Cultural Anthropology *(8-31). I noticed that one of Hokusai's motifs, specifically the one that's seen in the* Fisherman's Wife *(3-38) is present in that particular work.*

ShindoL: Oh, I wanted to draw something like that, and what came out of it was an octopus-looking thing. (laughs)

—How much did you know about the Fisherman's Wife?

ShindoL: I think most folks in America know the basics about it. The first time I saw it, it was less of a feeling of impact and more of one that was like, "Oh, so stuff like this exists too." Then, a few years ago, there was the *shunga* art exhibition in Tokyo, which was the first proper exhibit of its kind. (*The SHUNGA Exhibition* opened in Tokyo in 2015.) I remember thinking to myself, "Wow, so Japan has had eromanga for a really long time." I was genuinely impressed. There was a pamphlet being sold at the exhibition, and while there was mostly normal content inside of it, there were still themes and motifs which were decidedly not normal, too. I thought that it was like an old eromanga magazine.

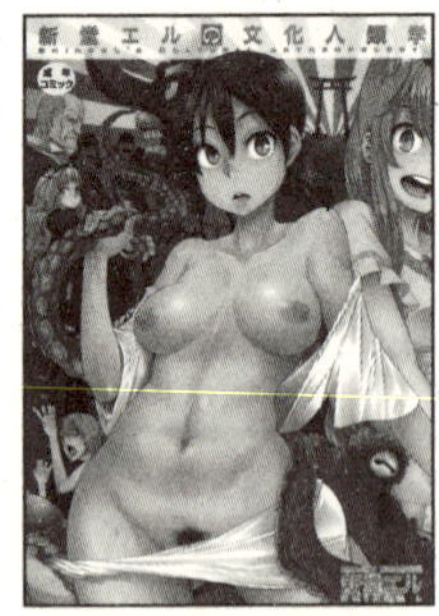

8-31: ***ShindoL's Cultural Anthropology*** (*ShindoL no Bunka Jinruigaku*; 2013, TI NET)

—Do you feel that as an American and an artist, that you are (culturally) inheriting a long, unbroken line of Japanese erotic history that dates back to the age of shunga?

ShindoL: When I'm drawing? No, not really. The thoughts that are foremost in my mind at that time are, "I want to read this sort of content, so I'll draw it too."

—*In the case of the* Fisherman's Wife, *eromanga is like an encoded version of those illustrations. Did you use the motifs found in that work to parody it more than use it as a tribute?*

ShindoL: Well… It's less of inserting that motif as a parody, but at the same time, it's not me using it as some sort of deep background for the work itself. It's more like, "Oh, this could be interesting if I throw it into my book." I'm sorry for treating it so nonchalantly in my own art. (laughs)

—*I think it's fine to have parodies of tentacles worldwide. I participated in an otaku event in the States last year, and the fans brought stuff like stuffed tentacle toys along with them. (laughs) Tentacles really have become a bit of a meme all over the world. The fact that this is happening and people around the world are recognizing tentacles really puts a feather in Toshio Maeda's hat as the progenitor of that trope. When you were younger, did you feel that there was general recognition of tentacles?*

ShindoL: When I was going through puberty, anime with tentacles were being churned out one after the other, so I'd say that it influenced me to a decent degree. When I talk with other Americans about that point in time, we all still get really excited over all of those anime, because they really were amazing.

—*Do you feel that there are any other differences between American comics and Japanese manga? If so, what are they?*

ShindoL: Just the fact that the amount of sound effects in Japanese is abundant. Of course, there are plenty that already exist on their own, but what's more amazing is that you're just free to make up your own if you want.

I honestly think it's cool. And you can change things up by throwing in all kinds of sound effects, too, so you don't get bored with them. It isn't just about the types and variety of words, either, but also if you change the way you draw them, I feel that you'll end up transmitting a different type of expression.

(Compiled November 2016)

The Freedom and Non-Freedom of Expressions

When I was younger (at least I think I was, at some point), being able to watch uncensored videos and read uncensored erotic books was my most important and difficult mission. The ink that made up those censored areas in those books would melt like butter...at least that's what all of the rumors said. So, I desperately pursued them, that's how utterly thirsty I was for uncensored content. It was at that time that I learned that uncensored pornographic content—books and videos—were being imported into Japan from the States. America seemed to be a magical place where one could freely create expressions without being under the yoke of censorship.

I yearned for that freedom. At the time, I thought that when it came to expressions and erotic content, Japan was so much of the opposite, not free at all. When it came to expressions, Japan was like a developing country when compared with the United States.

So when an eromanga artist came to Japan from America in order to pursue a career in eromanga, and said that Japan was in fact more free about expressions than America, it was, well, a shock.

Looking at all of it, I decided it wasn't erotic because I could see everything, as Japanese publishers have to purposely hide certain body parts (and this is taking into account that if one does not censor their work, they'll run into legal trouble). Eventually, I arrived at the conclusion that precisely because creators and publishers have to hide their work, that content was indeed erotic after all. The process it took for me to get to that conclusion was erotic, sound effects were erotic, Japanese eromanga expressions that authors created with such great creativity and then helped develop were erotic. Recklessly searching for genitalia was an act of resistance to this past younger self of mine, which in turn, I hoped would encourage me to keep going (and it was actually pretty fun).

Many American releases of eromanga are uncensored. For Japanese people, that's something to be envied. But the reason why eromanga earned such popularity in America was not because one could see everything uncensored, but rather because there were so many different expressions that the audience could enjoy. And it was at that time that I sincerely appreciated the level of freedom that eromanga creators had, as well as the sheer diversity of all of those expressions. Those minds burning with delusions helped overcome all national borders, extending joint ownership of that content to the world.

This time, like a California Roll, or a winning hand of seven pairs in mahjong, it may be that eromanga expressions cultivated and grown in the United States will migrate back to Japan, and earn their citizenship. It may be that this time, because the whole world is involved in the creation of these expressions, the age of eromanga gaining the possibility of spreading even further and spreading her wings has arrived.

To be more precise, are there American-developed eromanga expressions out there that have shocked all of Japan? For example, we touched upon this a bit earlier in this chapter, but the case of Kondom and the "insect rape" expression shocked the whole of the United States upon its release. As if developed as a counter-attack, what came out of that period was something known as the "dragon car sex" genre. As its name denotes, this genre involves dragons (or flying animals) having sex with cars (or inanimate objects). I'm not sure how this aroused people, but this is an actual genre that exists. I would love for you to put "dragon car sex" into a search engine so you can see examples of what this genre entails. But please take responsibility for whatever you may find and view, and if you get into this genre as a result, I sure as hell won't take responsibility for that. ❁

The History of Hentai Manga

CHAPTER NINE

Other Expressions

The special use expressions in this book that I've made an attempt to portray are just but a small section of the wide variety of them out there, and with great difficulty, I've assigned names to the ones with the highest level of public recognition (and there have been some that I've had to give names to, period). There are still many, many more special-use expressions out there. Much like an all-or-nothing gambler, a lot of these expressions have had an impact on fans. For those that are used frequently, some have undergone critical mass but have no names, and one can still find more that haven't been categorized as of yet. So, in this chapter, I'll be taking the opportunity to showcase some of these very unique expressions.

The Inside-Out Perspective

The *cross-section view* attempts to capture what's not visible in real life via round slices of what look like MRI images, but there's also one more expression that is also, in reality, hard to see. This expression is known as the "inside-out perspective" (*tainai shiten*). The *inside-out perspective*, much like the *cross-section view,* uses a visual point of view from within the body. One can use it to show areas within the vagina and anus, but also to show areas within the mouth facing outward from the body (9-1).

Its special characteristic is that it appears as if it's been taken by a small camera within the body. Patterns of use within stories include fingers prying open female genitalia. There are also many depictions where the person who is doing the opening of their partner's genitalia has their facial expression shown facing outward from the opened genitalia to their face visible to the audience as well. It makes the reader feel as if their eyes have been swallowed by this girl (who's having her genitalia opened) and are looking outward from her body, as if the reader is an erotic version of the main character from ***Fantastic Voyage.*** One could also say that it appears as if after male genitalia have been inserted by an impressive force into a girl's body, and you can see out of the now open organ towards the audience. This gives the reader front row seats to view the act of sexual intercourse, and possibly creates the effect where the reader can appreciate it as if it were a fine piece of art or wine.

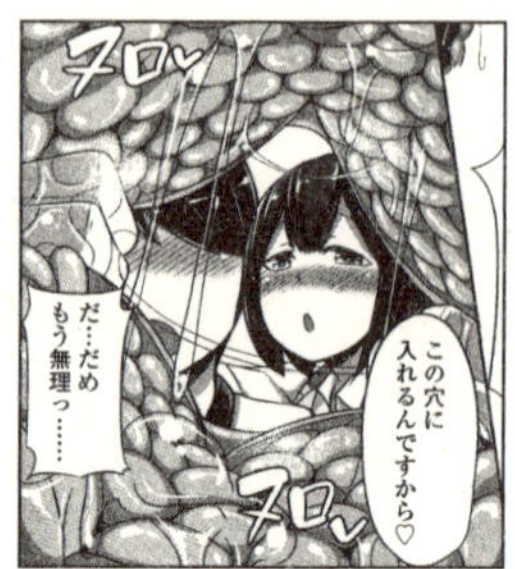

9-1: "Mate! Onaho wa Junbi Shitaka!?" (HANABi 2015, Akaneshinsha)

While I want to say that this is an experience exclusive to manga, advances in medical technology have produced tiny wireless cameras that can give people a look at the inside of the body. It's as if life is imitating science-fiction, and perhaps this is just a pipe dream, but it could be that one day we see the *cross-section view* made a possibility within the real world, too. Though that's probably me just overthinking it. (laughs)

Crystal Insertion

This expression was used in a specific chapter in Yamatogawa's work, ***Power Play!*** This expression is generally used in situations where a girl is wearing a swimsuit and an aqueous life form that is (or has turned) transparent rapes her with a gel-like male sex organ. We do not need to use the *cross-section view* in parallel with this expression, because we can physically see the moment of insertion of the male genitalia with the naked eye (since the creature is *transparent*, 9-2).

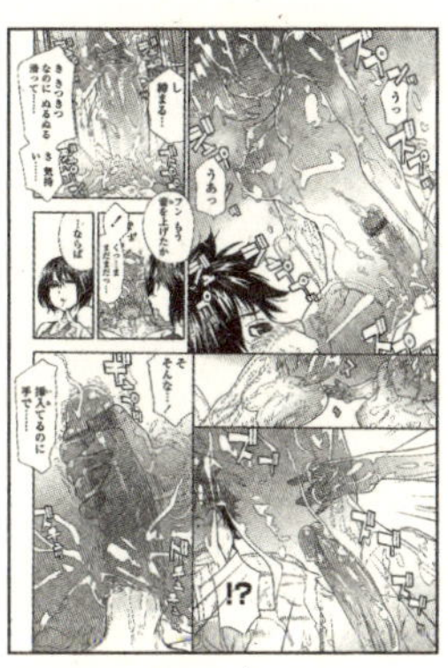

9-2: ***Power Play!*** (Yamatogawa 2012, Akaneshinsha/FAKKU)

Because this life form may be gel-like in nature, at the moment of insertion we can also see the heroine giving the organism a hand job at the same time. The end result are visuals that only Hollywood CG could otherwise properly render.

However, because the situation in which this expression can be used is so limited, I think that even the artist behind this expression realized that fact and as a result did not use it too many times in their own work.

Invisible Man

Speaking of transparent genitalia, in order to make the female partner stand out, in this case the male partner is made half-transparent. The term *danshari* is a pun on another word also pronounced "danshari," but written with different kanji, which usually refers to decluttering or minimalism. In this technique, the male partner is considered visual "clutter," or someone who is weak or deficient that must be culled to make the female partner stand out (9-3).

I touched lightly upon the *danshari* expression in the *cross-section view* chapter, but another way to use this expression is to emphasize the moment of insertion, as well. This expression was born from the male readers' desire to be the male partner in that moment and is mostly seen in male-targeted eromanga. This expression, for the most part, is not used within the *BL* and *TL* genres, which are largely female-targeted. Within this technique there are many different ways to "erase" the male partner, but

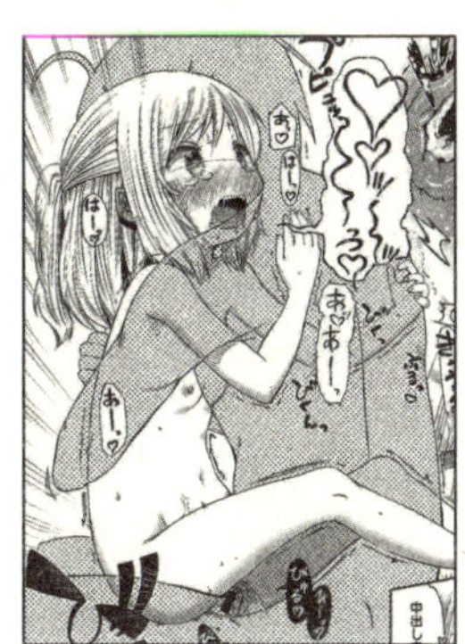

9-3: "Rabu^2 Spa" (Hota. 2017, Wanimagazine)

it's important to remember that making the male partner completely transparent would not satisfy the male readers' gaze, and thus, would have no meaning for using it as a technique. This expression fails when artists attempt to give the male partner a sense of agency, so it ends up being useless as a plot device in these cases.

In order to prove the male partner's existence in these scenes, techniques like making him half-transparent, using grayscale to make his body opaque, or using the round-slice technique that's seen a lot in the *cross-section view* are all used. In exceedingly rare scenes, however, it is the female partner whose existence is barely in the scene at all, making her half-transparent. Perhaps that version of those rare expressions should be called "joshari" (invisible woman).

There have also been cases where, in order to show the act of cunnilingus, the female partner is made half-transparent in order to show how desperately the male partner is eating her out (9-4). If the reader is only shown the male partner's head buried between her thighs, then one can't properly see this particular act. This expression is degrees away from the *cross-section view,* which is to say, it too exists for the sole reason of making the invisible visible to the reader.

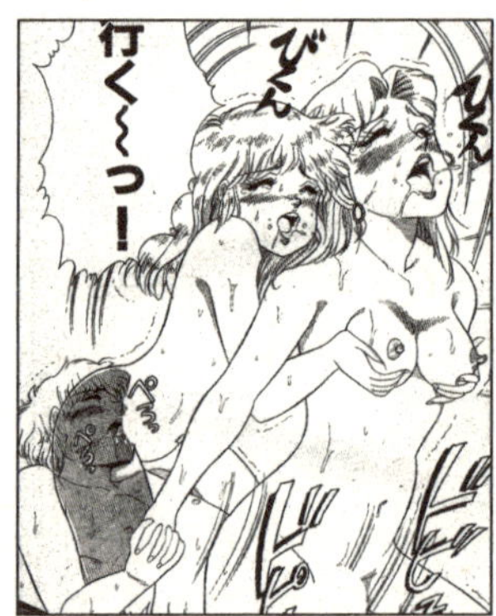

9-4: "Tasogare wa Moete..." (Erika Wada 1991, Tsukasa Shobo)

Heart Eyes

This is one expression that has exploded in use within eromanga in the last few years. In order to show a partner's sexual feelings of pleasure, joy, or expectation for the former two things, a heart mark is added to the pupil of the eye of that partner.

The "heart eyes" or "heart-in-eyes" expression is part of a long history of eye expressions in manga that have been there practically since day one (9-5, 6). Before the *heart eyes* technique was used in eromanga, it first appeared in shojo manga as an expression for love at first sight. By combining that history with a new, more erotic interpretation of the expression as used in eromanga, a new expression was not born, but rather a new version of an existing expression was developed.

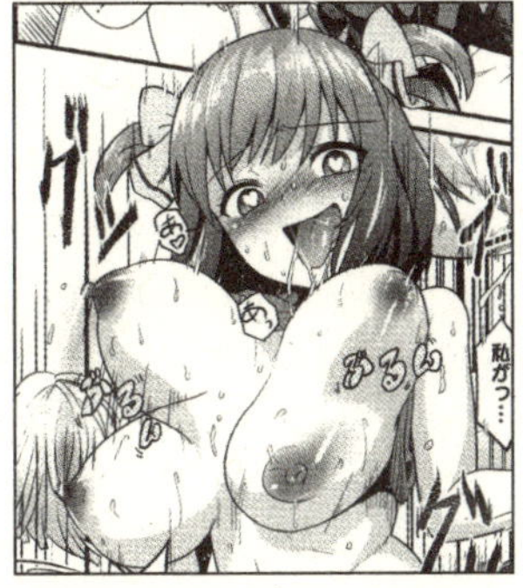

9-5: ***Un-Cheergirl*** (Wanao 2019, Akaneshinsha)

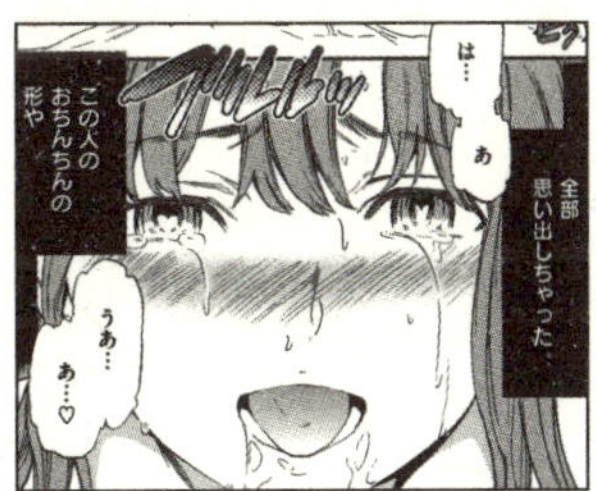

9-6: "Hidane" (Cuvie 2017, Wanimagazine)

There was a joke floating around a few years ago when manga-loving students from another country photoshopped heart marks onto the eyes of Michelangelo's ***David***, and the force with which it spread across social media was truly incredible. However, it's important to note that I was not able to confirm the pedigree of this social media phenomenon. (laughs)

However, I still cannot help but wonder about the obviously deep impression it made as an expression on others at the time.

Shimaji-style "Chinkoma"

Shimaji, the creator of this expression, originally used this in their self-published work ***Soku Hame Bicchinpo NY ni Iku*** (2015; 9-7) and it quickly became a much-talked about technique on how to divide comic panels. Its special characteristic is creating comic panels in the shape of male genitalia, and because of that, aside from its popular name taken from its creator, is called the *chinkoma* (dick panel).

Within the panel, the *otokonoko's* eyes have hearts in them, but that in itself is not what the reader should focus on. The marvelous thing about this expression is the closeup illustrated for the reader within the phallus outline.

It's usually at the part of the story when the receiving partner sees the giving partner's male genitalia and gets excited, and in this way, the *chinkoma* really brings the lust and excitement home to the reader.

It's fine to show that excitement by drawing the male genitals flopping out of the giving partner's pants, but the *chinkoma* is one of the few expressions that shows that transcendent moment of attraction. It's genius for doing this. I wonder if this expression that combines so many components of manga itself, sprinkled with some eroticism will continue to develop in the future.

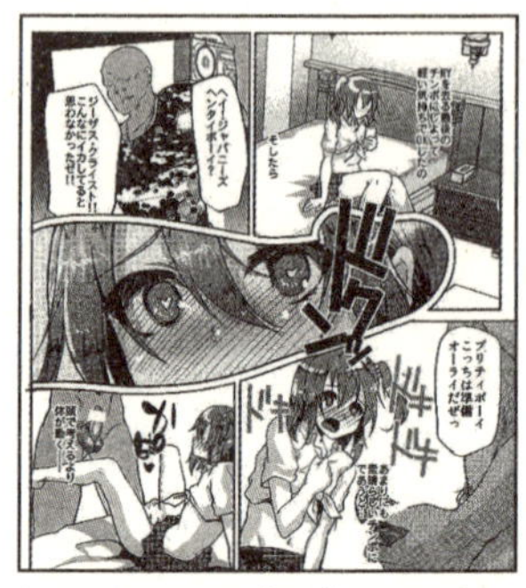

9-7: ***Soku Hame Bicchinpo NY ni Iku*** (Shimaji 2015, Cannabis)

Censorship Mark Art

This expression refers to the absolutely indispensable sticker that's slapped on every adult-oriented comic. Anyone under the age of eighteen cannot buy products with this mark on it and is used as a form of self-enforced censorship regulation within the adult media industry. The mark reads "seinen comic" (adult comic) on the materials it's printed upon, and surprisingly enough, though it's a piece of the self-enforced censorship machine, has actually been used as a meme. When done correctly, the mark is cleverly deployed as an expression and is used nonchalantly, but not in a way that would violate the self-enforced regulations. If it's a situation where it has to be displayed, it can become one of the several defiant expressions out there that shows the author's determination to their audience.

In Kenya Shishimaru's ***Eroribonhon*** (2001, Oakla Publishing), the adult comics mark is used as a way to cover up one of the female characters' genitalia in a very eye-catching and clever deployment of resources. In terms of the image itself, I don't think that there was much that needed to be covered up or hidden. Nonetheless, the author says by utilizing the mark in this manner, "This is eromanga!" in an obvious and defiant way.

But there's always someone there to outdo you. In the end, using the adult media mark in this way as a concept had become a technique.

In Hideyuki Matsurioka's ***Naka no Kabe*** (2010, Akaneshinsha, 9-8), the background is completely covered in the adult marks until the cover itself was packed to its capacity. He also covers the character's genitalia with them, too. This was a completely original design at the time. The marks seem to be authentic and were deployed on the lower right of the page. Because of that, strangely, the design isn't quite as eye-catching after that specific deployment of resources, and becomes a literal form of the aphorism, "seeing the forest for the trees."

Instead of the creator of this expression being a manga artist, it's more likely that they were tapped to handle the design for the book and were commissioned to produce these designs. Considering those factors, this validates the expression itself, even if it's trying to use self-regulation rules against themselves. When you think about that, it's actually quite funny.

The smattering of expressions I've introduced to you here make up but a tiny fraction of the infinite number of expressions I wish I could share with you. Now you can see how eromanga as a genre is positively overflowing with creativity. I can't help but wonder what new expressions will be born.

To general manga fans, I offer you the following question: obviously reading manga is fun, but why not take a stab at finding new expressions in your manga? I'm sure if you do, you'll have reactions like, "Wow, I had no clue this expression existed!" and, "This is a very common expression, but who thought it up in the first place?"

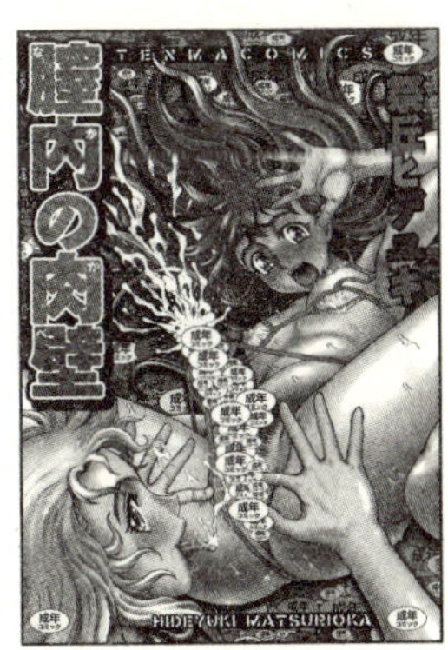

9-8: ***Naka no Kabe***
(Hideyuki Matsurioka 2010, Akaneshinsha)

The History of Hentai Manga

APPENDIX ONE

The Definition of Eromanga

In this book the term "eromanga" is used frequently, but exactly what kind of manga falls into this category?

To be honest, it is incredibly hard to give an answer to this question or explain it in a way that will satisfy everyone. However, if I were to define it to the best of my ability using a broad framework, I would say that eromanga can describe a Japanese comic that has adult-targeted, eros-themed stories at their core drawn in a way in order to excite arousal in the reader and whose purpose is to facilitate diffusion of those ideas and themes within those stories. To phrase it in a way that is easier to understand, I would say that it's manga designed to aid the process of masturbation on behalf of the reader, or even more simply, that it's "orgasm manga."

However, there are other genres where one can also find sexually charged stories that excite and arouse the reader, within the shonen, seinen, and even children's manga. The stories in those types of manga are not [thematically] strong enough to bring the reader to orgasm, and in these cases sexually charged can generally mean softcore scenes or mild panty-flashing. Though to be fair, however, considering which age cohort these magazines are targeted towards, people of shonen/seinen age (teen to young adult) might be sexually excited by these tamer elements.

The next question that arises is: are stories in those three categories, with their tamer scenes, included in the wider definition of eromanga? The answer to that may lie in one's opinion on the subject. If we go with the definition of "excites an arousal response in their readership" as the defining piece of this puzzle, then we can't exactly say it isn't eromanga.

In this way, depending on how the reader is "trapped" or "caught" and sucked into reading manga, the borderline of "is it eromanga or not" changes drastically.

One also must consider the reason why the manga exists. If the artist or editor helped create a story with the intent to excite an arousal response within the reader, even if the intent from that side of things was not to include [story] components that do so, it may as well be the same thing if the readership's interpretation of the material is that it appears sexually titillating. Opinions and the way people feel things differ from person to person, and when someone asks if a work is or can be considered eromanga, regardless if the answer is yes or no, that work is already changing.

Also, when one says "eromanga," one automatically links that term to its target audience, which are men. But even within female-targeted erotic manga genres, including *lady-comi,* and in recent years, both the aggressively expanding *BL* and *TL* genres (or basically, any genre that has women as its readership target) have contained sexually-coded expressions in extreme content that under these conditions can be called eromanga.

Female-targeted media is different than male-targeted media in terms of what content preferences are held by their readership. So if for example, one could make a blanket statement like "*BL* = eromanga," then I would say that's reckless. Even if a female-targeted work did have the ultimate goal of exciting arousal in its readership, unlike male-targeted media, there's no guarantee that work will automatically be masturbatory material. Additionally, it's difficult to state whether or not female-targeted masturbatory material can be argued, as the boundaries within female-targeted are completely different and more difficult to flesh out than that of their male counterparts'.

There is also the important point that industry-produced work isn't just the only thing that goes into the eromanga genre. There's amateur work, *doujinshi,* and webcomics to consider as well, and amongst all of those things you can definitely find work that can be safely considered as part of the eromanga genre.

So as you can see, the framework that helps define eromanga is incredibly vague, and much like clouds, the boundaries and borderlines of eromanga itself are fuzzy at best yet at the same time have been recognized by its readership. If anything, it may be accurate to say that the many readers out there have helped define eromanga as a genre. In order to exclude uncertain elements and narrow things down, we can also say that adult manga magazines with 18+ only content and anything else that bears the "adult manga" mark makes for a very concrete definition on what is considered eromanga (at least, in the industry's eyes). However, for material printed before 1991 and the advent of the mark, determining whether or not that material counts as eromanga becomes thorny at best.

So for the purposes of this book, I will be using the "adult manga" mark as the narrow framework to define what is eromanga and what isn't, and for eromanga and *bishojo comics* printed before 1991, it will be included in the adult mark definition as eromanga. ✿

The History of Hentai Manga

APPENDIX TWO

The Difference Between Eromanga and Bishojo Comics

One other term I use in this book nearly as much as eromanga is "bishojo comics." They have similar types of content and themes, however, the differences between them are more subtle.

Just as it's difficult to concretely provide a definition for eromanga, the definition of "bishojo comics" is similarly difficult to pin down. But of the two genres, I can say with confidence that a clear definition is especially hard to explain.

Ever since this term was put into use, its boundaries have been fuzzy at best, and it has continued to change over time, making it even more nebulous. If I were to explain it frankly, I would compare it to shonen manga insofar as the *bishojo* character (an attractive girl) is the core of the narrative—which depicts the girl's cuteness, charm, praiseworthiness, strength, as well as her activities—just as the genre name suggests.

This genre was born in the early 1980s in zine events like Comic Market and it soon became the center of *otaku* culture. Where it pulled in the most fans were with character designs; as these new characters were often very anime-like, cute, and sometimes super-deformed. It's also clear that a significant segment of manga fans at the time thought these characters were erotic in nature.

However, while the *bishojo* character was a sexually charged icon, depictions of erotic themes and sex weren't necessarily prerequisites of the genre. In that sense, in this softer, cloudier dawning era of adult comics, many of these works and their depiction of eros wasn't radical enough to be categorized as eromanga.

It's been said that the person who gave *bishojo* comics their name was none other than its founding father, artist Hideo Azuma. The genre made its Japanese debut in June 1982 with the first issue of the comic magazine *Lemon People* (AMATORIA). At the time of its debut, these works were called "lolicon comics," but Azuma didn't like that name, so instead he proposed the term "bishojo comics." Ever since, the name has consistently been in use. I'm not sure how Azuma grasped the genre, but in his written work, ***Animal Company*** (1980, Tokyo Sanseisha, A), the protagonist goes to his local bookstore to buy what he calls "bishojo comics," which solidifies the fact that Azuma already had a mental image of the content.

At this point in time, there was someone else who had a different idea of the image of the genre that Azuma had proposed. This person was an editor-in-chief of one of the major *bishojo* magazines at the time, *Manga Burikko* (which was initially self-published but later released by Byakuya-Shobo), Eiji Otsuka. The magazine began as a place to reprint *ero-gekiga* comics but after a streak of poor sales numbers, as a way to shore up the magazine he then pivoted to include *bishojo* material. At the time, those in charge of the magazine decided to meet with the then-freelance editor, Otsuka, and upon his advice, went ahead and reorganized the magazine and its structure. The first issue of the reformed version of the magazine was released in May 1983, and its slogan

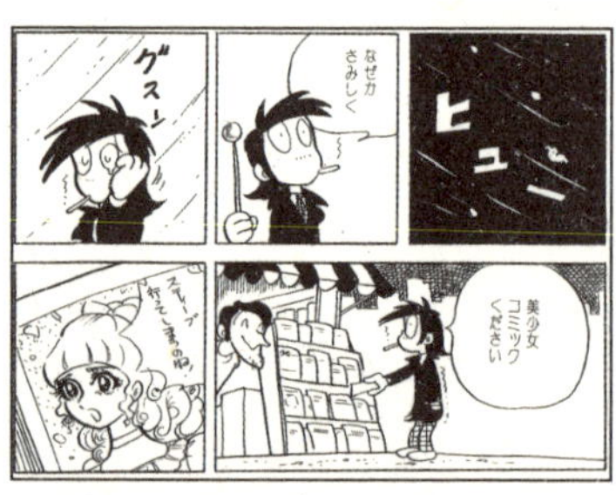

A: ***Animal Company*** (Hideo Azuma 1980, Tokyo Sanseisha)

was changed to, "A magazine for boys who dream about bishojo comics!" Otsuka's image of the magazine did not necessarily adhere to the principles Azuma held (that of the cute, anime-like girls, pillars of otaku culture) but rather he wanted to promote artists who used wisps of inspiration from shojo comic artists in their own work like: Yumi Shirakura, Kyoko Okazaki, Akira Kagami, and others.

However, this new crop of authors didn't necessarily subscribe to one or the other of the two warring ideals of what the *bishojo* was and should be. Instead, they tended to mix the two, creating an alloy of sorts. In the coming years, it was certain that publishers would find that new authors that popped up would increasingly superscript their own interpretation of that within the genre. If anything, at the beginning of this era when that first definition was asserted, both creators and readers independently combined their own interpretations. This was a time when creators and readers had a lot of fun with that particular process.

Within all of that, there were creators in the vein of Rei Aran, who worked with a lot of sci-fi themes like mecha, giant robots, and the like, whose anime-style characters and works were exceedingly polished by the time they rolled out into the market. Creators like Shinobu Hiromori (a.k.a. Miyasu Nonki), whose seemingly sole purpose was to torment and tease his *bishojo* characters, and also whose popular inside jokes seemed to sell the comics by themselves, who debuted at this time would absorb all of those components into their work and as they did so, helped amplify it amongst readers.

In its early years, this genre was exceedingly experimental and free about what content made the cut. This would be utterly unthinkable now, but it's been hypothesized that a lot of the artists that debuted at this time were minors, as were the readers who supported their work. These young parties just wanted to read comics featuring girls that were perhaps a little erotic, that they could not find in regular manga magazines. It was also thought that these young readers were having a lot of fun messing around with these comics (in a good way).

COMIC Lolipop published statistics about their readership, with most of them in their teens. As a result of having such a young readership, we can probably say that this was not a magazine with adult content in it even though it had been hypothesized as otherwise. Because of that, there was most likely some resistance to calling these *bishojo* works eromanga. But because these magazines were aimed at rabid fans of the genre, they slowly became more popularized, and as a result became more commercialized as well.

This new commercialized *bishojo* genre offered erotic content at a bargain, which as a result, started to sell increasingly more. This was obviously the market principle in action. And the artist who was at the vanguard of this increasingly erotic, popular, and commercialized the *bishojo* genre was Tou Moriyama. Most of his work became hits, and it was as if he was firing off continuously with his work. He created a large tide of hugely popular selling erotic *bishojo* content. A lot of the manga that decorated pages of these magazines were erotic but sold well regardless. However, that was definitely not necessarily the worst thing to happen to the genre and the industry that had formed around it. Instead, it excited people, and in terms of comic magazines, as long as artists held the belief that, "I can draw whatever the hell I want as long as I put *bishojo* characters in!" then they were given opportunities. Those attitudes came about due to the fact that magazines, seen as open spaces to experiment within, were allowed to retain that function during this time. Those places ended up birthing many different talents and abilities, and within them, *bishojo comics* as a genre developed a larger framework and was able to mature and advance.

At the beginning of the '90s, the genre suffered a huge blow due to increasingly stringent comic regulation. When the adult comics mark was born, the writing was on the wall. Readers recognized that now, *bishojo comics* were targeted specifically at only adults, and only adults read those. Nowadays, saying that these comics are eromanga isn't as problematic. If anything, I get the impression that people have stopped using the term, outside of events like Comic Market.

As things are now, the genre has become quite removed from the original idea spawned upon the genre's birth, as most titles now focus on cute girls doing everyday things. Furthermore, mature women, wives, even crossdressing boys who look like girls have infiltrated the genre, and the current visual style is more than just "anime." If anything, it's almost as if it's made a return to a style of depiction close to *gekiga* (often hyper-realistic visually or thematically). The priority for its readership is to use it mainly as masturbation material, and multiple other genres thrive and grow within it.

But the reason why the magazines still use the term *bishojo* in their copy is due to the historical custom of retaining vestiges of the past. And that is where the term eromanga comes in, denoting that now the genre has the framework of being fallen to becoming mere masturbation material targeted at a male readership. At the same time, I do not think that will bring the genre to a close, as it's a larger part of Japanese culture, though I do feel like the pride of all of these great artists has been hidden.

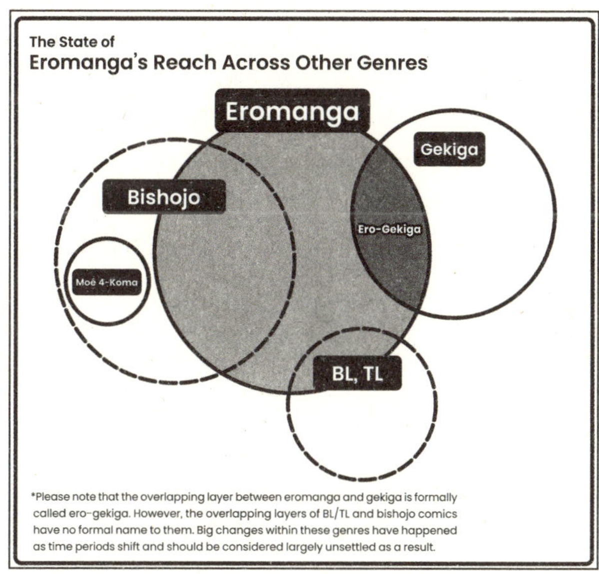

(ed.: 4-Koma refers to Japanese four-panel vertical comic strips.)

The History of Hentai Manga

END OF BOOK SUPPLEMENT

Girls' Only Eromanga Gathering

When discussing eromanga expressions, there are all sorts of people who take them in, and in many different ways. I've introduced many special-use expressions within this book, but there's no possible way eromanga fans would have universally accepted them all.

One expression that easily comes to mind is the *cross-section view,* where some fans think that it's actually pretty weak and unacceptable. The fans saying these things aren't rare either.

On the creator side of things, there are also many artists out there that greatly dislike certain expressions and feel that some of them like "ramee" and the *cross-section view* are just too far removed from reality for them to use.

However, it's true that the backdrop against which particular expressions evolved and were developed were only able to do so due to eromanga readers and fans accepting and recognizing them. Many artists and editors assume that most of these fans are male, and they have used manga that makes them feel good as a benchmark for growth and development. But even with male-targeted media, it's certain that there's also a group of women reading that content as well.

In recent years, I've heard several reports state that the pool of female fans has expanded rapidly. It's been thought that there are many reasons why this is happening, the first of which is due to these female fans being captured by the many different internet publications and curation services for manga online. Originally, most female-targeted genres included *BL, TL,* and *lady-comi,* among others. I can't help but wonder if before the internet age, having to physically go into a bookstore and buy things wasn't a huge hurdle that barred many women from reading male-targeted adult material. There's also the issue of disposing of those adult magazines after one's read them. But if one has a smartphone, all of those issues disappear, and everything is stored on the phone. No mess, no fuss, no having to go into bookstores or dispose of magazines that might make people talk.

During the karaoke-age bubble (the late '90s), when the earliest digital publications hit servers, the most popular products that women bought were softcore eromanga. I've heard that around nine at night, when office ladies got off from work, was when ebook retailers sold the most copies of their wares. It wasn't that women weren't into erotic media, but more that they were never really able to get their hands on it.

It could be said that during this era women were now able to cross a gendered media hedge that had divided them from men who liked the same content for so many years. Women were finally able to explore what stories and designs they liked in erotic media, and that had not happened before.

The opportunity to have an exchange of ideas with women about this very topic arose when I decided to open a space for them and have an all-girls' eromanga conference. So I gathered up eromanga fans from that ever-growing number of new female fans, and asked them to talk about their brightly burning passionate love of the genre.

Of course, I say all-girls here, but I was there to preside over that meeting, so I'd rather the audience not make jokes about it. Naming the meeting was just a formality. Talking to these ladies about their favorite eromanga was its purpose, but as I thought, the special-use expressions from male-targeted erotic media was also an opportunity for humor.

Please allow me to pull excerpts from this event, where we talked about the mysterious world of eromanga expressions that men rarely thought about. I also brought up a central concern from male eromanga fans, which is taboo material.

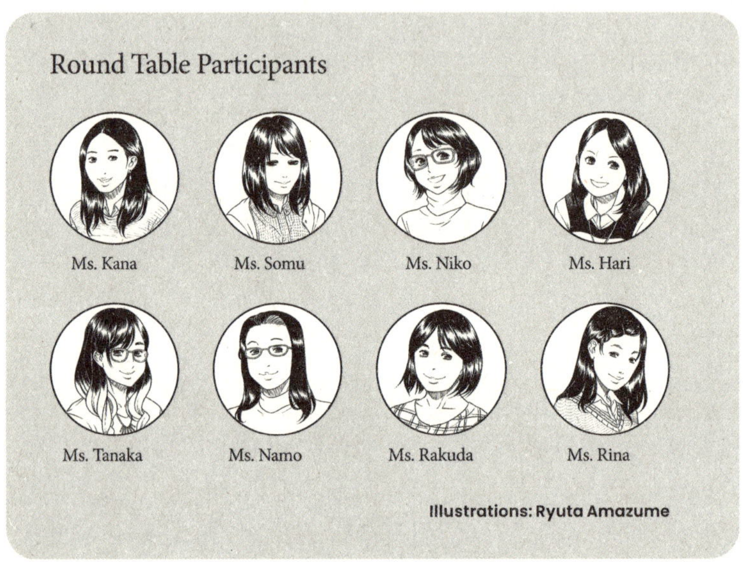

Round Table Participants

Illustrations: Ryuta Amazume

"Here's some weird eromanga."

—Everyone participating in this gathering is female, so let's start off with your impressions on eromanga. Could you tell me about situations where you had thoughts like, "This is really different from manga for women," or "That's the first time I've seen that," or "Like hell does that happen in real life!"

Namo: For me, I think it was a manga that showed lactation and mother's milk. It was a shock mostly because in real life, if you're not pregnant, you rarely ever lactate. It never just happens by rubbing your breasts, like the rumors say.

So, when I saw a scene that showed women lactating after (the implication of) conception, I was like, "It isn't milk, but it isn't anything else, either... What is this?" If anything, it got me worried. (laughs)

Another example is when a girl gets creampied and says, "Oh! It's so [physically] hot!" I don't think that can happen in real life, especially when you consider that semen is generally at body temperature.

There are other things that fire me up, of course, but I only really wanted to comment on those few things.

Oh, and this is coming from me as a parent, but that whole trope about raping a girl and she starts to enjoy it partway through, or really starts feeling it even after she's been kidnapped and confined, or any other kind of awful things like that... Truthfully, that makes me really uncomfortable. I think that's a little too extreme, and there should be a line that has to be drawn when it comes to content like that.

Hari: I'm pretty much cool with any expression but the *ahegao* with double peace signs... That's a no from me.

—Oh, I'd love to hear your take on the ahegao *as a woman, as it's definitely an expression that men seem to either love or hate.*

Rakuda: But isn't that expression less common these days?

Hari: Yeah, it does kind of feel like its use hasn't increased much lately.

Rina: I really *hated* it when it was in vogue, and it was the popular expression everyone used. But when I read material that had it after that fad started to fade, I really started to like it. (laughs) I heard a rumor about how when you really want to read *ahegao*-filled content, you can literally just go and buy all of the media with that expression in it. (laughs)

Rakuda: I mean, that whole expression itself isn't really very erotic in my book. There's a paper-thin difference between the *ahegao* genre and comedy. I myself prefer the *misakura-go* expression, but...

Kana: You really don't talk that much during sex, huh?

Namo: It's like you're narrating what's going on. Like, "Oh, you're hitting me so deep!" and stuff like that. I don't say that during sex. (laughs)

Niko: I mean, it's not like people can't figure out what's going on without narration, right? The act itself is pretty obvious.

Kana: I happen to think that it's sexier when your partner goes silent during sex. But I also feel a bit ambivalent about all of the dialogue during those scenes, too.

Tanaka: To make things easier to understand for the audience, they end up explaining so much of the act. I think it's an act of kindness on behalf of the manga itself when you see expressions like that.

—Instead of exposition, I wonder if it's what the female partner wants their partner to say to them? I have heard that some people actually feel that if their partner looks like they're about to make an ahegao *or start speaking in tongues that it's actually a buzzkill. (laughs)*

Hari: I think the reason why I don't like the *ahegao* is that it's the extreme opposite of Naoki Yamamoto's expressions. Like when I think about what I talk about during sex, the act itself is bookended by small talk about me and my partner's day, stuff like that.

Somu: Oh, I totally get that. It's stuff like, "Oh, I haven't done the laundry yet," and the like. It's small talk about how we lead our lives, and I think that domestic touch is pretty erotic.

Hari: Bingo. Exactly.

Yuriko: If it's too easy to understand, the effect is like a narcotic, you know? You end up reading too much of it and you feel paralyzed afterward.

Niko: When I was talking with a friend about porn recently, and I'm not sure if this is an effect from eromanga, we were talking about how we felt that depictions of anal sex have increased in recent years.

—You mean within porn itself?

Niko: Yes, that's right. Allegedly a lot of younger women want to have anal sex.

Hari: I happen to think it's the opposite. I think men are like, "Hm, I'm curious about it so I think I'll ask [my female partner] to try it on me." Apparently, a lot of young men are pleading with their girlfriends to try anal with them with the girl on the giving end.

Everyone: Whaaaat?!

—So how do these women do anal with their male partners on the receiving end?

Hari: With their fingers! So that's why a lot of people now have an interest in doing anal.

—Hm. The internal structure of the male anus is different in that it has an

organ where women do not, so it could be that that's where men and women see eye to eye, I suppose. (laughs)

Niko: I've heard that many women want their partners to shut up about it.

Rina: They want them to stop [asking]...

Niko: In manga, sex from behind often results in a tighter [receiving] partner, but I think that differs on personal experience.

Rakuda: I read something like that in a report. This was from a female, but apparently, she got too tight so she was advised to stop doing it from behind.

Somu: I mean you need to wash yourself out first before you can consider doing anal, you know!

Rina: And then there's the issue in manga where when the couple starts with anal sex but then shifts to vaginal sex... I really wish they wouldn't do that!

Namo: Yeah, you can get an infection that way!

Somu: Manga never shows that, either.

Rakuda: I think that when it comes to anal sex, there's more room for argument. (laughs)

—Let's talk more about that, then!

Rakuda: I would say that before you decide to try what's in the manga you read, you make sure that you're well-versed in how things work with anal.

Hari: Speaking of which, that reminds me. In Akira Kizuki and Nanki

Sato's ***Usotsuki Paradox*** (Hakusensha; B), there are three partners with two guys and one girl. The guys just kinda try to ram it in without any prep and there was one scene where I was like, "Oh, manga really is different, isn't it." That scene was the ideal of how sex should happen. Only in manga.

Kana: In Ryuta Amazume's ***Nana to Kaoru*** (Hakusensha; C), in order to try shibari-style rope bondage on a girl, the main character goes to a lot of trouble to learn how to do it! He even boils the hemp rope himself. He then goes as far as drying it, oiling it, even burns the fuzz off of it, and as a result, gets a nice, smooth rope comes out of it.

Amazume went ahead and drew the whole process of how to make proper ropes in his book and honestly, I thought it was both really interesting and amazing.

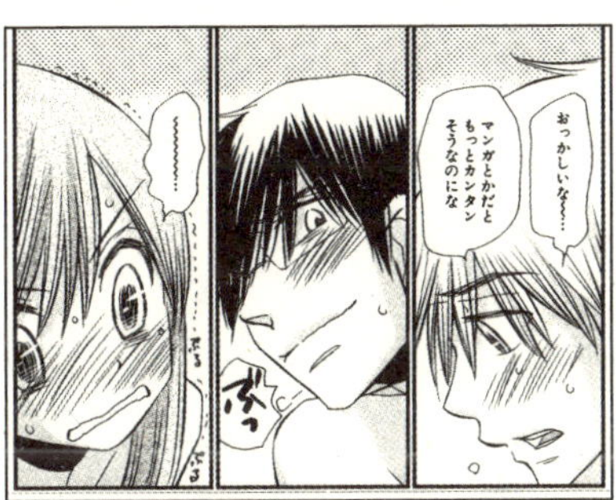

B: ***Usotsuki Paradox***, Vol. 9 (Nanki Sato & Akira Kizuki 2012, Hakusensha)

—Speaking of the differences between reality and ideals in eromanga, there are times when content is interesting because it's very much obviously a fantasy, and other times when it's interesting because it's very real, but then sometimes you get a work where you get the sense that both are interesting.

But getting back to manga expressions, what do women think of censorship in eromanga? The amount varies for different publications, but usually within the magazines one sees at the bookstore, the seaweed strip style of censorship is

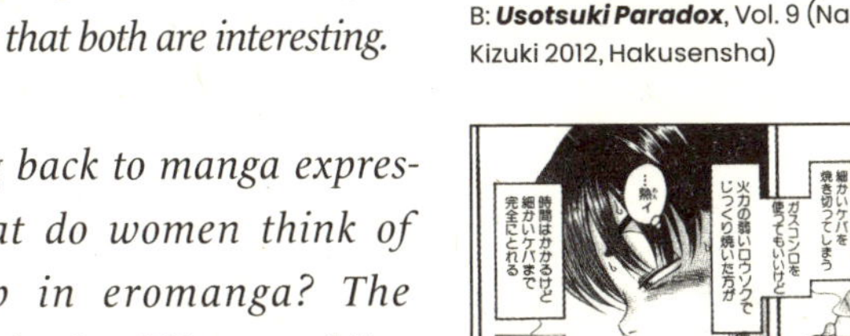
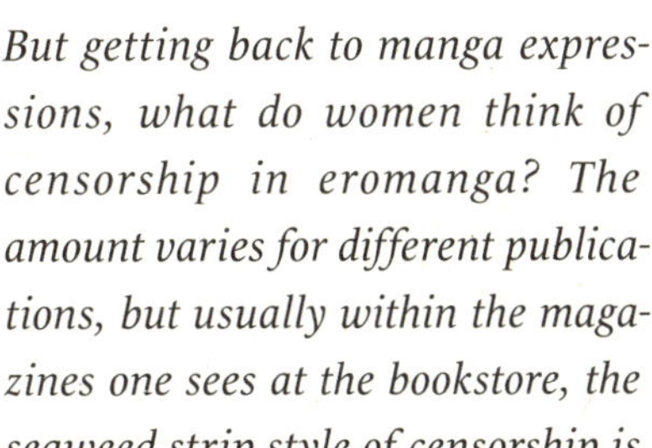

C: ***Nana to Kaoru***, Vol. 1 (Ryuta Amazume 2008, Hakusensha)

used. The magazines sold in convenience stores are a little more shrewdly censored.

What do you think?

Rina: I was actually kinda interested about that.

Kana: At least those magazines give the outside appearance that they're censoring material.

Tanaka: Do they even attempt to hide anything at all, with the degree of how far the censorship goes?

—When censorship was at its leanest, only the glans of the penis was censored, and that was it.

Rina: I don't really understand it, but I am interested. But why not censor the shaft of the penis vertically instead of just horizontally with the glans using so many strips?

Hari: There's no real meaning to that.

—It's not like just because there's a bit of censorship means that you can just sit back, relax, and read it. If it all went away and things didn't get any more erotic (by showing genitalia), then why are we censoring at all? At least, that's how I feel about it.

But now I know that in women's eyes, censorship has no meaning whatsoever. (laughs) So let's switch gears. How do we all feel about the cross-section view?

Rakuda: I rather like it.

Rina: I don't know if it's the *cross-section view,* but that expression where the female genitalia are opened and it's like you as the reader is looking out at their partner? I thought that was really interesting. It's like you as the reader are experiencing the penis's point of view.

Everyone: The penis's point of view! (laugh)

Tanaka: There's a situation where when one partner is licking the female partner's nipple and she has big breasts. In this case, the reader can see things from the inside of the male's mouth, so it's like we're seeing things from their teeth's point of view, right?

Rina: Wow!

Rakuda: There's a lot I've seen where the reader is looking at things as if the point of view is from the inside of that partner's mouth but not necessarily from their teeth's point of view.

Kana: Those expressions where, during oral sex, when the receiving partner ejaculates and pours semen down the giving partner's throat are really erotic!

—*There's the general thought that the reason why the* cross-section view *was developed as an expression was because people get curious about what's going on in their bodies.*

Niko: So, kind of like health and science education in school, then.

Hari: Oh, I get it. It kind of allows men to try to understand what's happening inside their female partner, right? I'm actually pretty happy there's something like that out there.

—*The* cross-section view *is indeed quite kind. (laughs)*

Forbidden questions for the girls' eromanga gathering

—So the theme of this next part is important. This is where we talk about a topic that I think that men all over the world want to ask about but often don't get the chance to do so. So as the representative on behalf of all of these men worldwide, allow me to ask: do women use eromanga as masturbation material?

Originally men used eromanga to do so, but do women use it for the same goal? And if not, why do women read eromanga at all? These questions seem exceedingly simple, but some men surprisingly seem to feel that this topic is very profound. I think that conversations about this question are very sensitive in nature, but if you could answer this for the sake of cluing in male readers, I think we'd all be quite grateful.

This is a voluntary question, and you don't need to answer if you don't want to.

Kana: Is it okay if I go for it?

—Yes, by all means, please do.

Kana: Personally, I don't. I get mentally fired up seeing the situations and expressions and dialogue, but it really doesn't affect me (sexually) much at all. I do stuff in the self-publishing world and make my own doujinshi, so I can see an expression and think, "Oh, this is really erotic," and reflect on it. Ultimately though, because it's only two-dimensional it doesn't really affect or arouse me.

—In other words, it can be useful as a tool to help erotically nourish your work. And instead of getting aroused, you can get mentally fired up and think it's really cute, or moé, *then consider using it in your work.*

Kana: I really don't use it for my own sake as a person. It's like when I watch porn, I can go, "Oh, that's so erotic! That's so good!" But that's about the extent of it. There's really no other effect on me from either in that way.

Niko: In my case when I was young, I would use it that way. It would really strike a chord with me, so I'd masturbate to it. But recently, I've stopped altogether. Perhaps it's because I became an adult. (laughs)

If I were to use it as masturbation material now, I would have to match up to a certain type of woman, but eromanga is drawn largely by and for the male gaze. If they included cuter elements so that the girl's body could enjoy intercourse more, I'd definitely be satisfied by that. By making it masturbatory material and knowing that it's drawn largely by and for the male gaze, those male fantasy components are personally just too strong for me.

Also, another issue I have is that recently, aren't all the girls in eromanga really adorable? Like the art for them is beautiful. Do men really ejaculate to that? It's really quite puzzling.

Hari: There are actually guys out there that say, "These pictures are too pretty! I can't cum to this!" you know.

—People who believe in drawing ability and fetish supremacy would probably understand your feelings here, I think.

Rina: I was actually dumbstruck when I found out that there are people out there who don't read eromanga in order to masturbate. If I'm swayed by a particular work in a certain way, I use it as masturbation material. Though depending on my emotional state, what I use for it tends to change. The times I just want to satisfy my desires, I go for doujin or illustrations that just have people fucking.

But there are times where I want a girl and a guy doing everyday stuff, and then I use material that's a blend of crying and cumming. In this situation, I don't care whether it's the guy or the girl, and the crying part doesn't necessarily need to stem from empathy [for the other partner's feelings]. Just wanting to observe their partner is also just fine. If I read something like that, I end up crying. The cuteness of that normal couple and their happiness makes me really happy. (sobs)

Kana: It's all about that third-person point of view.

—Have you ever found that professionally produced eromanga is difficult to masturbate to?

Rina: Nope! I've found that Fumi Minato's work has my ideal couples in it, so I often read those and cry. (laughs) Kerorin's virgin boy characters are super cute, too. There's also no use in arguing about Homunculus' work, I use it regardless. (laughs) So whether it's industry-produced or indie zines, if it has my favorite themes in it, that's key.

—I get the sense that as long as it meets your criteria for use, you tend to enjoy a lot of different things.

Rakuda: I personally use everything. (laughs) And of course, I really enjoy manga. I draw sometimes so I also use it for reference for my drawings. So I'd say it's all three of those things. I believe we briefly touched on the topic of an artist's drawing ability, but when the art is really gorgeous, it makes me really happy, so I just go full speed ahead and use it. I feel that when the quality of the art is high, I can usually find my favorite situations and themes are in those designs. I have a lot of fixations and ways to enjoy them, and just as we spoke of before, I'm constantly buying erotic content that seems to span all sorts of genres. So I basically use everything.

—By using that material to masturbate, reading it for fun, and then using it as drawing references... you may be the most male-like of the lot here.

Somu: I also only buy stuff that makes me cum!

Everyone: Whoa!

Somu: I think the only thing that doesn't make me shlick is Asami Sekiya's stuff. But Sakeru Kito's stuff really makes me go!

—You say that you only buy material that makes you cum but how do you know if it'll accomplish that without reading it first? What happens when you buy something and it doesn't?

Somu: I make it work.

Everyone: Wow!

—So you try to recover the cost of your investment? (laughs) It makes me want to cheer you on!

Hari: A long time ago, I used to be really sensitive to arousal, so pretty much anything made me cum. But as I became more literate regarding the topics that appear in eromanga, that stopped happening. So I do get a lot of enjoyment out of reading manga, but when I want to masturbate, I just search for the situations and stories I know that can get me there. Usually G-10's work gets me to that point.

Tanaka: I use different materials for different needs, I guess. However, the stuff I don't usually use, I'll maybe use once in a hundred times. This goes for when I'm prepared for anything, or when I just am hung up on the peace sign stuff.

—So your [physical] condition may also be linked to how you consume that material?

Tanaka: Usually when I buy a really great doujinshi or something that's on the level of being sacred, I usually sit and read it when I take baths. Like when I don't do something before [masturbating], it's like using a cleansing scrub to see how it works for you before you commit to using it in your skin care routine.

Everyone: (laughs)

Kana: Wait, is that when you do it?

Tanaka: No. It's when I'm reading something that's truly blessed, and I'm preparing my heart for it. It's when I'm at my best, like I'm sitting on the floor with perfect posture and ripping the plastic off of the comics so I can read them!

—I'm sure the creators of those works must be really happy you're so excited to read their new material. It's almost like it's your religion. (laughs)

So looking at the statistics so far, we can tell that roughly 60% of the ladies from this panel use manga for masturbatory purposes. But just as people need more than side dishes to survive, they need main courses, desserts and such, and there are components that equate to that in this situation. I'm glad at the fact that they can also enjoy other methods of consuming this material and I wonder if my guests understood that.

*(*The full text of this event can be found on my blog, though I also might self-publish it as well. I invite those that want to read more of it to check those sources.)* ✿

History of Eromanga Timeline

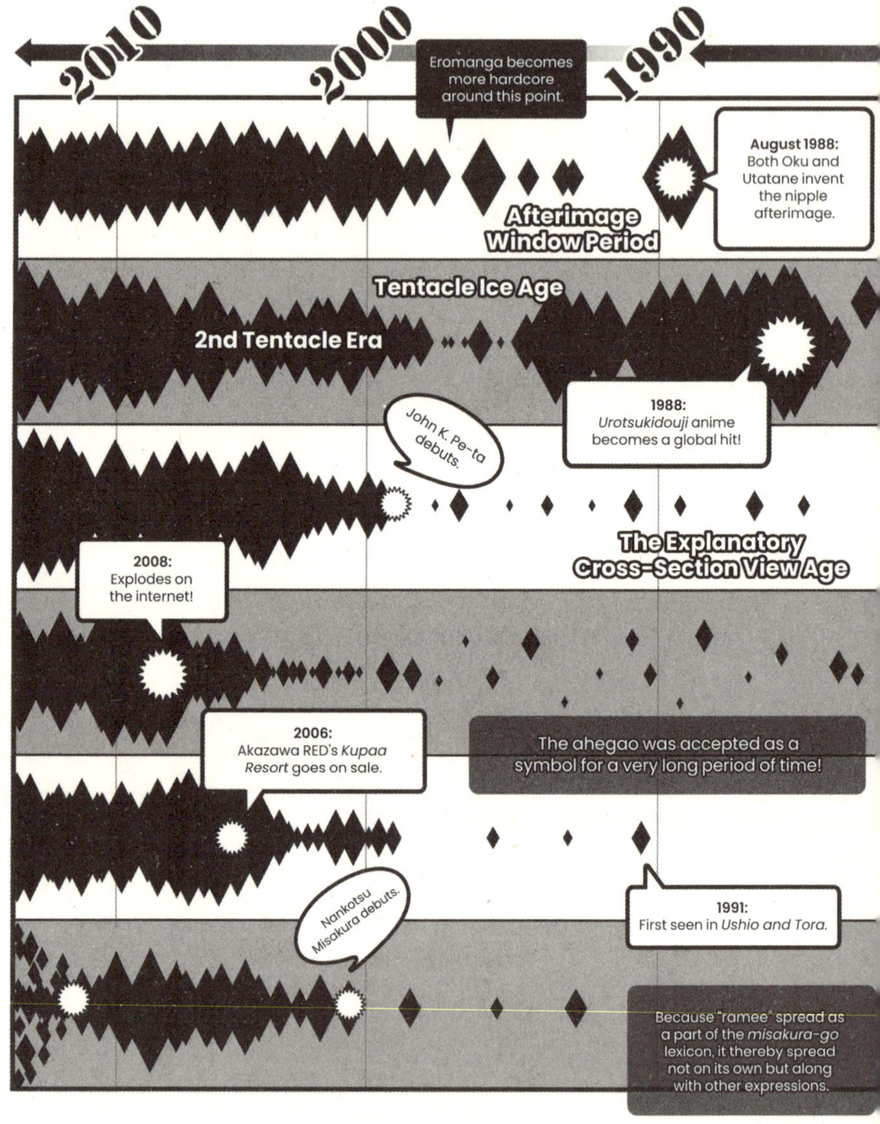

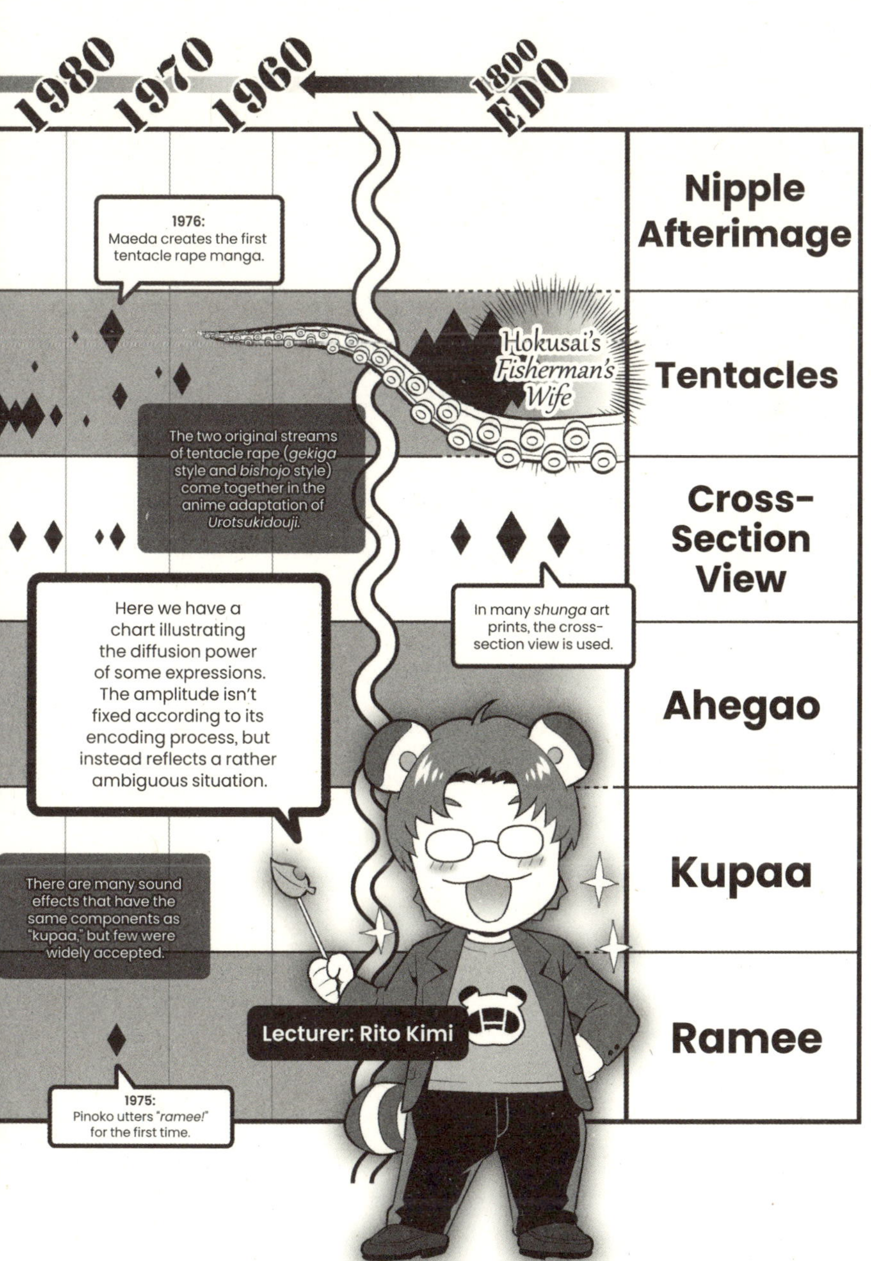
1980
1970
1960
1800
EDO
Nipple Afterimage
Tentacles
Cross-Section View
Ahegao
Kupaa
Ramee
1976:
Maeda creates the first tentacle rape manga.
Hokusai's Fisherman's Wife
The two original streams of tentacle rape (*gekiga* style and *bishojo* style) come together in the anime adaptation of *Urotsukidouji.*
In many *shunga* art prints, the cross-section view is used.
Here we have a chart illustrating the diffusion power of some expressions. The amplitude isn't fixed according to its encoding process, but instead reflects a rather ambiguous situation.
There are many sound effects that have the same components as "kupaa," but few were widely accepted.
Lecturer: Rito Kimi
1975:
Pinoko utters "*ramee!*" for the first time.

Afterword

It could be that people think me titling this book ***The History of Hentai Manga: An Expressionist Examination of Eromanga*** is an exaggeration, seeing as how expressions are limited to a certain sphere.

Well, they'd be right.

However, the real reason behind this title is that I want people to know that yes, this is a real field in which people seriously are doing academic research in. With this book, I wanted to explore in which way expressions are born, propagated, and spread and have that side by side with illustrations because even within the field of manga research, not many people have done work in this specific topic. It's a field that I dearly hope people after me will carry on developing in my stead. So, my publisher very generously allowed me to bestow this book with such a holistic title. I believe I have, with my work in this book, managed to maintain standards set before me. After this, I fully intend to continue my work widening this field and researching even more about expressions.

I do, however, fully expect angry fingers pointing out things to the tune of, "There was never an expression like this!" and "You didn't mention [insert random expression here]; what the hell kind of history of expressions is this?!" This research is in its infancy. But precisely because so many people participated in this research, this subject has been able to expand to the extent that it has. Getting all of your important opinions and your requests has made me unexpectedly very happy. So, by all means, please let the publisher know what you think!

Even within the special expressions of eromanga that I've introduced in this book, the artists who helped birth them and the readers who help spread them all had their own paths along with them. I'm sure to the artists that helped create these expressions, some of which hadn't been around until now, having their work be flagbearers must be a great honor. At the same time, watching these expressions be misinterpreted and morph into forms they never intended for them to take must be a very painful thing indeed. I'm sure that particular experience is not limited to those who have invented eromanga expressions, but to everyone who's created manga expressions.

Toshio Maeda, the so-called *Tentacle Master,* experienced this. There was a period when, much to his confusion (and exhaustion), he went around the world, and the only thing people wanted him to draw for them were tentacles and not much else. However now that he's no longer doing manga, the expression that he invented now connects him to many people. So instead of remaining confused and exhausted, he is grateful for the experience.

Nankotsu Misakura is one creator whose name is the shining diadem of their expression, yet remains baffled as to why their expression exploded and spread the way it did. Nevertheless, they're very positive about it regardless. They refuse to be captive to the ideas that belonged to their past self, and instead focus on churning out ever cuter girls and interesting expressions. While they repeatedly use the scrap and build strategy as their personal creative process, they nevertheless continue to create new works.

For Hiroya Oku and Hiroyuki Utatane, who both created versions of the *nipple afterimage,* they too were both so shocked that they never re-used their expressions again within their works. To these two mangaka that are constantly groping for new solutions with their expressions and concepts, their heads already so full of their next big idea, most likely know the awareness of the ideas they've created is fleeting at best. The moment their ideas started to spread, that was the moment that those expressions let go of their parents' hands and evolved in ways they never even dreamed. At that point, the spread was already out of their control.

Events like that have baffled and confined creators in the past, but there are creators like Akazawa RED and John K. Pe-ta, who have weaponized the expressions they developed and have allowed them to coexist alongside them. Admittedly, one of the most interesting parts of creating a history of manga expressions is the puzzle aspect of it, allowing the researcher to unravel the various transmission processes they all have. Researching them online raises the topic of the identity of their inventors, and all but a few that appear in this book were ever set in stone. I would like for everyone reading this book to understand that the true essence of these expressions can be different from what they became.

But some rather bothersome problems remain... When expressions are shared faster than expected, and the number of new ones that are unearthed when one gets their eyes on the research material.

To be truthful, the amount of time it took to finish this book was nearly half a year longer than my early predictions. The reason for that is of course, my own slow speed in writing it, but also, I was far too optimistic. Being lazy accounted for 80% of the problem, which I suppose is obvious, but also as I was writing this, I was provided a flowing stream of eromanga, and due to that, I kept finding brand new expressions one after the other. There was also the issue of organizing all my data and materials, and it was as if I were an archeologist continually unearthing new finds. So, no matter how much I wrote, that goalposts kept moving away from me.

A new reality emerged, one where I wouldn't let it get away either in the past or the present. I would finish writing the conclusion to a chapter, but then was met by the great misfortune of not being able to make any big changes to it. To put it another way, this field is one where if one were to slightly excavate such unexplored lands, who knew what treasure would be waiting beneath the earth? By the time this book is to be published, my conclusion may do a 180° turn, but if I just wait around, collecting new expressions, I may never be able to present my work. One must make a choice eventually. So, I decided in order to make sure everyone understood my field of research, I knew I had to polish material that pertained to more than one certain time period. After all, history itself is a study that will never be completed and is ever ongoing (and so I became serious about my efforts)!

Even so, this field is far too large for me to cover alone. But there was also another big problem that has worried researchers in all fields of study: what happens when you don't have a map to guide you?

For manga researchers, the most important materials one needs are comics. I needed the actual magazines that serialized it, which also funneled material into books that were later published. I thought that if I read the magazines as I went along, that would have been the most standard research method I could use. Compared to the past, the archive of regular manga really has really advanced.

But for eromanga, it's sad to say that I barely had enough to work with. For starters, an archive of eromanga magazines and books had not been established nor serviced over the years. I could barely count the number of libraries that had actual eromanga collections, but the ones I was able to find were half-heartedly put together at best. The approach to collecting primary sources was barely there at all either. If I couldn't figure out who presented what and when, then the place where I was to conduct my research had a fatal data deficit.

For basic research I had to get an overall perspective on eromanga magazines, but in order to do that I also had to put together a rough archive to pool my materials. It was a labor of love that took eight years to advance, but I finally got a feeling that I was able to see the whole picture. And not just of eromanga but also *bishojo comics,* as well. To be sure, that whole picture was vast. At first, I planned to start research only after getting the organization of the archive down and putting it all in order, but it seemed that reality wasn't so accommodating. I didn't have the time to do that.

And then it hit me. What if I were to make a publicly shared map, where other researchers could come to the continent of eromanga and have them help me research with what I needed?

However, one barrier that stood in the way of that strategy was the fact that… Oh, how should I put it? I had a severe data deficit, and if the amount of previous research to work with was minimal, I wouldn't fare much better as an expert on the topic without it. The first breakthrough would be getting everyone to pool data. If we were able to do that, imagine how much easier we could make getting into this field! Let's not mention being able to connect other subjects of research like sociology, expression theory, criticism, and others as well.

But organizing the archive I was to do for my eromanga research was further complicated by a physical barrier, which was trouble in sourcing the primary source magazines I so desperately needed for it, which erected another mental barrier in turn.

I called it the "Erotic Wall."

Wouldn't that lead to a situation where no matter how much I wanted to research eromanga, I would find excuses taking the lead? Surely, others wouldn't think that the reason why I set eromanga as my subject of research was so I could gather masturbation material, right? Would they acknowledge my subject of research at all? Will this hurt my chances at a job search? Surely, friends and family won't turn a cold shoulder at me for wanting to research this…right?

All I could think about were the negatives coiled around the subject of eromanga, and I couldn't help but get cold feet.

Just by being adjacent to the written word "ero" made one feel an unconscious sense of the taboo for no reason whatsoever. One wasn't supposed to touch it, allow it to touch you, or make it your primary subject of research.

Originally, eromanga is a subset of manga, and expressions become pieces of adjoined land it shares with other genres. There are big reciprocal influences they cast on each other, as I've said many times within this book. However, as one understands that truth, an invisible wall is erected, and you must pretend that you don't just see eromanga. While eromanga may not be as safe to handle as shonen manga, that does not mean one should blindly exclude it altogether. But their expressions, especially the erotic ones, are bad.

A few years back, the NHK's BS2 channel aired a program called

Manga no Genba, where manga artists of note are interviewed. It's a pretty hardcore program produced for manga fans. To the end, they never so much as touched eromanga authors. So perhaps out of a sense of rivalry, my self-published work, *Eromanga no Genba* was born.

That book that was born out of an impulse at that time has continued for eight years. I don't think NHK saw a book of it coming. Though I don't think that there was anyone more shocked about that than me. (laughs) Shortly thereafter, the NHK's ***Naoki Urusawa's Manben*** and ***SWITCH: Interview Tatsujin-tachi,*** to my utter shock and surprise, discussed Naoki Yamamoto's work, ***Bunkou no Hito-tachi*** (Ohta Books), which had recently been designated as an obscene book by the government. So, I guess I have to forgive them on this one.

I've gone off topic, but regardless, if you want to research eromanga, you'll need both physical and emotional resolve to see it through. But right now, I think that the map of the eromanga continent has progressed. However, I haven't put this map together all on my own.

Due to my predecessors' magnificent research, I've been able to start putting the map into place. This book, which became my chance to seriously pursue eromanga research was due to the critic, author, and sometimes-mangaka Kaoru Nagayama's book, *Erotic Comics in Japan.* His work includes a column in *Manga Hot Milk* magazine, and a ground-breaking eromanga news mook, *Comic Junkys*. I had pursued him personally, but that was in order to get an entertainment article for some academic reference material. I think I had been unconsciously rejected due to a link to my research. Consequently, when I read his book, I realized, "Oh, it's okay to talk about both grand and slightly difficult elements within eromanga after all!" It felt as if I was having a divine revelation. Nagayama and his work toppled my Erotic Wall, like the fall of the Berlin Wall.

His other work, the ***Manga Ronsoh*** series, and its platonic ideal of "let's really listen when someone speaks, let us lend an ear" inspired me. And it wasn't just the journals' scholarly data, but the columns with and by people who work in manga, too. I listened to the stories the insiders told, and truly absorbed the details covered, which allowed me to commit to the industry, and build a better style when it came to advancing research both within and outside of eromanga. As a result, without Yoshihiro Yonezawa's book, ***Sengo Eromangashi*** (2010, Seirin Kogeisha) to balance out Nagayama's approaches and help me combine both of their styles into something that worked for me, then this book may never have been born.

Mr. Nagayama in particular really helped me out with regard to writing, life, and my habits, and gave me a ton of advice for this book. I will repay your kindness...Well, now that I've raised you up this far, please go ahead and pay me a manuscript fee for each article I've produced for you. (laughs)

During the production of this book, I had a lot of collaboration and got a lot of advice. Adult media researcher Rio Yasuda helped with the chapter about breasts and gave me a lot of valuable information from the third dimension about the history of *kyounyu.* My senpai from our university science-fiction research circle helped with the tentacles chapter. Role-playing game designer and writer Yusuke Tokita helped me out with editing information about the Cthulhu mythos. I also have to thank the staff at Meiji University's Yoshihiro Yonezawa Memorial Library for giving me access to truly precious magazines (your subculture publication collection is much more reliable than that of the National Diet Library). Thank you to Ryuta Amazume, who always forgets the positions and titles of researchers and writers and just talks to me, and along with Edara provided the cute drawings of the women who participated in the girls-only event. I know you were busy, too. Thank you.

Thank you also to my second man in a three-legged race, who, more than anyone else, oversaw the development of this book from start to finish, Mr. Murakami. Whenever I lost sight of the issue at hand and became lost, you always pertinently led me back to where I needed to be. You were with me no matter whatever I wanted to write about, and whenever I went berserk with my chapters, you let me know what I needed to cut from them. When I fell into a slump and was so blocked I just couldn't write at all, you would send me gentle emails reminding me of where I needed to be in terms of progress on this book (and for a writer as lazy as I am, you always asserted just the right amount of pressure to whip me into shape).

Thank you to my designer for this book, to the lovely ladies who accompanied me for the roundtable, and to every editor who helped me out, too. Thank you.

Finally, let me take this opportunity to once more stand in front of all of the people in eromanga as an industry. Let me once again reiterate my gratitude for your hard work.

Now, then! This repetitive eromanga research really has only just begun. To those that feel the same, I invite you to come to a new continent and search for beautiful, charming bishojo girls with us. This vast plain, regardless of its rare, tumbling finds, holds no rivals for us to compete with. Let's go, eromanga! Let's make more erotic discoveries together! ✿

FAKKU Edition Exclusive Afterword

To those reading a translated version of this book abroad,

It's been three years since the original version of this book was published in Japan in 2017, and now you finally have the English version of *The History of Hentai Manga* in your hands. I would first and foremost like to thank the staff of FAKKU! for making topics like Japanese linguistic onomatopes and other such things so easy to understand for an English-speaking audience. In particular, the level of understanding that this company and their staff have of hentai itself is really remarkable, so I'm quite glad that I asked FAKKU! to handle the translation of this book.

Eromanga (that is to say, hentai) research, compared to regular manga research, is a field that is still very much within its infancy. In Japan, hentai's birthplace, there are so few books on this field that I can barely count them on one hand.

However, when you compare that to books published abroad on the same subject, it seems to be an embarrassment of riches. It would be appropriate to say that there are nearly zero books on this topic out in English or abroad as I write this afterword.

I feel strongly that with the publication of this book abroad, it will help speed along the research of other Japanese authors on the same topic far faster than before. Through the publication of this book, I would be thrilled and pleased beyond my wildest dreams if other readers were to pick up and continue this same field of research.

But I do not wish to only have this book translated in English. I hope that one day I'll see a translation released in Portuguese, German, and French as well. If you would like to see a translation of this book in your language, I strongly encourage you to contact Ohta Books or FAKKU! and let them know.

Also, I will accept any questions or consultations directly. In order to prime the pump for further hentai research, I would like to actively respond to requests for interviews or lectures anyone may have, so it would make me really happy if you were to contact me with such a request.

Finally, I would like to thank my kindred-spirit in hentai, FAKKU!'s Jacob Grady, for showing interest in licensing this book in the first place. Thank you so, so much! ❁

Bibliography

Chapter One

1-1: *Cybele* Vol. 5 (1980, Cybele editorial) doujinshi

1-2A: *Lemon People*, Feb. 1982 (AMATORIA) magazine

1-2B: ***Rasen Kairou*** (Waho Konoma; *Lemon People,* Nov. '83, AMATORITA)

1-3: ***Futari to 5-nin,*** Vol. 1 (Hideo Azuma 1974, Akita Shoten)

1-4: ***Kawaii GIRL no Kaki-kata Kyoshitsu*** (Aki Uchiyama; *Lemon People,* Oct. '83, AMATORIA)

1-5: ***Kuchu Rokaku no Majitsushi*** (Senno Knife; *Lemon People,* Aug. '82, AMATORIA)

1-6: ***Iczer One*** (Rei Aran; *Lemon People,* Oct. '83, AMATORIA)

1-7: ***Hades Project Zeorymer*** (Moriwo Chimi; *Lemon People,* Aug. '84, AMATORIA)

1-8: ***Joyful Koshinaka & "Eiken" Gang*** (Giyugun 1987, Shoubunkan)

1-9: ***Izumi-chan Graffiti,*** Vol. 1 (Tatsuo Kanai 1981, Shueisha)

1-10: ***Oh! Tohmei Ningen,*** Vol. 3 (Yasuhiro Nakanishi 1983, Kodansha)

1-11: ***Heart ♥ Catch Izumi-chan,*** Vol. 6 (Hikaru Tooyama 1986, Kodansha)

1-12: ***Miss Machiko,*** Vol. 1 (Takeshi Ebihara 1981, Gakken)

1-13: ***Ojama Yurei-kun,*** Vol. 2 (Susumu Yoshikawa 1980, Shogakukan)

1-14: ***Paradise Gakuen,*** Vol.1 (Masatoshi Kawahara 1985, Kodansha)

1-15: ***Yarukkya Nnight,*** Vol. 1 (Nonki Miyasu 1985, Shueisha)

1-16: ***Ikenai! Luna-sensei,*** Vol 1 (Sumiko Kamimura 1987, Kodansha)

1-17: ***Rough & Ready*** (Tou Moriyama 1986, Tsukasa Shobo)

1-18: *Kimiko Matsuzaka Photo Book Dekka~i no Mekke!* (1989, Big Man) mook

1-19: *Bachelor*, Feb. 1992 (Dia Press) magazine

1-20: ***Dokkin ♥ Minako-sensei*** (Wataru Watanabe 1987, Byakuya-Shobo)

1-21: ***Dokkin ♥ Minako-sensei,*** Vol. 2 (Wataru Watanabe 1987, Byakuya-Shobo)

1-22: ***Aphrodite no Yu-utsu*** (Kei Kitamimaki 1988, Byakuya-Shobo)

1-23: ***D-Cup LOVERS*** (Tohru Nishimaki 1993, Hit Publishing)

1-24: *D-Cup Collection,* Vol. 1 (1988, Byakuya-Shobo) magazine

1-25: *D-Cup Club,* Iss. 1 (1988, Outou Shobo) magazine

1-26: "Big Breast Emancipation Movement" (*D-Cup Collection,* Vol. 1, '88, Byakuya-Shobo) article

1-27: ***Ogenki Clinic,*** Vol. 1 (Haruka Inui 1987, Akita Shoten)

1-28: ***Kanojo wa Delicate!*,** Vol. 8 (Takeshi Kajiwara 1990, Kodansha)

1-29: ***Kyounyu Hunter*,** Right Breast (Kouichirou Yasunaga 1990, Shogakukan)

1-30: ***HEN***, Vol. 3 (Hiroya Oku 1992, Shueisha)

1-31: ***Piss Doll*** (Shiroi Gunpan 1988, Byakuya-Shobo)

1-32: ***Keiko-sensei no Kagai Jugyo*** (Minor Boy 1988, France Shoin)

1-33: ***Oshioki Bakunyu Nurse*** (Hiroshi Kawamoto 2002, Toen Shobou)

1-34: ***Ichigo ♥ Channel*,** Ch. 23 (Yu Asai; *Comic Yumi-chan,* Feb. '96, Cybele Publishing)

1-35: ***Midnight Program*** (Yoshimasa Watanabe 1992, Akaneshinsha)

1-36: "NyuMan" (Mugi Tokisaka; *Kairakuten Hoshigumi* Nov. '97, Wanimagazine)

1-37: ***NIGHT VISITOR*** (Kazuki Kotobuki 1994, Tsukasa Shobo)

1-38: "Futarikkiri no" (Kazu Tomonaga; *Comic Dolphin,* Sep. '93, Tsukasa Shobo)

1-39: ***PUNKY KNIGHT*** (Kozou Youhei 2001, Akaneshinsha)

1-40: ***Sensei no Tsuyabukuro*,** Vol. 1 (Kiyoshi Shimizu 2005, JC Publishing)

1-41: ***INSULT!!*** (Yumisuke Kotoyoshi 2001, Fujimi Publishing)

1-42: ***Mikaeru Keikaku***, Vol. 2 (DISTANCE 2002, JC Publishing)

1-43**: WITCH!,** Vol. 1 to ½ (Ryohta Magaki 1998, Tsukasa Shobo)

1-44: ***Innocent Children*** (miyabitsuzuru 2001, Tsukasa Shobo)

1-45: ***G-gai Kitan*** (Yuichirou Tanuma 2000, Core Magazine)

1-46: ***Encyclopedia of Tetsuyaro Shinkaida*** (Tetsuyaro Shinkaida 1989, Byakuya-Shobo)

1-47: *Comic Kairakuten*, Oct. 1997 (Wanimagazine) magazine

1-48: ***Engine Room*** (OH! Great 1999, Core Magazine)

1-49: ***Video Girl Ai*,** Vol. 3 (Masakazu Katsura 1990, Shueisha)

1-50: ***Meguri Kuru Haru*** (OKAMA 1998, Wanimagazine)

1-51: ***VAVA*** (Douman Seiman 1996, Hit Publishing)

1-52: ***Otome Kaihatsu*** (Tachibana Seven 2002, Oakla Publishing)

1-53: ***Muku na Tenshitachi*** (Heppoko-kun 2001, Shobunkan)

1-54: "Un, Yappari Nurse shika!!" (UonaTelepin; *Comic Megastore,* Apr. '01, Core Magazine)

1-55: ***CHI CHI POCKET*** (Kanikani 2001, Kubo Shoten)

1-56: ***Delusion Love Device*** (Kouichi Kusano. 2006, Hit Publishing)

A: ***TiTiKei*** (IshiKei 2013, Wanimagazine)

B: ***TiTiKei*** (IshiKei 2013, Wanimagazine)

C: ***TiTiKei*** (IshiKei 2013, Wanimagazine)

D: ***TiTiKei*** (IshiKei 2013, Wanimagazine)

E: *Comic Mo-e* (Oct. 2000, Shobunkan) magazine

1-57: ***KO · KO · RO...***, 0 (Rio Jinguji 2004, Aaru) video game

1-58: ***NINETEEN,*** Vol. 2 (Shou Kitagawa 2005, Shueisha)

1-59: ***GREASEBERRIES,*** Vol. 1 (Masamune Shirow 2014, GOT)

1-60: ***To LOVE Ru,*** Vol. 1 (Kentaro Yabuki & Saki Hasemi 2006, Shueisha)

1-61: ***Eiken,*** Vol. 10 (Seiji Matsuyama 2003, Akita Shoten)

1-62: ***Oppai no Yure ni Go-Chui kudasai*** (Wakachiko 2017, Sankosha)

1-63: ***Nihon Kyounuto*** (RaTe 2007, Wanimagazine)

Chapter Two

2-1: ***Ma-monogatari Aishi no Betty,*** Vol. 1 (Seisaku Kano & Kazuo Koike 1980, Shogakukan)

2-2: **Shikken Ningyo *Dummy Oscar*,** Vol. 3 (Seisaku Kano & Kazuo Koike 1979, Studio Ship)

2-3: ***Cobra***, Vol. 1 (Buichi Terasawa 1979, Shueisha)

2-4: ***DAICON IV: OP FILM*** (DAICON4 Executive Committee 1983) animation

2-5: ***DAISY!*** (Amatarou 2009, Core Magazine)

2-6: "Nao to Ecchi" (Kikurage; *Comic Anthurium,* Jun. '14, GOT)

2-7: "The Feeling of a Woman Begging for Bareback" (Nishi Iori; *Comic Kairakuten,* Jul. 2017, Wanimagazine)

2-8: ***Love Sign?*** (Uekan 2017, Core Magazine)

2-9: ***To Meet Someday*** (Jacky Kameyama 1994, Kubo Shoten)

2-10: "Natsu no Prelude" (Tohru Nishimaki; *D-Cup Collection*, Vol. 1, 1988, Byakuya-Shobo)

2-11: "Jukenshi Tina no Yutsu" (Hitoshi Funato; *D-Cup Collection*, Vol. 1, 1988, Byakuya-Shobo)

2-12: ***GANTZ***, Vol. 7 (Hiroya Oku 2002, Shueisha)

2-13: ***HEN*** (Hiroya Oku; *Young Jump,* Iss. 1-2, '89, Shueisha)

2-14: ***HEN*** (Hiroya Oku; *Young Jump,* Iss. 1-2, '89, Shueisha)

A: ***GANTZ***, Vol. 17 (Hiroya Oku 2005, Shueisha)

B: ***Maetel no Kimochi***, Vol. 3 (Hiroya Oku 2007, Shueisha)

C: ***HEN***, Vol. 2 (Hiroya Oku 1989, Shueisha)

D: ***HEN***, Vol. 3 (Hiroya Oku 1989, Shueisha)

2-15: ***COUNT DOWN*** (Hiroyuki Utatane; *TEA TIME*, 6, '92, Fujimi Publishing)

2-16: "MIRROR" (Hiroyuki Utatane 1989, Byakuya-Shobo)

E. *TEA TIME,* 6 (Hiroyuki Utatane 1992, Byakuya-Shobo) magazine

F. ***Countdown: Sex Bombs*** (Hiroyuki Utatane 1992, Fujimi Publishing)

G. **Seraphic Feather**, Vol. 9 (Hiroyuki Utatane 2005, Kodansha)

2-17: ***Countdown: Sex Bombs*** (Hiroyuki Utatane 1992, Fujimi Publishing)

2-18: ***Berserk***, Vol. 7 (Kentaro Miura 1995, Hakusensha)

2-19: "VIVID FANTASY" (Rei Arou; *Hana Ichimonme*, Jul. '93, Mediax)

2-20: "Jigoku Kyoshi O'en Senjuraku" (Heaven-11; *Manga Hot Milk*, Jun. '93, Byakuya-Shobo)

2-21: "SOAP" (Ran Hiryuu; *Penguin Club,* Apr. '94, Tatsumi Publishing)

2-22: "BATH COMMUNICATION" (Hiromi Egawa; *Hana Ichimonme,* Feb. '95, Mediax)

2-23: "HAPPY BIRTHDAY TO MY GIRL" (DISTANCE; *Comic PaPiPo*, Oct. '94, France Shoin)

2-24: "Ai no Tame ni" (Douman Seiman; *Comic Touhime*, Jul. '95, Hit Publishing)

2-25: "NyuMan" (Mugi Tokisaka; *Kairakuten Hoshigumi* Nov. '97, Wanimagazine)

2-26: ***Keiko-sensei no KagaiJugyo*** (Minor Boy 1988, France Shoin)

2-27: "NIGHT VISITOR" (Kazuki Kotobuki; *Comic Dolphin,* Sep. '93, Tsukasa Shobo)

2-28: ***Imoto Play*** (Seiji Aura 2002, France Shoin)

2-29: "Shiritsu Seishitan Gakuen Renai!? Senka" (Kengo Yonekura; *Comic Rise,* Aug. '98, Mediax)

2-30: ***Mama ni Dokkin*** (Wataru Watanabe 2001, Toen Shobou)

2-31: "Boku no Haigorei?" (Katsura Yoshihiro; *Comic Hot Milk*, Mar. '13, Core Magazine)

2-32: "Go-Keiyaku wa Kochira desu!" (Chiyoko Ayakase; *Comic Hot Milk*, Nov. '12, Core Magazine)

2-33: "Karate Ne-chan Monzetsu Suimin Kumite" (Drachef; *Angel Club,* Jan. '16, Angel Publishing)

2-34: "Real mo Game mo Kinshin Soukan" (Dai Uemukai; *Comic Grape,* Vol. 42 '17, GOT)

2-35: "Milky Queen" (Meguru Tsubakiya; *Ero Damashi*, Mar. 2014, Issuisha)

2-36: "Kanojo wa Joji Happyochu" (URAN; *Comic Megastore H,* Nov. '11, Core Magazine)

2-37: "Ani < Imoto" (Dorei Jackie; *Comic Megastore H*, Sep. '10, Core Magazine)

2-38: "Zankou" (Kuroarama Soukai; *Comic PaPiPo*, Dec. '99, France Shoin)

2-39: "Gyaku Rape Salon" (Saiyazumi; *Comic Milf*, Apr. '17, TI NET)

2-40: "METAMO SISTER" (Amatarou; *Comic Hot Milk*, Sep. '12, Core Magazine)

2-41: "NicoTama 2" (Yuki Takano; *Comic Aun*, Dec. '06, Hit Publishing)

2-42: "HHH" (DISTANCE; *Comic Megastore*, Feb. '09, Core Magazine)

2-43: Tooi Hi no Yakusoku (Nero Norakuro; *Comic Megastore H*, Jan. '07, Core Magazine)

2-44: ***Saishu Kareshi Dangi*** (Yutakamaru Kagura 2003, Akaneshinsha)

2-45: "Magnitude 10.0" (Dorei Jackie; *Comic Megastore H,* Apr. '10, Core Magazine)

2-46: "RUSH!" (Chitose Sakuragi; *Comic Kairakuten,* Apr. '96, Wanimagazine)

2-47: ***Netorare New Heroine*** (KONKIT 2014, Issuisha)

2-48: ***ToraChichi*** (KONKIT 2014, Fujimi Publishing)

2-49: ***Mai no Kyounyu Ranbo*** (Taiyo Nemuri. 2000, Cybele Publishing)

2-50: ***Bakunyu Jukujo Nikudan-Pai Panic*** (Taiyo Nemuri 2000, Toen Shobou)

2-51: ***Bakunyu Jukujo Nikudan-Pai Panic*** (Taiyo Nemuri 2000, Toen Shobou)

2-52: ***Mai no Kyounyu Ranbo*** (Taiyo Nemuri 2000, Cybele Publishing)

2-53***: Love Junkies,*** Vol. 2 (Kyo Hazuki 2015, Akita Shoten)

2-54: "Dare nimo Ienai" (Kanan Yamada 2002, Kousai Shobo)

2-55: ***Beyond the Friend, Under the Lover*** (Natsuki Kuriyama 2004, Shobunkan)

2-56: ***I Love You*** (Gyoe Suzumushi 2008, Shobunkan)

2-57: ***Bon-kyu-bon Danshi!*** (Kaya Aota 2014, Shusuisha)

2-58: ***Futon to Kotatu 3*** (Tonari Toyama 2013, Screamo)

2-59: ***To LOVE Ru: Darkness,*** Vol. 7 (Kentaro Yabuki & Saki Hasemi 2013, Shueisha)

2-60: ***Oyama! Kikunosuke,*** Vol. 14 (Takahiro Seguchi 1999, Akita Shoten)

2-61: **Suzuka**, Vol. 1 (Kouji Seo 2004, Kodansha)

2-62: Original illustration (Tooru Mitsumine, 2015)

Chapter Three

3-1A: ***Pandra 2: The Grimore,*** III (Erect Sawaru 2016, Kill Time Communications)

3-1B: ***LOAD OF TRASH***, Complete (A-10 2010, Core Magazine)

3-1C: "SECRET JOURNEY" (Po-Ju & Zappa Go; *Comic Megastore*, Oct. '09, Core Magazine)

3-1D: ***Hitozuma Jigoku Rou*** (Hoshizuki Melon 2014, Sanwa Publishing)

3-2: ***Kraken in Angola Bay*** (Pierre Denys de Montfort 1810; Robert Hale Ltd.) illustration

3-3: "The Dream of the Fisherman's Wife" (Katsushika Hokusai 1820; ***Kinoe no Komatsu***) print

3-4: ***Programme of Erotic Noh Plays*** (Kitao Shigemasa 1781) print

3-5: ***Lust of Many Women on One Thousand Nights*** (Shunsho Katsukawa 1786) print

3-6: *Planet Stories,* Spring (Alexander Leydenfrost 1942; Fiction House) magazine

3-7: ***The Call of Cthulhu and Other Weird Stories*** (H.P. Lovecraft & S.T. Joshi 1999, Penguin)

3-8: "Kibatsu! Sexy Kaiju Oabare" (*Weekly Manga Q,* Mar. 12, '68, Shinju Shobo)

3-9: "The Returnees" (Osamu Tezuka; *Play Comic*, Jan. 13, '73, Akita Shoten)

3-10: ***No Longer Human*** (Hideo Azuma 1978, Tokyo Sanseisha)

3-11: "Kaeri Michi" (Hideo Azuma 1981; ***Hizashi***, Kiso Tengaisha)

3-12: ***Nanako SOS,*** Vol. 1 (Hideo Azuma 1983, Koubunsha)

A: ***Urotsukidouji,*** Vol. 1 (Toshio Maeda 1986, Wanimagazine)

B. ***Urotsukidouji,*** Vol. 5 (Toshio Maeda 1987, Wanimagazine)

C. ***Urotsukidouji: Legend of the Overfiend*** (1987; Phoenix Entertainment) animation

3-13: "SEX Tearing" (Toshio Maeda; *Young Comic*, Jul. 16, '76, Shonengahosha)

3-14: "SEX Tearing" (Toshio Maeda; *Young Comic*, Jul. 16, '76, Shonengahosha)

3-15: "Gekisatsu! Uchuken" (Ryu Hurricane; *Lemon People,* Aug. '82, AMATORIA)

3-16: ***Dokkin ♥ Minako-sensei***, Vol. 2 (Wataru Watanabe 1987, Byakuya-Shobo)

3-17: "Oedo Ankokugai" (Irumakamiri; *Comic PaPiPo,* Oct. '98, France Shoin)

3-18: "Ashita naki Sekai, ♂ naki Jinrui" (Moriwo Chimi; *Lemon People,* Jan. '83, AMATORIA)

3-19: "Yakan" (Juzo Minazuki; *Comic PaPePo,* Jun. '92, France Shoin)

3-20: "Valis" (Ikuo Dodonpa; *Penguin Club*, Oct. '91, Tatsumi Publishing)

3-21: "Haru ga Kita!" (Momo Nakafusa; *Manga Hot Pants*, May '89, Tokyo Sanseisha)

3-22: ***Princess Quest Saga*** (Yui Toshiki 1994, Fujimi Publishing)

3-23: "Gody Britt" (Yu Tomiaki; *Comic BEAT,* Jan. '93, Tokyo Sanseisha)

3-24: "Slave Warrior Maya" (Conodonts; *Candy Time*, Dec. '89, Fujimi Publishing)

3-25: ***Rough & Ready*** (Tou Moriyama 1986, Tatsumi Publishing)

3-26: "Angel Heat" (Ikkou Sahara; *Potpourri Club,* Mar. '90, Taiyou Tosho)

3-27: "Fairy Saber" (Masaki Kamitou; *Penguin Club,* Oct. '93, Tatsumi Publishing)

3-28: ***Naizo Lady*** (Taro Nakayama 1988, Kubo Shoten)

3-29: ***Cream Lemon Part 3: Super-Dimension Legend Rall*** (1984, Fairy Dust) animation

3-30: ***TENTACLES*** (Kazumasa Ichikawa 1998, Tsukasa Shobo)

3-31: ***Shokushu ni Kisei-sareshi Otome no Katachi*** (2017, Kill Time Communication) anthology

3-32: ***Tentacle Lesbians*** (2017, Kill Time Communication) anthology

3-33: ***Marunomi Haramase Akume!*** (2017, Kill Time Communication) anthology

3-34: ***Moho Love*** (Sanpei Kamirenjaku 2009, Akaneshinsha)

3-35: ***Tale of 100 Vaginas*** (Shunsho Katsukawa, 1771) print

3-36: ***I Got Married to the Tentacle*** (Kitsune Miyashita 2016, Kaiohsha)

3-37: ***Perfect Planet*** (Iimo, 2016, Julian Publishing)

3-38: ***Shokushu Akume!*** (Soft On Demand, 2009) video

3-39: ***Amai Seikatsu,*** Vol. 7 (Hikaru Yuzuki 2015, Shueisha)

3-40: "Tonight, My Wife Will..." (Takashi Sano; *Manga Goraku Special*, Aug. '16, Nihon Bungeisha)

3-41: ***ShindoL's Cultural Anthropology*** (ShindoL 2016, TI NET)

3-42: ***GREASEBERRIES***, Vol. 1 (Masamune Shirow 2014, GOT)

3-43: ***To LOVE Ru: Darkness,*** Vol. 14 (Kentaro Yabuki & Saki Hasemi 2015, Shueisha)

3-44: ***Monster Musume,*** Vol. 9 (Oyakado, 2016, Tokuma Shoten)

Chapter Four

4-1: "Souma Kurumi no Hahaoya" (Kei Mizuryu; *Comic Hot Milk,* Dec. '16, Core Magazine)

4-2: "DokiDoki ★ Community Life", #3 (TakayaKi; *Comic E x E,* Jan. '17, GOT)

4-3: ***GANTZ,*** Vol. 1 (Hiroya Oku 2000, Shueisha)

4-4: ***Anatomical Drawings from the Royal Library*** (Leonardo Da Vinci 1492; Winsor Castle)

4-5: ***News from the Bedroom: The Pillow Library*** (Eisen Keisai 1823)

4-6: "Uchuujin Report: Sample A to B" (Mami Komori & Fujiko F. Fujio, *Bessatu Mondai Shosetsu*, 1977, Tokuma Shoten)

4-7: "Kiyoshi-ko no Yoru" (Hideo Azuma; *Play Comic*, Dec. '76, Akita Shoten)

4-8: "Sara ni Toki wa Midare" (Hideo Azuma, *Play Comic,* Mar. '78, Akita Shoten)

4-9: "Seishun Sanmyaku" (Tatsuhiko Yamagami, *Super Fiction*, Iss. 12, '82, Futabasha)

4-10: ***Ecstasy off Limits,*** Vol. 1 (Ai Shiraishi 1990, Shogakukan)

4-11**:** ***Manga Sutra,*** Vol. 25 (Katsu Aki 2004, Hakusensha)

4-12: ***Manga Sutra,*** Vol. 22 (Katsu Aki 2004, Hakusensha)

4-13: "Inmitsu Honeymoon" (Shigeru Tomita; *Manga Dynamite*, 1981, Tatsumi Publishing)

4-14: "Yukishoujo Densetsu" (Fumio Nakajima; *Gekiga Lolita*, May '82, Sun Publishing)

4-15: ***Eden no Kaze*** (Toshio Maeda 1990, Koike Shoin)

4-16: ***Penguin in Bondage*** (Tou Moriyama 1986, Tatsumi Publishing)

4-17: "Android wa Denkikokeshi no Yume wo Miruka?" (Kasumi Goto; *Manga Burikko,* Aug. '83, Byakuya-Shobo)

4-18: "Tadaima Benkyouchuu" (Juzo Minazuki; *Candy Time,* Apr. '91, Fujimi Publishing)

4-19: "Happy-ning Star" (Mizu-Youkan; *Penguin Club*, Dec. '91, Tatsumi Shobo)

4-20: "Utamai-chau" (HindenBURG; *Potpourri Club,* Apr. 91, Taiyou Tosho)

4-21: ***Mermaid ♥ Junction*** (Yui Toshiki 1987, Byakuya-Shobo)

A: ***Geki!! Monzetsu Operation*** (John K. Pe-ta 2005, Toen Shobou)

B: ***Tokimeki Monzetsu Vulcan!!*** (John K. Pe-ta 2008, Core Magazine)

C: ***Super Monzetsu Megabitch*** (John K. Pe-ta 2010, Core Magazine)

4-22: ***JKP's World*** (John K. Pe-ta 2005, Toen Shobou)

4-23: ***Juice of Girl*** (Type.90 2002, Shobunkan)

4-24: ***Freshness Abnormal*** (Henmaru Machino 2007, Toen Shobou)

4-25: ***Waku Waku Monzetsu Maison*** (John K. Pe-ta 2015, GOT)

4-26: ***B-Flat 38°C,*** Loveberry Twins (Jogi Tsukino 2004, Core Magazine)

4-27: ***Domin-8 Me!*** (Sessyu Takemura 2004, Core Magazine)

4-28: ***KinshinSoukan*** (Kinohitoshi 2004, Core Magazine)

4-29: ***MySlave*** (DISTANCE 2004, JC Publishing)

4-30: ***SEISO TSUI DANSHA*** (Shiwasu no Okina 2003, Hit Publishing)

4-31: "Suzuki-kun no Juunan" (Kengo Yonekura; *Comic Megastore*, Aug. '05, Core Magazine)

4-32: "Kairaku-G" (Fuusen Club; *Mangeki*, Mar. '04, TI NET)

4-33: ***PRETTY COOL*** (Sengoku-kun 2009, Akaneshinsha)

4-34: ***Netorare New Heroine*** (Kon-Kit 2013, Issuisha)

4-35: **Cheerful Eros Project** (Yuzuki N-Dash 2007, Akaneshinsha)

4-36: "Sexgiving Day" (Knuckle Curve; *Comic X-Eros*, Jun. '15, Wanimagazine)

4-37: "Natsu no NokoriKa" (Amayumi; *Penguin Club*, Sep. '16, Fujimi Publishing)

4-38: "Moso no Saki made..." (Edara; *Bishoujo Kakumei road*, Dec. '13, Issuisha)

4-39: "Under Lip Service" (Yumenotanuki; *Comic Bavel*, Dec. '15, Bunendo)

4-40: "12-ji made Matenai!" (Isonogi, *Comic E x E*, Sep. '16, GOT)

4-41: "Renai-gokko" (Hiryu Tawara; *Comic Tenma*, Mar. '16, Akaneshinsha)

4-42: "Ongaeshi no Tsuraoka-kun TS: Sakata" (Kei Narusawa; *Comic Aun*, Dec. '16, Hit Publishing)

4-43: "Onee-chan Book Camp!" (Rei Yuki; *Comic Mashou*, May '16, Sanwa Publishing)

4-44: "Sono Toko, Gakkou de", #1 (RAYMON; *Comic Megastore H*, Jan. '06, Core Magazine)

4-45: "Hito de Nashi no Koi" (Mitsuka Hattori; *Comic Toutetsu*, Apr. '15, Issuisha)

4-46: "Niku Maho no Okite" (CLONE Ningen; *Comic Megastore ALPHA*, Nov. '14, Core Magazine)

4-47: "Inchou vs The World" (GESUNDHEIT; *Keriberon*, Iss. 46, '16, LEED Publishing)

4-48: "Sisters Conflict" (Shindou; *Comic Hot Milk*, Jun. '14, Core Magazine)

4-49: "Futari no Tenkosei" (Takashi Shiran; ***Kyomi Ari,*** 2010, TI NET)

4-50: ***Confession de Miel Mére*** (CLONE Ningen 2015, Core Magazine)

4-51: ***Jyusei Ganbou*** (Meet Sido 2015, Sanwa Publishing)

4-52: ***Jinro Kyoshitsu*** (Kyotaro Suzuki 2016, Hit Publishing)

4-53: "OPEN THE GIRL" (Hidari Ogawa; *Comic LO*, Jul. '16, Akaneshinsha)

4-54: ***Yakeppachi's Maria*** (Osamu Tezuka 1996, Akita Shoten)

4-55: ***Sikorsky Tonight*** (F4U 2009, Core Magazine)

4-56: ***Sikorsky Tonight*** (F4U 2009, Core Magazine)

4-57: ***Chibitch Bitch*** (LOW 2014, Core Magazine)

4-58: "Hajimete no Hatsujo-ki" (LOW; *Comic Megastore H*, Oct. 2008, Core Magazine)

4-59: "Akumakko ♥ Sakyura" (Kousuke; *Comic Anthurium*, Jun. '16, GOT)

4-60: ***Punishment to Peeing Boy!*** (Ryo Sakurai 2014, Libre)

4-61: ***Chin ☆ COMPLETE*** (Chinzurena 2014, Mediax)

4-62: "3-nengo mo Koibito de Itai nodesu" (Ayato Sasakura; *Comic JUICY*, Apr. '17, Akaneshinsha)

4-63: "Passion Tsushin" (IZAYOI; *Comic Mao*, Aug. '99, Shinyusha)

Chapter Five

5-1: "Patissiere in the Dark" (Denshin Ameyama; *Angel Club*, Oct. '16, Angel Publishing)

5-2: ***Kanyo Shojo*** (Ippon Nagare 2015, Hit Publishing)

5-3: "Bijin OL Hame Hajime!" (Clock Asakura; *Comic Toutetsu*, Apr. '15, Issuisha)

5-4: *Muscat Note*, Feb 1994 (Taiyou Tosho) mook

5-5: "Hokago Nymphomania" (Shimon Tomomimi; *Comic Bavel*, Sep. '16, Bunendo)

5-6: "Elekutorea" (Kyoden Sanbun; *Comic Megastore ALPHA*, Sep. '13, Core Magazine)

5-7: ***Yutosei no MuchiMuchi Chigoku*** (Marukidou 2013, TI NET)

5-8: ***Sarashi-Ai*** (ShindoL 2010, TI NET)

5-9: ***Chikusha no Nushi*** (Hirohisa Onikubo 2011, Angel Publishing)

5-10: ***Miru mo Muzan*** (OYSTER 2011, Issuisha)

5-11: "Abareta Onna Kyoushi" (Tokisana 2012, Kill Time Communication)

5-12: "Kinen Satsuei" (Noji; *Comic X-Eros*, Jul. '17, Wanimagazine)

5-13: ***Futa Letter*** (2010, HarthNir) video game

5-14: "Ai ♥ Scraper" (Hiromitsu Takeda; Comic Megastore H, May '08, Core Magazine)

5-15: ***Lolikko Kiss*** (Mitsuru Bangaichi 1986, Nippon Shuppansha)

5-16: "Hatsujo Densetsu" (Tou Moriyama***; Yoiko Seikyoiku*** 1985, Shobunkan)

5-17: ***Orgasm King*** (Fuusen Club 1998, Tosho Shobo)

5-18: "Pla-Ude Sunlight: Kouhen" (Araya Shiki; *Comic Dolphin*, Feb. '93, Tsukasa Shobo)

5-19: ***B-flat 37°C*** (Jogi Tsukino 2002, Core Magazine)

5-20: ***Taimanin Asagi,*** Vol. 1 (PIXY - Lilith Soft 2007) anime

5-21: ***Ahegao Patchouli*** (Yukiman, www.pixiv.net/member_illust.php?mode=medium&illust_id=1140808; 2008) illustration

5-22: ***Ahegao template*** (Yukiman, www.pixiv.net/member_illust.php?mode=medium&illust_id=1185428; 2008) illustration

5-23: ***A-H-E*** (Fatalpulse 2008; Illustration by Asanagi)

5-24: ***Ecstasy at 3seconds.*** (Torajiro Sanagi 2013, Fujimi Publishing)

5-25: ***AheColle*** (Naoto Fukuyama 2014, Sanwa Publishing)

5-26: ***Chin ☆ COMPLETE*** (Chinzurena 2014, Mediax)

5-27: "Aru Natsu no Hiwai de Kirei de Yokoshima na One-san" (Bu-chan; *Angel Club*, Oct. '16, Angel Publishing)

5-28: "ToketeMite wa Ikaga Desu?" (Ryo Sakurai 2016, Libre Publishing)

5-29: "ToketeMite wa Ikaga Desu?" (Ryo Sakurai 2016, Libre Publishing)

5-30: ***Ahegao Minaide!*** (Shin Takahane & Kinohitoshi 2010, France Shobo)

5-31: ***Eromanga Mitai na Ahegao wo Sarashita Onna-tachi*** (2015, Moodys) video

5-32: ***Ahegao Double Peace Gakuen*** (2015, Rocket) video

Chapter Six

6-1: "Zangyou~Keibiin wa Mita!" (Tesshin Azuma; *Comic Kairakuten*, Feb. '17, Wanimagazine)

6-2: "Ippatsu Kaiketsu Onayami Soudan" (Kuroitsu Tsuruga; *Comic Kou*, Mar. '17, Akaneshinsha)

6-3: "Manga Mitai ni" (Sakamata Nerimono; *Comic MATE LEGEND*, Jun. '17, Issuisha)

6-4: "Peeping Mom" (D.P; *Comic PaPePo*, Nov. '04, France Shoin)

6-5: ***Radical ☆ Temptation*** (Yoshiharu Makita 2005, Akaneshinsha)

6-6: "Kagero" (Coupe; *COMIC Kairakuten BEAST*, Jul. '17, Wanimagazine)

6-7: "RinRin Ecchi" (Doku Denpa; *Comic Anthurium*, Jun. '17, GOT)

6-8: "Osanajimi no Eroge Seiyuu Motivation", Pt. 2 (Fujishima Seiichigou; *Comic Tenma*, Aug. '15, Akaneshinsha)

6-9: "Tissue Story" (Shikkarimono no Takeshi-kun; *Comic X-Eros*, Sep. '16, Wanimagazine)

6-10: ***Kupaa Resort*** (Akazawa RED 2006, Shinyusha)

6-11: ***Jealoussic Park*** (Akazawa RED 2009, MAX)

6-12: ***Loli-Pako: BrakKUPAA-ruzu***! (Akazawa RED 2014, Akaneshinsha)

6-13: ***Dekinboy*** (Shin Tamura 1978, Shogakukan)

6-14: ***Urusei Yatsura,*** Vol. 17 (Rumiko Takahashi 1983, Shogakukan)

6-15: "Nii-chan to Issho" (Akazawa RED; *Potpourri Club,* Jun. '04, Shinyusha)

6-16: ***Ushio and Tora,*** Vol. 4 (Kazuhiro Fujita 1991, Shogakukan)

6-17: ***Please Teach Me*** (Chokudokan 1998) doujinshi

6-18: ***KupaaBon*** (Chokudokan 2004) doujinshi

6-19: "Kaori Monogatari" (Aoi Makita; *Manga Hot Milk,* May '93, Byakuya-Shobo)

6-20: "A Slave", Pt. 2 (Rei Hidiri; *Natural High,* Mar. '97, Fujimi Publishing)

6-21: "Hisho no Himegoto" (Katsupiko Fuji; *Potpourri Club,* Sep. '97, Shinyusha)

6-22: **Dance of Desire** (Toshio Maeda 1983, Ichibankan Shobo)

6-23: "Sonna Hiromi wa Damasarete!" (Aki Uchiyama; *Petit Angel*, Aug. '95, Sun Publishing)

6-24: "Go-nenme no Natsu ni" (Shinkukan; *Comic ROAD*, Oct. '88, Tsukasa Shobo)

6-25: "Up-Name DANGER Miss Bunny!!" (Mitsune Ayasaka; *Comic Dolphin*, Jul. '92, Tsukasa Shobo)

6-26: "Sweet Candy" (Tamano Tamaki; *Comic KoppePan*, Aug. '89, Amikaru)

6-27: "Pururun ♥ Otome Hakusho" (Wataru Watanabe; *Comic Yumi-chan*, Aug. '95, Cybele Publishing)

6-28: "Stamina Ryori" (Morris; *Comic Homohime*, Sep. '02, Fujimi Publishing)

6-29: ***To LOVE Ru: Darkness***, Vol. 15 (Saki Hasemi & Kentaro Yabuki 2016, Shueisha)

6-30: "Yoshida to Mesu-buta Senpai" (John K. Pe-ta; *Comic Megastore ALPHA,* Jan. '16, Core Magazine)

6-31: "Sokai no HESO Kaizoku" (Hirodi Ishikawa; *Comic E x E*, Mar. '17, GOT)

6-32: "Onedari Santa ♥" (Mari Amo; *Potpourri Club,* Jan. '12, MAX)

6-33: "Cosplay wa Hajimemashita" (Ke-to; *Manga Bangaichi*, Jan. '09, Core Magazine)

6-34: "Wakaretemo, Suki na Sensei" (Tsubura Hase; *Comic Megastore H*, Dec. '05, Core Magazine)

6-35: "X-Swap!" (Yume-no-Tanuki; *Comic PuruMelo*, Sep. '13, WAKOH Publishing)

6-36: ***Don't be Hard on Me*** ♥ (Shimaji 2015, Wanimagazine)

6-37: "Neko ni Saretai ♥" (Kazuki Hiro; *Comic PuruMelo*, Jun. '13, WAKOH Publishing)

6-38: ***Binzume Imouto-tachi 2*** (Nankotsu Misakura 2001, HarthNir) doujinshi

6-39: ***G.A.I.g (f)*** (Nankotsu Misakura 2008, HarthNir) doujinshi

6-40: ***Gotai Choo Manzoku*** (Nankotsu Misakura 2001, Outou Shobo)

6-41: ***Hikikomori Kenkoho*** (Nankotsu Misakura 2003, Core Magazine)

6-42: ***Black Jack*** (Osamu Tezuka; *Shonen Champion*, Jul. 7, '75, Akita Shoten)

6-43: ***Any Questions*** (RaTe 1993, Tsukasa Shobo)

6-44: "Maka Fushigi Shukusei Shinshi Jiken" (Takashi Sano; *Manga Zettai Manzoku*, Nov. '96, Kasakura Publishing)

6-45: "Wakaitte Subarashii" (Nankotsu Misakura; *kikasuma,* Jul. '02, Shobunkan)

6-46: ***To LOVE Ru: Darkness,*** Vol 3 (Saki Hasemi & Kentaro Yabuki 2011, Shueisha)

6-47: ***Hayate the Combat Butler!,*** Vol. 36 (Kenjiro Hata 2013, Shogakukan)

6-48: ***Zeppin! Ramen Musume,*** Vol. 1 (Kazuyoshi Tomoki 2012, Kodansha)

6-49: ***Kiss Him, Not Me!,*** Vol. 9 (Junko 2016, Kodansha)

6-50: ***Kichiku, Encount*** (Owal 2014, Takeshobo)

Chapter Seven

7-1: "NewMen" (Go Zappa; *Penguin Club Special Edition,* Jan. '93, Tatsumi Publishing)

7-2: "Yura Yura Paradise" (Aura Seiji; *Penguin Club,* Oct. '93, Fujimi Publishing)

7-3: "Waitress" (Ruka Umino; *Namaiki,* Apr. '09, Takeshobo)

7-4: "Chikan Yuugi", Play Case 2 (Harumi Shimamoto; *Young Kyun!,* Mar. '17, Cosmic Publishing)

7-5: "Konnichiwa Ochinchin" (Yukiu Con; *Comic Kou,* Mar. '17, Akaneshinsha)

7-6: ***EroDamashi!,*** Vol. 1 (Dirty Matsumoto 2003, Oakla Publishing)

7-7: ***Towarare Penguin*** (Tou Moriyama 1986, Tatsumi Publishing)

7-8: ***Yaruki Manman,*** Vol. 1 (Masamichi Yokoyama & Jiro Gyu 1980, Kodansha)

7-9: ***Manga Sutra,*** Vol. 22 (Katsu Aki 2003, Hakusensha)

7-10: ***Dan Kong*** (Reijiro Kato 1993, Wanimagazine)

7-11: ***ChinTsubu,*** Vol. 2 (Nase Yamato 2004, Jitsugyou no Nihonsha)

7-12: ***Shikken Ningyo: Dummy Oscar,*** Vol. 3 (Seisaku Kano & Kazuo Koike 1979, Studio Ship)

7-13: "Koton a la Mode" (Kojiki Ohji; *Comic Megastore,* Mar. '00, Core Magazine)

7-14: ***Watashitachi no Hajimari*** (Menea the Dog 2017, Core Magazine)

7-15: "Yamagami-san ga Kureta Yome" (Kaiduka; *Comic Anthurium*, Jun. '17, GOT)

7-16: "Naisho no Shinro Soudan" (Migu Fujiyama; *Boys Pierce,* Mar. '13, Junet)

7-17: "Uchuu Keiji GALVAN" (Yuko Minami; *Penguin Club,* Feb. '87, Tatsumi Publishing)

7-18: **Daa-san no Tame ni Okita Ayako 32-sai B107** (Okina Keikaku 2011) doujinshi

7-19: "Konami-chan Dai-Pinch" (Yoshimasa Watanabe; *Penguin Club Special Edition*, Feb. '92, Tatsumi Publishing)

7-20: "Genki ni Narisou" (Ogami Wolf; *Candy Time,* Jun. '91, Fujimi Publishing)

7-21: "Nene Taifu" (Chisato Takanabe; *Penguin Club Special Edition*, May '92, Tatsumi Publishing)

7-22: "Tadaima Benkyouchuu" (Juzo Minazuki; *Candy Time,* Apr. '91, Fujimi Publishing)

7-23: "CLUB ART PHAPSODY" (Natsuma; *Candy Time,* Jun. 1991 Fujimi Publishing)

7-24: "Complex Girl" (Mizu Youkan; *Penguin Club,* Jan. '93, Tatsumi Publishing)

7-25: "Genki ni Narisou" (Ogami Wolf; *Candy Time,* Jun. '91, Fujimi Publishing)

7-26: "K no Truck" (Tou Moriyama, *Comic PaPePo,* May '92, France Shoin)

7-27: "Byouin Kamen" (Masayoshi Watanabe; *Penguin Club,* May '93, Tatsumi Publishing)

7-28: "Muchimuchi Purin" (Rei Shinozaki; *Comic BEAT,* Mar. '92, Tokyo Sanseisha)

7-29: "Muchimuchi Purin" (Rei Shinozaki; *Comic BEAT,* Mar. '92, Tokyo Sanseisha)

7-30: "Minerva Road" (Yu Tomiaki, *Comic BEAT,* Dec. '91, Tokyo Sanseisha)

7-31: "Hurdle wo Koete" (Kanna Amazaki ; *Comic Dolphin,* Dec. '03, Tsukasa Shobo)

7-32: *Comic Lolipop,* Jun 1990 (Kasakura Publishing) magazine

7-33: *Manga Hot Milk,* Nov 1994 (Byakuya-Shobo) magazine

7-34: *Comic Touhime,* Feb 1996 (Hit Publishing) magazine

7-35: *Comic JUMBO,* Jan 1989 (Toen Shobo) magazine

7-36: *Comic JUMBO,* Aug 2005 (Toen Shobo) magazine

7-37: ***Konya, Tonikaku XX ga Mitai.*** (Kenji Kishizuka 2009, Fujimi Publishing)

7-38: ***Konya, Tonikaku Ryoujoku ga Mitai***. (Kenji Kishizuka 2002, Fujimi Publishing)

7-39: **Henachoko DaiSakusen Z,** Vol. 11 (Hideo Nishimoto 2002, Kodansha)

7-40: ***Hell Teacher Nube*** (Takeshi Okano & Sho Makura; Shonen Jump, Iss. 44 '94, Shueisha)

7-41: ***Yuuna and the Haunted Hot Springs*** (Tadahiro Miura; *Shonen Jump,* Iss. 42 '16, Shueisha)

7-42: ***Yuuna and the Haunted Hot Springs,*** Vol. 4 (Tadahiro Miura 2016, Shueisha)

7-43: ***I"s*** (Masakazu Katsura; *Shonen Jump,* Iss. 39 '97, Shueisha)

7-44: ***I"s,*** Vol. 3 (Masakazu Katsura 1999, Shueisha)

7-45: ***I"s*** (Masakazu Katsura; *Shonen Jump,* Iss. 40 '98, Shueisha)

7-46: ***I"s,*** Vol. 5 (Masakazu Katsura 1999, Shueisha)

7-47: ***To LOVE Ru: Darkness,*** Vol. 3 (Kentaro Yabuki & Saki Hasemi 2011, Shueisha)

7-48: ***To LOVE Ru: Darkness,*** Vol. 5 (Kentaro Yabuki & Saki Hasemi 2011, Shueisha)

7-49: ***Eromanga no Genba*** (Kimi Rito 2016, Sansai Books)

7-50: ***Eromanga no Genba*** (Kimi Rito 2016, Sansai Books)

Chapter Eight

8-1: ***Urotsukidouji: Legend of the Overfiend,*** Movie Edition (1989, Kitty Media) Blu-ray/ DVD set

8-2: ***Heroes for Hire 2,*** #13 (Sana Takeda & Fred Van Lente, Zeb Wells 2007, Marvel)

8-3: "Anime Expo panel" (Kimi Rito 2016) photograph

8-4: ***Alice's Nightmare,*** Part 2 (Cyberunique & ADM 2014)

8-5: @oniakako (www.twitter.com/oniakako/status/829917115935191041 2016, twitter) photograph

8-6: @DollyLoveHallyu (www.twitter.com/DollyLoveHallyu/status/846824486800441346

2016, twitter) photograph

8-7: ***Countdown: Sex Bombs,*** #1 (Hiroyuki Utatane 1995, Fantagraphics)

8-8: ***Princess of Darkness,*** #1 (Yuichiro Tanuma 1995, Fantagraphics)

8-9: ***Sexhibition,*** #1 (Gari Suehiro 1995, Fantagraphics)

8-10: ***Hot Tails,*** #1 (Yui Toshiki 1996, Fantagraphics)

8-11: ***Sexcapades,*** #1 (Dirou Chiba's 1996, Fantagraphics)

8-12: ***Secret Plot,*** #7 (NeWMeN 1997, Fantagraphics)

8-13: ***SECRET PLOT DEEP*** (NeWMeN 1998, Fujimi Publishing)

8-14: ***Secret Plot Deep,*** #6 (NeWMeN 1999, Fantagraphics)

8-15: ***Bondage Fairies,*** #2 (Kondom 1994, Antarctic Press)

8-16: ***Bondage Fairies***, #2 (Kondom 1994, Antarctic Press)

8-17: ***After School Sex Slave Club*** (Tuna Empire 2008, Icarus Publishing)

8-18: *COMIC AG Digital,* 03 (2008, Icarus Comics) magazine

8-19: ***Pink Sniper*** (Kengo Yonekura 2006, Fantagraphics)

8-20: ***Domin-8 Me!*** (Sessyu Takemura 2007, Fantagraphics)

8-21: ***Milk Mama*** (Yuki Yanagi, 2007, Fantagraphics)

8-22: ***Domin-8 Me!*** (Sessyu Takemura 2007, Fantagraphics)

8-23: ***Renai Sample*** (Homunculus 2014, FAKKU)

8-24: ***Curiosity XXXed the Cat*** (F4U 2016, FAKKU)

8-25: Uncensored mark from Anime Expo (Kimi Rito 2015) photograph

8-26: ***Power Play!*** (Yamatogawa 2012, Digital Manga)

8-27: ***Renai Sample*** (Homunculus 2014, FAKKU)

8-28: ***Tayu Tayu*** (Yamatogawa 2009, Akaneshinsha)

8-29: ***Boing Boing*** (Yamatogawa 2013, Digital Manga)

A: ***Junai Irregulars*** (ShindoL 2014, TI NET)

B: ***Henshin*** (ShindoL 2016, Wanimagazine)

C: ***Metamorphosis*** (ShindoL 2017, FAKKU)

D: ***Henshin*** (ShindoL 2016, Wanimagazine)

8-30: ***PLAYMATE OF THE APES*** (DA HOOTCH 2006) doujinshi

8-31: ***ShindoL's Cultural Anthropology*** (ShindoL 2013, TI NET)

Chapter Nine

9-1: "Mate! Onaho wa Junbi Shitaka!?" (HANABi; *Girls for M,* Oct. '15, Akaneshinsha)

9-2: ***Power Play!*** (Yamatogawa 2012, Akaneshinsha)

9-3: "Rabu² Spa" (Hota.; *Comic X-Eros,* Jan. '17, Wanimagazine)

9-4: "Tasogare wa Moete..." (Erika Wada; *Comic JUMBO,* Sep. '91, Tsukasa Shobo)

9-5: "Un-Cheergirl" (Wanao; ***UnCheergirl,*** 2019, Akaneshinsha)

9-6: "Hidane" (Cuvie; *Comic Kairakuten,* Oct. '17, Wanimagazine)

9-7: ***Soku Hame Bicchinpo NY ni Iku*** (Shimaji 2015, Cannabis)

9-8: ***Naka no Kabe*** (Hideyuki Matsurioka 2010, Akaneshinsha)

Appendices

A: ***Animal Company*** (Hideo Azuma 1980, Tokyo Sanseisha)

B: ***Usotsuki Paradox,*** Vol. 9 (Nanki Sato & Akira Kizuki 2012, Hakusensha)

C: ***Nana to Kaoru,*** Vol. 1 (Ryuta Amazume 2008, Hakusensha)

The History of Hentai Manga
An Expressionist Examination of Eromanga

First Published in Japan in November, 2017 by Ohta Publishing Co.

Thrid Printed Edition
English Edition published in August 2021 by FAKKU, LLC.

Translation: Molly Rabbit
Proofreading: Chris Champoux
Production: Brittany Elise, Dominique Lief
Supervision: Eduardo Manuel Chavez
Digital: Taneli Vatanen

EROMANGA HYOUGENSHI

English translation rights arranged with Ohta Publishing Co.
through Tuttle-Mori Agency, Inc., Tokyo

FAKKU!

FAKKU, LLC.
contact@fakku.net

ISBN-13:978-1-63442-254-3
Library of Congress Control Number: 2020952211